Regulating Hedge Funds in the EU

European Company Law Series

VOLUME 18

Editor

Steef M. Bartman, Attorney-at-Law, Emeritus Professor of Company Law at Leiden Law School and Professor of Corporate Group Liability at Maastricht University, the Netherlands.

Introduction

The European Company Law Series is closely linked to the bimonthly journal European Company Law, also published by Kluwer Law International.

Contents/Subjects

The series covers subjects of company law in a broad sense, including insolvency, co-determination and securities law. Topical issues such as merger control, corporate governance, and piercing the corporate veil have been covered.

Objective of Series

Analysis of topical or complex subjects in European company law.

Readership

Academics; regulators; practitioners.

The titles published in this series are listed at the end of this volume.

Regulating Hedge Funds in the EU

Alexandros Seretakis

Wolters Kluwer

Published by:
Kluwer Law International B.V.
PO Box 316
2400 AH Alphen aan den Rijn
The Netherlands
E-mail: international-sales@wolterskluwer.com
Website: www.wolterskluwer.com/en/solutions/kluwerlawinternational

Sold and distributed by:
Wolters Kluwer Legal & Regulatory U.S.
7201 McKinney Circle
Frederick, MD 21704
United States of America
E-mail: customer.service@wolterskluwer.com

ISBN 978-94-035-3512-8

e-Book: ISBN 978-94-035-3513-5
web-PDF: ISBN 978-94-035-3514-2

About the Author

Alexandros Seretakis is an Assistant Professor of Law at Trinity College Dublin where he served as the founding Director of the MSc in Law and Finance. Alexandros holds a law degree from the Aristotle University of Thessaloniki, an LLM in Banking and Finance from the University College of London, an LLM in Corporation Law from New York University. He completed his PhD at the University of Luxembourg. Alexandros has served as a research fellow at the NYU Pollack Center for Law and Business and the Institute of Advanced Legal Studies in London. He is admitted to practise law in Greece and the State of New York. He is a guest lecturer at the University of Piraeus, the University of Luxembourg and the Institute of Banking in Ireland. Moreover, Alexandros has served as a consultant and advisor to start-ups and investment fund companies.

Table of Contents

List of Abbreviations

Advisers Act	Investment Advisers Act
AFM	Netherlands Authority for the Financial Markets
AIF	Alternative Investment Fund
AIFM	Alternative Investment Fund Manager
AIFMD	Alternative Investment Fund Managers Directive
AIMA	Alternative Investment Management
Association Amaranth	Amaranth Advisors LLC
AIG	American International Group
AMF	Autorité des marchés financiers
AUM	Assets under Management
ACP	Autorité de Contrôle Prudentiel
BAFIN	Bundesanstalt für Finanzdienstleistungsaufsicht
BRRD	Bank Recovery and Resolution Directive
BCBS	Basel Committee on Banking Supervision
BHC	Bank Holding Company
CDO	Collateralized Debt Obligation
CDS	Credit Default Swap
CFTC	Commodity Futures Trading Commission
CLO	Collateralized Loan Obligation
CME	Coordinated Market Economy
CRMPG	Counterparty Risk Management Policy Group
CSSF	Commission de Surveillance du Secteur Financier
CFPB	Consumer Financial Protection Bureau
Dodd-Frank Act	Dodd-Frank Wall Street Reform and Consumer Protection Act of 2010
ECB	European Central Bank

EFSF	European Financial Stability Fund
Enhanced Leverage Fund	High-Grade Structured Credit Strategies Enhanced Leverage Fund
ERM	Exchange Rate Mechanism
ESM	European Stability Mechanism
ESMA	European Securities and Markets Authority
EMIR	European Market Infrastructure Regulation
ESCB Statute	European System of Central Banks Statute
ESRB	European Systemic Risk Board
Exchange Act	Securities and Exchange Act of 1934
FATF	Financial Action Task Force
FCA	Financial Conduct Authority
FCIC	Financial Crisis Inquiry Commission
FDIC	Federal Deposit Insurance Corporation
FED	Federal Reserve
FRB	Federal Reserve Board
FSA	Financial Services Authority
FSB	Financial Stability Board
FSOC	Financial Stability Oversight Council
GAO	Government Accounting Office
Hedge Fund Rule	Registration Under the Advisers Act of Certain Hedge Fund Advisers; Final Rule
HFSB	Hedge Funds Standards Board
High-Grade Fund	High-Grade Structured Credit Strategies Fund
IMF	International Monetary Fund
Vickers Commission	Independent Commission on Banking
Investment Company Act	Investment Company Act of 1940
IOSCO	International Organization of Securities Commissions
JOBS Act	Jumpstart Our Business Startups Act of 2012 XIII
LBO	Leveraged Buyout
LCFI	Large Complex Financial Institution
LCR	Liquidity Coverage Ratio
LME	Liberal Market Economy
Liikanen Report	Report of the High-Level Expert Group on Reforming the Structure of the EU Banking Sector
LLC	Limited Liability Company
LLP	Limited Liability Partnership
LTCM	Long-Term Capital Management
MAD	Market Abuse Directive
MAR	Market Abuse Regulation

MBS	Mortgage-Backed Security
MFA	Managed Funds Association
MiFID	Markets in Financial Instruments Directive
MiFIR	Markets in Financial Instruments Regulation
MTF	Multilateral Trading Facility
NAV	Net Asset Value
NBFC	Nonbank Financial Company
NSFR	Net Stable Funding Ratio
OCC	Office of the Comptroller of the Currency
OECD	Organisation for Economic Co-operation and Development
OFR	Office of Financial Research
OLA	Orderly Liquidation Authority
OTC	Over the Counter
OTF	Organized Trading Facility
PRA	Prudential Regulation Authority
PWG	President's Working Group
Repo	Repurchase Agreement
SBAI	Standards Board for Alternative Investments
SEC	Securities and Exchange Commission
Securities Act	Securities Act of 1933
Short Selling Regulation	EU Regulation on Short Selling and Certain Aspects of Credit Default Swaps
SINBFC	Systemically Important Non-bank Financial Company
SIFI	Systemically Important Financial Institution
SSM	Single Supervisory Mechanism
SSM Regulation	Single Supervisory Mechanism Regulation
SRB	Single Resolution Board
SRF	Single Resolution Fund
SRM	Single Resolution Mechanism
SRM Regulation	Single Resolution Mechanism Regulation
Stat Arbs	Statistical Arbitrageurs
TBTF	Too Big to Fail
TFEU	Treaty for the Functioning of the European Union
UCITS	Undertakings for Collective Investment in Transferable Securities

Foreword by Steef M. Bartman

As the main editor of the CECL book series on European Company Law, I am extremely happy to welcome this book written by Alexandros Seretakis as new part of the series. The author seeks to introduce the reader into the sometimes as rather 'mystical' perceived world of hedge funds, their history and background, their achievements, and disasters, as well as their current regulatory environment. On the basis of a thorough comparison between hedge fund regulation in the US (*Dodd-Frank Act*, 2010) and in the EU (*AIFM Directive*, 2011), he concludes that the US response to the threats hedge funds may pose on the financial stability is in some respects superior to the EU response. Hence, the author proposes additional legislation in the EU, *inter alia* aimed at the designation of non-bank financial institutions like hedge funds as systematically important, combined with the inclusion of such institutions into the EU special resolution regime for banks (*Bank Recovery and Resolution Directive*, *Single Resolution Mechanism*). Moreover, he suggests the creation of a centralized supervisory regime instead of the current supervision by national authorities.

Purely from a financial stability point of view all these proposals sound necessary and effective to me. However, environmental threats are increasingly mounting pressure on big companies to decarbonize their operations. Collective interest groups are using all instruments available, including legal action, in an attempt to speed up that process. Hedge funds seem to adapt rapidly to this new development. By letter of 27 October 2021, the New York-based hedge fund Third Point has urged Royal Dutch Shell to split into multiple companies in order to increase its performance and market value. The idea of the involved fund manager, Mr Daniel Loeb, is that Shell's (future) investments in non-fossil energy sources have a negative impact on the results of its traditional fossil energy business. The one would do much better without the other. Shell's management has responded that the proposed break-up would severely hinder the company in realizing its green goals set for the near future. It seems that the existence and actions of hedge funds will continue to pose challenges to company directors and lawyers alike. Alexandros Seretakis' study is a fine illustration of that statement.

Steef M. Bartman, professor of corporate group liability,
Maastricht University, the Netherlands, 2 November 2021

Foreword by Blanaid Clarke

The hedge fund industry has grown significantly since the 1990s and now stands at almost USD 2,500 billion. Hedge funds are available to high worth individuals and professional investors, and as a result, until recently they were subject to low levels of regulatory scrutiny and transparency. This led in turn to a poor public understanding of their role in the global financial system and an often time's cynical view of hedge funds as opportunistic investors. *Regulating Hedge Funds in the EU* provides much-needed clarity by explaining in an extremely clear and accessible manner what these investment funds are and the contribution, both positive and negative, they make to the financial system and to the economy more broadly. Students and newcomers to the subject are always surprised to learn that despite the importance of the subject and the swathe of regulation which now exists, there is no precise statutory definition. In the US and the EU, hedge funds are defined by reference to what they are not rather than what they are – tending thus to be either overinclusive or under-inclusive. In Chapter 1, the author explores the cause of this elusive definition attributing it to the wide variety of investment strategies employed by hedge funds, the diversity in their legal and business structures and the similarities in the practices of hedge funds and other private equity – all of which are described within the book. He then proceeds to provide a useful working definition centred upon their distinguishing industry-wide characteristics and investment strategies. This in itself provides a useful contribution to our understanding of this topic. The chapter also provides a fascinating examination of the major incidents involving hedge funds providing a rich narrative to facilitate an assessment of the extent to which hedge funds have acted as a destabilizing factor in the world's financial system before concluding that their negative role has been overstated.

That said, hedge funds are considered to be carriers of substantial risks, including systemic ones. Past materialisations of systemic risk including the circumstances surrounding the demise of the Long Term Capital Management fund and the role of hedge funds in the Global Financial Crisis of 2008-2009 reconfirmed the relevance of these perceptions. The book explores these risks and provides excellent insights into the rationale for hedge fund regulation and the appropriate form of regulation. The author is well placed then to make a cogent argument for greater regulatory intervention in the case of large systemically important hedge funds and hedge funds housed within systemically important financial institutions on the basis that systemic risk is the sole plausible reason supporting regulatory intervention in the hedge fund industry.

The text provides a rigorous comparative law analysis of hedge fund regulation in the US and EU in the aftermath of the Global Financial Crisis. Drawing on this analysis, and research on credit institution regulation in the EU, the author proposes a prohibition on EU credit institutions and other systemically important institutions sponsoring and investing in hedge funds and suggests that a Eurozone-wide systemic risk supervisor be appointed to the industry. Arguing that national bankruptcy procedure is ill-equipped to deal with the failure of a systemically important hedge fund, he also suggests the introduction of a special resolution regime for such hedge funds as a means of enhancing financial stability and ensuring such funds are permitted to fail in an orderly manner. This is an ambitious programme of reform and one which would require significant political will and momentum. In putting forward these solutions to manage the risk associated with the hedge fund industry, I commend my colleague for this important contribution to the ongoing regulatory and legislative debate.

Professor Blanaid Clarke
McCann FitzGerald Chair of Corporate Law,
Trinity College Dublin

Acknowledgements

First and foremost, I would like to extend my gratitude to my parents, Stavroula and my late father Leonidas, for their support. Special thanks go to Professor Nikos Psimmenos of the University of Ioannina for his support and advice. Special gratitude also goes to Professor Emilios Avgouleas of the University of Edinburgh for his great guidance and encouragement. I would also like to take this opportunity to express my appreciation to my PhD supervisor, Professor André Prüm, since the present book is in part based on the research conducted during my doctoral studies, which were funded by the National Research Fund of Luxembourg (FNR). Moreover, I am grateful to Professor Blanaid Clarke of Trinity College Dublin for her encouragement and support. Furthermore, I would like to thank Professor Steef Bartman of Maastricht University for his support and vote of confidence in my research. I am also indebted to Professor Corrado Malberti of the University of Trento, Professor Ryan Bubb and Professor Florencia Marotta-Wurgler of NYU School of Law for their help in various phases of my academic life. Furthermore, I am grateful to Professor René Smits of the University of Amsterdam, Etienne de Lhoneux of the Central Bank of Luxembourg, Dr Thomas Papadopoulos of the University of Cyprus and Dr Mariia Domina Repiquet of the University of Lorraine for sharing their views and expertise. A vote of thanks should also be extended to Dr Olivier Hance for his practical insights. Thanks also go to the staff at Wolters Kluwer for transforming the initial manuscript into a book and to Alexandra Shilov for proofreading. Finally, I would like to thank my colleagues and students at Trinity College Dublin for very stimulating discussions.

Introduction

> Hedge funds are the vehicles for loners and contrarians, for individualists whose ambitions are too big to fit into established institutions[1]

BACKGROUND

From Soros' landmark bet against the British pound in 1992 to John Paulson's big short against the US housing market in 2007, hedge funds have long attracted the covert admiration and suspicion of politicians, regulators and the public. The opaque nature of the industry, its alleged role in major crises around the world and a perceived lack of investor protection have repeatedly led to calls for greater regulation of hedge funds. Nonetheless, it was not until the recent financial crisis that hedge fund regulation gained momentum. The result was the adoption of legislation, which will radically transform the hedge fund industry. The Dodd-Frank Act[2] and the AIFM Directive[3] are the first successful attempts of regulators across both sides of the Atlantic to bring hedge funds onto their regulatory radar.

Hedge funds lack a formal or universally accepted definition. A widely used definition was offered by the PWG, which defined hedge funds as 'any pooled investment vehicle that is privately organized, administered by professional investment managers, and not widely available to the public'.[4] Nonetheless, taking into account the shortcomings of the various definitions offered, a working definition of hedge funds centred upon their unique industry-wide characteristics that demarcate

1. Sebastian Mallaby, *More Money Than God: Hedge Funds and the Making of a New Elite* (Penguin Books, 2010), 4.
2. Dodd-Frank Wall Street Reform and Consumer Protection Act, Pub. L. No. 111-203, 124 Stat. 1376.
3. Directive 2011/61/EU of the European Parliament and of the Council of 8 June 2011 on Alternative Investment Fund Managers and Amending Directives 2003/41/EC and 2009/65/EC and Regulations (EC) No. 1060/2009 and (EU) No. 1095/2010, 2011 O.J. (L 174) 1.
4. The President's Working Group on Financial Markets, *Hedge Funds, Leverage, and the Lessons of Long-Term Capital Management* (April 1999), 1.

them from other investment vehicles, most notably mutual funds, is the second-best alternative to a concrete and unambiguous definition.[5]

First and foremost, hedge funds are able to operate unconstrained in liquid public markets following a wide variety of short-term investment strategies and employing sophisticated investment techniques, such as short selling, derivatives and leveraged investing. Furthermore, unlike mutual funds, whose performance is measured by reference to some market index, hedge funds seek absolute returns. This pursuit is enhanced by the high-powered performance-based compensation of hedge fund managers. Apart from the management fee equal to 1-2% of AUM, hedge fund managers charge investors an incentive fee, usually set at 20% of the fund's profits, widely known as carried interest. Moreover, hedge funds offer limited liquidity to their investors. Finally, due to regulatory constraints, hedge funds are open only to sophisticated investors.

Hedge funds owe their existence to Alfred Winslow Jones back in 1949 although it was not until after 2000 that hedge funds witnessed an exponential growth with assets reaching USD 2.89 trillion in 2016.[6] Soros' bet against the sterling first showed that the industry was a powerful force in financial markets. The Asian financial crisis of 1997 resulted in a populist outrage with hedge funds criticized for speculating against national currencies. The near failure of LCTM, a star overleveraged hedge fund, and the collapse of Amaranth, the biggest hedge fund failure to date, were the next worrying incidents. Furthermore, various commentators have long argued that the opaqueness and complexity of the industry create a ripe opportunity for fraud and opportunism on the part of hedge fund managers against hedge fund investors. Regulation, it is argued, is warranted by the high informational asymmetries, potential conflicts of interests and agency costs between investors in hedge funds and their managers.[7] Another common criticism levelled against the industry concerns the growing incidents of insider trading and the propensity of hedge funds to engage in market manipulation.[8]

Furthermore, the failure of LCTM and the 2008 financial crisis alarmed regulators regarding the risks that the industry poses to financial stability. The standard two channels, widely documented academic literature, through which hedge funds may contribute to systemic risk are the credit and the market channels.[9] The credit channel refers to the impact that the failure of a large fund or a group of small- and medium-sized funds could have on its creditors and other counterparties. Systemic risk through the market channel can arise when adverse market movements lead to withdrawal of credit, tightening of collateral requirements, collateral calls and investor

5. *See generally* Lee Peter Getmansky Mila and Lo Andrew, 'Hedge Funds: A Dynamic Industry in Transition', *National Bureau of Economic Research Working Paper* No. w21449 (August 2015): 2-8.
6. John Authers and Mary Childs, 'Hedge Funds: Overpriced, Underperforming', Financial Times, https://next.ft.com/content/9bd1150e-1b76-11e6-b286-cddde55ca122.
7. Ryan Sklar, 'Hedges or Thickets: Protecting Investors from Hedge Fund Managers' Conflicts of Interest', *Fordham Law Rev.* 77 (2009): 3251-3277.
8. Lynn Stout, 'How Hedge Funds Create Criminals', *Harvard Business Review* (13 December 2010).
9. *See* Deutsche Bundesbank, 'Hedge Funds and Their Role in the Financial Markets', *Monthly Report* (March 1999): 37-38.

redemptions forcing a leveraged hedge fund or multiple small- and medium-sized funds to liquidate their positions at a loss leading to a death spiral of fire sales. Moreover, the collapse of Bear Stearns revealed the perils of housing hedge funds within SIFIs.[10] Finally, hedge funds have been forcefully criticized for contributing to systemic risk via their short selling activities.[11]

However, it was not until the 2008 financial crisis and the ongoing sovereign debt crisis that hedge fund regulation became an alarming priority for regulators across the Atlantic. The AIFM Directive in Europe brings hedge funds under a single regulatory framework. Seeking to enhance investor protection, the Directive contains numerous onerous requirements for hedge fund managers, including greater transparency towards investors, arrangements for managing conflicts of interests, remuneration restrictions and depositary and valuation requirements. Furthermore, disclosure requirements towards supervisors, risk management and liquidity management requirements and the ability of national authorities to impose limits on funds, such as leverage limits, in order to protect financial stability are clearly aimed at tackling systemic risk. Moreover, in 2014, the European Commission adopted the Proposal on Bank Structural Reform,[12] which was subsequently withdrawn, banning hedge fund sponsorship and investments by banking institutions.

In contrast to the EU regulatory regime and in particular the AIFM Directive, which contains stringent investor protection provisions, the Dodd-Frank Act in the US predominantly targets systemic risk. The Volcker Rule bans depositary institutions and other systemically important institutions from investing in or sponsoring hedge funds. Furthermore, Dodd-Frank requires hedge funds to register with the SEC and continuously disclose information to it. The SEC must share this information with the FSOC, which has the power to designate a hedge fund as a SIFI and subject it to the supervision of the FED, which has the authority to impose enhanced risk-based capital, liquidity requirements, limits on short-term debt and debt-to-equity limits. Finally, hedge funds, whose failure could jeopardize financial stability, may be placed into a special resolution procedure administered by the FDIC, also known as OLA. This special resolution procedure displaces a disorderly bankruptcy procedure for a systemically important institution.

Research Theme of the Book

The main aim of the present book is to offer proposals for reforming the current EU supervisory and regulatory framework for hedge funds by tackling the contribution of the industry to systemic risk. The book begins by offering an introduction to the world of hedge funds, namely their definition, main characteristics, organizational structure,

10. Ben Bland, 'Bear Stearns Hedge Funds Wiped Out', The Telegraph, http://www.telegraph.co.uk/finance/markets/2812344/Bear-Stearns-hedge-funds-wiped-out.html.
11. Bill Saporito, 'Are Short Sellers to Blame for the Financial Crisis', Time, http://content.time.com/time/business/article/0,8599,1842499,00.html.
12. 'Proposal for a Regulation of the European Parliament and of the Council on Structural Measures Improving the Resilience of EU Credit Institutions', COM 2014 (29 January 2014).

investment strategies and their benefits. Furthermore, the popular image of hedge funds has been tainted by the alleged role that they have played in major crises around the world. Thus, the major incidents involving hedge funds and financial crises will be documented and examined, in order to assess the extent to which hedge funds have acted as a destabilizing factor in the world financial system.

After having demystified hedge funds, this book will seek to explore the dangers posed by hedge funds and assess the rationales for their regulation. Investor protection, market abuse and the contribution of hedge funds to systemic risk are the main rationales offered for their regulation.[13] Furthermore, the rise of hedge fund activism has created deep scepticism regarding the destructive effects of activist hedge funds on companies' long-term value.[14] As the analysis in Chapter 2 will reveal, systemic risk is the sole plausible reason supporting regulatory intervention in the hedge fund industry. However, regulatory intervention is warranted only in the case of large systemically important hedge funds and hedge funds housed within SIFIs.

Having settled the issue regarding the need for regulation, its purpose and its scope, another interesting question is posed. What form should regulation take? Two different regulatory models are available: self-regulation and government regulation.[15] Another crucial distinction in the hedge fund literature is the difference between direct regulation of hedge funds and indirect regulation, namely their regulation via financial institutions, which are the creditors and counterparties of hedge funds.[16] Overall, the book will advocate for direct government regulation in the area of systemic risk recognizing though the supplementary role of indirect regulation and self-regulation.

Furthermore, recent legislative developments in the US and EU will be compared and assessed. The EU's main piece of legislation in the area of hedge funds, namely the AIFM Directive, was adopted based on a perceived lack of adequate investor protection and the role of hedge funds in aggravating systemic risk, while the Dodd-Frank Act adopts a more nuanced approach towards investor protection regulation focusing predominantly on systemic risk regulation. Starting from the premise that systemic risk is the sole rationale justifying a regulatory intervention in the hedge fund industry, a comparative examination of the hedge fund regulatory regimes in the US and the EU will reveal that certain elements of the Dodd-Frank Act, namely the Volcker Rule, the ability of the FSOC to designate non-bank financial institutions as systemically important and the introduction of a resolution regime for non-bank financial institutions, deal more effectively with the issue of systemic risk.

Consequently, the weak points of the EU's regulatory regime and the concomitant strengths of the Dodd-Frank Act will be explored. For instance, the ability of banking institutions in Europe to sponsor and/or invest in hedge funds significantly

13. Luis A. Aguilar, 'Speech by Sec Commissioner: Hedge Fund Regulation on the Horizon – Don't Shoot the Messenger', news release, 18 June 2009.
14. *See generally* Frank Partnoy, 'US Hedge Fund Activism', in *Research Handbook on Shareholder Power*, ed. Jennifer G. Hill & Randall S. Thomas (Edward Elgar, 2015).
15. Peter Grajzl & Peter Murrell, 'Allocating Lawmaking Powers: Self-Regulation Versus Government Regulation', *Journal of Comparative Economics* 35, no. 3 (2007).
16. Randy Haight, 'Community of Support: Moving Toward Indirect Regulation of the Hedge Fund Industry', *Marshall Global Markets Law Journal* 3, no. 1 (2014).

compromises financial stability by offering incentives to hedge funds to exploit the implicit government guarantee of their parents and increase their leverage. The failure of a hedge fund will also put the existence of the parent company at risk as evidenced by the failure of Bear Stearns, which was partially triggered by problems in two of its hedge funds. Furthermore, a major weakness of the AIFM Directive is the entrustment of the supervision of systemic risk stemming from hedge funds with national supervisors. National supervisors frequently do not possess the relevant expertise in analysing and tackling systemic risk. What is more, neither the AIFM Directive nor the EU resolution regime tackles the systemic risk posed by the failure of a systemically important hedge fund. As a result, national ordinary insolvency law will apply in case of a hedge fund failure. However, a national bankruptcy procedure is ill-equipped to deal with the failure of a systemically important hedge fund. A special resolution regime will significantly enhance financial stability by ensuring the orderly failure of a hedge fund.

Based on the above-mentioned examination, the book will present a proposal for enhancing the current supervisory and regulatory framework and strengthening systemic risk supervision and regulation. The proposal has three main building blocks. First, I will advocate the introduction of a ban on hedge fund sponsoring and investing by EU banking institutions and other systemically important institutions. Second, I will argue in support of the creation of a Eurozone-wide systemic risk supervisor. Finally, I will propose the creation of a special resolution procedure for systemically important hedge funds whose failure could jeopardize financial stability. More specifically, I will propose the inclusion of hedge funds into the EU special resolution regime, namely the BRRD and the SRM.

The ban on investing in and sponsoring of hedge funds by banking institutions and other systemically important institutions is a simple step towards enhancing financial stability in Europe and seems to be a pretty straightforward exercise. As a result, the stance of the EU, which has withdrawn the Proposal on Bank Structural Reform, will be criticized.

Furthermore, the book will argue in favour of the creation of a single supervisory framework for systemically important hedge funds in the Eurozone. Taking into account the recent creation of a SSM and the relevant expertise of the ECB in monitoring financial stability, it will be argued that the SSM should be extended to also cover systemically important hedge funds. The ECB should therefore have the exclusive competence to supervise hedge funds, which pose a threat to financial stability.

Pursuant to the book's proposal, the ESRB would have the authority to designate large hedge funds as systemically important institutions and subject them to the ECB's enhanced prudential supervision and regulation. The determination should be made according to the contribution of funds to systemic risk and by adopting clear and reasonable standards. Once a systemically important institution is brought under the ECB's supervision, enhanced prudential standards will immediately apply. The enhanced standards should seek to ensure the institution's solvency and liquidity. In particular, the imposition of leverage limits will enhance the ability of systemically important hedge funds to sustain losses. In addition, by reducing solvency risk, leverage limits reduce the likelihood of liquidity problems sparked by solvency concerns of creditors and investors in hedge funds. Moreover, the contagion caused through asset sales is minimized since the fraction of assets that a hedge fund may have to sell after losses in order to recover its equity ratio is smaller if it has more equity. Furthermore, the imposition of liquidity requirements will further enhance the resilience of a systemically important hedge fund to panicked withdrawals by its investors, counterparties and creditors. In addition, stress testing requirements conducted by the ECB should form an integral component of the ECB's toolkit. Finally, the mandatory imposition of gates by the ECB would curb panicked withdrawals by hedge fund investors.

While prudential regulation minimizes the probability of hedge fund failures, it does not deal with the *ex post* effects of the failure of a systemically important hedge fund. Taking into account the adverse effects of a hedge fund failure on the financial system, the disruptions, costs and delay associated with the application of ordinary national insolvency procedures and the moral hazard and enormous costs created by outright government bailouts, a comprehensive resolution regime for systemically important hedge funds is essential for the protection of systemic stability. Thus, the book will also explore the case for extending the BRRD[17] and the SRM[18] to cover systemically important hedge funds.

Structure of the Book

The book is divided into four chapters. Chapter 1 will serve as an introduction to the world of hedge funds. Chapter 2 will examine the main rationales for hedge fund regulation and the main modes of hedge fund regulation. Chapter 3 will offer a comparative examination of hedge fund regulation in the US and the EU. Finally, Chapter 4 will offer our proposals for reforming the current EU hedge fund supervisory and regulatory regime.

More specifically, the first chapter will serve as a primer on hedge funds, offering an overview of their history, their unique characteristics, the main organizational and operational structures commonly used by hedge funds and their investment strategies. Moreover, the chapter will discuss the benefits brought by hedge funds. Finally, it will also offer an examination of the most important instances in the history of hedge funds where hedge funds have come under the public spotlight.

Chapter 2 will seek to explore the dangers posed by hedge funds, assess the rationales for their regulation and determine the appropriate regulatory response. The

17. Directive 2014/59/EU of the European Parliament and of the Council of 15 May 2014 Establishing a Framework for the Recovery and Resolution of Credit Institutions and Investment Firms and Amending Council Directive 82/891/EEC, and Directives 2001/24/EC, 2002/47/EC, 2004/25/EC, 2005/56/EC, 2007/36/EC, 2011/35/EU, 2012/30/EU and 2013/36/EU, and Regulations (EU) No. 1093/2010 and (EU) No. 648/2012, of the European Parliament and of the Council, 2011 O.J. (L 173) 1.
18. 'Regulation (EU) No 806/2014 of the European Parliament and of the Council of 15 July 2014 Establishing Uniform Rules and a Uniform Procedure for the Resolution of Credit Institutions and Certain Investment Firms in the Framework of a Single Resolution Mechanism and a Single Resolution Fund and Amending Regulation (EU) No 1093/2010 O.J. (L 225) 1'.

chapter will examine the rationales for hedge fund regulation offered in academic literature, namely the need to protect investors in hedge funds, the danger to market integrity posed by hedge funds, their contribution to systemic risk, the short-term mentality provoked by hedge fund activists and the destabilizing effects of hedge fund short-selling activities. The analysis suggests that the systemic risk posed by large systemically important hedge funds and hedge funds housed within SIFIs is the only plausible reason supporting a regulatory intervention in the hedge fund industry. Furthermore, I will argue that direct government regulation is the optimal response to hedge funds' contribution to systemic risk recognizing though the important role of self-regulation and indirect regulation.

Chapter 3 offers a comparative examination of hedge fund regulation in the US and the EU. The reader will be introduced to the main provisions of the AIFM Directive, which aims to create a harmonized regulatory framework for hedge funds. Further, Chapter 3 will examine the abandoned European Commission Proposal on Bank Structural Reform, which prohibited the largest EU banks from sponsoring and investing in hedge funds. Finally, the chapter will analyse the developments in the area of resolution of financial institutions. The examination will proceed with an analysis of regulatory developments in the US. The Dodd-Frank Act enacted in the aftermath of the financial crisis requires the registration of hedge fund managers with the SEC. In addition, Dodd-Frank gives the FSOC the authority to designate non-bank financial institutions, including hedge funds, as SIFIs. Designation places a SIFI under the prudential supervision and regulation of the FED. Moreover, hedge funds, whose failure would pose a significant risk to the financial stability of the US, may be placed into a special resolution procedure administered by the FDIC. Finally, the Volcker Rule curbs banks' engagement in the hedge fund business. In concluding the examination of regulatory developments in the US, I will also highlight the positive elements of the regime introduced in the US compared to the approach taken by European regulators.

The final chapter of the book will offer proposals for improving the current EU supervisory and regulatory regime. Specifically, the book will advocate the introduction of a US-style Volcker Rule in Europe, which was moving towards the US model with the withdrawn Proposal on Bank Structural Reform. Furthermore, the book will propose the creation of a single supervisory framework for hedge funds in the Eurozone and the allocation of supervisory powers with regard to systemically important hedge funds to the ECB. Finally, Chapter 4 will make the case for the introduction of a special resolution regime for hedge funds.

CHAPTER 1

The Hedge Fund Phenomenon

1.1 INTRODUCTION

Not only praised as prototypical arbitrageurs correcting inefficiencies and providing liquidity in financial markets but also criticized for driving short-termism, creating asset bubbles and falling on companies like 'swarms of locusts',[19] hedge funds remain the most controversial vehicles of the AIFs universe. Despite the tremendous growth of the hedge fund industry, particularly after the late 1980s when a group of prominent global macro managers, including George Soros, Paul Tudor Jones and Julian Robertson, were able to generate market-beating returns by aggressively speculating on global macroeconomic trends, the world of hedge funds is still shrouded in a veil of mystery largely due to the highly complex and dynamic trading strategies employed by hedge funds and the scarcity of information about them. The alleged contribution of hedge funds to various crises around the world and their perceived ability to move markets and influence economic developments have amplified the mystique and provoked the suspicion and frustration of politicians, regulators and the public.

The purpose of this chapter is to offer the reader a better understanding of the hedge fund industry and disentangle the myths from the realities of the hedge fund universe. Section 1.2 of the chapter will serve as a primer on hedge funds and offer an

19. The description of hedge funds as 'swarms of locusts' belongs to the former Chairman of the Social-Democratic Party of Germany Frank Muntefering following the outcry provoked by the shareholders' rebellion against Deutsche Boerse's bid for the London Stock Exchange (LSE), which resulted in the collapse of the bid and the resignation of Deutsche Boerse's Chief Executive Officer and Chairman of the Board of Directors. UK-based hedge fund The Children's Investment Fund (TCI) led the revolt, which marked the advent of Anglo-Saxon aggressive shareholder activism in the traditionally closed and insider-dominated German corporate system commonly referred to as 'Deutschland AG'. For an excellent overview of this landmark revolt and its effects on German corporate governance, *see generally* Sudi Sudarsanam and Tim Broadhurst, 'Corporate Governance Convergence in Germany Through Shareholder Activism: Impact of the Deutsche Boerse Bid for London Stock Exchange', *Journal of Management & Governance* 16, no. 2 (2012).

overview of the history of hedge funds, the unsuccessful attempts of various regulatory bodies and legal instruments to accurately define them and the unique characteristics of hedge funds that distinguish them in practice from other investment vehicles. What is more, it will introduce the reader to the organizational and operational structures commonly used by hedge funds and their investment strategies. Furthermore, the main benefits brought by hedge funds will also be examined. Section 1.3 offers an examination of the most important instances in hedge fund history where hedge funds have come under the public spotlight. The first such instance was Soros' landmark bet against the British pound, which forced the UK to exit the ERM. Hedge funds were further fiercely criticized for provoking the East Asian currency and financial crisis, which destabilized Asian economies. The near demise of LTCM and the failure of Amaranth drew widespread attention to the potential financial stability implications of hedge fund failures. Finally, hedge funds were once again vilified for aggravating the financial and sovereign debt crises. These instances offered politicians fertile ground for raising their accusatory finger towards the hedge fund industry criticizing hedge funds for earning extraordinary profits at the expense of ordinary investors, national economies and global financial stability. An examination of these episodes will further the goal of demystifying hedge funds and assess the extent to which their negative image is warranted.

1.2 HEDGE FUNDS: A PRIMER

1.2.1 A Brief Overview of the History of Hedge Funds

The predecessors of modern hedge funds were investment trusts, which made their appearance in the US in the 1920s.[20] These investment vehicles offered their investors the ability to pool their investments and achieve higher returns through the enhanced employment of leverage.[21] Alfred Winslow Jones' investment fund A.W. Jones & Co, launched in 1949, is generally credited with being the first hedge fund.[22] Jones' private investment partnership exhibited certain unique characteristics, which would later be widely adopted by the hedge fund industry.[23] In order to escape restrictive SEC regulation and thereby obtain maximum flexibility in structuring his portfolio, Jones established his fund as a general partnership. In contrast to other equity investment vehicles, most notably mutual funds, which took exclusively long positions in stocks,

20. Heesang Chai Dominic Buchanan John & Deakin Simon, *Hedge Fund Activism in Japan: The Limits of Shareholder Primacy* (Cambridge University Press, 2012), 62.
21. *Ibid*. The concept of pooled investment developed initially in the UK was previously unknown to the US market. John Kenneth Galbraith, *The Great Crash, 1929* (Mariner Books, 1955), 52-65.
22. Daniel A. Strachman, *Getting Started in Hedge Funds*, 3rd ed. (Wiley, 2005), 24. Contrary to the general consensus that credits Alfred Winslow Jones with creating the first hedge fund, Warren Buffett, the legendary investor, has argued that Benjamin Graham, the father of value investing, built and managed the first hedge fund in the mid-1920s. Warren Buffett, 'Letter to the Editor', *Financial History* (Summer 2006), 86.
23. For an excellent overview of Jones' investment style and philosophy and the structure of his hedge fund *see* Mallaby, *More Money Than God: Hedge Funds and the Making of a New Elite*, 15-39.

Jones combined his long positions with short positions allowing him to hedge away his portfolio's market risk.[24] Furthermore, Jones amplified his fund's returns by prudently utilizing leverage. Jones' model of combining short selling with leverage, along with his superior stock-picking ability, generated spectacular profits for which he charged a 20% performance fee. A host of imitators soon sprang up and the second half of the 1960s witnessed a large number of new hedge fund launches.[25] The new hedge funds defied Jones' investment approach leveraging their long positions significantly while de-emphasizing the utilization of short sales.[26] As a result, they suffered massive losses during the bear market of the early 1970s, which put an end to the boom of the nascent hedge fund industry.[27]

The hedge fund industry did not recover from its previous bust until the late 1980s and after the widespread publicity of Julian Robertson's Tiger Fund's impressive performance.[28] Julian Robertson departing from Jones' original investment approach, which rested on the employment of a sophisticated hedging policy, implemented a global macro investment strategy based on the analysis of macroeconomic developments and the placing of unhedged opportunistic directional bets in fixed-income, equity, currency and commodity markets.[29] The late 1980s and the 1990s were the golden age of global macro managers.[30] The revolution in the over-the-counter derivatives markets, with the proliferation of novel financial derivatives, significantly expanded the range of trading opportunities that hedge fund managers could exploit.[31]

24. Short selling refers to the practice of selling a security without the seller actually owning it at the time of the sale. In a short sale, the seller will sell a security borrowed by a third-party lender and purchase an identical security at a later date to be returned to the lender. The short seller stands to profit from any decline in the price of the security between the sale and the repurchase. *See* Jennifer Payne, 'The Regulation of Short Selling and Its Reform in Europe', *European Business Organization Law Review* 13, no. 3 (2012): 414-15.
25. Mallaby, *More Money Than God: Hedge Funds and the Making of a New Elite*, 36-37. According to Caldwell, a 1968 Securities and Exchange Commission survey recorded 215 investment fund partnerships in the US out of which 140 were hedge funds. Ted Caldwell, 'Introduction: The Model for Superior Performance', in *Hedge Funds: Investment and Portfolio Strategies for the Institutional Investor*, ed. Jess Lederman & Robert A. Klein (Burr Ridge, Ill.: Irwin Professional Publishing, 1995).
26. Mallaby, *More Money Than God: Hedge Funds and the Making of a New Elite*, 37-38.
27. *Ibid.*, 40-41.
28. Julie Rohrer in an article in *Institutional Investor* was the first to document Tiger Fund's extraordinary performance, which was able to generate a 43% compound annual return from its launch in 1980 until 1986. Julie Rohrer, 'The Red-Hot World of Julian Robertson', *Institutional Investor*, May 1986.
29. For an introduction to Julian Robertson's biography and investment approach *see* Daniel A. Strachman, *Julian Robertson: Tiger in the Land of Bulls and Bears* (John Wiley and Sons, 2004).
30. The hedge fund industry in 1990 counted approximately six hundred hedge funds worldwide managing approximately USD 20 billion of assets. *See* François-Serge Lhabitant, *Hedge Funds: Myths and Limits* (Wiley, 2002), 12.
31. Derivatives are financial contracts whose value is derived from an underlying financial asset or underlying reference index or rate. Derivatives are used for risk management purposes enabling the transfer of risks to the entities best able to handle them. One can distinguish between exchange-traded and over-the-counter derivatives. Exchange-traded derivatives are standardized and fungible. Their trading on an organized exchange ensures a high level of transparency and regulatory oversight. In contrast, over-the-counter derivatives are privately negotiated bilateral contracts that can be tailored to the counterparties' needs. Trading in the over-the-counter market is dominated by a handful of dealer-banks. While over-the-counter markets

George Soros' bet against the British pound in 1992 further enhanced the reputation of global macro managers as market movers.[32] Hedge funds came once again under the public spotlight during the financial crisis that hit East Asian countries in mid-1997.[33] Global macro managers were portrayed as the driving force behind the widespread collapse of asset prices in East Asian economies. The default by Russia on its rouble-denominated debt in 1998 further rattled financial markets leading to the near collapse of LTCM, a hedge fund with more than USD 100 billion of assets. The year 1998 was a turning point for the hedge fund industry with several hedge funds failing and the industry as a whole undergoing a reshuffle.[34]

The impressive performance of hedge funds amid the bursting of the Internet bubble[35] enhanced the industry's reputation for delivering returns uncorrelated to equity markets and increased its attractiveness, particularly among institutional investors.[36] While stock markets around the world suffered massive drops during 2000-2002, the global hedge fund industry was able to deliver a compound return of

allow for the creation of innovative financial instruments, they suffered, until the recent reforms in derivatives markets in both the US and the EU, from a lack of transparency and regulation. On the concept of derivatives, their evolution and the different types of derivatives *see generally* René M Stulz, 'Financial Derivatives', in *The Milken Institute Review, Third Quarter* (2005); Bruce G Carruthers, 'Diverging Derivatives: Law, Governance and Modern Financial Markets', *Journal of Comparative Economics* 41, no. 2 (2013).

32. Due to their extraordinary success in predicting and profiting from economic developments, global macro managers were quickly accepted as public intellectuals. The most notable example was George Soros who in his 1987 book *The Alchemy of Finance* forcefully attacked the then prevailing paradigm that unregulated financial markets ensure an optimal allocation of resources and highlighted the proclivity of financial markets to boom and bust cycles. *See* George Soros, *The Alchemy of Finance: Reading the Mind of the Market* (Wiley, 1987).
33. The East Asian financial crisis started in Thailand after the Thai government was forced to abandon its fixed-exchange rate regime and devalue the baht. The crisis soon spread to other East Asian countries including Malaysia, Indonesia, the Philippines and South Korea.
34. Even though the strains in financial markets caused by Russia's default and the near collapse of LTCM resulted in severe losses for numerous hedge funds and significant fund failures, the overall performance of the hedge fund industry remained positive. *See* Richard A. Opper Jr., 'Not Such a Bad Year for Hedge Funds', New York Times, 31 January 1999.
35. The Internet Bubble refers to the speculative bubble that developed during the two-year period leading up to March 2000 and was characterized by increased speculation in the shares of companies in the information technology sector. The bubble developed initially in the US but quickly spread to virtually all industrialized economies. At the height of the bubble companies without any revenues and any reasonable prospect of generating revenues in the future were rewarded with extraordinarily high valuations by investors. *See* Burton G Malkiel, *A Random Walk Down Wall Street: The Time-Tested Strategy for Successful Investing (Revised and Updated)* (Norton, 2012), 80-98. The bubble burst on 10 March 2000 after the Nasdaq Composite, which had rose to 5.408,62 points, started to fall hitting a low of 1.314.85 points in August 2002. Anna Scherbina, 'Asset Price Bubbles: A Selective Survey', *IMF WP/13/45* (February 2013): 7. Robert Shiller whose book *Irrational Exuberance* was published in March 2000 a few days before the collapse of the Internet Bubble attributed the bubble to irrational investor optimism driven by the Internet revolution, the rise of online trading, the election of a pro-business Republican Congress in the US, the predominance of materialistic values in Western societies, the expansion of the volume of trade and the growth of mutual funds and defined benefit contribution plans. Furthermore, Shiller highlighted the crucial role played by the media in reinforcing the irrational euphoria among investors. *See generally* Robert J Shiller, *Irrational Exuberance* (Princeton University Press, 2005).
36. As Scholes notes, hedge funds did not initially seek to attract institutional capital. Instead, they mostly targeted high net worth. Myron S. Scholes, 'The Future of Hedge Funds', *Journal of*

30%.[37] Disappointed by the performance of equity markets, investors quickly turned to hedge funds, which proved their ability to offer positive returns even under the most stressful market circumstances. The growing appeal of hedge funds to institutional investors opened up the opportunity for hedge fund managers to tap a vast source of capital. The attraction of institutional capital would prove crucial for the industry's growth during the following years. As Sebastian Mallaby notes, 'hedge funds grew larger, slicker and more methodical in style. They were emerging as a real industry'.[38]

The growth in the number of hedge funds and the amount of AUM continued apace during the years following the Internet bubble. By 2007, over 7.000 hedge funds were operating worldwide, managing assets reaching USD 2 trillion.[39] An interesting development was the proliferation of the hedge fund industry in Europe.[40] A deeply rooted entrepreneurial culture, which ensured a vast pool of talented investment professionals, and the liquidity of its equity markets, allowed the US to monopolize the hedge fund industry for years.[41] Nonetheless, the 2000s witnessed the emergence of Europe as an attractive alternative for hedge fund managers.[42] The development of the hedge fund industry in Europe was spurred by the maturing of the US market, where

Financial Transformation 10 (1997): 8. The benefits of incorporating hedge funds into institutional investors' portfolios became widely recognized after Yale University and several other endowments, which had allocated part of their portfolios to hedge funds, outperformed during the Internet Bubble other institutional investors which had followed the then prevailing 60/40 equity/bond allocation model. Citi Prime Finance Business Advisory Services, *Institutional Investment in Hedge Funds: Evolving Investor Portfolio Construction Drives Product Convergence* (June 2012), 3.

37. Simon A Lack, *The Hedge Fund Mirage: The Illusion of Big Money and Why It's Too Good to Be True* (Wiley, 2011), 35-36.
38. Mallaby, *More Money Than God: Hedge Funds and the Making of a New Elite*, 266.
39. Ludwig Chincarini, 'Hedge Funds – An Introduction', in *Research Handbook on Hedge Funds, Private Equity and Alternative Investments*, ed. Phoebus Athanassiou (Edward Elgar, 2012), 14.
40. In the beginning of 2006, the European hedge fund industry countered around 1.250 funds managing an amount of capital in excess of USD 325 billion. *See* Internal Market and Services DG European Commission, *Report of the Alternative Investment Expert Group: Managing, Servicing and Marketing Hedge Funds in Europe* (July 2006), 13.
41. *See* Lhabitant, *Hedge Funds: Myths and Limits*, 22.
42. While the US remains the world's leading location for hedge fund management with over 70% global hedge fund assets managed out of the US, Europe managed to increase its share from 13% in 2002 to around 20% of global assets under management in 2017. New York remains the favourite location for US hedge fund managers with approximately 34% of global hedge fund assets managed from New York. The leading centre for hedge fund management in Europe is the UK. At the start of the COVID pandemic, nearly 13% of global hedge fund assets under management were managed from the UK. The overwhelming majority of UK managers are based in London, making it thus a leading hedge fund centre. 'How Brexit and Covid-19 Combined to Hit UK Hedge Funds', Financial Times, https://www.ft.com/content/1583f02f-2973-4597-942d-98a25c158a65; 'Preqin Special Report: Hedge Funds in Europe', June 2017. London is also the leading centre for hedge fund service providers including prime brokers, custodians and auditors. Popular jurisdictions for hedge fund domiciliation are the Cayman Islands, the British Virgin Islands, Bermuda, the US, Luxembourg and Ireland. For instance, under a typical hedge fund structure in Europe, a UK-based hedge fund manager or a US fund manager willing to access the European market will set up a fund or multiple funds in Luxembourg or Ireland. In choosing the jurisdiction of domiciliation investment managers will pay attention to the expertise offered by the relevant jurisdiction, its reputation with investors, the flexibility of its legal regime and the availability of reputed service providers. Fanny Sergent, 'Luxembourg: A Hedge Fund Center "Par Excellence"', *HFM Week Special Report: Luxembourg 2015* (2015): 6-7.

a growing number of hedge fund managers had to fiercely compete for a limited number of opportunities.[43] Another important factor was the financialization[44] of Europe during the 2000s. Europe saw its financial sector grow exponentially with European countries embracing the latest innovations in finance. European policymakers promoted the liberalization of the financial sector and the integration of European financial markets, which were previously highly fragmented along national lines.[45] The development of integrated and deep financial markets allowed hedge fund managers to deploy their strategies freely across the European continent.

The industry's boom ended abruptly with the bursting of the housing bubble in the US and the subsequent credit crunch, which paralysed the global financial system. Even though hedge funds were able to navigate the early stages of the financial crisis with the average hedge fund gaining 10.4 % in 2007,[46] the collapse of Lehman Brothers in September 2008 and the ensuing panic had a severe impact on the industry. Faced with a drying up of funding liquidity due to withdrawals from panicked investors,[47] collateral calls, and the freezing of credit markets, hedge funds were forced to deleverage and exit their positions at a loss.[48] The losses led to more investor withdrawals and margin calls, thus creating a vicious cycle. The hedge fund industry reported a 19 % annual loss in 2008,[49] while approximately 1,500 funds underwent liquidation representing an astonishing 15 % of the total number of hedge funds.[50] In 2009, hedge funds were able to recoup a substantial part of the losses suffered during the financial crisis gaining on average 18.6 % and achieving their best annual performance in a decade.[51]

43. *Ibid.*
44. As Epstein notes 'financialization means the increasing role of financial motives, financial markets, financial actors and financial institutions in the operation of the domestic and international economies'. Gerald A Epstein, *Financialization and the World Economy* (Edward Elgar, 2005), 3.
45. The integration of financial markets was one of the goals included in the Lisbon Agenda, as it was considered a means of enhancing the efficient allocation of capital, thereby promoting growth and employment. *See* Presidency Conclusions, Lisbon European Council (23 March 2000). The process of integration of European financial markets involved the deregulation of financial markets across Europe with the dismantling of restrictions on cross-border financial transactions and the repeal of regulations limiting the operation of foreign market participants in domestic financial markets. *See* Mads Andenas, 'Who Is Going to Supervise Europe's Financial Markets', in *Financial Markets in Europe: Towards a Single Regulator*, ed. Mads Andenas and Yannis Avgerinos (Kluwer Law International, 2003), 16.
46. Katherine Burton & Jenny Strasburg, 'Jpmorgan, Renaissance Trail Hedge-Fund Gains in 2007', Bloomberg, http://www.bloomberg.com/apps/news?pid=newsarchive&sid=aF2.5PL13F4o.
47. Redemption requests reached a staggering 20 % of client funds in the last quarter of 2008. *See* United States Financial Crisis Inquiry Commission, *The Financial Crisis Inquiry Report: Final Report of the National Commission on the Causes of the Financial and Economic Crisis in the United States* (2011), 361.
48. Noreen Clancy Lloyd Dixon and Krishna B. Kumar, *Rand Corporation, Hedge Funds and Systemic Risk* (Rand Corporation, 2012).
49. Credit Suisse/Tremont Hedge Index, *One for the History Books: Hedge Fund Performance in 2008* (2009), 1.
50. Hedge Fund Research, *Record Number of Hedge Funds Liquidate in 2008.*
51. Credit Suisse/Tremont Hedge Fund Index, *Hedge Funds Hit a High Note 2009 Industry Review* (2010), 1.

The intensification of the sovereign debt crisis and the turmoil in financial markets marked another challenging period for the hedge fund industry with hedge funds posting disappointing returns in 2010 and 2011.[52] Hedge funds continued their lacklustre performance, severely underperforming equity markets in 2012 and 2013. The industry's dismal performance continued during the following years with several high-profile institutional investors, such as the California Public Employees' Pension Scheme, axing their investments in hedge funds.[53] The underperformance of the industry has been attributed to the strong performance of equity and bond markets, stricter regulation and competition from mutual fund vehicles replicating hedge fund investment strategies, called liquid alternatives.[54] The year 2020 saw a resurgence in interest in hedge funds driven by the industry's best performance in over a decade.[55] Several high-profile fund managers were able to successfully navigate the market volatility caused by the coronavirus pandemic and deliver spectacular gains.[56]

Overall, one should note that recent years have seen a radical transformation of the hedge fund industry. With the exception of 2008, hedge funds have constantly underperformed equity markets since 2003, throwing their reputation for delivering market-beating returns into doubt.[57] The lacklustre performance of the industry has been accompanied by a reorientation of its profile and investment style with hedge fund managers stressing their ability to offer their investors long-term stable investment returns.[58] The increased allocations of institutional investors, which place diversification above outsized returns, have significantly contributed to this shift.[59] The influx of institutional capital has contributed to the industry's rapid growth, despite its subpar performance. At the end of 2020, hedge fund AUM surged to USD 3.6 trillion, approximately double the total from 2008.[60] Furthermore, the hedge fund

52. Emily Chasan, 'Hedge Funds Offered Weak Returns in 2010', Reuters, http://www.reuters.com/article/2010/12/31/us-hedgefunds-yearend-idUSTRE6BU1W720101231; Sue Chang, '2011 Was a Year of Horrors for Hedge Funds', The Wall Street Journal, http://www.marketwatch.com/story/2011-was-a-year-of-horrors-for-hedge-funds-2011-12-23.
53. John Authers and Mary Childs, 'Hedge Funds: Overpriced, Underperforming', Financial Times, https://www.ft.com/content/9bd1150e-1b76-11e6-b286-cddde55ca122.
54. Joseph A. McCahery and Alexander de Roode, 'The Lost Decade for Hedge Funds: Three Threats', *European Corporate Governance Institute Working Paper* No. 486 (2019).
55. Aliaj Ortenca, 'Hedge Fund Industry Assets Surge to Record $3.6tn', Financial Times, https://www.ft.com/content/6d757883-2800-469a-a719-af085568b53d.
56. Lawrence Fletcher, 'Top Hedge Funds Reap Biggest Gains in a Decade During Pandemic', Financial Times, https://www.ft.com/content/2d106227-d6e7-4ea2-9772-abb0da694e70.
57. 'Hedge Funds: Going Nowhere Fast', The Economist, http://www.economist.com/news/finance-and-economics/21568741-hedge-funds-have-had-another-lousy-year-cap-disappointing-decade-going.
58. *Ibid.*
59. Indeed, in a survey conducted by Deutsche Bank, 79% of institutional investors participating in the survey reported that their expected returns from hedge fund portfolios ranged from 5% to 10%. Deutsche Bank Markets Prime Finance, *Eleventh Annual Alternative Investment Survey* (2013), 7. Institutional capital accounted in 2012 for approximately 60% of global assets under management. KPMG/AIMA, *KPMG/AIMA Global Hedge Fund Survey: The Evolution of an Industry* (2012), 5.
60. Stephen Foley, 'Hedge Holdings Soar Despite Returns Trailing Behind Equities', Financial Times, http://www.ft.com/intl/cms/s/0/5ed8bd60-61a5-11e3-916e-00144feabdc0.html#axzz3BWm0pIlK; Rob Copeland, 'Hedge Funds Drive to Another Record', The Wall Street Journal, http://online.wsj.com/news/articles/SB10001424052702304049904579516132458546194. *See*

industry has witnessed a high level of consolidation, particularly during the last decade, with the largest funds controlling the majority of hedge fund assets.[61] Another interesting development is the slow but gradual globalization of the hedge fund industry. While the US and Europe remain by far the leading markets for hedge fund management, the tremendous growth of the Asian-Pacific economies has significantly boosted the local hedge fund industry, which reached USD 121 billion of AUM.[62] Hong Kong and Singapore have emerged as regional hubs for hedge fund managers seeking to enter the Asian-Pacific market,[63] while Chinese authorities have opened their market to foreign competitors and are moving aggressively to develop Shanghai into a global hedge fund centre.[64] Brazil and South Africa represent two additional upcoming hedge fund centres, especially for hedge fund managers operating in Latin America and Africa, respectively.[65]

1.2.2 Hedge Funds: Definition and Characteristics

1.2.2.1 In Search of a Definition of Hedge Funds

Despite the exponential growth of the industry since its inception in 1949, its popularity and esteem with the investment community and the attention it has garnered from regulators and the public alike, hedge funds lack a formal, universally accepted

Barth et al. estimate that the net assets under management of the hedge fund industry are much larger than regulators' and industry experts' estimates. The authors estimate that in 2016 hedge funds had at least USD 5.2 trillion assets under management. *See also* Daniel Barth et al., 'The Hedge Fund Industry Is Bigger (And Has Performed Better) Than You Think', *OFR Working Paper* 20-01 (March 2021).

61. As of the first quarter of 2011, 5.2% of all hedge funds managed 62.3% of total industry assets. *See* David Stowell, *Investment Banks, Hedge Funds, and Private Equity* (Academic Press, 2012), 227. Ibbotson et al. measuring the performance of about 8.400 hedge funds from January 1995 until December 2009 find that the largest 1% of hedge funds were able to substantially outperform smaller hedge funds delivering a compound annual return net of fees of 11.59%. In contrast, the smallest 50% of hedge funds delivered a compound annual return net of fees of just 6.85%. *See* Roger G Ibbotson, Peng Chen and Kevin X Zhu, 'The ABCs of Hedge Funds: Alphas, Betas, and Costs', *Financial Analysts Journal* 67, no. 1 (2011).
62. Preqin, *Global Hedge Fund Report* (2014), 25; Mia Lamar, 'Hedge Funds Multiply in Asia, Pursuing Flood of Cash', http://online.wsj.com/news/articles/SB10001424052702303704304579382243771070218. *See also* 'Global Hedge Fund Report' (Preqin, 2020), 15-16.
63. Preqin, *Preqin Special Report: Asia-Pacific Hedge Funds Potential for Record Growth* (September 2013), 10.
64. 'China Hedge Funds Add $200 Billion, Trouncing Wall Street', Bloomberg, https://www.bloomberg.com/news/articles/2021-02-07/china-hedge-funds-add-200-billion-trouncing-wall-street-rivals. For instance, the government of Shanghai's Hongkou district launched the Shanghai Hedge Fund Zone with the ambition for Hongkou to compete with Mayfair in London or Manhattan in New York. The attraction of the Hedge Fund Zone for hedge fund managers lies in the generous tax and other benefits provided to hedge fund management companies. Rusell Flannery, 'Former Shanghai Ghetto District Moves to Turn Itself into China's Hedge Fund Hub', http://www.forbes.com/sites/russellflannery/2013/10/19/former-shanghai-ghetto-moves-to-turn-itself-into-china-hedge-fund-hub/.
65. Preqin, *Global Hedge Fund Report*, 46.

definition.[66] The difficulty in devising an accurate definition of hedge funds stems from the wide variety of investment strategies employed by them,[67] the diversity in their legal and business structures[68] and the fact that hedge funds and other institutional investors often engage in the same practices, thereby making any efforts to distinguish between them impracticable.[69] Further confusion is caused by the inclusion of the word 'hedge', leading one to assume that a defining characteristic of hedge funds is the use of hedging strategies pursuant to the original Jones model. One should note that even though hedge funds do commonly engage in trading strategies seeking to insulate their investors from adverse market movements,[70] this is not always the case. For instance, directional strategies, a popular category of hedge fund investment strategies, including dedicated short selling and global macro investing, are based on the placing of aggressive bets on the future direction of markets or securities with no or minimal utilization of hedging to reduce market risk.

Various regulatory authorities, international organizations, industry associations and academics have sought to define hedge funds either by focusing on the broad characteristics that hedge funds share, which distinguish them from other investment vehicles, most notably mutual funds, or by describing them by reference to what they are not rather to what they are.[71] Nonetheless, the definitions proposed tend to be either overinclusive or under-inclusive and therefore unsuccessful in providing an accurate and unambiguous definition of hedge funds. An example of a widely used overinclusive definition was offered by PWG, which defined hedge funds as 'any pooled investment vehicle that is privately organized, administered by professional investment managers, and not widely available to the public'.[72] While the above-mentioned definition captures essential characteristics of hedge funds, it fails to clearly

66. Andrew Crockett, 'The Evolution and Regulation of Hedge Funds', *Banque de France, Financial Stability Review: Special Issue Hedge Funds* 10 (2007): 20.
67. Barry Eichengreen and Donald Mathieson, 'Hedge Funds, What Do We Really Know?', *IMF Economic Issues* 19 (1999).
68. International Organization of Securities Commissions, *Hedge Funds Oversight: Final Report* (2009).
69. Eichengreen and Mathieson, 'Hedge Funds, What Do We Really Know?'.
70. Examining a large sample of hedge funds, Chen finds that the majority of hedge funds trade derivatives. The use of derivatives is associated with lower fund risks such as return volatility, downside risk, and extreme event risk, as well as lower risk of fund failure in severe market conditions. These characteristics indicate that hedge funds trade derivatives for hedging purposes. Yong Chen, 'Derivatives Use and Risk Taking: Evidence from the Hedge Fund Industry', *Journal of Financial and Quantitative Analysis* 46, no. 4 (2011).
71. Negative definitions of hedge funds stress their ability to operate outside the regulatory framework for retail collective investment schemes. *See* Eilis Ferran, 'After the Crisis: The Regulation of Hedge Funds and Private Equity in the EU', *European Business Organization Law Review* 12, no. 3 (2011): 380. For an overview of various definitions offered by regulatory authorities, international organizations, industry associations and individual commentators *see* Phoebus Athanassiou, *Hedge Fund Regulation in the European Union: Current Trends and Future Prospects* (Kluwer Law International, 2009), 13-14. David A. Vaughan, 'Selected Definitions of "Hedge Fund"', *Comments for the U.S. Securities and Exchange Commission Roundtable on Hedge Funds* (2003).
72. Markets, *Hedge Funds, Leverage, and the Lessons of Long-Term Capital Management*, 1.

distinguish between hedge funds and other similar AIFs such as private equity funds.[73] Other frequently used definitions stress the employment of short-term investment strategies as a defining characteristic of hedge funds[74] disregarding the evolution of the hedge fund industry and the broadening of their investment strategies. Recent years have seen a considerable degree of convergence of the strategies of private equity and hedge funds, with hedge funds pursuing typical private equity style long-term investments such as LBOs of public and private companies and activist investing.[75]

The financial crisis of 2007-2008 triggered calls for tougher regulation of hedge funds. The result was the adoption of the AIFM Directive and the Dodd-Frank Act, which radically transformed the regulatory landscape for the hedge fund industry. These two pieces of legislation tentatively move closer towards providing a statutory definition of hedge funds. The Dodd-Frank Act introduces the concept of 'private funds' requiring all advisers to private funds to register with the SEC. A private fund is defined as any issuer that would be an investment company under section 3 of the Investment Company Act[76] but for the exemptions provided in section 3(c)(1) or

73. Private equity is a generic term encompassing a wide variety of investments. The customary characteristic of private equity investments is illiquidity since private equity involves unregistered securities. *See* Joseph A McCahery and Erik PM Vermeulen, *Corporate Governance of Non-Listed Companies* (Oxford University Press, 2010), 171. Private equity includes venture capital, development capital, mezzanine capital, leveraged buyouts and distressed investing. Venture capital funds provide financing to start-up and early state firms. Development capital involves the provision of funds to existing companies to support their expansion. Mezzanine funds provide financing to leveraged buyouts in the form of subordinated debt with equity participation in the form of warrants to subscribe for shares in the borrower while distressed debt investors purchase debt of troubled companies at a discount and use their rights as debtholders to influence the restructuring of the company gaining potentially control. The most well-known category of private equity funds is leveraged buyout funds which acquire controlling stakes in private companies or public companies which are subsequently taken private with the aim of increasing their long-term value. *See* Peter Temple, *Private Equity: Examining the New Conglomerates of European Business* (Wiley, 1999), 4. & Cyril Demaria, *Introduction to Private Equity: Venture, Growth, LBO and Turn-around Capital* (Wiley, 2013), 117-21. Private equity investments are channelled through specialized intermediaries that are usually organized as limited partnerships, commonly known as private equity funds. Private equity firms such as KKR, Blackstone, and TPG periodically establish private equity funds in the form of limited partnerships where they serve as general partners. The general partner is responsible for managing the fund. *See* George W Fenn, Nellie Liang and Stephen Prowse, *The Economics of the Private Equity Market*, Staff Series (Board of Governors of the Federal Reserve System (US), 1995), 28. In order to evade onerous regulatory requirements, private equity funds are closed to retail investors and impose a high minimum investment threshold. Financial Services Authority, 'Private Equity: A Discussion of Risk and Regulatory Engagement', Discussion Paper 06/6 (2006): 23.
74. *See*, for instance, Davis Polk and Wardwell, 'A Fund by Any Other Name: The Convergence of Hedge Funds and Private Equity Funds', *Private Equity Newsletter* (2006): 1.
75. Jonathan R. Macey, *Corporate Governance: Promises Kept, Promises Broken* (Princeton University Press, 2010), 244-51. Activist hedge funds acquire large non-controlling stakes in public companies and use their influence to advocate for changes in the governance, capital structure and operating performance of target firms. As Shadab notes 'even though hedge fund activists do not manage portfolio companies as closely as private equity funds do, activist hedge funds are much closer strategically and structurally to private equity funds'. Houman B. Shadab, 'Coming Together after the Crisis: Global Convergence of Private Equity and Hedge Funds', *Northwestern Journal of International Law and Business* 29, no. 3 (2009): 612.
76. Lynn A Stout, 'The Mechanisms of Market Inefficiency: An Introduction to the New Finance', *Journal of Corporation Law* 28, no. 4 (2002).

3(c)(7) of the Investment Company Act.[77] Furthermore, the Volcker Rule explicitly defines hedge funds along with private equity funds as any issuer that would be an investment company but for the use of the above-mentioned exemptions.[78] Even though virtually all hedge funds in the US take advantage of the exemptions granted by section 3(c)(1) and 3(c)(7) in order to evade the onerous regulatory requirements imposed by the Investment Company Act,[79] one should note that these exemptions are utilized not only by a variety of AIFs including private equity funds, venture capital funds and commodity funds but also by other mainstream corporate entities such as joint ventures and acquisition vehicles.[80] As a result, the definition provided by the Dodd-Frank Act suffers from being overinclusive and fails to address the specific characteristics associated with hedge funds.

A more substantive definition of hedge funds, which captures some of their essential characteristics, has been adopted by the SEC in connection with the imposition of disclosure requirements on hedge funds. For the purposes of Form PF, the SEC has defined hedge funds as any private fund that exhibits any of the following characteristics: (a) charges a performance fee that takes into account market gains instead of only realized gains, (b) high leverage, or (c) short selling.[81] While the definition offered by the SEC represents a marked improvement over previous definitions, it neglects key characteristics of hedge funds, most notably that they are open strictly to sophisticated investors.

European regulators have not fared much better than their US counterparts in their quest for a substantive and accurate definition of hedge funds. The AIFM Directive adopted in the aftermath of the financial crisis creates a pan-European regulatory framework for AIFMs managing or marketing funds in the EU. An AIFM is defined as any entity managing AIF as a regular business.[82] An AIF is considered any 'collective investment undertaking' which raises capital from a number of investors in

77. Dodd-Frank Act, section 402(a)(29), 15 U.S.C. §80b-2(a)(29). Section 3(c)1 of the Investment Company Act exempts an issuer that has hundred or fewer holders of its securities and that does not engage or propose to engage in a public offering of securities. Section 3(c)(7) of the Investment Company Act exempts an issuer whose security holders are all qualified purchasers and that does not engage or propose to engage in a public offering of securities. *See* Investment Company Act of 1940, Pub. L. No. 76-768, Ch. 686, Title 1, 54 Stat. 789 (Codified as Amended at 15 U.S.C. §§80a-L-80a-64), §3c(1) & (7), 15 U.S.C.§80(a)-3(c)(1) & (7).
78. Dodd-Frank Act, section 619, §13(h)(2), 12 U.S.C. §1851(h)(2).
79. The Investment Company Act of 1940 severely limits the ability of investment companies to utilize leverage, derivatives and short selling which are key investment tools used by hedge funds, in order to implement their investment strategies.
80. Kevin Petrasic, 'The Volcker Rule Proposal-Many Questions, Few Answers', *Paul Hastings Memorandum* (November 2011); Financial Stability Oversight Council, *Study & Recommendations on Prohibitions on Proprietary Trading & Certain Relationships with Hedge Funds & Private Equit Funds* (January 2011), 60-61.
81. Commodities Futures Trading Commission and Securities and Exchange Commission, *Reporting by Investment Advisers to Private Funds and Certain Commodity Pool Operators and Commodity Trading Advisors on Form Pf* (2011), 22-29. Form PF is a report filed periodically by registered hedge fund advisers containing information regarding the funds managed. *See* 17 C.F.R. §275.204(b)-1 (requiring private fund advisers to file Form PF with the SEC periodically).
82. Directive 2011/61/EU of the European Parliament and of the Council of 8 June 2011 on Alternative Investment Fund Managers and Amending Directives 2003/41/EC and 2009/65/EC and Regulations (EC) No. 1060/2009 and (EU) No. 1095/2010, 2011 O.J. (L 174) 1 Art. 8, at 21.

order to invest it according to a defined investment policy and does not require authorization pursuant to Article 5 of Directive 2009/65/EC (commonly known as UCITS Directive).[83] The above-mentioned definition certainly encompasses hedge funds as collective investment vehicles falling outside the UCITS regulatory regime. Nonetheless, the concept of AIFs as introduced by the AIFM Directive captures all non-UCITS funds, including private equity funds, real estate funds, commodity funds, venture capital funds and retail non-UCITS funds.[84]

1.2.2.2 Common Characteristics

As Nabilou and Pacces note, despite the difficulties associated with defining hedge funds in a manner which is adequately inclusive and sufficiently exclusive of all their aspects, a working definition is necessary in order to make progress in studying them.[85] A working definition of hedge funds centred upon their unique industry-wide characteristics that demarcate them from other investment vehicles, most notably mutual funds, is the second best to a concrete and unambiguous definition.[86]

First and foremost, hedge funds are able to operate unconstrained in public and private markets following a wide variety of actively managed[87] investment strategies[88] and employing sophisticated investment techniques such as short selling, derivatives trading and leveraged investing techniques, which are severely curtailed or even prohibited for mutual fund managers. The Investment Company Act of 1940 in the US

83. *Ibid.*, Art. 4(1)(a), at 16. The UCITS Directive creates common minimum regulatory standards for UCITS. Directive 2009/65/EC of the European Parliament and of the Council of 13 July 2009 on the Coordination of Laws, Regulations and Administrative Provisions Relating to Undertakings for Collective Investment in Transferable Securities (UCITS), 2009 O.J. (L 302) 32. Pursuant to Art. 1 of the UCITS Directive, UCITS are defined as undertakings with the sole object of collective investment in enumerated transferable securities and liquid financial assets, which raise their capital from the public, operate in accordance with the principle of risk-spreading and whose investors may upon request freely redeem their units. Collective investment schemes, which are authorized in accordance with the Directive, are allowed to freely market their units across the European Union. The overwhelming majority of European mutual funds are established as UCITS funds and authorized pursuant to the Directive, reaping thus the benefits of the Pan-European passport. For an overview of the UCITS regime and its history *see* Kevin R Johannsen, 'Jumping the Gun: Hedge Funds in Search of Capital under UCITS IV', *Brooklyn Journal of Corporate Financial and Commercial Law* 5, no. 2 (2010).
84. Stephen Robinson, 'The AIFMD Unveiled', in *Hedge Funds: Jurisdictional Comparisons*, ed. Stephen Ball (Sweet and Maxwell, 2013); Deloitte, *Alternative Investment Fund Managers Directive: Meeting the Challenge* (Deloitte, 2013).
85. Hossein Nabilou and Alessio M Pacces, 'Hedge Fund Regulation Dilemma: Direct vs. Indirect Regulation', *William and Mary Business Law Review* 6, no. 1 (2015): 185.
86. Athanassiou, *Hedge Fund Regulation in the European Union: Current Trends and Future Prospects*, 15-16.
87. The active management of hedge funds can be contrasted with index funds, a popular category of mutual funds, which passively replicate an index without seeking to influence it. *See* Macey Jonathan Carnell Richard Scott and Miller Geoffrey, *The Law of Financial Institutions*, 4th ed. (Wolters Kluwer, 2013), 738-39.
88. On the contrary, long-only mutual funds, which comprise the majority of the mutual fund universe, follow a single investment strategy of buying and holding assets usually public equities or bonds.

prohibits open-end registered investment companies[89] from using leverage except for bank debt subject to an asset coverage ratio of 300%,[90] while it severely restricts derivatives trading and short selling.[91] Furthermore, the UCITS Directive prohibits UCITS funds from borrowing and engaging in short sales.[92] Nonetheless, these limitations do not bite as short selling and leverage can be undertaken through the use of derivatives with leverage acquired through derivatives capped at a maximum of 100%.[93]

What is more, unlike mutual funds whose performance is measured by reference to a market index, hedge funds seek absolute returns irrespective of market movements or 'alpha', which stands for managerial skill.[94] This pursuit is enhanced by the high-powered performance-based compensation of hedge fund managers. Pursuant to industry practice, the compensation of a hedge fund manager consists of an annual management fee, typically set at 2% of AUM along with an incentive fee usually set at 20% of the fund's annual profits, which is widely known as 'carried interest'.[95]

Another important feature of hedge funds, which distinguishes them from mutual funds, is the limited liquidity offered to their investors. In contrast to mutual funds, which offer daily liquidity to their investors, hedge funds restrict the ability of fund investors to withdraw their capital. Redemption restrictions seek to avoid catastrophic runs by hedge fund investors, which destabilize the fund's liquidity and endanger its investment strategy. Hedge funds accept new investor subscriptions usually at the

89. Mutual funds in the US typically take the form of open-end investment companies registered under the Investment Company Act.
90. Section 18 of the Investment Company Act limits the ability of a registered investment company to issue 'senior securities'. Section 18(g) defines a 'senior security' as 'any bond, debenture, note or similar obligation or instruments constituting a security or evidencing indebtedness, and any stock of a class having priority over any other class as to distribution of assets or payment of dividends'. Investment Company Act §18(g), 15 U.S.C. §80a-18(g). Open-end investment companies are prohibited from issuing any 'senior security' but are allowed to borrow from a US-regulated bank provided that an asset coverage ratio of at least 300% is maintained. Investment Company Act of 1940 §18(f), 15 U.S.C. §80a-18(f).
91. The SEC has extended the concept of 'senior security' to short sales and certain derivative transactions such as future contracts, options and currency forwards. SEC staff interpretations of the Investment Company Act require a registered investment engaging in short sales and certain derivatives transactions to either hold an offsetting long position in the financial instrument or to segregate an amount of liquid assets sufficient to offset the relevant short position or position in derivatives. *See* Emerald Mgmt. Co., SEC No-Action Letter, 1978 SEC No-Act. 502, at 2 (21 January 1978) & Thomas Harman Georgia Bullitt, Christopher Menconi, Bill Zimmerman and Christopher Jackson, 'Legal Considerations for Registered Investment Companies Investing in Derivatives: Part I', *The Investment Lawyer* 17, no. 8 (2010): 14-16.
92. Directive 2009/65/EC of the European Parliament and of the Council of 13 July 2009 on the Coordination of Laws, Regulations and Administrative Provisions Relating to Undertakings for Collective Investment in Transferable Securities (UCITS), 2009 O.J. (L 302) 32, Art. 83, at 93-94.
93. Exposure arising from derivative instruments must not exceed the total net value of the fund's portfolio. *Ibid.*, Art. 51(3), at 71.
94. 'Alpha' refers to the excess return of a hedge fund relative to the return offered by investing in the stock, bond market or other active investment vehicles. *See* Houman B Shadab, 'Hedge Fund Governance', *Stanford Journal of Law, Business, and Finance* 19, no. 1 (2013): 187.
95. Mutual fund managers on the contrary are compensated solely with a management fee and are not entitled to any share in the funds' profits. *See* 'Hedge Funds and the Financial Market', *Committee on Oversight and Government Reform, Hedge Funds and the Financial Markets* (2008): 4.

beginning of calendar months and may close themselves to new subscriptions if they have reached their desired level of AUM.[96] In addition, investors are allowed to redeem their capital only on a periodic basis with current market practice being at the end of each quarter.[97] Other widely used liquidity management tools are 'lock-ups', 'gates', and 'side pockets'. Lock-ups prevent investors from withdrawing their capital for a minimum period after their investment usually set at one year or longer, while gates limit withdrawals to a specified percentage of the fund's overall capital.[98] Hedge fund managers may also retain the right to completely suspend investor redemptions, albeit only in the most dire circumstances.[99] Furthermore, in order to protect the value of illiquid investments from investor withdrawals, hedge fund managers increasingly use 'side pockets'. Side pockets are sub-accounts where illiquid investments are placed.[100] Investors are not able to redeem their capital until the liquidation of the investments subject to the side pocket.[101]

Finally, due to regulatory constraints, hedge funds are open only to sophisticated investors,[102] although recent years have seen the spread of products seeking to offer the benefits of hedge fund investing to retail investors.[103] Investors in hedge funds are subject to minimum investment thresholds typically starting as low as USD 25.000 and reaching as high as USD 1 million.[104] Regulatory constraints limiting hedge fund investing to sophisticated investors are grounded in a public concern that the complex and volatile nature of hedge fund investment strategies and the superior bargaining power of hedge fund managers make hedge funds unsuitable for retail investors who are unable to 'fend for themselves' lacking the requisite skills, experience and wealth to understand the risks associated with hedge fund strategies, conduct adequate due

96. Scott J. Lederman, *Hedge Fund Regulation*, 2nd ed. (Practicing Law Institute, May 2016), para. 2.2.4.
97. Moreover, investors must typically give a thirty to ninety day's advance notice of their intention to redeem their shares. *See* Lhabitant, *Hedge Funds: Myths and Limits*, 17.
98. Lederman, *Hedge Fund Regulation*, paras 2.3.3. D(3)(a) & D(3)(b).
99. Stowell, *Investment Banks, Hedge Funds, and Private Equity*, 214.
100. Lederman, *Hedge Fund Regulation*, para. 2.3.3. E(1).
101. *Ibid.*
102. For a review of the US regulations that hedge funds seek to evade *see* the relevant discussion in section 1.2.3. Furthermore, the AIFM Directive regulates the marketing of hedge funds to professional investors across the EU. Nevertheless, in accordance with Art. 43 of the AIFM Directive individual Member States have the freedom to decide whether to allow the marketing of hedge funds to retail investors in their territory and impose stricter requirements than the ones imposed by the Directive.
103. The most widespread products are funds of hedge funds, namely funds that invest in multiple individual hedge funds. Recent developments include: the initial public offerings of hedge fund managers, the proliferation of exchange-traded funds and indexes seeking to track the performance of hedge funds, and the offering of hedged mutual funds namely mutual funds which use hedge-fund-like strategies. *See generally* Steven Davidoff, 'Black Market Capital', *Columbia Business Law Review* 2008, no. 1 (2008).
104. Julie Steinberg, 'Funds of Hedge Funds Come with Heaps of Fees', The Wall Street Journal, http://online.wsj.com/news/articles/SB10001424052702304448204579183973097089350. Mi nimum investment thresholds can reach exorbitant levels for the most sought-after funds. For instance, in its heyday Long-Term Capital Management had a minimum investment threshold of USD 10 million. *See* Mark Jickling, 'Lessons of Long-Term Capital Management and Amaranth Advisors', in *Research Handbook on Hedge Funds, Private Equity and Alternative Investments*, ed. Phoebus Athanassiou (Edward Elgar Publishing, Inc., 2012), 26.

diligence, purchase the services of sophisticated purchaser representatives, protect their interests against opportunistic behaviour by hedge fund managers and absorb the losses arising from poor investment decisions.[105]

1.2.3 Hedge Fund Organizational Structures and Service Providers

In its most basic format, a hedge fund structure is in essence a two-tiered organization consisting of two entities: the fund itself and the investment management firm managing the fund, commonly termed the 'hedge fund manager'.[106] Hedge fund management firms establish hedge funds in the form of limited partnerships,[107] where they serve as general partners. The general partner is responsible for managing the fund. Furthermore, the general partner solicits capital from investors, who are the limited partners of these funds. A limited partnership limits the liability of limited partners to the extent of their invested capital, with the general partner being liable for the partnership's obligations.[108] In order to retain their limited liability protection,

105. Prohibition of Fraud by Advisers to Certain Pooled Investment Vehicles; Accredited Investors in Certain Private Investment Vehicles, 72 Fed. Reg. 400, 406 (proposed 4 January 2007) (SEC's proposal to increase the 'accreditor investor standards' under Regulation D) & Houman B Shadab, 'Fending for Themselves: Creating a US Hedge Fund Market for Retail Investors', *New York University Journal of Legislation and Public Policy* 11, no. 2 (2007): 290-94.
106. It would be a rather futile endeavour to try to provide a complete examination of the various structures used by hedge funds around the world. Taking into account that the US remains the largest market for hedge fund management and one of the largest markets for hedge fund domiciliation, our discussion will be limited to the structure used by US hedge fund managers managing US-based funds, the US domestic-only single fund structure. In practice, US hedge fund managers utilize a variety of structures in order to meet the needs of their investors. Non-US investors and US tax-exempt investors, such as endowments, foundations and pensions, prefer investing in offshore funds due to tax considerations. In contrast, US-taxable investors gravitate towards domestic funds as investing in offshore funds carries adverse tax consequences. Since it is impossible to organize a single fund catering to the needs of every type of investor, US hedge fund managers utilize a variety of multiple fund structures. In a parallel fund structure, the fund manager will organize and operate two different funds, a domestic one and an offshore one. US taxable investors will invest in the domestic fund, while non-US investors and US tax-exempt investors will invest in the offshore fund. Alternatively, the fund manager may decide to use a 'master-feeder' structure. In a 'master-feeder' structure, the fund manager will establish a domestic 'feeder' fund raising capital from US-taxable investors and an offshore 'feeder' fund raising capital from non-US investors and US tax-exempt investors. The funds will then contribute their capital into a master fund, which will hold and manage the investment portfolio. For an excellent overview of the different hedge fund structures utilized by US hedge fund managers *see* Lederman, *Hedge Fund Regulation*, paras 2-4, 2-6, 2-20 to 2-38.
107. Funds are organized as limited partnerships, in order to take advantage of the pass-through treatment of partnership profits. Tax liability on partnership profits is not incurred at the entity level, but is rather passed on to the individual investors. *See* Alan L Kennard, 'The Hedge Fund Versus the Mutual Fund', *The Tax Lawyer* 57, no. 1 (2003). An increasing number of hedge funds are structured as limited liability companies, a new form of business organization offered under state law. Limited liability companies enjoy pass-through tax treatment, while they also afford their members and managers limited liability. *See generally* Larry E Ribstein, 'Uncorporation and Corporate Indeterminacy', *University of Illinois Law Review* (2009).
108. In order to limit its liability for the partnership's obligations, the general partner will itself be usually organized as a limited partnership, a limited liability company or a Subchapter S corporation. A Subchapter S corporation is a corporation, which elects to be taxed under

limited partners are prohibited from participating in the fund's management. The general partner owes fiduciary duties to the limited partners, which can be restricted or even completely eliminated by the partnership's operating agreement.[109] The operating agreement delineates the precise rights and duties between the general partner and the limited partners, including the general partner's compensation and the limited partners' exit rights.

US federal law also indirectly impacts the structure of hedge funds. The main statutes applicable to hedge funds are the Securities Act,[110] the Exchange Act,[111] the Investment Company Act[112] and the Advisers Act.[113] The Securities Act regulates the offering and sales of securities to the public. Companies raising capital in the public markets are required to file a registration statement with the SEC and deliver to purchasers a prospectus containing information about the issuer and the securities being offered.[114] Furthermore, the Securities Act places restrictions on the dissemination of information regarding the offering and sale of securities, which is not part of the registration statement or the prospectus.[115] Hedge funds raise capital by issuing limited partnership or LLC-member interests to prospective investors. Since interests in hedge funds are considered securities for the purposes of federal securities law,[116] hedge funds are subject to the Act's registration and prospectus delivery requirements.

In order to avoid the costly and time-consuming registration process, hedge funds structure their offerings and sales of interests pursuant to a private placement exempted from the registration and prospectus delivery requirements under section 4(2) or Rule 506 of Regulation D. Section 4(2) exempts 'transactions not involving any public offering'.[117] As the term 'public offering' is not defined in the Securities Act, its interpretation is left to the SEC and the courts. As developed by case law, the courts will consider a variety of factors in determining whether the offering is public or private in nature, including the sophistication of the offerees, their access to information, their ability to bear economic risk and the size and manner of the offering.[118] Alternatively,

---

Subchapter S of the Internal Revenue Code. In order to be eligible to make a subchapter S election, a corporation must meet certain requirements, including a hundred-shareholder limit. Subchapter S corporations resemble partnerships in that they do not pay any entity-level taxes and their profits pass through to their shareholders. *See generally* Martin J. McMahon and Daniel L. Simmons, 'When Subchapter S Meets Subchapter C', *The Tax Lawyer* 67, no. 2 (2014).

109. Winnifred A. Lewis, 'Waiving Fiduciary Duties in Delaware Limited Partnerships and Limited Liability Companies', *Fordham Law Review* 82, no. 2 (2013).
110. Securities Act of 1933 Pub. L. No. 73-22, 48 Stat. 74 (Codified at 15 U.S.C. §77a).
111. Securities Exchange Act of 1934, Pub. L. No. 73–291, 48 Stat. 881, Enacted 6 June 1934 (Codified at 15 U.S.C. §78a).
112. Investment Company Act of 1940, Pub. L. No. 76-768, Ch. 686, Title 1, 54 Stat. 789 (Codified as Amended at 15 U.S.C. §§80a-L-80a-64).
113. Investment Advisers Act of 1940, Pub. L. No. 76-768, Ch. 686, Title II, 54 Stat. 847 (Codified as Amended at 15 U.S.C. §§80b-L-80b-21).
114. Securities Act §5(a)-(c), 15 U.S.C. §§77e(a)-(c) & Stephen Jung Choi and Adam C Pritchard, *Securities Regulation* (Foundation Press, 2008), 468-70.
115. *Ibid.*
116. Securities Act, §4(1), 15 U.S.C. §77b(a)(1). *See Sec V. W.J. Howey Co.*, 328 US 293, 301 (1946).
117. Securities Act §4(2), 15 U.S.C. §77d(a)(2).
118. *See* Lederman, *Hedge Fund Regulation*, para. 4-4.

hedge funds may rely on Rule 506 of Regulation D, which provides a safe harbour for issuers of securities relying on section 4(2). Rule 506(b) allows sales of hedge fund interests to an unlimited number of 'accredited investors'[119] and up to thirty-five 'non-accredited investors'.[120] Furthermore, offerings made pursuant to Rule 506(b) must not involve any form of general solicitation or advertising.[121] Nonetheless, hedge funds may avoid the ban on general solicitation and advertising if they limit sales of their securities to accredited investors and take steps to verify that the purchasers of such securities are accredited investors.[122] Offers and sales of securities that satisfy the conditions of Rule 506(b) & (c) 'shall be deemed to be transactions not involving any public offering within the meaning of section 4(2)'. As a matter of practice, hedge funds prefer to utilize the safe harbour offered under Regulation D, instead of relying on the ambiguous section 4(2) case law.

Hedge funds may also be subject to the Exchange Act, which imposes registration and periodic reporting requirements on publicly traded companies. However, section 12(g) of the Exchange Act exempts from registration any issuer having at the end of its most recent fiscal year assets not exceeding USD 10 million or a class of equity security held of record by fewer than two thousand persons or five hundred persons who are not accredited investors.[123] Registration under the Exchange Act subjects registrants to

---

119. Rule 501(a) defines 'accredited investors' as banks, insurance companies, mutual funds, certain other institutional investors, family offices with assets in excess of USD 5,000,000, directors, executive officers and natural persons who are knowledgeable employees of the issuer, natural persons holding in good standing certain 'professional certifications or designations or credentials' designated by order of the SEC, any natural person whose individual net worth, or joint net worth with that person's spouse, excluding that person's primary residence, at the time of his purchase exceeds USD 1,000,000 and any natural person who had an individual income in excess of USD 200,000 in each of the two most recent years or joint income with that person's spouse in excess of USD 300,000 in each of those years and has a reasonable expectation of reaching the same income in the current year. *See* 17 C.F.R. 1 230.501(a)(1).
120. Non-accredited investors, either alone or with a purchaser representative, must be sophisticated – that is, they must have sufficient knowledge and experience in financial and business matters to make them capable of evaluating the merits and risks of the prospective investment. Rule 506(b)(2)(ii).
121. While the case law analysing section 4(a)(2) focuses on offerees, Rule 506 focuses on actual purchasers. Rule 506(b) provides only a limitation on the number of non-accredited investors, whose number cannot exceed thirty-five. Therefore, in principle, hedge funds may offer their securities to an unlimited number of investors, irrespective of whether they are accredited or non-accredited, sophisticated or non-sophisticated, as long as there are no more than thirty-five non-accredited actual purchasers. However, offerings of hedge fund interests are constrained by the ban on general solicitation and advertising, including advertisements published in newspapers and magazines, public websites, communications broadcasted over television and radio, and seminars where attendees have been invited by general solicitation or general advertising. One should note that the terms 'general solicitation' and 'general advertising' are not restrictively defined under Rule 502(c). The SEC has stated that an offering will not involve a general solicitation if the issuer has a reasonable belief that the offerees are accredited investors or are otherwise sophisticated focusing on the prior relationship between the offerees and the issuer in order to determine whether such a reasonable belief exists. Bradley Berman et al., *General Solicitation and General Advertising*, Harvard Law School Forum on Corporate Governance, https://corpgov.law.harvard.edu/2021/06/21/general-solicitation-and-general-advertising/.
122. 17 CFR 230.506(c).
123. Exchange Act §12(g)(1)(A), 15 U.S.C §78l(g)(1)(A).

periodic reporting requirements, requirements for proxy solicitations and tender offers, insider reporting of stock trades and short-swing profits rules.[124] Even though hedge fund interests fall within the definition of equity security,[125] hedge funds can evade registration by having fewer than 2,000 investors. Since hedge funds limit their investor base to accredited investors, the 499 non-accredited investor cap is practically not applicable to them.

Furthermore, hedge funds fall within the definition of an 'investment company' under the Investment Company Act,[126] which requires investment companies to register with the SEC, file periodic reports and comply with onerous investment restrictions. In order to avoid the application of the Investment Company Act, hedge funds rely on the safe harbour rules of section 3(c)(1) or 3(c)(7). Section 3(c)(1) exempts from the definition of investment company hedge funds that do not offer and sell their securities in a public offering and have fewer than hundred beneficial owners.[127] Furthermore, section 3(c)(7) exempts any issuer, the outstanding securities of which are owned exclusively by persons who at the time of acquisition of such securities are 'qualified purchasers' and which is not making and does not at the time propose to make a public offering of such securities.[128] Hedge funds tend to use the exemption provided by section 3(c)(7) as it does not limit the number of investors in

---

124. *See* Exchange Act §13, 15 U.S.C. §78m, Securities Act §14, 15 U.S.C. §78n & Exchange Act §16, 15 U.S.C. §78p. Short-swing profits liability is established under section 16(b) of the Exchange Act, which seeks to prevent abusive behaviour by insiders. According to section 16(b), any profit realized by any person, who is directly or indirectly the beneficial owner of more than 10% of any class of any equity security registered pursuant to section 12 of the Exchange Act, from any purchase and sale, or any sale and purchase, of any equity security of such issuer within any period of less than six months must be disgorged to the issuer. Section 16(b) does not cover transactions where such beneficial owner was not such at the time of the purchase and sale, or the sale and purchase. Exchange Act §16(b), 15 U.S.C. §78p(b).
125. Securities and Exchange Commission, *Implications of the Growth of Hedge Funds* (Washington, Dc: Securities and Exchange Commission, 2003), 18-19.
126. Section 3(a)(1)(A) of the Investment Company Act defines an investment company as 'an issuer, which is or holds itself out as being engaged primarily, or proposes to engage primarily, in the business of investing, reinvesting or trading in securities', while section 3(a)(1)(C) of the Act also defines an investment company as 'an issuer that is engaged or proposes to engage in the business of investing, reinvesting, owning, holding or trading in securities, and owns or proposes to acquire investment securities having a value exceeding 40 percent of the value of its total assets on an unconsolidated basis'. *See* Investment Company Act §3(a)(1)(A), (C), 15 U.S.C. §80a-3(a)(1)(A), (C).
127. Investment Company Act §3(c)(1), 15 U.S.C. §80a-3(c)(1).
128. Investment Company Act §3(c)(7), 15 U.S.C. §80a-3(c)(7). *See also* Investment Company Act §2(a)(51), 15 U.S.C. §80a-2(a)(51) defining a 'qualified purchaser' as '(i) any natural person (including any person who holds a joint, community property, or other similar shared ownership interest in an issuer that is excepted under section 3(c)(7) with that person's qualified purchaser spouse) who owns not less than $5.000.000 in investments, as defined by the Commission; (ii) any company that owns not less than $5.000.000 in investments and that is owned directly or indirectly by or for 2 or more natural persons who are related as siblings or spouse (including former spouses), or direct lineal descendants by birth or adoption, spouses of such persons, the estates of such persons, or foundations, charitable organizations, or trusts established by or for the benefit of such persons; (iii) any trust that is not covered by clause (ii) and that was not formed for the specific purpose of acquiring the securities offered, as to which the trustee or other person authorized to make decisions with respect to the trust, and each settlor or other person who has contributed assets to the trust, is a person described in clause (i), (ii), or (iv); or (iv) any person, acting for its own account or the accounts of other

the fund. One should note, however, that in order to avoid the application of the Exchange Act of 1934, hedge funds limit the number of investors to two thousand.

Finally, the Advisers Act requires investment advisers to register with the SEC and comply with the provisions of the Advisers Act, which mandate, among other things, periodic filings to the SEC, the maintenance of business records and the disclosure of information to the advisers' clients.[129] Hedge fund managers managing a fund's portfolio are captured by the broad definition of investment adviser of the Advisers Act and are therefore required to register under the Advisers Act,[130] unless they are prohibited from registering under the Advisers Act or an exemption from registration applies. Prior to the adoption of the Dodd-Frank Act, hedge fund managers were able to avoid registration under the Advisers Act by relying on the private adviser exemption provided by section 203(b)(3) that exempted an investment adviser that had fourteen or fewer clients during the preceding twelve months, did not hold itself out to the public as an investment adviser and did not advise a registered investment company. Hedge funds were able to count as clients the individual funds, rather than the individual investors in the funds. As a result, hedge fund managers evaded registration by managing fewer than fifteen individual hedge funds. Nonetheless, Title IV of the Dodd-Frank Act repealed the private adviser exemption contained in section 203(b)(3). As a result, hedge fund managers must register with the SEC and comply with the provisions of the Advisers Act.

A number of third-party service providers are involved in the day-to-day operations of hedge funds. The most significant service providers are prime brokers, which are part of major financial institutions, such as Goldman Sachs, JP Morgan Chase, Morgan Stanley, Credit Suisse and Deutsche Bank. The services offered by prime brokers include the financing of hedge funds' trades, clearing and settlement services, acting as global custodians of funds' assets, securities lending to cover short sales, and capital introduction services, which assist hedge fund managers in their capital raising activities by introducing them to potential investors. Prime brokerage services represent a major source of revenue for financial institutions and are utilized, apart from hedge funds, by a number of market participants, including private equity funds, venture capital funds, mutual funds and corporations. Another important hedge fund service provider is the custodian, which is responsible for safekeeping hedge fund

qualified purchasers, who in the aggregate owns and invests on a discretionary basis, not less than $25.000.000 in investments'.

129. Investment Advisers Act §203(a), 15 U.S.C. §80b-3(a). A detailed examination of the provisions of the Advisers Act and the amendments introduced by the Dodd-Frank Act will be discussed extensively in Chapter 3.

130. An 'investment adviser' is defined in section 202(a)(11) of the Advisers Act as 'any person who, for compensation, engages in the business of advising others, either directly or through publications or writings, as to the value of securities or as to the advisability of investing in, purchasing, or selling securities, or who, for compensation and as part of a regular business, issues or promulgates analyses or reports concerning securities'. Investment Advisers Act §202(a)(11), 15 U.S.C. §80b-2(a)(11).

assets.[131] Finally, administrators offer independent pricing and NAV calculation services. They also perform a number of administrative services, such as accounting and bookkeeping, legal support and investor relations.

1.2.4 Hedge Fund Investment Strategies

As the hedge fund industry has grown and matured, hedge funds have deviated from the original Jones' approach to investing, adopting a wide variety of investment strategies with divergent risk and return profiles. Categorizing hedge fund investment strategies has proven to be a challenging endeavour. For instance, Fung and Hsieh offer a classification of hedge fund strategies by virtue of the type of positions that the fund manager is taking (referred to as the investment strategy's 'style') and the asset class that the fund concentrates its investments in (referred to as the investment strategy's 'location').[132] Another popular approach is to distinguish between market neutral and directional investment strategies.[133] While market neutral strategies exhibit a low correlation with the market, directional strategies are based on the placing of aggressive one-way bets on market movements. Hedge funds are also often categorized according to whether they employ systematic or discretionary investment strategies.[134] Hedge funds adopting systematic strategies employ sophisticated computer programs in order to spot market opportunities, with limited human intervention. In contrast, discretionary trading is based on the hedge fund manager's skills, experience and judgment. Despite the discord with regard to the classification of hedge fund strategies, one can distinguish four broad categories of investment strategies: equity-related, arbitrage and relative value strategies, event-driven strategies and directional strategies.[135]

Equity-related strategies can be divided into two subcategories: long-short equity and non-hedged equity. The long-short equity investment approach was originally pioneered by Alfred Winslow Jones and is based on the combination of long and short positions in equities with the aim of reducing market risk. Hedge fund managers

131. The failure of major hedge fund prime brokers housed within large financial institutions in recent years, such as Bear Stearns, Lehman Brothers and MF Global, has alerted hedge funds to the risks of entrusting the custody of their assets to prime brokers. For instance, hedge fund clients of Lehman Brother's London-based prime brokerage unit, Lehman Brothers International Europe, saw their assets frozen when LBIE entered into administration enduring a year-long effort to retrieve them. *See* Rob Copeland, 'Returns from Activist Hedge Funds Are Causing a Stir', The Wall Street Journal, http://online.wsj.com/articles/returns-from-activist-hedge-funds-are-causing-a-stir-1404773120. As a result, there has been a notable shift towards the use of third-party custodians, which are not involved in the prime brokerage business. The largest third-party custodians are the Bank of New York Mellon and State Street Corporation.
132. William Fung and David A Hsieh, 'Empirical Characteristics of Dynamic Trading Strategies: The Case of Hedge Funds', *Review of Financial Studies* 10, no. 2 (1997).
133. Gregory Connor and Mason Woo, 'An Introduction to Hedge Funds', *Discussion Paper, 477. Financial Markets Group, London School of Economics and Political Science* (2004): 23.
134. *Ibid.*
135. Stowell, *Investment Banks, Hedge Funds, and Private Equity*, 219. One should also stress the increased popularity and solid performance of multi-strategy funds, which dynamically allocate capital among investment strategies.

adopting a long-short equity investment strategy apply fundamental analysis, in order to identify overvalued and undervalued stocks seeking to achieve strong returns through strong security selection on both the long and short side. What is more, introducing short sales to the portfolio has the effect of reducing overall market exposure. A variant of the long-short investment approach is equity market neutral investing, which seeks to eliminate market exposure typically by allocating an equal amount of capital in long and short positions.[136] Furthermore, the long-short equity strategy has evolved considerably with an increasing number of hedge fund managers adopting a sector-oriented approach and/or developing more quantitative strategies. In contrast to long-short equity, non-hedged equity hedge funds concentrate their investments solely in long positions generating returns by relying on their superior stock-picking ability.[137] Even though hedging is not an integral part of their investment strategy, non-hedged equity funds may, depending on market circumstances, introduce hedging positions in their portfolio.[138]

Relative value or arbitrage strategies exploit price inefficiencies between closely related or correlated financial instruments based on the belief that these discrepancies will disappear over time.[139] Hedge funds focusing on relative value strategies exhibit remarkable diversity in the financial instruments traded and the tools employed. Popular relative value strategies include fixed-income, convertible and statistical arbitrage.[140] Fixed-income arbitrage funds generate returns by arbitraging away pricing anomalies between related fixed-income instruments such as bonds, futures, options and interest rate swaps.[141] For instance, yield curve trades seek to profit from unusual patterns and anticipated changes to the yield curve,[142] while spread trades exploit the difference in yields between two fixed-income instruments.[143] The convertible arbitrage strategy involves the simultaneous placing of a long position in a company's

136. Eric Stokes, *Market Neutral Investing: Build Consistent Low-Risk Profits by Creating Your Own Hedged Portfolio* (Kaplan Business, 2004), 91-93; J.P. Morgan Asset Management, *Investment Insights: Spotlight on Market Neutral Investing* (2012), 2.
137. Stowell, *Investment Banks, Hedge Funds, and Private Equity*, 221.
138. Armelle Guizot, *The Hedge Fund Compliance and Risk Management Guide* (2006), 11.
139. Roger Ferguson and David Laster, 'Hedge Funds and Systemic Risk', *Banque de France, Financial Stability Review: Special Issue Hedge Funds*, no. 10 (2007): 47.
140. Securities and Commission, *Implications of the Growth of Hedge Funds*, 35-36.
141. *Ibid.*, 36.
142. The yield curve is a representation of the relationship between yield (interest rate) and the remaining time to maturity of fixed-income instruments. *See* Arturo Estrella and Mary R Trubin, 'The Yield Curve as a Leading Indicator: Some Practical Issues', *Current Issues in Economics and Finance* 12, no. 5 (2006).
143. A classic spread trade, which was also one of LTCM's first trades, involves the exploitation of price differentials between 'on the run' and 'off the run' Treasury bonds. 'On the run' Treasury bonds are the most recently issued bonds of a particular maturity, while the bonds of the same maturity issued at previous auctions are termed 'off the run' bonds. 'On the run' bonds, for instance, recently issued thirty-year Treasuries, usually trade at a premium to 'off the run' bonds, for example, thirty-year Treasuries with a remaining maturity of 29.5 years and similar cash flows, due to their superior liquidity. An arbitrageur can capture the spread between 'on the run' and 'off the run' bonds by buying the cheaper 'off-the-run' bonds and selling the more expensive 'on the run' securities since their price should converge within six months (with the 'on the run' bond becoming 'off the run'). In essence, the arbitrageur collects a fee for

undervalued convertible bonds and the short sale of its overvalued common shares.[144] Finally, *Stat Arbs* utilize complex mathematical and statistical models to spot pricing discrepancies between securities whose prices have deviated from their historical/statistical relationship based on the premise that their prices will return to their long-term average level.[145]

Hedge funds focusing on event-driven strategies exploit price fluctuations stemming from extraordinary events in a corporation's lifetime such as bankruptcies, spin-offs, mergers and takeovers. Hedge funds engaging in distressed investing seek to profit from a company's bankruptcy or financial distress either passively or actively. Passive managers are more trading-oriented, simply buying the undervalued distressed securities of the company, typically debt and/or equity, waiting for them to rise in value and selling them at a profit.[146] In contrast, activist distressed investors acquire a position in a company's distressed debt and use their rights as debtholders in order to influence corporate affairs.[147] Mergers and takeovers are another major type of corporate transactions, which event-driven hedge funds seek to exploit. Merger or risk arbitrage increased exponentially during the merger boom of the 1960s catching the public spotlight during the 1980s with the rise and fall of one of Wall Street's most infamous arbitrageurs, Ivan Boesky.[148] Merger arbitrage is premised on the exploitation of the so-called arbitrage spread in connection with a merger or takeover offer. In a cash merger or takeover offer, the arbitrageur will evaluate the likelihood of the deal going through, take a long position in the target's stock and capture the 'arbitrage spread', the difference between the target's share price and the offer price,[149] if the deal

supplying liquidity. *See* Roger Lowenstein, *When Genius Failed: The Rise and Fall of Long-Term Capital Management* (Random House, 2000), 42-43.

144. Securities and Commission, *Implications of the Growth of Hedge Funds*, 35.
145. A more formal definition of statistical arbitrage is offered by Lo according to whom statistical arbitrage 'refers to highly technical short-term mean-reversion strategies involving large numbers of securities (hundreds or even thousands, depending on the amount of risk capital), very short holding periods (measured in days to seconds), and substantial computational, trading, and information technology (IT) infrastructure'. *See* Andrew W Lo, *Hedge Funds: An Analytic Perspective* (Princeton University Press, 2010), 260.
146. For instance, securities of firms in financial distress which have entered or are expected to enter into bankruptcy proceedings often trade below their fundamental value due to investor risk aversion and/or irrationality and legal rules, which require institutional investors to hold highly rated securities. *See* Lhabitant, *Hedge Funds: Myths and Limits*, 100.
147. *See generally,* Michelle M Harner, 'Corporate Governance and Public Policy Implications of Activist Distressed Debt Investing', *The Fordham Law Review* 77, no. 2 (2008): 717.
148. Until the announcement on 14 November 1986 that he had pleaded guilty to insider trading in connection with pending mergers and acquisitions, Ivan Boeksy was considered one of Wall Street's shrewdest investors. The unravelling of Boesky's insider trading scheme, which implicated prominent financiers including Michael Milken, sent ripples across Wall Street and marked the beginning of the end of Drexel Burnham and Lambert one of the leading US investment banks and pioneer in the development of the market for junk bonds. *See* Connie Bruck, *Predator's Ball* (Penguin, 2013), 317-29.
149. Until the deal is completed the target market price will generally stay below the offer price with the 'arbitrage spread' reflecting the risk that the deal will not be completed due to a host of different factors including defensive actions of the target, antitrust clearance, lack of approval by the target's shareholders and adverse changes in market conditions. *See* Stanley B Block, 'Merger Arbitrage Hedge Funds', *Journal of Applied Finance* 16, no. 1 (2006): 89-90.

is eventually consummated.[150] In case of a stock-for-stock deal, where the acquirer offers to swap a fixed number of its shares for a fixed quantity of shares of the target, merger arbitrageurs are exposed not only to the risk that the deal will fall through but also the risk that the acquirer's stock price will decline between the announcement of the offer and the completion of the transaction.[151] In order to lock in the 'arbitrage spread', the arbitrageur will buy the stock of the target and simultaneously short the shares of the acquirer.[152] Activist investing is another event-driven strategy, which has witnessed remarkable growth during the last few years. The success of activist campaigns and the attractive returns offered by activist hedge funds have led to a surge in investor allocations.[153] Chapter 2 provides a more complete examination of hedge fund activism and its impact on investors and companies.

Hedge funds pursuing directional strategies place one-way unhedged bets on the direction of movements in individual securities or the broader market. Global macro fund managers profit by analysing macroeconomic and geopolitical developments and taking long and short positions in equities, bonds, derivatives, currencies, real estate and commodities around the globe.[154] In their heyday in the early 1990s, global macro fund managers dominated the hedge fund industry managing approximately 70% of total hedge fund assets.[155] However, by 2008 their share of the industry's total assets had declined to 8%.[156] Another directional strategy, which regularly receives the attention of policymakers and the public alike, is dedicated short selling.[157] Dedicated short funds are specialized in identifying and short selling overvalued securities,

150. *Ibid.*
151. Numerous empirical studies have documented that the announcement of a takeover or merger results in a decline in the acquirer's share price. For an exhaustive review of the relevant literature *see* Marina Martynova and Luc Renneboog, 'A Century of Corporate Takeovers: What Have We Learned and Where Do We Stand?', *Journal of Banking & Finance* 32, no. 10 (2008): 2154-58. The negative market reaction lends support to two distinct hypotheses, the hubris hypothesis and managerial empire building. According to the hubris hypothesis, managers of bidding firms infected by hubris overpay for acquisitions believing that they can manage the target better than its current management. *See* Richard Roll, 'The Hubris Hypothesis of Corporate Takeovers', *Journal of business* 59, no. 2 (1986). Pursuant to the empire building hypothesis, managers implement acquisitions in order to maximize the size of their firms allowing them to reap additional pecuniary and non-pecuniary benefits such as increased compensation and prestige. Dennis C Mueller, 'A Theory of Conglomerate Mergers', *The Quarterly Journal of Economics* 83, no. 4 (1969); Michael C Jensen, 'Agency Costs of Free Cash Flow, Corporate Finance, and Takeovers', *The American Economic Review* 76, no. 2 (1986).
152. Ivan F. Boesky, *Merger Mania, Arbitrage: Wall Street's Best Kept Money-Making Secret* (Holt Reinhart and Winston, 1985).
153. Copeland, 'Returns from Activist Hedge Funds Are Causing a Stir'.
154. Filippo Stefanini, *Investment Strategies of Hedge Funds* (Wiley, 2006), 239-41.
155. *Ibid.*, 241.
156. Eurekahedge, *The Eurekahedge Report* (11 January 2009).
157. A famous dedicated short seller and guru investor is James Chanos, founder of Kynikos Associates. Chanos became famous for uncovering Enron's accounting irregularities, leading to the exposure of a spectacular corporate scandal. President James Chanos and Kynikos Associates, *Prepared Statement for the U.S. Securities and Exchange Commission Roundtable on Hedge Funds* (15 May 2003) (offering a first-hand account of how hedge fund manager James Chanos uncovered Enron's accounting fraud).

mostly shares. Despite the widespread attention that they receive, dedicated short funds are nowadays extremely rare.[158]

1.2.5 The Benefits of Hedge Funds

The increased popularity of hedge funds can be attributed to the considerable benefits that they bring to financial markets and their participants. By trading in and out of markets constantly buying and selling securities, hedge funds provide much needed 'market liquidity'[159] to financial markets.[160] Indeed, Aragon and Strahan find that stocks held by Lehman connected funds that suffered substantial losses as a result of Lehman's bankruptcy, experienced larger declines in market liquidity than stocks not held by these funds during the last quarter of 2008 indicating that hedge funds act as providers of liquidity even during adverse market conditions.[161] Apart from market liquidity, hedge funds also contribute to 'funding liquidity'[162] by directly extending loans to cash-strapped firms and providing repo financing to corporations and financial intermediaries.[163] What is more, operating unconstrained by burdensome regulation and with high-powered performance incentives, hedge funds are induced to exploit profitable albeit risky opportunities when other market participants are unwilling to do so, thereby adding to risk diversification in the financial system.[164]

158. According to Fung and Hsieh, dedicated short funds represented in 2004 a mere 1% of the overall number of hedge funds and 0.2% of total hedge fund assets. Peter Dodd, 'Merger Proposals, Management Discretion and Stockholder Wealth', *Journal of Financial Economics* 8, no. 2 (1980): 9.
159. According to Nikolaou, market liquidity is defined as 'the ability to trade an asset at short notice, at low cost and with little impact on its price'. Kleopatra Nikolaou, 'Liquidity (Risk) Concepts Definition and Interactions', *European Central Bank Working Paper Series* No. 1008 (2009): 18.
160. Timothy F. Geithner, President & CEO, Fed. Reserve Bank of NY, Keynote Address at the National Conference on the Securities Industry: Hedge Funds and Their Implications for the Financial System (17 November 2004).
161. George Aragon and Philip E Strahan, 'Hedge Funds as Liquidity Providers', *Journal of Financial Economics* 103, no. 3 (2012).
162. Pursuant to Foucalt et al., funding liquidity refers to the ability of financial intermediaries or companies to meet their obligations either by having sufficient cash or by obtaining credit at acceptable terms. Pagano Marco Foucault Thierry and Roell Ailsa, *Market Liquidity: Theory, Evidence, and Policy* (Oxford University Press, 2013), 9.
163. Tracy Alloway and Arash Massoudi, 'Hedge Funds Step into the Shadows', Financial Times, http://www.ft.com/intl/cms/s/0/b7e2de34-29e4-11e3-9bc6-00144feab7de.html?siteedition=intl#axzz37SMH17Yl. Repurchase agreements or 'repos' are financial contracts, which rese mble a secured loan. In a repo transaction, one party 'the borrower' sells securities to the other party 'the lender' in exchange for cash with the securities serving essentially as the collateral for the loan. The borrower assumes the obligation to repurchase the securities at the original price plus an additional amount, representing effectively the interest rate charged by the lender, at a specified future date. The lender will request collateral with a market value greater than the amount of cash lent, with the difference termed 'haircut' or 'margin', in order to protect itself against a borrower default. Michael J Fleming and Kenneth Garbade, 'The Repurchase Agreement Refined: GCF Repo', *Current Issues in Economics and Finance* 9, no. 6 (2003): 1-2.
164. Ben S. Bernanke, Chairman Fed. Reserve Board of Governors, Speech at the New York University School of Law: Financial Regulation and the Invisible Hand (11 April 2007).

Furthermore, hedge funds play a unique role in promoting the efficiency of markets. Acting as prototypical 'arbitrageurs'[165] or 'rational speculators', they constantly gather and analyse information in order to identify and exploit security mispricings, thus bringing security prices closer to their fundamental value. Indeed, the arbitrage mechanism is a key building block of 'the efficient capital market hypothesis'.[166] To the extent that 'noise traders', irrational investors who trade on sentiment, cause security prices to move away from their fundamental value, fully informed traders such as hedge funds sensing a profit opportunity will quickly buy the undervalued securities or short the overvalued ones. In the long run, irrational investors will lose their wealth due to their bad bets, while rational speculators will reap the profits stemming from their arbitrage activity.[167] As a result, arbitrageurs will, over time, drive irrational investors out of the market.[168] Consistent with the hypothesis that hedge funds perform the role of arbitrageurs, Cao et al. document that stocks bought by hedge funds experience an improvement in informational efficiency compared with stocks sold by hedge funds.[169] Furthermore, the authors find that stock buying by hedge funds increases informational efficiency significantly more than buying by mutual funds and banks.

Nonetheless, one should note that the role of arbitrageurs in contributing to market efficiency is more limited than usually acknowledged. Pursuant to its academic definition, arbitrage is an investment strategy that offers riskless profits at no cost. For instance, if an arbitrageur determines that a particular security is undervalued relative to its fundamental value, it will buy the underpriced security and simultaneously hedge its bet by selling short an essentially similar security, thus earning a profit without taking any risk. However, real-world arbitrage typically involves the assumption of risk. Arbitrage, as defined in academic literature, is premised upon the availability of close substitutes of mispriced securities allowing arbitrageurs to lay off risks. In practice, substitute securities may not exist and existing substitutes may be highly

165. According to Sharpe and Alexander, arbitrage is defined as 'the simultaneous purchase and sale of the same, or essentially similar, security in two different markets at advantageously different prices'. William Sharpe and Gordon Alexander, *Investments*, 4th ed. (Prentice Hall, 1990).
166. Economists distinguish three forms of market efficiency. Pursuant to the weak form of market efficiency, market prices reflect the information contained in past prices. The second form of market efficiency is termed 'the semi-strong form of market efficiency'. According to this form of market efficiency, market prices, in addition to past prices, also reflect all other published information. Finally, in its strongest form, the efficient capital markets hypothesis states that prices reflect all information both public and private. Brealy Richard A, Myers Stewart C. and Allen Franklin, *Corporate Finance*, 8th ed. (McGraw-Hill, 2006), 337. The efficient capital markets hypothesis is further broken down into informational and fundamental efficiency. The three forms of market efficiency analysed above belong to the first aspect of market efficiency termed 'informational efficiency'. According to the second aspect of the ECMH, also referred to as fundamental efficiency, the market price of a widely traded security reflects its fundamental value. *See* Ronald J Gilson & Reinier Kraakman, 'Market Efficiency after the Financial Crisis: It's Still a Matter of Information Costs', *ECGI Law Working Paper No. 242/2012* (2014): 12.
167. Shleifer Andrei, Bradford De Long, Lawrence Summers and Robert Waldmann, 'Noise Trader Risk in Financial Markets', *Journal of Political Economy* 98, no. 4 (1990): 704.
168. *Ibid.*
169. Liang Bing Cao Charles, Lo Andrew and Petrasek Lubomir, 'Hedge Fund Holdings and Stock Market Efficiency', *Finance and Economics Discussion Series, Federal Reserve Board, Washington D.C.* (May 2014).

imperfect. Barberis and Thaler offer an illustrative example of an arbitrageur who determines that the price of Ford's stock is undervalued. The arbitrageur will buy the undervalued Ford stock and hedge its bet by shorting a substitute security such as General Motors. However, General Motors is a highly imperfect substitute security. While the arbitrageur by shorting General Motors is protected from bad news about the automobile industry as a whole, it still remains exposed to fundamental risk as its short position does not offer a hedge against firm-specific adverse news about Ford.[170]

Furthermore, arbitrageurs bear the risk that mispricings will worsen in the short run causing them to suffer steep losses, a risk referred to in finance literature as 'noise trader risk'.[171] If the arbitrageur is a professional portfolio manager whose capital is raised from multiple investors, for instance, a hedge fund manager, its investors may lack the specialized knowledge to evaluate the manager's skill.[172] Consequently, they may interpret the negative returns not as the result of bad luck, but rather as evidence of bad judgment.[173] Investors may accordingly decide to withdraw their funds forcing the arbitrageur to liquidate its positions. The fear of such a scenario may make the arbitrageur less willing to correct the mispricing in the first place.[174] Moreover, if overly optimistic investors dominate the market, a rational speculator may determine that the most profitable strategy is to ride the bubble and exit its positions before it bursts rather than try to correct it.[175] Indeed, Brunnermeier and Nagel examining hedge fund US holdings during the period of 1998 to 2000 document that hedge funds were heavily invested in technology stocks indicating that they were riding the technology bubble.[176] Furthermore, skilfully anticipating price declines of individual technology stocks, hedge funds were able to avoid the downturn by reducing their holdings before prices of individual stocks collapsed and simultaneously increasing their positions in technology stocks that continued to rise.[177]

What is more, hedge funds bring substantial benefits to their investors. Despite the industry's lacklustre performance during the last few years, on a long-term basis hedge funds have managed to deliver 'alpha' to their investors reflecting the superior skill of hedge fund managers. For instance, from 1994 to 2011, the hedge fund industry recorded a return of 9.97% after fees compared to 7.18% for stocks and 6.25% for

170. Nicholas Barberis and Richard Thaler, 'A Survey of Behavioral Finance', *National Bureau of Economic Research* No. w9222 (2002): 5.
171. Andrei Shleifer and Lawrence H Summers, 'The Noise Trader Approach to Finance', *The Journal of Economic Perspectives* 4, no. 2 (1990): 21.
172. Andrei Shleifer, *Inefficient Markets: An Introduction to Behavioral Finance* (Oxford University Press 2000), 89.
173. Andrei Shleifer and Robert W Vishny, 'The Limits of Arbitrage', *The Journal of Finance* 52, no. 1 (1997): 36-37.
174. *Ibid.*
175. Dilip Abreu and Markus K Brunnermeier, 'Bubbles and Crashes', *Econometrica* 71, no. 1 (2003): 173-74.
176. Markus K Brunnermeier and Stefan Nagel, 'Hedge Funds and the Technology Bubble', *The Journal of Finance* 59, no. 5 (2004): 2014.
177. *Ibid.*

bonds.[178] Moreover, in their study Barth et al. argue that the degree of underperformance of the industry has been exaggerated.[179] Studies measuring performance typically rely on data found in public hedge fund databases. Examining public hedge fund data and regulatory filings from 2013 to 2016, the authors document that the returns of publicly reporting hedge funds are considerably lower than the returns of non-publicly reporting funds. The total return of non-publicly reporting funds is 26.6% over the sample period, while the return of publicly reporting funds is 9.4%. As a result, the authors claim that performance estimates based on publicly reporting funds significantly underestimate the true performance of the industry. In addition, hedge funds have also been able to consistently outperform other active investment vehicles, such as hedged mutual funds. Examining the performance of hedge funds relative to hedged mutual funds during the period 1994-2004, Agarwal et al. find that hedge funds with investment styles similar to those used by hedged mutual funds significantly outperformed hedged mutual funds by roughly 3.3% per year after fees.[180]

Apart from delivering superior returns, hedge fund managers are also skilled at offering returns with low systematic risk helping investors achieve better-diversified portfolios.[181] Their ability to utilize leverage, short selling and derivatives allows hedge funds to adopt a variety of investment strategies with a low correlation to the overall market. While hedge funds have not been able to consistently outperform equity markets, they exhibit a unique ability to generate positive returns in both up and down markets. Shadab comparing yearly hedge fund returns to the returns of the S&P 500 from 1996 to 2003 finds that hedge funds posted negative returns only in 1998 recording positive returns in all other years even as the stock market was suffering losses.[182] Furthermore, even though at the peak of the financial crisis in 2008 hedge funds suffered substantial losses reaching 19%, they were still able to outperform equity markets, which witnessed an extraordinary decline with the MSCI World Index and the S&P 500 losing 42% and 37% of their value, respectively.[183]

Finally, hedge funds play a unique role in the promotion of good corporate governance. Referred to as 'financial detectives', short selling hedge funds have exposed some of the biggest corporate frauds through their diligent research and their willingness to stand up against corporate management.[184] Indeed, Massa et al.

178. Imperial College Center For Hedge Fund Research, London, *The Value of the Hedge Fund Industry to Investors, Markets and the Broader Economy* (2012).
179. Daniel Barth, Juha Joenvaara, Mikko Kauppila, and Russell R. Wermers, 'The Hedge Fund Industry Is Bigger (and Has Performed Better) Than You Think', *OFR Working Paper* 20-01 (March 2021).
180. Vikas Agarwal, Nicole M Boyson and Narayan Y Naik, 'Hedge Funds for Retail Investors? An Examination of Hedged Mutual Funds', *Journal of Financial and Quantitative Analysis* 44, no. 2 (2009).
181. Houman B Shadab, 'The Law and Economics of Hedge Funds: Financial Innovation and Investor Protection', *Berkeley Business Law Journal* 6 (2009): 269-72.
182. *Ibid.*, 268-69.
183. Credit Suisse/Tremont Hedge Fund Index, *One for the History Books: Hedge Fund Performance in 2008* (January 2009), 2.
184. Apart from Chanos' uncovering of Enron's accounting fraud, hedge fund short sellers have also assumed a leading role in detecting other spectacular corporate scandals. A case which made the headlines across the globe was Bill Ackman's, then owner of hedge fund firm Gotham

confirming the disciplinary effect of short selling find that the threat of short selling reduces the incentives of management to engage in earnings manipulation.[185] In a separate study, the same authors document that the threat of short selling attacks leads to a significant improvement in internal governance, an increase in the sensitivity of management compensation to performance, a boost in the monitoring role of the Board and an improvement in firm profitability.[186] Moreover, the new breed of activist hedge funds is further shaking up the cosy atmosphere that pervades boardrooms. As it will be explained in Chapter 2, shareholder activism as practised by hedge funds results in substantial benefits for investors and target companies alike.

1.3 HEDGE FUNDS IN POPULAR IMAGINATION (AND CRISES)

1.3.1 Hedge Funds and Currency Crises

1.3.1.1 Black Wednesday

The 1992 ERM crisis was the first episode that raised concerns about the destabilizing effects of hedge fund speculators on financial markets. The ERM was established in 1979, and pursuant to its rules, the currencies of the European countries joining the ERM were allowed to fluctuate against one another within predetermined trading ranges.[187] In the early 1990s, inflationary pressures resulting from the costs of German reunification forced Germany's central bank to sidestep its role as ERM's anchor and raise interest rates at a time when other participating countries were facing a recession calling for a policy of low interest rates.[188] Rising interest rates in Germany caused investors to pour money into Deutsche marks and dump other currencies.[189] The downward pressure exerted on weaker European currencies resulted in their trading at the lower end of the band permitted by the ERM. Taking into account the refusal of the Bundesbank to lower its interest rates, the only options available to European governments whose currencies were under pressure were either to increase their

Partners LP, bet against MBIA, an overleveraged AAA-rated bond insurer that was engaging in accounting manipulation. MBIA suffered huge losses during the financial crisis, and its rating was lowered to junk status. As a result, Ackman was able to profit handsomely from MBIA's near demise. For an excellent description of Bill Ackman's crusade against MBIA *see* Christine S Richard, *Confidence Game: How Hedge Fund Manager Bill Ackman Called Wall Street's Bluff* (Bloomberg Press, 2010).

185. Massimo Massa, Bohui Zhang and Hong Zhang, 'The Invisible Hand of Short Selling: Does Short Selling Discipline Earnings Management?', *Review of Financial Studies* 28, no. 6 (2015).
186. 'Governance Through Threat: Does Short Selling Improve Internal Governance?', *INSEAD Working Paper* No. 2013/83/FIN (2013).
187. The main purpose of the ERM was to dampen exchange rate variability within Europe and prepare the countries participating in the European Community for a future monetary union and the introduction of a single European currency. As Ferguson and Schlefer note, 'the ERM was thus a halfway house between freely floating exchange rates and a single currency'. Niall Ferguson and Jonathan Schlefer, 'Who Broke the Bank of England?', *Harvard Business School BGIE Unit Case No. 709-026* (2009): 1.
188. *Ibid.*, 7.
189. Mallaby, *More Money Than God: Hedge Funds and the Making of a New Elite*, 152.

interest rates in order to attract more capital or to support their currencies via their central banks' intervention in the markets.[190] After determining that recession-battered countries such as Italy and the UK would be reluctant to raise their interest rates and that their central banks lacked the firepower to support their currencies, speculators started their attack against weaker currencies betting on their devaluation and their exit from the ERM. The defining moment of the crisis was Britain's decision to exit the ERM. After massive selling of the pound with Soros' Quantum Fund at the forefront, the BOE abandoned its defence of the currency and the British government announced on 16 September 1992 that it was withdrawing from the ERM.[191]

Hedge funds immediately became the targets of politicians with the French finance minister even calling for their guillotining. It is beyond doubt that a small group of hedge funds, most notably the Quantum Fund, played a crucial role in the ERM crisis of 1992 with their bearish bets significantly affecting the prices of European currencies. Nonetheless, one should note that the actions of hedge funds were not the sole cause of the price declines of European currencies. Another important contributor was the unwinding of the so-called convergence play,[192] which had caused, during the period from 1987 to 1991, a spectacular increase in capital flows into higher-yielding ERM currencies.[193] The unwinding of convergence trades due to fears of devaluation resulted in massive investor outflows from certain currencies such as the Italian lira, the British pound and the Spanish peseta.[194] Finally, one should note that the currency readjustments that hedge funds accelerated were inevitable since the exchange rate pegs introduced by the ERM were inconsistent with the macroeconomic fundamentals of the respective countries.[195]

---

190. *Ibid.*
191. A less publicized bet was Soros' short positions in the Swedish krona, which forced Sweden to devalue its currency and withdraw from the ERM. For an excellent account of Soros' landmark bets against both the British pound and Swedish krona, *see Ibid.*, 159-71.
192. According to the IMF, the 'convergence play' reflected the growing perception by international investors that the macroeconomic fundamentals of the member countries of the ERM were on a path to eventual convergence. Investors grew increasingly confident that the steady progress towards a European Monetary Union would cause interest rates within the ERM area to fall to the level of interest rates prevailing in low-interest-rate countries, most notably Germany, and that there would be no substantial exchange rate adjustments. International Monetary Fund, *International Capital Markets: Part II, Systemic Issues in International Finance, World Economic and Financial Surveys* (1993), 49. The convergence trade involved investors borrowing in a currency with a low interest rate, mainly the German mark, and investing in assets denominated in high yield currencies such as the Italian lira, British pound or Spanish peseta. As interest rates fell, the long positions would appreciate in value. The trade made money, as long as the high yielding currencies, whose exchange rates were pegged according to the rules of the ERM, did not depreciate by more than the interest rate differential. William Fung, David A Hsieh and Konstantinos Tsatsaronis, 'Do Hedge Funds Disrupt Emerging Markets?', *Brookings-Wharton Papers on Financial Services*, no. 1 (2000).
193. *See International Capital Markets: Part I. Exchange Rate Management and International Capital Flows, World Economic and Financial Surveys*, 8.
194. Fung, Hsieh and Tsatsaronis, 'Do Hedge Funds Disrupt Emerging Markets?', 381.
195. Maria Strömqvist, 'Hedge Funds and Financial Crises', *Sveriges Riksbank Economic Review* (2009).

1.3.1.2 *The East Asian Currency and Financial Crisis*

During the second half of the 1980s, the majority of East Asian countries enjoyed a period of fast economic growth. Nonetheless, severe weaknesses lay under the surface. East Asian economies ran large current-account deficits financed with short-term external debt, which made them vulnerable to a sudden loss of investor confidence.[196] Encouraged by currency pegs to the US dollar, corporations and financial intermediaries increasingly relied on short-term dollar-denominated borrowing, becoming thus exposed to substantial exchange rate risk.[197] What is more, inadequate supervision and regulation of financial intermediaries resulted in the adoption of risky lending practices with lending decisions taken on the basis of personal, business or governmental connections.[198] The misallocation of credit was aggravated by implicit government guarantees.[199]

Beginning in the mid-1990s, the devaluation of the Chinese renminbi and the Japanese yen, and the fall in semiconductor prices caused an economic slowdown and a drop in asset prices, most notably stock and land prices, in several East Asian economies.[200] The first signs of the impending crisis came in early 1997. In South Korea, prominent industrial conglomerates declared bankruptcy, putting banks, which had extended credit to them, under significant stress.[201] Meanwhile, in Thailand, the failure of Samprasong Land signalled the financial difficulties facing non-bank financial companies, which had become overexposed to an overvalued property market.[202] The decision of the Thai government in June 1997 to pull its support from Finance One, a large financial company, caused investors to lose confidence in the Thai economy and massively withdraw their capital, forcing the government to abandon its exchange rate peg.[203] The baht's subsequent depreciation led investors to question the stability of exchange rate pegs and financial systems in the region, triggering widespread capital outflows.[204] During the following months, Malaysia, Indonesia, South Korea and the Philippines were hit by severe currency crashes and stock market declines.[205]

196. Nouriel Roubini and Brad Setser, *Bailouts or Bail-Ins* (Peterson Institute for International Economics, 2004), 33-34.
197. Galina Hale, 'Could We Have Learned from the Asian Financial Crisis of 1997-98?', *FRBSF Economic Letter* 2011 (2011).
198. Janet Yellen, 'The Asian Financial Crisis Ten Years Later: Assessing the Past and Looking to the Future, Speech to the Asia Society of Southern California', news release, 6 February 2007.
199. Paul Krugman, 'What Happened to Asia?', http://web.mit.edu/krugman/www/DISINTER.html.
200. Moreno Ramon, 'What Caused East Asia's Financial Crisis', *Federal Reserve Bank of San Fransisco Economic Letters* (7 August 1998).
201. Steven Radelet and Jeffrey Sachs, 'The Onset of the East Asian Financial Crisis', *National Bureau of Economic Research* No. w6680 (1998): 32.
202. *Ibid.*
203. *Ibid.*, 33. Prior to the collapse of Finance One, investors assumed that the government would aid faltering non-bank financial institutions. David Marshall, 'Understanding the Asian Crisis: Systemic Risk as Coordination Failure', *Federal Reserve Bank of Chicago, Economic Perspectives* 22 (1998).
204. Ramon, 'What Caused East Asia's Financial Crisis'.
205. One should note that the academic literature revolves around two competing, but not mutually exclusive, explanations of the causes of the Asian currency and financial crisis. Sachs and

Hedge funds were once again vilified for orchestrating concerted attacks against the currencies of East Asian countries. Mahathir Mohammad, then Prime Minister of Malaysia, famously characterized hedge funds as 'highwaymen of the global economy' bankrupting whole regions in their quest for extravagant profits.[206] Nonetheless, the empirical evidence indicates that the allegations against hedge funds were unfounded. Examining the exposures of ten major global currency hedge funds from 1993 to 1997, Brown et al. find no evidence that hedge funds' positions caused the depreciation of the Malaysian ringgit relative to the US dollar.[207] Instead, they find that during the period of June to August 1997 when the ringgit dropped by 10%, hedge funds held long positions in the currency.[208] These results suggest that hedge funds acted as liquidity suppliers in a falling market. Furthermore, in their analysis of the funds' exposure to a basket of Asian currencies, including the Malaysian ringgit, the Thai baht, the Philippine peso and the Indonesian rupiah, the authors document no relationship between hedge fund positions and current, past or future moves in exchange rates.[209] In a related study, Fung et al. conclude that the aggregate short positions of twelve large hedge funds in Asian currencies at the onset of the crisis were too small to have precipitated the currencies' crash.[210] Overall, the evidence strongly indicates that hedge funds played no crucial role in the widespread currency declines during the East Asian crisis. In contrast, the downward pressures on Asian currencies were predominantly the result of short and long sales by domestic corporations and banks and international commercial and investment banks.[211]

1.3.1.3 When Genius Failed: The Rise and Fall of Long-Term Capital Management

LTCM's near collapse was surely as spectacular as its rise. Founded in February 1994 and armed with the stellar reputation of its founders, which included two Nobel Prize-winning economists, LTCM was characterized as the 'Rolls Royce' of hedge

---

Radelet advance the view that even though the macroeconomic performance of the Asian countries was showing signs of deterioration, the triggering of the crisis and its propagation were the result of panic on the part of domestic and international investors. Steven Radelet and Jeffrey Sachs, 'The Onset of the East Asian Financial Crisis'. According to the competing view supported by Corsetti et al., the crisis should be mainly attributed to vulnerabilities in the economic fundamentals of the countries of the region. Nonetheless, they also stress the role of market overreaction and herding which caused the crisis, once triggered, to be more severe than warranted by the deteriorating fundamentals. *See* Giancarlo Corsetti, Paolo Pesenti and Nouriel Roubini, 'What Caused the Asian Currency and Financial Crisis? Part I: A Macroeconomic Overview', *National Bureau of Economic Research Working Paper* No. w6834 (1998).

206. Mahathir Mohammad, 'Highwaymen of the Global Economy', *The Wall Street Journal*, 23 September 1997.
207. Stephen J Brown, William N Goetzmann and James Park, 'Hedge Funds and the Asian Currency Crisis of 1997', *National Bureau of Economic Research* No. w6427 (1998): 8-10.
208. *Ibid.*, 9.
209. *Ibid.*, 11-12.
210. Fung, Hsieh and Tsatsaronis, 'Do Hedge Funds Disrupt Emerging Markets?', 397.
211. *See* Barry Eichengreen, 'Understanding Asia's Financial Crisis', *Clemens Lecture Series No. 10* (1998): 10-11.

funds.[212] Its main strategy was fixed-income arbitrage with the fund taking long positions in bonds it considered to be undervalued, while shorting bonds it deemed overvalued, betting that their prices would converge.[213] LTCM's bet was founded on the belief that credit or liquidity spreads between riskier or illiquid and low-risk or liquid bonds would eventually narrow. LTCM also entered into derivatives contracts that replicated buying or selling the underlying bonds. For instance, LTCM was a counterparty in interest rate swaps agreeing to make payments to its counterparty if spreads between different bonds widened while having the right to receive payments from its counterparty if spreads narrowed.[214] The fund held positions in a variety of markets, including government bond markets, MBSs markets, corporate bond markets, futures exchanges, OTC derivatives markets and foreign exchange markets. As profit opportunities in the fixed arbitrage business were drying up due to increased competition, and LTCM's returns were shrinking, its partners decided to adopt higher risk strategies allocating large amounts of capital to merger arbitrage and the shorting of equity volatility.[215] Furthermore, in order to enhance its returns, LTCM resorted to an aggressive use of leverage. At the end of August 1998, LTCM had over USD 125 billion in assets supported by an equity cushion of approximately USD 4.8 billion dollars, while the notional value of its derivatives contracts, the majority of which were over the counter, reached USD 1.4 trillion dollars.[216] Furthermore, the fund's market footprint had grown enormously. LTCM had reportedly entered into over six thousand trades with several dozen counterparties.[217]

Despite LTCM's initial success, the intensification of the Asian currency and financial crisis and the default by Russia in August 1998 on its rouble-denominated debt provoked a worldwide flight to quality with investors shunning risky, illiquid securities and pouring into low-risk, liquid securities causing spreads between them to widen dramatically. Faced with devastating losses and collateral calls by creditors and derivatives counterparties,[218] LTCM was forced to resort to a bailout by its major

212. Peter H Huang, Kimberly D Krawiec and Frank Partnoy, 'Derivatives on TV: A Tale of Two Derivatives Debacles in Prime-Time', *Green Bag 2d* 4 (2001). Formally, Long-Term Capital Management LP, a Delaware limited partnership headquartered in Greenwich Connecticut, was the management company operating a single fund, Long-Term Capital Portfolio LP, a Cayman Island incorporated partnership.

213. *See* Franklin R Edwards, 'Hedge Funds and the Collapse of Long-Term Capital Management', *The Journal of Economic Perspectives* 13, no. 2 (1999): 198.

214. *Ibid.*, 197-98.

215. LTCM shorted equity volatility by shorting large amounts of options on the S & P 500 stock index and on the indices of the major exchanges in Europe. The trade was premised on the belief that the market's expectation of future volatility of stocks was wrong. *See* Lowenstein, *When Genius Failed: The Rise and Fall of Long-Term Capital Management*, 100-02 & 23-42.

216. Markets, *Hedge Funds, Leverage, and the Lessons of Long-Term Capital Management*, 11-12.

217. *Ibid.*, 11 & 17-18.

218. In order to mitigate counterparty credit risk, derivatives counterparties are required to post margin (collateral) which may be cash or securities easily convertible to cash. Essentially all exchange-traded derivatives are cleared through a clearinghouse applying predetermined rules requiring counterparties to post 'initial' and 'variation margin'. Initial margin refers to the collateral that the counterparty must post when entering into the transaction and is collected based on the potential future credit exposure of the clearing house to the counterparty. In contrast, variation margin refers to the collateral used to limit the build-up of current exposures. The clearing house will calculate daily the mark-to-market value of the derivatives

creditors and counterparties under the auspices of the FED avoiding a formal bankruptcy procedure. A fourteen-member consortium comprising LTCM's most important creditors and counterparties agreed to inject USD 3.625 billion in exchange for 90% of LTCM's equity.[219] While the involvement of creditors and counterparties was rooted in their self-interest, since they were themselves the parties most exposed to the fund's default, the FED's intervention was based on the belief that the disorderly failure of LTCM would destabilize the financial system.[220] After the rescue, the consortium took over day-to-day control with the aim of unwinding the fund's portfolio. By the end of 1999, aided by recovering markets, LTCM's new shareholders were able to recoup their USD 3.625 billion investment and make a small profit.[221]

The LTCM debacle received widespread popular attention and, according to the view of the author, represents the sole incident in hedge fund history in which hedge funds, or more accurately the failure of a single hedge fund, threatened to jeopardize financial stability. The importance of LTCM's near collapse in justifying a regulatory intrusion in the hedge fund industry on 'systemic risk'[222] grounds will be examined extensively in Chapter 2.

---

contract and allocate gains and losses. If the market value of the contract moves against the counterparty, then the clearing house will issue a 'margin call' requiring the counterparty to post additional collateral equal to the amount owed to it by the counterparty. In non-cleared OTC derivative contracts, the posting of initial or variation margin rests upon the parties' agreement. OTC derivatives are, however, typically documented under the ISDA master agreement, which regulates margin requirements in its Credit Support Annex. *See generally* Darrell Duffie, Ada Li and Theo Lubke, 'Policy Perspectives on OTC Derivatives Market Infrastructure', *Staff Report, Federal Reserve Bank of New York* (2010). Furthermore, while the majority of OTC derivatives were until recently non-cleared, recent reforms in both the US and the EU mandate the central clearing of as many OTC derivatives as possible and their trading on organized exchanges or comparable trading facilities. *See* David Felsenthal, 'Regulation of OTC Derivatives Markets - EU vs US Initiatives', Harvard Law School Forum on Corporate Governance and Financial Regulation, http://blogs.law.harvard.edu/corpgov/2012/09/23/regulation-of-otc-derivatives-markets-eu-vs-us-initiatives/.

219. *See* Markets, *Hedge Funds, Leverage, and the Lessons of Long-Term Capital Management*, 13-14.
220. *See* William J. McDonough, 'Statement Before the Committee on Banking and Financial Services us House of Representatives', news release, 1 October 1998.
221. Philippe Jorion, 'Risk Management Lessons from Long-Term Capital Management', *European Financial Management* 6, no. 3 (2000): 284.
222. According to Schwarcz, systemic risk is defined as the risk 'that a trigger event, such as an economic shock or institutional failure, causes a chain of bad economic consequences - sometimes referred to as a domino effect. These consequences could include (a chain of) financial institution and/or market failures. Less dramatically, these consequences might include (a chain of) significant losses to financial institutions or substantial financial-market price volatility. In either case, the consequences impact financial institutions, markets, or both'. *See* Steven L Schwarcz, 'Systemic Risk', *Georgetown Law Journal* 97, no. 1 (2008): 198.

1.3.1.4 *The Collapse of Amaranth*

The next spectacular hedge fund failure was Association Amaranth,[223] a hedge fund that collapsed in September 2006 after suffering heavy losses stemming from misplaced bets in natural gas derivatives. Amaranth was founded in 2000 by Nicholas Maounis as a multi-strategy fund focusing mainly on convertible bond arbitrage.[224] After reporting lacklustre returns, Amaranth expanded into higher-yielding markets, especially the US energy market. The success of its energy trading bets resulted in the spectacular growth of Amaranth, which by 2006 was managing approximately USD 8 billion of assets and employing more than four hundred people in major financial centres, including London and Singapore.[225] Amaranth's principal trading strategy was calendar spread trading using natural gas swaps, futures and options.[226] According to Cinciarini, Amaranth's complex spread trades 'could be summarized as a general bet that winter natural gas prices would rise relative to non-winter natural gas prices, referred to as the long winter, short non-winter spread trade'.[227]

Amaranth expected that going into 2007 winter, natural gas prices would be sharply higher than summer gas prices due to increased hurricane activity.[228] Based on this intuition, Amaranth pursued two trading strategies. It took long positions in natural gas futures contracts expiring in January 2007, while it shorted futures contracts expiring in November 2006, betting that January natural gas prices would be higher than November prices.[229] Furthermore, it bought futures contracts for March 2007 while it sold short futures contracts for April 2007, expecting that March prices would be higher than April prices.[230] Nonetheless, predictions of a mild winter and a meek hurricane season caused the market to turn against Amaranth in August 2006 with its positions sharply falling in value.[231] Faced with devastating losses and collateral calls from its brokers, Amaranth sold its energy portfolio to JP Morgan Chase & Co. and Citadel Investment Group, another hedge fund, with the rest of Amaranth's investments disposed in an orderly liquidation.[232]

223. Formally, Amaranth Advisors headquartered in Greenwich Connecticut and incorporated in Delaware was the management company for various funds with the Amaranth LLC fund being its principal fund.
224. For an excellent account of Amaranth's rise and eventual demise *see* Barbara Dreyfuss, *Hedge Hogs: The Cowboy Traders Behind Wall Street's Largest Hedge Fund Disaster* (Random House, 2013).
225. US Congress, Senate Permanent Subcommittee on Investigations, *Excessive Speculation in the Natural Gas Market* (2007), 56.
226. *See Ibid.*, 9-47 for a description of the complex structure and operation of the US natural gas markets including the natural gas swaps, options and futures markets.
227. Ludwig Chincarini, 'A Case Study on Risk Management: Lessons from the Collapse of Amaranth Advisors LLC', *Journal of Applied Finance* 18, no. 1 (2008): 152.
228. *See* Congress, *Excessive Speculation in the Natural Gas Market*, 51-52.
229. *Ibid.*
230. *Ibid.*
231. Jickling, 'Lessons of Long-Term Capital Management and Amaranth Advisors', 300 & Henny Sender Ann Davis and Gregory Zuckerman, 'What Went Wrong at Amaranth', The Wall Street Journal, http://online.wsj.com/news/articles/SB115871715733268470.
232. In fact, JP Morgan quickly sold many of the energy positions acquired by Amaranth to Citadel earning a profit of more than USD 725 million. Henny Sender and Gregory Zuckerman Ann

Overall, it should be stressed that unlike the LTCM episode, the collapse of Amaranth, which remains the largest failure in hedge fund history,[233] did not have any impact on financial markets and was resolved rapidly via a private sector initiative. Despite the legitimate fears raised by LTCM's near collapse regarding the potential contribution of hedge funds to systemic risk, the Amaranth debacle demonstrated the ability of the hedge fund industry to find creative solutions to its own problems. However, the investigation into Amaranth's demise launched by the US Senate Permanent Subcommittee on Investigations concluded that Amaranth's large-scale trades in US natural gas financial markets distorted market prices and increased price volatility.[234] Furthermore, the distortions in financial markets caused by Amaranth's trading resulted in inflated natural gas prices for end-users.[235] Amaranth's collapse was followed by a wave of market manipulation charges with its star natural gas trader, Brain Hunter, receiving a USD 30 million fine from the Federal Energy Regulatory Commission for manipulating the natural gas futures market.[236]

1.3.1.5 Hedge Funds and the Financial Crisis

The seeds of the 2007-2008 financial crisis can be traced back to the housing and credit bubble in the US, which peaked during the five-year period from 2002 to 2007.[237] The crisis was triggered in February 2007 when a rise in subprime mortgage defaults was first observed.[238] In the months leading up to Lehman's collapse, a number of significant financial institutions exposed to the subprime mortgage market, including Bear Stearns, Fannie Mae and Freddie Mac, were rescued by the US government.[239] The bankruptcy of Lehman Brothers on 15 September 2008 marked the defining moment of the crisis sparking a contagious run by short-term creditors, which propagated among institutions and markets indiscriminately.[240] The loss of investor confidence was

---

Davis, 'Amid Amaranth's Crisis, Other Players Profited', The Wall Street Journal http://online.wsj.com/news/articles/SB117012628156391989.

233. At the end of August 2006, shortly before its collapse, Amaranth had USD 9.668 billion of assets under management, an amount considerably higher than the USD 5 billion that LTCM was managing before its demise. Furthermore, the trading losses suffered by Amaranth reached USD 6.6 billion, approximately one-third more than LTCM's USD 4.4 billion trading losses. Houman B Shadab, 'The Challenge of Hedge Fund Regulation', *Regulation* 30, no. 1 (2007): 40.
234. Congress, *Excessive Speculation in the Natural Gas Market*, 1-7, 114-19.
235. *Ibid.*
236. Dreyfuss, *Hedge Hogs: The Cowboy Traders Behind Wall Street's Largest Hedge Fund Disaster*, 237-43.
237. From 2002 to 2007 US housing prices rose at an annual rate of 11% while the ratio of debt to US national income grew from 3.75:1 to 4.75:1. Viral V Acharya and Matthew Richardson, 'Causes of the Financial Crisis', *Critical Review* 21, no. 2-3 (2009): 195-96.
238. Markus K Brunnermeier, 'Deciphering the Liquidity and Credit Crunch 2007-2008', *Journal of Economic Perspectives* 23, no. 1 (2009): 82-83. The author also offers a short but meaningful narrative of the crisis.
239. *Ibid.*, 83-89.
240. Hal Scott, 'Interconnectedness and Contagion', *Committee on Capital Market Regulation* (2012): 106-36. According to Scott, the contagious run resulted from: (a) the perception created to market participants that by letting Lehman fail the US government was no longer willing to stand behind ailing financial institutions, (b) market uncertainty regarding the direct impact of

aggravated by the announcement one day later that the FED was extending a USD 85 billion bailout loan to AIG, which was facing a severe liquidity crisis.[241] The following days witnessed the freezing of the interbank lending, repo and commercial paper markets and a run on major financial institutions by their customers.[242] Furthermore, money market mutual funds witnessed an unprecedented amount of withdrawals after a major money market mutual fund, the Reserve Primary Fund, 'broke the buck' because of its holdings of Lehman debt.[243] The credit crunch rapidly spread across the globe forcing governments and central banks to resort to extraordinary fiscal and monetary stimulus and bailouts of financial and non-financial institutions.

In 2008, at the height of the crisis, hedge funds were fiercely criticized for aggravating market declines by spreading false rumours about the health of financial institutions and short selling their stocks, thus engaging in so-called bear raids.[244] After intense lobbying by the banking industry, governments around the world imposed bans on short selling. On 18 September 2008, the SEC and the UK's FSA introduced bans on short sales of financial stocks.[245] The majority of governments around the world adopted similar actions.[246] The bans severely impacted hedge funds since many of their trading strategies, such as convertible arbitrage, rely on short selling.[247] Moreover, numerous studies have concluded that the short selling bans slowed price discovery and dampened liquidity without successfully supporting the prices of financial stocks.[248] Even the SEC has acknowledged that it was mostly long sellers that drove the severe price declines during September 2008.[249]

Lehman's collapse on its counterparties. However, Skeel rejects the popular belief that Lehman's collapse was the cause of the subsequent paralysis that swept over the credit markets and provides evidence that market reactions to AIG's rescue loan were of equal - or even greater - magnitude to reactions to Lehman's bankruptcy filing. *See* David Skeel, *The New Financial Deal: Understanding the Dodd-Frank Act and Its (Unintended) Consequences* (Wiley and Sons, 2011), 23-25.

241. For an excellent overview of AIG's liquidity crisis and bailout *see* William K. Sjostrom, 'The AIG Bailout', *Washington and Lee Law Review* 66, no. 3 (2009).
242. *See* Scott, 'Interconnectedness and Contagion', 121-37.
243. Money market mutual funds are a subset of mutual funds investing in short-term debt issued by borrowers of high credit quality and offering their investors a stable USD 1 per share price. Breaking the buck refers to the inability of a fund to maintain its USD 1 share price. *See generally* Jill Fisch and Eric Roiter, 'A Floating Nav for Money Market Funds: Fix or Fantasy', *University of Illinois Law Review* (2012).
244. Bill Saporito, 'Are Short Sellers to Blame for the Financial Crisis', Time, http://www.time.com/time/business/article/0,8599,1842499,00.html.
245. Emergency Order Pursuant to section 12(k)(2) of the Securities Exchange Act of 1934 Taking Temporary Action to Respond to Market Developments, Exchange Act Release No. 58,592, 73 Fed. Reg. 55,169 (18 September 2008); FIN. SERVS. AUTH., SHORT SELLING (NO. 2) INSTRUMENT 2008, FSA 2008/50 (18 September 2008) (relating to UK financial sector companies).
246. *See* Dechert, *International Short Selling Regulation: Recent Developments* (2008).
247. Louise Story, 'A Debate as a Ban on Short-Selling Ends: Did It Make Any Difference?', The New York Times, http://www.nytimes.com/2008/10/08/business/08short.html?_r=0.
248. *See* Ekkehart Boehmer, Charles M Jones and Xiaoyan Zhang, 'Shackling Short Sellers: The 2008 Shorting Ban', *Review of Financial Studies* 26, no. 6 (2013); Alessandro Beber and Marco Pagano, 'Short-Selling Bans Around the World: Evidence from the 2007-09 Crisis', *The Journal of Finance* 68, no. 1 (2013).
249. Memorandum from Office of Economic Analysis, U.S. Sec. & Exch. Comm'n to Distribution List on Analysis of the July Emergency Order Requiring a Pre-Borrow on Short Sales (14 January 2009).

Hedge funds have also been accused of fuelling the credit and real estate boom by purchasing CDOs, the instruments at the heart of the subprime crisis.[250] Nonetheless, the total that hedge funds devoted to CDO trading was calculated to be around USD 7 billion as of July 2007, which represented only a small percentage of the overall CDO market.[251] Indeed, banks continue to be the main holders of CDO securities.[252] Furthermore, one has to take into account the reasons behind the growth of the CDO market. The CDO market was in essence created in response to the growing demand of institutional investors for highly rated securities offering attractive returns. Unlike institutional investors who were the main investors in the highly rated tranches of CDO deals, hedge funds concentrated their investments in the more speculative lower-rated tranches and equity tranches.[253]

Another criticism levelled against hedge funds relates to their role in aggravating the financial crisis through 'fire sales'.[254] Various commentators have argued that the massive deleveraging by hedge funds that took place during the financial crisis exerted a downward pressure on asset prices.[255] Furthermore, the failure of Bear Stearns, the then fifth largest investment bank in the US, resulting from the collapse of two highly leveraged internal hedge funds, alerted regulators to the perils of hedge funds' interconnectedness with SIFIs. Even though the dangers of hedge funds' interconnectedness with SIFIs are now widely recognized and regulators in the US have taken steps to break this link, the available empirical evidence does not support the view that hedge funds' deleveraging during the crisis adversely affected asset prices.[256]

1.3.1.6 Hedge Funds and the Sovereign Debt Crisis

The current sovereign debt crisis in Europe started in 2010 when fears regarding the solvency of Greece led investors to flee Greek sovereign bonds, shutting the country out

---

250. *See* Photis Lysandrou, 'The Primacy of Hedge Funds in the Subprime Crisis', *Journal of Post Keynesian Economics* 34, no. 2 (2011). A collateralized debt obligation – commonly referred to as a CDO – is a debt security issued by a special purpose vehicle and backed by fixed-income assets such as mortgage-backed securities or corporate bonds. The debt securities are usually divided into several tranches with different seniorities and different ratings. Frank Partnoy and David A Skeel Jr, 'Promise and Perils of Credit Derivatives', *The University of Cincinnati Law Review* 75 (2006): 1027-32.
251. Shadab, 'Hedge Funds and the Financial Market'. The size of the CDO market in the US, the main market for CDOs, was estimated at around USD 900 billion in 2007. International Monetary Fund, *Global Financial Stability Report: Financial Market Turbulence: Causes, Consequences and Policies* (2007), 16.
252. Alternative Investment Management Association, *The Role of Credit Hedge Funds in the Financial System: Asset Managers, Not Shadow Banks* (March 2012), 1.
253. *Hearings, supra* note 251, at 9 (written testimony of Houman B. Shadab). In a CDO deal, the equity tranche represents the most speculative tranche, which stands to be wiped out first in case of default or losses in the underlying fixed-income assets backing the debt securities. *See* Gunter Meissner, *Credit Derivatives: Application, Pricing, and Risk Management* (Wiley, 2009), 45.
254. Shleifer and Vishny define a fire sale as a 'forced sale of an asset at a dislocated price'. Andrei Shleifer and Robert W Vishny, 'Liquidation Values and Debt Capacity: A Market Equilibrium Approach', *The Journal of Finance* 47, no. 4 (1992).
255. *See infra*. Ch. 2.
256. *See infra*. Ch. 2.

of financial markets and forcing it to resort to a joint EU-IMF bailout.[257] Markets soon turned their attention to Ireland and Portugal, which in turn had to resort to a bailout package.[258] The crisis spread to the core of the Eurozone with Spain and Italy facing increased borrowing costs and the Eurozone showing real signs of financial disintegration.[259] The threat of a disorderly Greek exit from the Eurozone, as well as questions about the ability and/or willingness of Europe's richest countries to bail out Spain and Italy, put the very existence of the euro and the Eurozone in doubt.[260] The years following the onset of the crisis saw the adoption of hastily conceived and unrealistic bailout packages,[261] a never-ending saga of Greek bailouts, debt restructurings and buybacks, profound changes to the Eurozone's institutional arrangements, and the slowing of the Eurozone economy.

Hedge funds soon became a target blamed for causing and/or aggravating the sovereign debt crisis by using wolf-pack tactics[262] to attack the euro and individual countries' bonds. European politicians led a campaign against hedge fund speculators and the use of naked CDS on sovereign debt, accusing them of driving up the funding costs of European governments.[263] During the crisis, European regulators adopted uncoordinated measures banning naked CDS of Eurozone government bonds and short

257. Alkman Granitsas Charles Forelle, 'Greece Asks for $60 Billion Bailout', The Wall Street Journal, http://online.wsj.com/news/articles/SB100014240527487037098045752013309375722258?mg=reno64-wsj.
258. Patricia Kowsmann, 'Portugal Bailout Plan Detailed', http://online.wsj.com/news/articles/SB10001424052748703937104576302883922114642?mg=reno64-wsj; Forelle Charles and Enrich David Walker Marcus, 'Ailing Ireland Accepts Bailout', The Wall Street Journal, http://online.wsj.com/news/articles/SB10001424052748703567304575628362883493310?mg=reno64-wsj.
259. Matthew Saltmarsh Liz Alderman, 'Worries Rise over Spain and Italy Debt', http://www.nytimes.com/2011/08/03/business/global/pressure-builds-on-italy-and-spain-over-finances.html?pagewanted=all&_r=0.
260. David Gauthier-Villars & Charles Forelle, 'Downgrades Fan Fresh Euro Fears', The Wall Street Journal, http://online.wsj.com/news/articles/SB100014240529702037353045771628320158835 36?mg=reno64-wsj.
261. A prominent example is the first Greek bailout package. In return for obtaining funds from the EU and the IMF, Greece committed to adopt painful austerity measures and structural reforms aimed at cutting its budget deficit from an astronomical 13.6% to 3% in just three years. Lefteris Papadimas & Jan Strupczewski, 'EU, Imf Agree $147 Billion Bailout for Greece' (Reuters), http://www.reuters.com/article/2010/05/02/us-eurozone-idUSTRE6400PJ20100502. Various commentators immediately criticized the plan as unworkable arguing that front-loaded austerity would depress demand and increase unemployment thereby diminishing any gains from spending cuts and tax increases. Martin Feldstein, 'Why Greece Will Default', Project Syndicate, http://www.project-syndicate.org/commentary/why-greece-will-default.
262. In this context, a wolf-pack tactic can be defined as hedge funds acting together to make coordinated bets against securities in order to drive down their prices. Nick Dunbar, 'An Imaginary Wolf-Pack', Nick Dunbar, http://www.nickdunbar.net/articles-and-reviews/an-imaginary-wolf-pack/.
263. Tracy Corrigan, 'Attacking Speculators Is a Good Bet for Troubled Politicians', The Daily Telegraph, http://www.telegraph.co.uk/finance/financialcrisis/7423145/Attacking-speculators-is-a-good-bet-for-troubled-politicians.html. A naked credit default swap is a credit default swap in which the buyer does not own the underlying debt against which protection is sought. Stulz, 'Financial Derivatives', 58,70.

selling of financial stocks.[264] Nonetheless, the allegations that speculative trading of CDS on sovereign debt was driving the drop in the underlying bond prices (thereby increasing borrowing costs for Eurozone governments) had little to do with reality. The overwhelming majority of studies, including, most importantly, the report of the European Commission's intra-service task force (a group set up to examine the effects of CDS trading on the sovereign debt crisis), have concluded that either the changes in spreads in sovereign CDS and bond markets were mainly contemporaneous or, in the case that price changes in the CDS markets did actually lead changes in the underlying bond markets, the changes in CDS spreads were linked to fundamentals responding to country-specific events.[265]

1.4 CONCLUSION

Despite the constant growth of the hedge fund industry and its increasing appeal with investors, the world of hedge funds is still shrouded in a veil of mystery with politicians, regulators and the public pointing to the difficulty in devising an accurate definition of hedge funds, the diversity in their legal and business structures and the complexity of their investment strategies. The present chapter has sought to demystify hedge funds by offering an in-depth overview of the history of the hedge funds, their unique characteristics, their organizational and operational structures, their investment strategies and the benefits that they bring to financial markets and their participants. What is more, I have endeavoured to disentangle the myths from the realities of the hedge fund universe by examining various episodes in hedge fund history where hedge funds have been vilified for acting as a destabilizing factor in the global financial system. As my analysis suggests, the criticism against hedge funds was, in most cases, unwarranted with hedge funds taking the blame for the failures of politicians, regulators and mainstream financial institutions.

264. Brooke Masters, 'European Short-Selling Ban Comes under Attack', Financial Times, http://www.ft.com/intl/cms/s/0/763a185e-c4e1-11e0-9c4d-00144feabdc0.html.; Alan Crawford, 'Germany to Temporarily Ban Naked Short Selling, Some Swaps of Euro Bonds', Bloomberg, http://www.bloomberg.com/news/2010-05-18/germany-to-start-temporary-ban-on-naked-short-selling-of-euro-bonds-banks.html.

265. *See* Degabriel Laurent Criado Sarai, Lewandowska Magdalena, Lindén Staffan and Ritter Peer, *Report on Sovereign CDS* (2010). The authors of the study find no evidence of mispricing in either the bond or CDS markets and that spread changes in these two markets were mainly contemporaneous. In addition, the German central bank, in its monthly report, concluded that although the CDS markets of peripheral countries were leading their bond markets in price discovery, the changes in CDS prices were the result of country-specific events. *See* Deutsche Bundesbank, *Monthly Report* (December 2010).

CHAPTER 2

Regulating Hedge Funds?

2.1 INTRODUCTION

Having demystified hedge funds in Chapter 1, Chapter 2 will seek to explore the dangers posed by hedge funds, assess the rationales for their regulation and determine the appropriate regulatory response. Section 2.1 will examine the main rationales offered by proponents of stricter hedge fund regulation seeking to build their case in favour of regulatory intervention, namely: (1) investor protection; (2) market integrity; and (3) systemic risk.[266] The investor protection rationale premises regulation on the need to protect investors against hedge fund managers' opportunism and fraud, while market integrity concerns revolve around the propensity of hedge funds to engage in market manipulation and insider trading. The contribution of hedge funds to systemic risk exemplified by LTCM's near collapse remains the most frequently invoked rationale by those seeking to justify a stringent regulatory regime for hedge funds. In light of the spectacular growth and success of hedge fund activists, the traditional justifications for hedge fund regulation should be supplemented with novel fears raised by critics of activists regarding their role in provoking a destructive short-term mentality inside corporate boardrooms. Overall, my analysis suggests that systemic risk is the sole plausible reason supporting a regulatory intervention in the hedge fund industry. However, as it will be argued, regulatory intervention is warranted only in the case of large systemically important hedge funds and hedge funds housed within SIFIs.

Having settled the issue regarding the need for regulation, section 2.2 of this chapter seeks to offer an answer to another interesting question: What form should the regulation of hedge funds on systemic risk grounds take? Various regulatory models are available: self-regulation or government regulation? Another crucial distinction in the hedge fund literature is the difference between direct regulation of hedge funds and

266. Christian Noyer, 'Hedge Funds: What Are the Main Issues', *Banque de France, Financial Stability Review: Special Issue Hedge Funds*, no. 10 (2007): 107-09.

indirect regulation, namely their regulation via their creditors and counterparties, mainly prime brokers. Overall, my thesis will advocate for direct government regulation in the area of systemic risk, recognizing though the important role of self-regulation and indirect regulation.

2.2 THE DARK SIDE OF HEDGE FUNDS

2.2.1 Investor Protection

Pursuant to the investor protection rationale, regulation is warranted by the high informational asymmetries, potential conflicts of interests, and agency costs that exist between investors in hedge funds and their managers.[267] Proponents of hedge fund regulation on investor protection grounds routinely point to the limited information disclosed to hedge fund investors, the growing incidences of managerial fraud through misreporting of the fund's returns, asset values or risk-taking and the overcompensation of hedge fund managers. Several empirical studies echo these concerns. In their separate studies, Cassar and Gerakos, Getmansky et al., and Banzaca find that hedge funds holding illiquid assets or assets over which managers have a wide discretion in their valuation are more likely to underestimate the volatility of their returns.[268] In a related study, Bollen and Poll find evidence of misreporting in the hedge fund industry with hedge fund managers exploiting the discretion afforded to them when valuing illiquid securities by reporting small gains as opposed to small losses.[269] Furthermore, Agarwal and Ray document that young and smaller hedge funds increase the fees charged to investors after a period of good performance but do not decrease them after poor performance.[270] Additionally, they find that these funds fail to deliver superior returns after fees are increased. The results of Agarwal and Ray's study suggest that hedge fund managers appropriate hedge funds' profits at their investors' expense by opportunistically increasing their fees. Finally, in their study of the returns and fees earned by approximately six thousand funds over a twenty-two-year period, Ben-David et al. document that investors earned only 36 cents for each dollar of gross profits with the rest collected by hedge fund managers as management fees and carried interest.[271]

267. Franklin R Edwards, 'Hedge Funds and Investor Protection Regulation', *Economic Review-Federal Reserve Bank of Atlanta* 91, no. 4 (2006): 36-38.
268. Jennifer Banzaca, 'Key Considerations for Hedge Fund Managers in Organizing and Operating Valuation Committees', *Hedge Fund Law Report* 5, no. 32 (August 2012); Mila Getmansky, Andrew W Lo and Igor Makarov, 'An Econometric Model of Serial Correlation and Illiquidity in Hedge Fund Returns', *Journal of Financial Economics* 74, no. 3 (2004); Gavin Cassar and Joseph Gerakos, 'Hedge Funds: Pricing Controls and the Smoothing of Self-Reported Returns', *Review of Financial Studies* 24, no. 5 (2011).
269. Nicolas PB Bollen and Veronika K Pool, 'Do Hedge Fund Managers Misreport Returns? Evidence from the Pooled Distribution', *The Journal of Finance* 64, no. 5 (2009).
270. Vikas Agarwal and Sugata Ray, 'Determinants and Implications of Fee Changes in the Hedge Fund Industry', https://papers.ssrn.com/sol3/papers.cfm?abstract_id=2024362.
271. Itzhak Ben-David, Justin Birru and Andrea Rossi, 'The Performance of Hedge Fund Performance Fees', *Charles A. Dice Center for Research in Financial Economics Working Paper* 2020-14 (2020).

Proponents of hedge fund regulation specifically criticize the secretive nature of the hedge fund industry. Inadequate disclosure of hedge fund holdings and investment strategies facilitates fraud on the part of hedge fund managers. In addition, the lack of disclosure allows hedge fund managers to mislead investors with regard to the investment strategies employed and the riskiness of their investment. The implosion of Bayou Management LLC, a Connecticut based hedge fund firm, in 2005, vividly illustrated the perils of limited disclosure.[272] Bayou's implosion is perhaps the most notorious hedge fund fraud in history. Bayou was able to raise approximately USD 450 million from investors over the course of its existence. Nonetheless, shortly after its inception in 1996, the hedge fund started recording large losses and its managers began misappropriating and dissipating investor capital. Bayou's managers sought to conceal the losses and misappropriation of investor monies by lying to investors regarding the fund's performance and the value of the investors' accounts. The fraud was uncovered in 2005 by the CFTC. Bayou filed for bankruptcy in 2006, while its managers were sentenced to multi-year prison terms.

Indeed, major regulatory actions in the hedge fund field, such as the adoption of the AIFM Directive in Europe and the Hedge Fund Rule in the US, were premised on the need to enhance investor protection. The investor protection rationale for regulating hedge funds is mostly prevalent in Europe where there is a widespread consensus among European politicians and regulators that investor protection is a legitimate rationale for regulating hedge funds. On the contrary, the approach adopted by US regulators with the enactment of the Dodd-Frank Act predominantly focuses on the systemic risk implications of hedge funds.

The major fallacy of the investor protection rationale is that investors in hedge funds are sophisticated having both the expertise and the bargaining power to adequately protect their interests.[273] Indeed, regulatory constraints limiting hedge fund investing to sophisticated investors are premised on the unsuitability of hedge funds for retail investors in contrast to sophisticated investors who are deemed able to 'fend for themselves'.[274] Despite concerns over the limited information available to hedge fund investors, the growing incidence of fraud in the hedge fund industry and the overcompensation of hedge fund managers, a robust reputational market for investment management services, ensures that hedge fund managers pay attention to investor

272. *See* Kathleen E Lange, 'New Antifraud Rule: Is Sec Enforcement the Most Effective Way to Protect Investors from Hedge Fund Fraud', *The Fordham Law Review* 77, no. 2 (2008): 851-53.

273. *See generally* Troy A Paredes, 'On the Decision to Regulate Hedge Funds: The Sec's Regulatory Philosophy, Style, and Mission', *University of Illinois Law Review* (2006): 990-97.

274. Athanassiou, *Hedge Fund Regulation in the European Union: Current Trends and Future Prospects*, 23-24.

concerns with hedge fund investors standing ready to withdraw[275] or not commit their capital in response to inadequate governance.[276]

Investors conduct extensive due diligence prior to their investments and during a fund's life, demanding information on the fund's risk, positions, strategy and compensation arrangements.[277] Furthermore, hedge fund managers design and implement robust risk management systems and controls in order to alleviate investor concerns over excessive risk-taking.[278] There is also substantial evidence that investors are able to negotiate significant improvements in other areas as well such as the valuation and custody of fund assets, an independent compliance function and the management of internal controls and conflicts. For instance, instead of relying on prime brokers and their in-house operations, hedge funds are increasingly utilizing independent and non-conflicted service providers for the valuation and custody of fund assets and other administrative and operational functions.[279] Investors also expect an independent, well-documented and adequately resourced compliance function, documentation with respect to internal controls and conflicts and disclosure of 'side letters' to all existing and potential investors.[280]

The hedge fund industry has also been extremely creative in devising innovative compensation arrangements, which limit performance-based fees and ensure an

275. Scholars have only recently recognized the powerful disciplinary effect of hedge fund investors' exit rights and their crucial role in lowering managerial agency costs. *See* Shadab, 'Hedge Fund Governance', 150. *See also* John Morley, 'The Separation of Funds and Managers: A Theory of Investment Fund Structure and Regulation', *Yale LJ* 123, no. 5 (2014): 1243-47, 52-54.

276. *See* Shadab, 'Hedge Fund Governance', 176 & Alternative Investment Management Association, *A Guide to Institutional Investors' Views and Preferences Regarding Hedge Fund Operational Infrastructures* (May 2011) (reporting that 'governance has become a "break or make" area in the investment decision-making process').

277. This is especially true after the negative experiences of investors during the financial crisis of 2008. *See* State Street, *Hedge Funds: Rebuilding on a New Foundation* (August 2011), 4-5; Diane Harrison, 'A Battle Cry for Hedge Funds: Separate but Not Equal', FINAlternatives (3 April 2012); Securities and Commission, *Implications of the Growth of Hedge Funds*, 47-49. According to a survey conducted by PriceWaterHouseCoopers over 85% of the hedge funds managers participating in the survey reported that they made at least monthly disclosures to their investors. PriceWaterHouseCoopers, *Transparency Versus Returns: The Institutional Investor View of Alternative Assets* (March 2008), 50.

278. Dan Awrey, 'The Limits of EU Hedge Fund Regulation', *Law and Financial Markets Review* 5, no. 2 (2011): 122.

279. Cassey Quirk and Bank of New York Mellon, *The Hedge Fund of Tomorrow* (April 2009), 15-16.

280. The term 'side letter' refers to a written agreement supplementing a fund's constitutional documents which grant preferential treatment to an investor with respect to his investment in a fund and may include a reduction in management fees and/or performance-based compensation, provision of more favourable liquidity terms such as waivers of gates or lock-ups and provision of quantitatively more and qualitatively better information. Side letters have come under criticism for offering special treatment to investors with superior bargaining power such as big institutional investors. Narayan Naik, 'Hedge Funds: Transparency and Conflicts of Interest', *Policy Department Economics and Scientific Policy, European Parliament* (2007): 33. The disclosure policy of the existence side letters to all existing and potential investors that the hedge fund industry seems to be adopting is the optimal approach to alleviating the concerns posed by this practice. Informed about the existence of side letters, investors may decline to invest their capital, while existing investors may demand the extension of the special terms granted to certain investors to them too.

alignment of interests between fund managers and their investors. A common provision in hedge fund management contracts is the 'high-water mark', which allows a hedge fund manager to claim the 'carried interest' only after previous losses of the fund have been recouped.[281] 'Hurdle rates' further limit managerial performance-based compensation requiring the hedge fund manager to exceed a designated rate of return before receiving the 'carried interest'.[282] Traumatized by the 2008 downturn and the severe losses suffered by hedge funds, investors are increasingly insisting on clawback provisions, which require the return of any incentive fee paid after the fund experiences subsequent losses.[283] Managerial co-investments in the funds are an additional powerful device for aligning the interests between managers and investors. Indeed, Agarwal, Daniel & Naik estimate that the mean (median) managerial ownership is 7.1% (2.4%) of hedge fund AUM.[284] Investors have also been successful in pressuring hedge fund managers to reduce management and performance-based fees. While a 2% management fee and an incentive allocation of 20% of fund profits has long been considered to be the industry standard, recent years have seen, according to industry insiders, the rise of a new industry normal with management fees dropping to 1.65% and the 'carried interest' reduced to 18%.[285] In fact, only a third of hedge funds today follow the 2 and 20 fee model.[286]

According to supporters of stricter hedge fund regulation, the sweeping retailization of the hedge fund industry further strengthens the case for regulatory intervention on investor protection grounds.[287] The proliferation of novel products, particularly funds of hedge funds,[288] and the spectacular rise in allocations by institutional investors, most notably pension funds, have resulted in the indirect exposure of ordinary investors to the hedge fund universe. As Edwards points out, the above-mentioned concern 'indirectly raises the principal-agent problems that may occur when retail investors delegate decision-making authority to professional fund advisers

281. William N Goetzmann, Jonathan Ingersoll Jr and Stephen A Ross, 'High Water Marks', *National Bureau of Economic Research* No. w6413 (February 1998): 1-2.
282. Lederman, *Hedge Fund Regulation*, para. 2-11.
283. Timothy Spangler, 'Clawbacks Becoming Fashionable on Wall Street', Forbes, http://www.forbes.com/sites/timothyspangler/2013/05/28/clawbacks-becoming-fashionable-on-wall-street/.
284. Vikas Agarwal, Naveen D Daniel and Narayan Y Naik, 'Role of Managerial Incentives and Discretion in Hedge Fund Performance', *The Journal of Finance* 64, no. 5 (2009): 2231.
285. Juliet Chung Gregory Zuckerman and Michael Corkery, 'Hedge Funds Cut Back on Fees', The Wall Street Journal, http://www.wsj.com/articles/SB1000142412788732389300457905495280 7556352.
286. Tom Teodorczuk, 'Only a Third of Hedge Funds Charge "2 and 20" Fees, Says Expert', *Financial News*, n.d., https://www.fnlondon.com/articles/only-a-third-of-hedge-funds-charge-2-and-20-fees-says-expert-20181108.
287. Phoebus Athanassiou, 'The Conceptual Underpinnings of Onshore Hedge Fund Regulation: A Global and European Perspective', *Journal of Corporate Law Studies* 8, no. 2 (2008): 258.
288. Funds of hedge funds are investment funds investing in other hedge funds. The benefits of funds of hedge funds are the diversification benefits achieved by investing in different hedge funds and the superior skill of fund of hedge fund managers in identifying skilled hedge fund managers and monitoring their performance. Funds of hedge funds may be unregistered or registered investment vehicles open to retail investors, such as funds registered under the Investment Company Act of 1940 in the US or under the UCITS Directive in Europe. *See* Edwards, 'Hedge Funds and Investor Protection Regulation', 44-46.

or managers'.[289] For instance, fund managers seeking to ramp up fund returns and increase their compensation may decide to aggressively expand their investments in hedge funds, thus exposing retail investors unwillingly to the high risks of the hedge fund industry. Furthermore, retail investors may suffer steep losses as a result of poor monitoring by fund managers of their hedge fund investments. Nonetheless, the approach of proponents of hedge fund regulation misses the mark. The optimal solution to address the principal-agent conflicts arising from the delegation of responsibilities to fund managers is not to regulate hedge funds but rather to strengthen existing oversight and governance mechanisms for monitoring and disciplining professional fund managers.[290]

Finally, the most significant shortcoming of regulating hedge funds on investor protection grounds is the creation of a false sense of security to investors.[291] Hedge fund regulation manipulates the perceptions of investors, causing them to believe that the rules imposed adequately address the risks associated with investing in hedge funds.[292] As a result, it disincentivizes them from conducting careful due diligence and monitoring hedge fund managers. Furthermore, it inhibits the negotiation and conclusion of mutually beneficial bargains between self-interested parties, namely hedge fund investors and managers, which curb hedge fund managers' opportunism.

Overall, our analysis suggests that regulating hedge funds on investor protection grounds makes little sense in so far as investors in hedge funds are sophisticated. Nonetheless, recent years have seen the breakdown of regulatory barriers limiting hedge fund investing to sophisticated investors. For instance, acting in accordance with Article 43 of the AIFM Directive, numerous European countries have extended the marketing of hedge funds to retail investors in their territory.[293] In cases where retail investors are allowed to directly invest in hedge funds, imposing appropriate regulation on hedge funds aimed at protecting investors from the high investment and operational risks of hedge funds is warranted.

289. *Ibid.*, 47.
290. *Ibid.*
291. *See* Houman Shadab, 'Houman Shadab Testifies Before Congress on Hedge Funds and the Financial Crisis', (Youtube, 2009).
292. Modern legal scholarship, and in particular Law and Economics scholarship, focuses on law's role in manipulating incentives. A recent strand of scholarship pioneered by Amitai Aviram highlights the important impact that law has on behaviour by manipulating perceptions. Aviram defines this behavioural effect of law as the 'placebo effect of law'. *See* Amitai Aviram, 'Placebo Effect of Law: Law's Role in Manipulating Perceptions', *The George Washington Law Review* 75, no. 1 (2006): 54 ('Although manipulating incentives certainly explains some of law's impact on behavior (e.g., increasing airport security may deter some airplane hijackers), law has an equally important impact on behavior by manipulating perceptions (e.g., causing the public to believe that the risk of airplane hijacking has diminished as a result of the law that increased airport security)').
293. An example is Luxembourg which has elected to extend the marketing of alternative investment funds, including hedge funds, to retail investors. *See* Art. 46 of the Law of 12 July 2013 on alternative investment fund managers.

2.2.2 Market Integrity

As Athanassiou notes, the protection of market integrity is 'a key determinant of the investors' ability to transact their business within an environment of fairness, transparency and non-discrimination, where the prices of financial assets reflect market fundamentals, unadulterated from market manipulation, collusion or other abusive behaviour'.[294] Indeed, the protection of market integrity is widely regarded as a key element for fostering capital market development and has therefore been a cornerstone of modern financial regulation.[295] Market integrity concerns have gained prominence in recent years due to the increased involvement of hedge funds in insider trading and market manipulation. A wave of insider trading and market manipulation investigations in the US has resulted in the indictment of star hedge funds and their managers[296] with empirical research suggesting that concerns regarding widespread insider trading and market manipulation by hedge funds are well founded. Examining the trading pattern of hedge funds around mergers and acquisitions, Dai et al. find evidence consistent with hedge funds trading on the basis of private information.[297] Their study reports that short-term holdings[298] of target shares by hedge funds in the quarter prior to the announcement of a merger or acquisition are positively associated with the transaction's premium and negatively associated with deal completion. What is more, the authors find that the pre-announcement target stock price run-up is significantly higher for targets with high short-term hedge fund holdings. In addition, they document that abnormal short selling in the acquirer's stock and put buying prior to the public announcement of a stock deal is negatively associated with the acquirer's stock returns following the public announcement especially when hedge funds hold higher short-term positions in the target. Furthermore, Ben-David et al. document that hedge funds engage in market manipulation by bidding up the prices of stocks they hold on critical reporting dates in order to inflate their performance.[299]

294. Athanassiou, *Hedge Fund Regulation in the European Union: Current Trends and Future Prospects*, 61.
295. Constructing an index of the stringency of insider trading laws in thirty-three countries, Beny finds that countries adopting more stringent insider trading laws exhibit more liquid stock markets, more informative stock prices and widespread equity ownership. Laura Nyantung Beny, 'Insider Trading Laws and Stock Markets Around the World: An Empirical Contribution to the Theoretical Law and Economics Debate', *Journal of Corporation Law* 32, no. 2 (2006).
296. *See*, for instance, Susan Pulliam and Chad Bray, 'Trader Draws Record Sentence', The Wall Street Journal, http://online.wsj.com/news/articles/SB10001424052970203914304576627191081876286 (detailing the sentencing of Raj billionaire hedge fund manager Raj Rajaratnam for insider trading); Juliet Chung, 'Falcone Admits Wrongdoing, Agrees to Five-Year Ban', The Wall Street Journal, http://online.wsj.com/news/articles/SB10001424127887323608504579023123351192450 (reporting the SEC's action against Philip Falcone a billionaire hedge fund manager accused of illegal market manipulation).
297. Massoud Nadia Dai Rui, Nandy Debarshi and Saunders Anthony, 'Hedge Funds in M&A Deals: Is There Exploitation of Private Information?', (Working Paper, 2010).
298. The authors define short-term holdings as holdings in the target that did not exist over the prior year but were acquired within one quarter prior to the public announcement of the merger or acquisition. According to the authors of the study, such short-term pre-announcement entry of a hedge fund suggests that it is privy to insider information. *Ibid.*, 4.
299. Franzoni Francesco Itzhak Ben-David, Landier Augustin and Moussawi Rabih, 'Do Hedge Funds Manipulate Stock Prices?', *The Journal of Finance* 68, no. 6 (2013).

The propensity of hedge funds to engage in insider trading and market manipulation stems from the structure and business model of hedge funds. The overriding majority of hedge funds are owner-managed small or midsize companies lacking the necessary infrastructure to combat the mismanagement of inside information such as 'Chinese Walls'.[300] In addition, as Jennifer Arlen notes, hedge funds operate in 'an industry where to survive they must be seeking out information other people do not have so they are always bumping up against both the temptation to break the law and the risk of accidentally violating the law'.[301] The high-powered incentives to generate profits created by the unique structure of hedge fund compensation whereby the manager is rewarded with a share of the profits further aggravates the temptation of hedge fund managers to engage in insider trading and market manipulation.

Nonetheless, insider trading and market manipulation are by no means exclusive to the hedge fund industry but are common phenomena in financial markets. Hedge funds are not fundamentally different from other financial market participants, including ordinary investors, which regularly succumb to the allure of quick profits generated by trading on inside information or manipulating markets. Recognizing the importance of the protection of market integrity for capital market development, virtually all developed economies including the US and the EU have already put in place a comprehensive legislative framework in order to combat insider trading and market manipulation, with developing economies following suit.[302] As a result, the enforcement of existing rules is sufficient to safeguard market integrity rather than the adoption of new rules targeting hedge funds.[303] Indeed, regulators, most prominently the SEC, have, in the aftermath of the financial crisis, stepped up their enforcement efforts against insider trading and market manipulation by hedge funds. It follows, therefore, that regulators around the world, including European regulators, would emulate the example of the SEC and increase their enforcement actions. To the extent that market participants devise innovative tactics in order to circumvent rules against insider trading and market manipulation, regulators should update the relevant rules. For instance, in response to the spectacular growth of over-the-counter markets and

300. Noyer, 'Hedge Funds: What Are the Main Issues', 106.
301. *See* 'The Forum: Insider Trading: Hedge Funds in the Crosshairs, Nyu School of Law Forum', (Youtube, 2013).
302. Insider trading and market manipulation in the EU are regulated by MAD and MAR *see* Directive 2014/57/EU of the European Parliament and of the Council of 16 April 2014 on Criminal Sanctions for Market Abuse (Market Abuse Directive), 2014 O.J. (L 173) 179; 'Regulation (EU) No. 596/2014 of the European Parliament and of the Council of 16 April 2014 on Market Abuse (Market Abuse Regulation) and Repealing Directive 2003/6/EC of the European Parliament and of the Council and Commission Directives 2003/124/EC, 2003/125/EC and 2004/72/EC, 2014 O.J. (L 173) 1'. For an overview of US prohibitions against insider dealing and market manipulation *see* Marco Ventoruzzo, 'Comparing Insider Trading in the United States and in the European Union: History and Recent Developments', *No. 257 European Corporate Governance Institute (ECGI)-Law Working Paper* No. 257 (2014); Sarah Dunn Davis, 'Market Manipulation Annotated Bibliography', (2010).
303. Noyer, 'Hedge Funds: What Are the Main Issues', 107. On the importance of enforcement *see* Utpal Bhattacharya and Hazem Daouk, 'The World Price of Insider Trading', *The Journal of Finance* 57, no. 1 (2002). The authors report that even though the cost of equity in a country remains unaffected by the introduction of an insider trading prohibition, it falls significantly after the first enforcement of that country's prohibition.

alternative trading venues, the EU has extended the prohibition on insider trading and market manipulation, previously applicable solely to financial instruments admitted to trading on EU 'regulated markets', to instruments traded over the counter, on MTFs and on OTFs.[304]

2.2.3 Systemic Risk

The most commonly invoked rationale for justifying regulatory intervention in the hedge fund industry is the repercussions that the distress of a large hedge fund or multiple small or medium-sized hedge funds could have on the stability of the financial system.[305] Regulatory authorities and academic researchers have recognized that hedge funds contribute to systemic risk via two channels, the credit channel and the market channel.[306] The credit channel refers to the impact that the failure of a large hedge fund or multiple smaller funds could have on creditors and other financial institutions that act as counterparties. Systemic risk through the market channel can arise when adverse market movements lead to the withdrawal of credit, tightening of collateral requirements, margin calls, and investor redemptions, forcing a large hedge fund or multiple smaller funds to liquidate their positions at fire-sale prices. The resulting decline in security prices leads to a further freezing of credit and investor withdrawals prompting a new round of forced sales. If this 'death spiral' continues and spreads to other investors who happen to hold the same assets, a financial crisis can

304. The original MAD prohibited insider dealing and market manipulation with respect to financial instruments admitted to trading on a regulated market or for which a request for admission to trading on such a market has been made. MAR, which repealed the original MAD, extends the prohibition to financial instruments traded on MTFs and OTFs. Furthermore, MAR applies to: (a) financial instruments not admitted to trading on a regulated market or traded on MTFs and OTFs the price or value of which depends on or has an effect on the price or value of a financial instrument admitted to trading on a regulated market or traded on MTFs and OTFs including, but not limited, to over-the-counter credit default swaps and contracts for difference; (b) trading in spot commodity contracts which could have an impact on the price of a financial instrument admitted to trading on a regulated market, traded on MTFs and OTFs or a financial instrument not admitted to trading on a regulated market or traded on MTFs and OTFs the price or value of which depends on or has an effect on the price or value of a financial instrument admitted to trading on a regulated market or traded on MTFs and OTFs; (c) trading in financial instruments including over-the-counter derivative contracts which could have an impact on the price of spot commodity contracts where the price or value depends on the price or value of those financial instruments. 'Regulation (EU) No 596/2014 of the European Parliament and of the Council of 16 April 2014 on Market Abuse (Market Abuse Regulation) and Repealing Directive 2003/6/EC of the European Parliament and of the Council and Commission Directives 2003/124/EC, 2003/125/EC and 2004/72/EC, 2014 O.J. (L 173) 1', Art. 1(d) & Art. 2(a) & (b) at 16-17. The definitions of a regulated market, MTF and an OTF are to be found in the MiFID II. *See* Directive 2014/65/EU of the European Parliament and of the Council of 15 May 2014 on Markets in Financial Instruments and Amending Directive 2002/92/EC and Directive 2011/61/EU, 2014 O.J. (L 173) 1.
305. Lloyd Dixon, *Rand Corporation, Hedge Funds and Systemic Risk*, 4.
306. *See Ibid.* & Financial Stability Board and IOSCO, *Assessment Methodologies for Identifying Non-Bank Non-Insurer Global Systemically Important Financial Institutions, Consultative Document* (January 2014), 29-30.

quickly develop.[307] One should add to the standard two channels, two other channels through which hedge funds may contribute to systemic risk: the impact of the failure of an internal hedge fund run by a systemically important bank or non-bank financial institution on the stability of its parent[308] and the impact of hedge funds' short selling activities on the stability of the financial system.

The analysis of hedge funds' contribution to systemic risk will be mostly based on an examination of three incidents where hedge funds have been forcefully criticized, rightly or wrongly, for contributing to systemic risk. The LTCM episode raised concerns regarding the destabilizing effects of the failure of a large hedge fund. Furthermore, hedge funds, as a group, have been accused of contributing to the financial crisis through the market channel with widespread forced sales by leveraged funds exerting a downward pressure on asset prices. The failure of Bear Stearns, triggered by problems in two of its internal hedge funds, exposed the perils of housing hedge funds within SIFIs. Finally, I will examine the potential adverse effect of hedge fund short selling activities on financial stability.

2.2.3.1 Too Big to Fail: LTCM

The involvement of the FED in the rescue of LTCM was prompted by fears that the failure of LTCM would have a destabilizing effect on financial markets. The collapse of LTCM threatened to generate systemic risk mostly through the market channel. As far as the credit channel is concerned, a default by LTCM would certainly impose severe losses on its creditors and counterparties. The exposures of LTCM's creditors and counterparties, which were mostly major banks, arose from OTC derivatives transactions, repos, prime brokerage, futures clearing and lending.[309] Furthermore, some banks held substantial equity investments in LTCM.[310] Upon LTCM's bankruptcy, counterparties would rush to close out their positions, liquidate their collateral, consisting of LTCM's positions, and rebalance their portfolios.[311] The massive liquidation of LTCM's assets against the background of stressed market conditions would send

307. Andrei Shleifer and Robert Vishny, 'Fire Sales in Finance and Macroeconomics', *Journal of Economic Perspectives* 25, no. 1 (2011): 30.
308. Smith Roy Richardson Matthew and Walter Ingo, 'Large Banks and the Volcker Rule', in *Regulating Wall Street: The Dodd-Frank Act and the New Architecture of Global Finance*, ed. Viral Acharya et al. (Wiley, 2010), 204-05.
309. Shleifer, *Inefficient Markets: An Introduction to Behavioral Finance*, 12.
310. One of LTCM's biggest investors was UBS. In June 1997, the bank entered into a transaction with LTCM's partners under which a group of partners agreed to pay UBS a premium of USD 289 million. In exchange for the premium, UBS was obliged to pay the partners the profits made on an equity interest in the fund with a notional value of USD 800 million over a period of seven years. In order to hedge its exposure, UBS invested directly USD 800 million in LTCM and was granted the option to increase its investment by USD 266 million. *See* Lowenstein, *When Genius Failed: The Rise and Fall of Long-Term Capital Management*, 108.
311. Markets, *Hedge Funds, Leverage, and the Lessons of Long-Term Capital Management*, 17-19. In the US, as in most countries with well-developed capital markets, financial contracts, such as repos and derivatives, are granted special treatment under insolvency laws. The US Bankruptcy Code exempts a bankrupt debtor's financial contract counterparty from core provisions of the Code, such as bankruptcy's automatic stay, the limitations on a nondebtor's ability to set off

their prices plummeting, exaggerating their losses. Furthermore, as counterparties simultaneously sought to replace their positions, markets would move sharply, leaving them unable to establish offsetting positions. It was estimated that in case of LTCM's failure, individual firms risked losing from USD 300 million to USD 500 million each, with the aggregate losses to LTCM's top seventeen counterparties ranging from USD 3 billion to USD 5 billion.[312] Even though financial regulators considered that the losses would not have threatened the solvency of LTCM's creditors and counterparties, they could still have provoked a credit crunch.[313]

Nonetheless, the direct effects of LTCM's failure on its creditors and counterparties were not the principal concern of the FED.[314] The FED's main concern was that widespread fire sales of LTCM positions might disrupt the functioning of the market. As losses on its positions were deepening, LTCM was faced with withdrawals by panicked investors and margin calls by its short-term creditors and derivatives counterparties.[315] Unable to meet their demands, LTCM was forced to liquidate its positions in a fire sale.[316] The resulting price declines inflicted losses on other leveraged market participants who happened to hold the same positions, including hedge funds, initiating a new round of forced sales.[317] The destructive process was halted by the FED-engineered bailout of LTCM. According to FED officials, the bankruptcy of LTCM would have severely amplified fire sales.[318] The widespread close-out of positions and liquidation of collateral by its counterparties, especially derivatives counterparties,

obligations that the nondebtor owes to the debtor against obligations that the debtor owes the nondebtor, the trustee's power to avoid preferences and fraudulent transfers ('trustee-avoiding powers') and rules invalidating *ipso facto* clauses. In contrast to ordinary creditors, the non-defaulting party may, upon the bankruptcy of its counterparty, immediately terminate all outstanding contracts, calculate the gains and losses on each contract, set them off against each other ('close-out netting') and immediately liquidate any assets held as collateral. Furthermore, payments and collateral received prior to the bankruptcy are exempted from the trustee-avoiding powers. *See* Thomas H Jackson and David A Skeel Jr, 'Dynamic Resolution of Large Financial Institutions', *Harvard Business Law Review* 2 (2012): 158-59. Similar special privileges have been introduced in the EU. Directive 98/26/EC on Settlement Finality in Payment and Securities Settlement Systems, 1998 O.J. (L 166) 45; Directive 2002/47/EC of the European Parliament and of the Council of 6 June 2002 on Financial Collateral Arrangements, 2002 O.J. (L 168) 43; Directive 2009/44/EC of the European Parliament and of the Council of 6 May 2009 Amending Directive 98/26/EC on Settlement Finality in Payment and Securities Settlement Systems and Directive 2002/47/EC on Financial Collateral Arrangements as Regards Linked Systems and Credit Claims, 2009 O.J. (L 146) 37. One should note that as the fund, Long-Term Capital Portfolio LP, was incorporated in the Caymans Islands, there was considerable uncertainty as to whether the bankruptcy proceedings would take place in the Caymans Islands courts under Cayman law or in US courts under US law. In case the proceedings were opened in the Cayman Islands, it was unclear whether financial contract counterparties would be able to close out their contracts and liquidate their collateral. Markets, *Hedge Funds, Leverage, and the Lessons of Long-Term Capital Management*, 26-28.

312. GAO, *Long-Term Capital Management: Regulators Need to Focus Greater Attention on Systemic Risk* (October 1999), 12.
313. Edwards, 'Hedge Funds and the Collapse of Long-Term Capital Management', 202.
314. McDonough, 'Statement Before the Committee on Banking and Financial Services US House of Representatives'.
315. Shleifer and Vishny, 'Fire Sales in Finance and Macroeconomics', 37.
316. *Ibid.*
317. *Ibid.*
318. Edwards, 'Hedge Funds and the Collapse of Long-Term Capital Management', 201-02.

would cause steep price declines and a substantial reduction in liquidity in many markets where LTCM held sizable positions. The drop in prices would set off a cascade of forced liquidations by investors with no relationship to LTCM. The crisis would spread to a number of credit and interest rate markets, which might 'cease to function for a period of one or more days and maybe longer'.[319]

With the LTCM debacle, large hedge funds entered the wider class of entities considered as TBTF. Even though FED officials sought to downplay their involvement in the rescue of LTCM,[320] the FED was sufficiently concerned to assemble LTCM's creditors and counterparties and organize their meetings. Furthermore, the FED's mere presence at the meetings is likely to have had an implicit coercive influence on the parties involved.[321] Despite the absence of an explicit taxpayer bailout of LTCM, the FCIC correctly observes that 'the FED's orchestration raised a question: How far would it go to forestall what it saw as a systemic crisis?'[322]

One can draw a number of lessons from the near collapse of LTCM. First, LTCM's near failure threatened to paralyse the financial system due to the fund's extraordinary use of leverage, the sheer size and illiquidity of its positions and its interconnectedness with the rest of the financial system. The fund's high leverage resulted in the rapid erosion of its capital base, the infliction of heavy losses on its creditors and counterparties and the exacerbation of fire sales.[323] In addition, the scale of its positions, its substantial investments in opaque and illiquid OTC derivatives markets and its concentrated positions in certain markets, such as in US and foreign futures exchanges,[324] made it difficult for LTCM or its counterparties to liquidate their positions without causing steep price declines. Furthermore, LTCM was highly interconnected, with the spillovers from its collapse affecting numerous counterparties and markets.

319. McDonough, 'Statement Before the Committee on Banking and Financial Services US House of Representatives'.
320. William McDonough, then President of the New York FED, forcefully stated that 'no Federal Reserve official pressured anyone, and no promises were made. Not one penny of public money was spent or committed'. *See ibid.*
321. Edwards, 'Hedge Funds and the Collapse of Long-Term Capital Management', 204.
322. Financial Crisis Inquiry Commission, *The Financial Crisis Inquiry Report: Final Report of the National Commission on the Causes of the Financial and Economic Crisis in the United States*, 57.
323. An example will make the importance of the amount of leverage utilized in exacerbating fire sales clearer. Imagine a hedge fund with USD 10 million in investor capital, which decides to set its leverage target ratio at 7 to 1. The fund will borrow USD 70 million and purchase assets worth USD 80 million. Furthermore, suppose that its assets lose value and are now worth only USD 75 million. The fund's capital will now fall to USD 5 million. In order to maintain a leverage ratio of 7 to 1, the fund must sell assets worth USD 40 million. That would bring its assets holdings down to USD 40 million, which will be financed with USD 35 million debt and USD 5 million in investor capital equal to a leverage ratio of 7 to 1. In contrast, if the fund decides to have a leverage ratio of 3 to 1 (USD 30 million in debt and USD 10 million in investor capital = USD 40 million in assets), then a USD 5 million decrease in the value of its assets will result in the sale of only USD 20 million in assets. The fund will now have assets worth USD 20 million financed with USD 5 million investor capital and USD 15 million debt.
324. Some of LTCM's futures positions on US and foreign exchanges represented over 10% of open interest while, according to the Bank of International Settlements, LTCM was the single largest user of interest rate swaps in the world. GAO, *Long-Term Capital Management: Regulators Need to Focus Greater Attention on Systemic Risk*, 7 & Bank for International Settlements, *69th Annual Report* (7 June 1999).

Second, the LTCM debacle illustrates the hazards of over-reliance on creditors and trading counterparties in monitoring and disciplining hedge funds. Poor counterparty credit risk management by banks and securities firms that provided credit and served as counterparties to LTCM allowed the fund to build up a staggering level of leverage and engage in excessive risk-taking. The stellar reputation and personal connections of its principals and competitive pressure between banks and securities firms to secure fees and commissions enabled LTCM to negotiate favourable credit terms with its creditors and counterparties.[325] LTCM provided these parties with minimal information regarding the fund's overall risk profile and the scale of its activities in certain markets.[326] While each counterparty imposed trading limits on its own exposures to the fund, none of LTCM's creditors and counterparties had the necessary information to monitor the fund's overall activities.[327] What is more, margin agreements with repo and derivative counterparties offered LTCM significant credit enhancements, including zero haircuts, zero initial margin and two-way margining.[328] Collateral arrangements against current credit exposures created a false sense of security for LTCM's creditors and counterparties resulting in an inadequate assessment, pricing and collateralization of the parties' potential future exposures.[329] Creditors and counterparties were thus left vulnerable to the extreme stress that markets witnessed in 1998 and the rapid deterioration of LTCM's creditworthiness.

Third, LTCM's collapse raised important questions about the systemic risk implications of the special insolvency treatment of derivatives and repos. Derivatives and repo safe harbours are traditionally justified by the need to mitigate the risk of contagion arising from the failure of a market participant. In the absence of the safe harbours, a debtor's bankruptcy could have a knock-on effect on its derivatives and

325. GAO, *Long-Term Capital Management: Regulators Need to Focus Greater Attention on Systemic Risk*, 6. Apart from Nobel Prizewinners Myron Scholes and Robert Merton, LTCM's principals included other prominent figures on Wall Street such as John Meriwether, the head of the Salomon Brothers' famous bond-trading desk, and David Mullins, a former vice-chairman of the Federal Reserve and Assistant Secretary of the Treasury. Many senior executives at the banks and securities firms, which lent funds and acted as counterparties to LTCM, were also significant investors in the fund. For instance, the CEO of Bear Stearns, LTCM's prime broker, had personally invested USD 10 million in the fund. Peter Huang, Kimberly Krawiec and Frank Partnoy, 'Derivatives on TV: A Tale of Two Derivatives Debacles in Prime-Time', 4.

326. The information that LTCM provided to counterparties and creditors consisted mostly of balance sheets and income statements, which did not capture the fund's exposure in certain markets, most importantly the OTC derivatives markets. Markets, *Hedge Funds, Leverage, and the Lessons of Long-Term Capital Management*, 15.

327. *Ibid.*, 16.

328. *See* Jorion, 'Risk Management Lessons from Long-Term Capital Management', 280; GAO, *Long-Term Capital Management: Regulators Need to Focus Greater Attention on Systemic Risk*, 6. Under two-way margining arrangements, both parties to a derivatives transaction are required to post collateral. Two-way margining arrangements are typical when both counterparties are established market participants. In contrast, under one-way margining arrangements, the obligation to post collateral applies only to one of the counterparties, usually the counterparty with the weakest credit profile. John Hull, *Risk Management and Financial Institutions* (Wiley, 2012), 738.

329. Markets, *Hedge Funds, Leverage, and the Lessons of Long-Term Capital Management*, 15.

repo counterparties, provoking widespread market instability.[330] The special protections granted to these counterparties allow them to rapidly exercise their close-out and netting rights, liquidate their collateral and enter into new contracts, thereby limiting their exposure to the debtor's distress.[331] Yet, the LTCM debacle illustrates that instead of mitigating systemic risk, the safe harbours may actually aggravate financial instability by facilitating runs on distressed financial institutions, sparking a systemic liquidity shortage that spreads to other firms and markets.[332] Indeed, the FED's intervention was motivated by fears that the bankruptcy of LTCM would cause its counterparties to rush to close out and net their positions and liquidate their collateral. Even though the PWG recognized the potential of the special privileges granted to derivatives and repo counterparties to provoke catastrophic runs, its report counterintuitively recommended the strengthening of the safe harbours.[333]

Overall, the LTCM episode raised legitimate concerns regarding the financial stability implications of a large hedge fund failure. Nonetheless, in seeking to deemphasize the potential contribution of hedge funds to systemic risk, opponents of hedge fund regulation routinely contrast LTCM's near collapse with the failure of Amaranth, which was successfully resolved via a private sector initiative having little impact on financial markets. One should stress, though, that Amaranth's orderly failure can be attributed to a number of mitigating circumstances. Unlike the stressed market conditions prevailing at the time of LTCM's near collapse,[334] Amaranth's failure occurred in a benign market environment.[335] Another important factor was the existence of market players having the financial wherewithal to acquire Amaranth's distressed energy portfolio and bet on its recovery.[336] In addition, Amaranth's activity was concentrated in the relatively small and isolated natural gas financial markets.[337]

330. Seth Grosshandler, 'Statement Before the House Subcommittee on Regulatory Reform, Commercial & Antitrust Law of the House Committee of the Judiciary', news release, 26 March 2014.
331. *See generally* Edward R Morrison, Mark J Roe and Christopher S Sontchi, 'Rolling Back the Repo Safe Harbors', *Business Lawyer* 69, no. 4 (2014).
332. Franklin R Edwards and Edward R Morrison, 'Derivatives and the Bankruptcy Code: Why the Special Treatment', *Yale Journal on Regulation* 22, no. 1 (2005): 104. 09-13.
333. Markets, *Hedge Funds, Leverage, and the Lessons of Long-Term Capital Management*, 40-41 & E(1).
334. Lucas Papademos, 'Opening Remarks at the Press Briefing on the Occasion of the Publication of the December 2006 ECB Financial Stability Review', news release, 11 December 2006. *See* McDonough noting that the extraordinary stress that markets were witnessing in August 2008 played a crucial role in the FED's determination that the collapse of LTCM would cause extreme market dislocations. McDonough, 'Statement before the Committee on Banking and Financial Services US House of Representatives'.
335. Deutsche Bundesbank, *Financial Stability Review* (November 2006).
336. In their model, Shleifer and Vishny show that assets sold in fire sales fetch heavily discounted prices because specialist industry buyers, who would be the natural candidates for acquiring the relevant assets, are themselves facing financial constraints due to an industry or economy-wide shock. With specialist buyers unable to bid, the assets in liquidation will be eventually acquired by industry outsiders who, having less expertise with the relevant assets, will bid for prices far below value in best use. *See* Shleifer and Vishny, 'Fire Sales in Finance and Macroeconomics'. The robust market conditions prevailing at the time of its collapse allowed Amaranth to unload its energy portfolio to specialists, namely Citadel and JP Morgan, who were unhindered by financial constraints. In contrast, LTCM's near collapse and the forced liquidation of its portfolio unravelled in the midst of extraordinary market stress. Specialist

2.2.3.2 Too Many to Fail: Hedge Funds, the Financial Crisis and Fire Sales

In their account of the financial crisis, Shleifer and Vishny argue that investor redemptions and the withdrawal of financing caused hedge funds to liquidate their holdings in a falling market.[338] Similarly, Ben-David et al. find that funding constraints due to withdrawals by investors and the tightening of credit led hedge funds to reduce their equity holdings by approximately 15%, on average, in each of the third and fourth quarters of 2008.[339] The authors conclude that the massive sell-off by hedge funds 'may have amplified the initial negative shocks to asset prices, and it certainly did not stabilize markets'.[340] In addition, Brown, Green and Hand present evidence consistent with hedge fund liquidations of their holdings increasing the severity of the decline in the overall market during the financial crisis.[341] The report of the FCIC in the US further criticizes hedge funds for sending prices plummeting. According to the report, hedge funds, in the years leading up to the crisis, heavily bought MBSs and CDOs using them as collateral in repo agreements.[342] However, when the spike in mortgage delinquencies and defaults caused credit rating agencies to downgrade these securities, repo lenders started demanding more collateral from hedge funds.[343] Faced with margin calls, hedge funds were forced to sell at distressed prices contributing to market stress.[344]

Despite the widespread criticism that hedge funds contributed to the financial crisis, a careful analysis reveals that hedge funds' role in aggravating the crisis through either the credit or market channel was rather limited. First of all, there is a dearth of evidence that hedge funds contributed to market instability through the credit channel. Indeed, the widespread hedge fund losses and failures did not have a destabilizing impact on their creditors and counterparties. The losses suffered by creditors and counterparties were too small to threaten their solvency.[345]

As far as their contribution to the financial crisis through the market channel is concerned, one should note that the impact of forced liquidations by hedge funds on asset prices has been greatly exaggerated. Most importantly, the extent of fire sales of assets by a market participant depends on the amount of leverage utilized. In contrast

buyers, such as hedge funds and financial institutions, who were the natural candidates for acquiring LTCM's portfolio, were suffering the same market-wide shock as LTCM and were also engaging in fire sales. As a result, the only available buyers for LTCM's portfolio were low-valuation industry outsiders.

337. Ferguson and Laster, 'Hedge Funds and Systemic Risk', 51.
338. Shleifer and Vishny, 'Fire Sales in Finance and Macroeconomics', 40.
339. Franzoni Fransesco Itzhak Ben-David and Moussawi Rabih, 'Hedge Fund Stock Trading in the Financial Crisis of 2007-2009', *Review of Financial Studies* 25, no. 1 (2012): 2-3.
340. *Ibid.*, 54.
341. Gregory W Brown, Jeremiah Green and John RM Hand, 'Are Hedge Funds Systemically Important?', *The Journal of Derivatives* 20, no. 2 (2012): 18.
342. Financial Crisis Inquiry Commission, *The Financial Crisis Inquiry Report: Final Report of the National Commission on the Causes of the Financial and Economic Crisis in the United States*, 135.
343. *Ibid.*, 213.
344. *Ibid.*
345. European Union Committee House of Lords, *Directive on Alternative Investment Fund Managers, Volume 1: Report* (10 February 2010), 20.

to popular beliefs, hedge funds utilize leverage in a prudent manner. Ang et al., investigating actual leverage ratios of 208 hedge funds obtained by a fund of hedge funds, find that average gross leverage including derivatives exposure from December 2004 until October 2009 was at a modest 2.1 times NAV.[346] What is most interesting is that, comparing hedge fund and finance sector leverage, the authors show that not only before the outbreak of the financial crisis in mid-2007 but also during the heights of the crisis in 2008 and 2009, hedge funds were actually reducing their leverage, while the leverage of banks, investment banks and the entire finance sector was shooting up.[347]

What is more, Ben-David et al. report that during the crisis hedge funds were more likely to sell the most liquid stocks, indicating that they sought to minimize the price impact of their fire sales.[348] Discretionary liquidity restrictions used by hedge funds managers during the crisis, such as the creation of side pockets for illiquid assets, the imposition of gates and the suspension of investor redemptions, further limited the extent of forced liquidations.[349] Aiken et al. document that by the first quarter of 2009 nearly a third of hedge funds had enacted discretionary liquidity restrictions.[350] Consistent with the hypothesis that hedge fund managers establish discretionary liquidity restrictions in order to avoid catastrophic runs by their investors and value-destroying fire sales, the authors find that funds that utilize discretionary liquidity restrictions tend to perform worse, experience larger outflows, have more liquidity risk and illiquid assets than funds that do not enact restrictions.

Indeed, researchers have recognized that the severe price declines witnessed during the crisis were caused by fire sales by mainstream institutional investors, most notably mutual funds. According to Hau and Lai, losses on their holdings of financial stocks forced equity funds to sell non-financial stocks in their portfolios driving down their prices.[351] The authors estimate that approximately 10% of the 53% decline in the US stock market related to the crisis could be attributed to forced sales by mutual funds.

---

346. Andrew Ang, Sergiy Gorovyy and Gregory B Van Inwegen, 'Hedge Fund Leverage', *Journal of Financial Economics* 102, no. 1 (2011). Examining over 100 hedge funds with USD 380 billion of assets, the FSA finds that aggregate gross hedge fund leverage remained modest at 3.8 times NAV from April 2010 until March 2012, with leverage for the median fund being around 2.2 times NAV. *See* Financial Services Authority, *Assessing the Possible Sources of Systemic Risk: A Report of the Findings of the FSA's Hedge Fund Survey and Hedge Fund as Counterparty Survey* (August 2012), 13. In its 2014 survey, the FCA, examining 106 hedge funds with USD 345 billion of assets, reports that in September 2013, the gross leverage of the mean fund amounted to 40 times NAV, while the gross leverage of the median fund equalled 4.2 times NAV. According to the survey, the mean is skewed by a limited number of very large funds, which apply substantial leverage. Gross leverage is expressed as the ratio of the gross notional exposure of a fund to its NAV. Gross notional exposure is the absolute sum of a fund's long and short exposure, including derivatives exposure. *See* Financial Conduct Authority, *Hedge Fund Survey* (March 2014), 16 (UK).
347. Ang et al. document that US listed investment banks and banks reached, in 2009, extraordinary leverage ratios of approximately 39 to 1 and 29 to 1, respectively. *See* Ang, Gorovyy and Van Inwegen, 'Hedge Fund Leverage', 32-55.
348. Itzhak Ben-David, 'Hedge Fund Stock Trading in the Financial Crisis of 2007-2009'.
349. *See* Lloyd Dixon, *Rand Corporation, Hedge Funds and Systemic Risk*, 54.
350. Adam L. Aiken, Christopher P. Clifford and Jesse A. Ellis, 'Hedge Funds and Discretionary Liquidity Restrictions', *Journal of Financial Economics* 116, no. 1 (April 2015): 197-218.
351. Harald Hau and Sandy Lai, 'The Role of Equity Funds in the Financial Crisis Propagation', *Review of Finance* 21, no. 1 (1 March 2017): 77-108.

Similarly, Manconi et al. find that fire sales by bond mutual funds caused the contagion of the financial crisis from the securitized bond market to the corporate bond market.[352] The authors' analysis suggests that in the years leading up to the financial crisis, the high returns and liquidity offered by securitized bonds induced bond mutual funds to acquire large amounts of these assets. When securitized bonds became toxic and illiquid in August 2007, bond mutual funds faced with large redemption requests decided to retain their holdings of illiquid securitized bonds and sell their holdings of liquid corporate bonds. The massive sell-off by mutual funds contributed to a sharp increase in credit spreads of corporate bonds and particularly junk bonds.

Overall, the experience of the financial crisis indicates that the simultaneous distress of multiple hedge funds is unlikely to have an impact on the stability of the financial system through either the credit or the market channel. Despite the wide-spread criticism that hedge funds contributed to the financial crisis, a careful analysis reveals that hedge funds' role in aggravating the crisis through either the credit or market channel was rather limited.

2.2.3.3 Hedge Funds and SIFIs: The Case of Bear Stearns

Bear Stearns was founded in 1923 by Joseph Bear, Robert Stearns and Harold Mayer.[353] The firm originally focused on equity-trading, seeking to capitalize on the 1920s bull market. It quickly cultivated a reputation as an aggressive risk-taking firm and came to dominate bond trading. Headquartered in New York City, the firm grew to become one of the largest and most successful investment banks in the world. By 2007, it was one of the leading mortgage bond underwriters and prime brokers in the US. During the 1990s, Bear Stearns, sensing the profit potential offered by the rise of the hedge fund industry, decided to start sponsoring its own funds.[354] In early 2003, the firm launched the High-Grade Fund, which soon grew to become its largest hedge fund managing more than USD 1.5 billion in investor capital. The fund aimed to offer investors modest but steady returns by making investments in highly rated CDOs. The success of the High-Grade Fund led Bear Stearns to create, in August 2006, a second fund, the Enhanced Leverage Fund, which employed a strategy similar to the High-Grade Fund's one. In order to generate higher returns than the High-Grade Fund, the Enhanced

352. Alberto Manconi, Massimo Massab and Ayako Yasuda, 'The Role of Institutional Investors in Propagating the Crisis of 2007-2008', *Journal of Financial Economics* 104, no. 3 (2012).
353. For an excellent account of the history of Bear Stearns from its founding until its eventual demise *see* William D Cohan, *House of Cards: A Tale of Hubris and Wretched Excess on Wall Street* (Anchor, 2010).
354. *See* Stowell, *Investment Banks, Hedge Funds, and Private Equity*, 455. Formally, Bear Stearns Companies Inc. was the holding company for various Bear Stearns' subsidiaries including Bear Stearns & Co Inc., the investment banking arm of the group, which was registered with the SEC as a broker-dealer. Internal hedge funds were managed by Bear Stearns Asset Management, which was a wholly owned subsidiary of Bear Stearns Companies Inc. and acted as the general partner of the funds. Bear Stearns Securities Corp. served as the prime brokerage unit of Bear Stearns and was a wholly owned subsidiary of Bear Stearns & Co. Inc. *See Complaint, Securities and Exchange Commission V. Ralph Cioffi and Matthew M. Tannin*, 5-6 (2008).

Leverage Fund allowed for a much more aggressive use of leverage.[355] Both funds financed their positions by entering into repo transactions with Bear Stearns, pledging the CDO assets as collateral for the repos.[356]

During 2006, seeking to boost returns, the funds started buying high-risk CDO assets backed by subprime mortgages.[357] The decline in the subprime mortgage market in early 2007 caused enormous losses to Bear's hedge funds, which were, through their CDO positions, indirectly exposed to subprime mortgages. Panicked investors massively withdrew their capital, while creditors refused to roll over their debt and seized collateral, consisting of the funds' CDO assets, putting it up for sale.[358] In an effort to avoid a fire sale of the funds' assets and repair its tarnished reputation, Bear Stearns agreed to extend a USD 3.2 billion collateralized loan to the High-Grade Fund and entered into negotiations with the lenders of the Enhanced Leverage Fund in order to stave off a widespread liquidation of the collateral held by them.[359] Nonetheless, Bear Stearns was not able to salvage its ailing hedge funds, which eventually filed for bankruptcy protection.

The failure of Bear's internal hedge funds imposed severe losses on the firm and irreversibly damaged its reputation setting the stage for its eventual collapse and humiliating acquisition by JP Morgan for a consideration of USD 10 per share.[360] Even though Bear's original investment in the funds was only USD 40 million, its real exposure, on a reputational basis, was much higher.[361] The firm's loan to the High-Grade Fund was never repaid, while the fund's CDO assets that Bear Stearns accepted as collateral in return for the loan rapidly lost virtually all of their value.[362] Furthermore, the failure of the funds led investors, customers and creditors to question the financial health of the firm.[363] The massive withdrawal of funds that followed

355. Both funds used a substantial amount of leverage. The High-Grade Fund maintained a target leverage ratio of 10 to 1, while the Enhanced Leverage Fund targeted a ratio of 12 to 1. Financial Crisis Inquiry Commission, *The Financial Crisis Inquiry Report: Final Report of the National Commission on the Causes of the Financial and Economic Crisis in the United States*, 135.
356. *In Re Bear Stearns Companies, Inc. Securities, Derivatives, and Erisa Litigation*, 22.
357. *Complaint, Securities and Exchange Commission V. Ralph Cioffi and Matthew M. Tannin*, 12.
358. Kate Kelly and Serena Ng, 'Bear Stearns Bails out Fund with Big Loan', The Wall Street Journal, http://online.wsj.com/articles/SB118252387194844899.
359. *Ibid.* & Matthew Goldstein, 'Bear Stearns to the Rescue-Sort of "BusinessWeek"', http://www.businessweek.com/stories/2007-06-22/bear-stearns-to-the-rescue-sort-ofbusinessweek-business-news-stock-market-and-financial-advice. One should note that, even though Bear Stearns agreed to extend USD 3.2 billion, the firm ultimately lent only USD 1.6 billion. Kate Kelly, 'Bear Stearns Hedge Fund Managers May Face Indictments', The Wall Street Journal, http://online.wsj.com/news/articles/SB121358606462876535?mg=reno64-wsj.
360. For a short narrative of Bears' last days *see* Marcel Kahan and Edward Rock, 'How to Prevent Hard Cases from Making Bad Law: Bear Stearns, Delaware, and the Strategic Use of Comity', *Emory Law Journal* 58 (2008): 717-21.
361. Hal Scott, *Written Testimony of Hal Scott Before the Committee on Financial Services, United States House of Representatives*, vol. 1 (June 2011), 16.
362. Bear Stearns had initially valued the CDO assets it received as collateral as high as USD 2 billion. *See In Re Bear Stearns Companies, Inc. Securities, Derivatives, and Erisa Litigation*, 49-52.
363. Interestingly, one of the main contributors to Bear's cash drain were its hedge fund clients, which massively withdrew their assets from their prime brokerage accounts at the firm. *See* Squam Lake Working Group on Financial Regulation, *Prime Brokers and Derivatives Dealers* (April 2010), 2.

trapped Bear in a liquidity squeeze. With its cash reserves drained, the firm was forced to accept a government-orchestrated takeover by JP Morgan. The deal was made possible only due to the extraordinary decision of the FED to purchase USD 29 billion of Bear Stearns' troubled assets, thus putting US taxpayers at considerable risk.[364] Bear was the first major financial institution to fall victim of the subprime crisis with its bailout representing, according to some observers, a milestone in the development of the financial crisis.[365] The decision of the US government to bail out Bear Stearns sent a signal to market participants that the government was willing to bail out distressed financial institutions if it considered that their failure could jeopardize financial stability. Heeding the government's message, TBTF financial institutions, including Lehman Brothers, avoided taking the necessary steps to repair their balance sheets or plan for their bankruptcies.

2.2.3.4 Hedge Funds and Short Selling

Short sellers remain one of the most unpopular market participants by regulators, politicians and the public alike. The recent GameStop saga serves as the latest example of popular resentment against hedge funds and their short selling activity. Hedge funds shorting the stock of GameStop, a struggling video game retailer, faced the rage of retail investors who accused short selling funds of engineering the demise of the company. In a show of support to the embattled company, an army of small traders coordinating on social media sites massively bought shares in the company causing its share price to surge. The price increase forced hedge funds to unwind their short positions at steep losses with some of the industry's biggest names falling victim to the short squeeze.[366]

The roots of modern-day resentment towards short sellers can be traced back to the 2007 financial crisis. Criticism against hedge fund short selling activity and its contribution to systemic risk began to build during the 2007-2008 financial crisis as the demise of banks was attributed in part to short selling and especially to 'bear raids'. In a 'bear raid', short sellers, such as hedge funds, engage in massive short selling of a firm's stock, intending to drive its stock down by igniting panic among the firm's counterparties and investors. As Pais and Stork note, 'the initial drop in price impacts the fundamentals of the firm, which generates a feedback effect that further increases

364. *See* Thomas C Baxter Jr and David Gross, 'The Federal Reserve's Response to the Crisis: Doing Whatever It Takes within Its Legal Authority', in *International Monetary and Financial Law: The Global Crisis*, ed. Mario Giovanoli and Diego Devos (Oxford University Press, 2010), 302-04; Christian A. Johnson, 'Exigent and Unusual Circumstances: The Federal Reserve and the US Financial Crisis', in *Law Reform and Financial Markets*, ed. Alexander Kern and Niamh Moloney (Edward Elgar, 2010), 300-03.

365. According to Skeel, it was the government bailout of Bear Stearns and not the bankruptcy of Lehman Brothers that marked the defining moment of the financial crisis. *See* David Skeel, 'The Euro Crisis: Lessons from Bear Stearns', The Wall Street Journal, http://online.wsj.com/articles/SB10001424052970204002304576626932530739412.

366. A short squeeze refers to the situation where the price of a stock rises sharply, forcing investors who have sold the stock to rush to buy it in order to close their positions, thus driving the prices even higher and amplifying their losses. *See* Sarah Marsh, 'Short-Sellers Make VW the World's Priciest Company', Reuters, http://www.reuters.com/article/2008/10/28/us-volkswagen-idUSTRE49R3I920081028.

pressure on the share price'.[367] Since the stock price incorporates information about the firm's profitability, a decrease in the stock price leads capital providers to downgrade their expectations of the firm's profitability.[368] Capital providers are then unwilling to extend capital to the firm lowering thus its performance and value.[369] This vicious cycle may lead to the eventual demise of the firm. Financial institutions are particularly susceptible to predatory 'bear raids', taking into account that their resilience depends on continued public confidence and the financial industry is vulnerable to runs by panicked investors and counterparties. 'Bear raids' have been blamed for causing the fall of Bear Stearns and Lehman Brothers and jeopardizing the stability of other financial institutions during the financial crisis. Indeed, Misra et al. provide a detailed account of the 'bear raid' against Citigroup's stock.[370] In response to the perceived risks of short selling activity, regulatory authorities around the world quickly imposed bans on short selling of financial firms. The SEC's and FSA's bans were followed by bans in numerous other jurisdictions, including Australia and the Netherlands. The euro area sovereign debt crisis again brought to the fore hedge funds' short selling activities with hedge funds being blamed for the elevated volatility of bank stocks.

The financial and sovereign debt crises led numerous countries to enact stringent regulation of short selling. An example is the European Short Selling Regulation introduced in response to the sovereign debt crisis. The Regulation, which came into force on 14 March 2012,[371] seeks to regulate speculative activity in EU government bonds as well as covered and naked short selling of shares admitted to trading on an EU regulated market or MTF.[372] Its main aims are to enhance transparency by forcing market players to disclose their positions, address settlement failure risk,[373] and prevent negative price spirals.

Under the Short Selling Regulation, significant net short positions in shares must be disclosed to both supervisory authorities and the market.[374] Furthermore, seeking to

367. Amelia Pais and Philip A Stork, 'Short-Selling, Leverage, and Systemic Risk', http://papers.ssrn.com/sol3/papers.cfm?abstract_id=2350125.
368. Itay Goldstein, Emre Ozdenoren and Kathy Yuan, 'Trading Frenzies and Their Impact on Real Investment', *Journal of Financial Economics* 109, no. 2 (2013): 567.
369. *Ibid.*, 567.
370. Marco Lagi Vedant Misra and Yaneer Bar-Yam, 'Evidence of Market Manipulation in the Financial Crisis', *arXiv preprint arXiv:1112.3095* (2011).
371. 'Regulation No. 236/2012 of the European Parliament and of the Council of 14 March 2012 on Short Selling and Certain Aspects of Credit Default Swaps, 2012 O.J. (L 86) 1'.
372. In a covered short sale, the seller will already have borrowed the security or entered into arrangements to borrow the security at the time of the sale. In a naked short sale, on the other hand, the seller will not have borrowed the security or entered into any arrangements to do so at the time of the sale. The seller hopes that he will be able to borrow and deliver the security to the buyer at the settlement date, which is usually three business days after the date of the sale. Abusive naked short selling occurs when the seller does not intend to borrow and deliver the security to the buyer but instead seeks to create artificial supply in order to drive down its price.
373. One should note that settlement failure risk can also occur, apart from abusive naked short selling, in instances where the lending market has become illiquid, leaving the naked short seller unable to borrow the shares.
374. Net short positions in shares, obtained after deducting any long positions from any short positions, must be disclosed to regulators once they reach 0.2% of the issued share capital and for any 0.1% increase thereafter. Disclosures to the public must be made at a higher 0.5%

address settlement failure risk and abusive naked short selling, the Regulation introduces a 'super locate' rule-making naked short sales considerably more difficult to execute.[375] Short selling is allowed only when the seller has borrowed or entered into an agreement to borrow the share or has an arrangement with a third party confirming that the share has been located and settlement can reasonably be expected to be effected.[376] Furthermore, a mandatory buy-in procedure is introduced for settlement failures. If the seller fails to deliver the shares within four days of settlement being due, the central counterparty must buy in the shares in order to ensure smooth settlement.[377] Where a buy-in is not possible, cash compensation is paid to the buyer.[378] The seller must reimburse the central counterparty for the costs of the buy-in or cash compensation.[379]

In response to the perceived role of short selling in aggravating market declines, national regulators are granted additional powers in exceptional circumstances. In case of adverse market developments threatening financial stability, national regulators may impose additional disclosure obligations for net short positions, request any party lending financial instruments to send notice of any change in the fees requested for such lending, or impose bans on short selling and sovereign credit default transactions.[380] Furthermore, the Regulation introduces a circuit breaker mechanism granting national authorities the power to ban or restrict short selling in a financial instrument if there is a significant decline in the price of the relevant instrument. The ban is temporary and lasts until the next trading day, following the day on which the price decline occurs.[381]

Even though short selling carries with it a negative connotation, numerous academic studies have documented the benefits that it brings to financial markets. Contrary to the image of short sellers as manipulative speculators, Boehmer et al. argue that short sellers are informed traders trading on value-relevant information.[382] Short selling contributes to the efficient allocation of capital by facilitating price discovery. In particular, short sellers can prevent the formation of price bubbles and correct overvaluation of securities. Consistent with the hypothesis that short selling controls overpricing, Jones and Lamont find that stocks that are expensive to short have low

threshold and for each 0.1% above that. Short and long positions also include derivative positions. 'Regulation No. 236/2012 of the European Parliament and of the Council of 14 March 2012 on Short Selling and Certain Aspects of Credit Default Swaps, 2012 O.J. (L 86) 1', Arts 5(2), 6(2), 3(1)-(2), at 9-11. Notifications in relation to net short positions in shares must be made no later than 3:30 PM the following trading day. *Ibid.*, Art. 9(2), at 11.

375. *See ibid.* Art. 17, at 15-16.
376. *See ibid.*, Art. 12(1), at 12-13, Art. 13(1), at 1.
377. *Ibid.*, Art. 15(1)(a), at 14.
378. *Ibid.*, Art. 15(1)(b), at 14.
379. *Ibid.*, Art. 15(1)(c), at 14.
380. *Ibid.*, Arts 19-21, at 16-17.
381. *Ibid.*, Art. 23(1), at 17. National regulators also have the power to extend the ban for an additional two days if the price continues to significantly drop in value at the end of second trading day. *Ibid.*, Art. 23(2), at 17.
382. Ekkehart Boehmer et al., 'What Do Short Sellers Know?', *Review of Finance* 24, no. 6 (1 November 2020): 1203-35.

subsequent returns and high valuations.[383] Furthermore, short selling promotes market efficiency by facilitating the rapid adjustment of prices to negative information. Biais, Biseres and Decamps document that under short sale constraints, negative information is slower to be reflected in prices.[384]

Furthermore, empirical research has univocally shown that bans on short selling enacted during the financial crisis had detrimental effects on price discovery and liquidity while failing to successfully support the prices of financial stocks.[385] Fabbri, Beber and Pagano document that short selling bans utterly failed to fulfil their original goal, namely to stabilize the stock prices of vulnerable banks and lower their probability of default.[386] On the contrary, they report that in both the financial and sovereign debt crises, short selling bans were associated with an increase in the volatility of stock prices and the probability of default for the banks with a weak capital position, higher systemic risk and less stable funding. The authors conclude that the evidence indicates that market participants may have interpreted the bans as a signal that regulators possessed strongly negative information about the solvency of banks. Moreover, Hasan et al. document that during the financial crisis, short sellers acted as rational and informed traders trading on fundamental information, contrary to criticism that they were engaging in 'bear raids'.[387] Indeed, their study shows that short selling activity was significantly higher for financial companies with subprime-related exposures and higher insolvency risk. Finally, they found that there was no significant difference between short selling activities for financial and non-financial firms.

Despite the considerable efficiency gains that short selling brings to financial markets, short selling has the potential to create downward spirals and destabilize orderly markets. As Avgouleas notes, a drop in the price of a security initially triggered by short sales may quickly evolve into a dangerous downward spiral due to investors' herding behaviour.[388] Downward spirals can have negative effects on both the issuers of the securities and the marketplace in general. Issuers whose securities are in free fall will lose the confidence of investors and creditors, who will refuse to contribute shareholder capital and extend credit. Moreover, the downward pressure in the price of a security may spread to other securities resulting in widespread destabilization of the market.

As far as the EU's Regulation on short selling is concerned, the adoption of the Regulation was heavily influenced by the experience of the financial and sovereign

383. Charles M Jones and Owen A Lamont, 'Short-Sale Constraints and Stock Returns', *Journal of Financial Economics* 66, no. 2 (1 November 2002): 207-39.

384. Bruno Biais, Christophe Bisiere and Jean Paul Decamps, 'Short-Sales Constraints, Liquidity and Price Discovery: An Empirical Analysis on the Paris Bourse', *European Financial Management* 5 (1999): 395-409.

385. *See* Beber and Pagano, 'Short-Selling Bans Around the World: Evidence from the 2007-09 Crisis'.

386. Alessandro Beber et al., 'Short-Selling Bans and Bank Stability', *The Review of Corporate Finance Studies* 10, no. 1 (1 March 2021): 158-87.

387. Nadia Massoud Iftekhar Hasan, Anthony Saunders and Keke Song, 'Which Financial Stocks Did Short Sellers Target in the Subprime Crisis?', *Journal of Banking & Finance* 54 (2015).

388. Emilios Avgouleas, 'A New Framework for the Global Regulation of Short Sales: Why Prohibition Is Inefficient and Disclosure Insufficient', *Stanford Journal of Law, Business and Finance* 15, no. 2 (2010): 403-4.

debt crises and in particular the perceived role that hedge fund short selling played in aggravating the crises. The problematic aspects of the Regulation are the very low disclosure thresholds and the bans it authorizes. While disclosure of short positions enhances market efficiency, the threshold has been set at unacceptably low levels. Considering that long positions have higher disclosure requirements, the EU in essence treats two market participants - long buyers and short sellers - in different ways, thus distorting markets and the efficient allocation of capital.

A low disclosure threshold is likely to chill short selling activity in Europe.[389] On the one hand, a low disclosure threshold will quickly alert company executives and market competitors of the short seller's activities, allowing them to retaliate in a variety of ways, including legal actions and short squeezes. On the other hand, the short seller's profits depend on the short position he is able to build until his activity becomes public, at which point other market participants will capitalize on the short seller's research and prices will adjust to reflect the new information. By setting a low disclosure threshold, short sellers may not be able to gain substantial profits in order to recoup the considerable costs of their activities, including the costs of amassing their short position and conducting research. Finally, as illustrated above, bans on short selling have a detrimental effect on financial instruments and markets. However, the introduction of a circuit breaker mechanism should be seen as a welcome development. Circuit breakers are considered to be an effective mechanism in containing the negative price spirals that short selling can create. Indeed, in its assessment of the impact of circuit breakers, ESMA documented that the use of circuit breakers dampens price volatility without negatively affecting the price discovery process.[390]

2.2.3.5 Hedge Funds and Systemic Risk: Lessons Learned

The three case studies offered and the analysis of short selling activity by hedge funds illustrate that the hedge fund industry may contribute to systemic risk either through the failure of a large hedge fund or through the collapse of an internal hedge fund housed within a SIFI. The LTCM debacle served as a wake-up call as regards the risks posed by the collapse of a large hedge fund. Nonetheless, it is frequently argued that our financial system has come a long way since LTCM's near collapse. In particular, major reforms in OTC derivatives markets aimed at improving transparency and reducing counterparty risk have substantially lessened the likelihood of an LTCM-like

389. A study by Oliver Wyman elaborates on these points and finds that short selling disclosure hampers liquidity by lowering trading volumes and increasing bid-ask spreads. *See* Oliver Wyman, *The Effects of Short Selling Public Disclosure of Individual Positions on Equity Markets* (2011), 5. Indeed, disclosure is associated with a large drop in short selling activity. Although the study seems to suggest that any public disclosure would be detrimental, we advocate for a disclosure regime for short selling activity comparable to the regime for long positions. Such a disclosure regime will promote market efficiency while allowing short sellers to profit from their activity. In addition, a disclosure regime will also chill manipulative activity by short sellers.
390. Cyrille Guillaumie et al., 'Market Impacts of Circuit Breakers - Evidence from EU Trading Venues', *ESMA Working Paper* No. 1 (2020).

hedge fund failure.[391] What is more, it appears that, in the aftermath of LTCM's demise, financial institutions have significantly strengthened their counterparty risk management practices vis-à-vis hedge funds, with creditors and trading counterparties prudently managing their exposures to hedge funds. For instance, shortly after the LTCM debacle, in January 1999, the BCBS published a set of sound practices for banks' interactions with hedge funds. At the same time, a group of twelve major commercial and investment banks announced the formation of the CRMPG, which published its own recommendations for improving financial institutions' counterparty risk management practices vis-à-vis hedge funds.[392] In its 2005 report, a new CRMPG noticed a marked improvement in the management of counterparty risk by financial institutions and significant progress in the implementation of the original recommendations.[393]

Even though the complete overhaul of derivatives markets should be seen as a welcome development, certain segments of the derivatives markets, most notably total return swaps, still suffer from a lack of transparency. What is more, hedge funds can still obtain leverage through other opaque and unregulated markets, most notably the repo market. The repo market remains essentially unregulated, with repo lenders being

---

391. The Dodd-Frank Act in the US and EMIR in the EU mandate the clearing and reporting of a broadly defined class of OTC derivatives. EMIR requires the clearing of OTC derivatives only if a central counterparty is authorized or recognized to clear them and ESMA determines that they should be cleared. In making the determination, ESMA will consider the degree of standardization of the relevant class of OTC derivatives, its liquidity and the availability of fair, reliable and generally accepted pricing information. The clearing obligation applies to both financial and non-financial counterparties, subject to certain exemptions for non-financial counterparties. The Dodd-Frank Act requires a swap to be cleared if the CFTC determines that it must be cleared and a clearing organization accepts it for clearing. Only end-users that are using derivatives for the purpose of hedging risks are exempt from the clearing obligation. A major benefit of clearing houses is their ability to mitigate counterparty risk by imposing robust initial and variation margin requirements. William Sharpe, Gordon Alexander, and Jeffery V Bailey, 'Investments, Englewood' (Prentice Hall, 1990), 231-32. Had LTCM cleared its OTC derivatives trades, then the clearing house would have demanded adequate initial margin preventing thus LTCM from building a substantial amount of leverage. EMIR and the Dodd-Frank Act also introduce margining and collateralization requirements for uncleared OTC derivatives. Furthermore, seeking to enhance the transparency of derivatives markets, EMIR requires all counterparties and central counterparties to report derivatives contracts, cleared or uncleared, to a registered trade repository. What is more, MiFIR grants ESMA the authority to determine the classes of derivatives subject to a clearing obligation, which must be traded on a regulated market, MTF or OTF. Similarly, Dodd-Frank provides for the reporting of any swap, cleared or uncleared, to a swap data repository. In addition, Dodd-Frank mandates the trading of all swaps that are subject to mandatory clearing trade on an exchange or swap executive facility. One should note that LTCM was able to amass an extraordinary degree of leverage largely due to the inability of its counterparties and regulators to monitor its massive positions in OTC derivatives. The reporting of derivatives to trade repositories and the shift of OTC derivatives to trading venues will allow regulators and market participants to monitor the build-up of risks in derivatives markets and prevent any market participant, including a hedge fund, from acquiring sizable positions in these markets. For a detailed examination of the relevant reforms in derivatives markets *see* Clifford Chance and ISDA, *Regulation of OTC Derivatives Markets* (September 2012).
392. *See* Counterparty Risk Management Policy Group, *Improving Counterparty Risk Management Practices* (June 1999); Basel Committee on Banking Supervision, *Sound Practices for Banks' Interactions with Highly Leveraged Institutions* (January 1999).
393. *See* Counterparty Credit Risk Management Policy Group, *Toward Greater Financial Stability: A Private Sector Perspective* (July 2005).

able to freely decide the haircut applied to the collateral used in repo transactions. It should be stressed that in the aftermath of the financial crisis and in order to address the risks posed by the build-up of leverage outside the banking system, the FSB has adopted recommendations that include a framework of numerical haircut floors for repo transactions, where banks provide financing to non-banks against collateral other than government securities and where non-banks provide financing to non-banks against collateral other than government securities.[394] Nonetheless, the recommended numerical haircuts, acting as a floor, are set at a rather low level. Furthermore, even though the European Union has adopted legislation, which seeks to enhance the transparency of repo markets by mandating the reporting of all repo transactions to a trade repository, the biggest market for Repos, the US market, remains unmonitored.[395] Finally, despite the witnessed improvements in financial institutions' counterparty risk management practices, one should not rule out the possibility that creditors and trading counterparties will once again imprudently extend credit to a large fund, lured by the reputation of its principals and the high fees generated by dealing with the fund.

The recent Archegos debacle justifies such concerns. Archegos Capital Management, whose name comes from the Greek word for leader Αρχηγός, is a family office set up by Bill Hwang, a former protégé of hedge fund legend Julian Robertson. Hwang formed his family office after his hedge fund Tiger Asia Management became embroiled in an insider trading scandal relating to Chinese stocks. Archegos, which managed about USD 10 billion of Hwang's own money, was able to build up trading positions reaching USD 50 billion through the use of total return equity swaps, including positions in US media companies, such as ViacomCBS and Discovery, and Chinese tech companies, such as Baidu and Tencent.[396] A total return equity swap is a derivative contract that replicates the cash flows of an investment in shares of a company.[397] In a typical swap, the long party will obtain the economic returns on a notional amount of shares, namely cash distributions such as dividends and an amount equal to any appreciation in the market value of the shares, by the short party without owning them. The short party on its side is entitled to receive an amount equal to any depreciation in the market value of the shares and a negotiated interest rate. The short party, usually an investment bank that seeks to obtain a return from the interest rate charged, will typically hedge its exposure by buying the referenced shares.

394. Financial Stability Board, *Regulatory Framework for Haircuts on Non-centrally Cleared Securities Financing Transactions* (14 October 2014); *Regulatory Framework for Haircuts on Non-centrally Cleared Securities Financing Transactions* (12 November 2015).
395. *See* Regulation 2015/2365 on transparency of securities financing transactions and of reuse and amending Regulation (EU) No. 648/2012.
396. Katie Martin, Lawrence Fletcher and Robin Wigglesworth, '"They Can Do What They Want": Archegos and the $6tn World of the Family Office', Financial Times, https://www.ft.com/content/c319839d-d185-4e8a-bbc7-659bebe58031.
397. For an in-depth analysis of total return swaps and the decoupling of economic and voting ownership *see* Henry T. C. Hu and Bernard Black, *'Debt, Equity and Hybrid Decoupling: Governance and Systemic Risk Implications'*, European Financial Management 14, no. 4 (September 2008): 663-709; Henry T C Hu and Bernard Black, *'The New Vote Buying: Empty Voting and Hidden (Morphable) Ownership'*, Southern California Law Review 79 (2006): 811-908.

Following losses on its investment in ViacomCBS, Archegos was faced with margin calls by panicked prime brokers. The margin calls triggered a cascade of forced liquidations of Archegos positions by the fund and its prime brokers, which could face up to USD 10 billion in losses.[398] Even though the wider market fallout from the implosion of Archegos was contained, the debacle raises some uncomfortable questions about the quality of prime brokers' risk management. Prime brokers, including Goldman Sachs, Morgan Stanley, Credit Suisse and Nomura, allowed Archegos to build up significant exposure to shares of multiple companies while underestimating the losses that they could potentially suffer from the forced liquidation of Archegos' positions. Moreover, Archegos was able to conceal the true extent of its exposure through the use of total return swaps. Even though European regulators have amended their disclosure rules to capture financial instruments that give investors economic exposure to companies, including total return swaps, such instruments still escape disclosure requirements in the US.[399]

Indeed, empirical evidence seems to indicate that regulators should focus their attention on the monitoring of financial stability risks posed by large hedge funds. The FCA's March 2014 survey of hedge fund managers operating in the UK found that certain funds have been able to significantly expand their activities in financial markets, with the top ten funds managing an average of USD 1.9 trillion in gross notional exposure.[400] Furthermore, the survey documents that these funds tend to utilize a substantial amount of leverage obtained primarily through the use of

398. Gillian Tett, 'Archegos Avalanche Shows Cracks Are Hidden Under the Surface', Financial Times, https://www.ft.com/content/4459a6b2-b842-4d21-b19b-bda138a5bfdf.

399. The Transparency Directive mandates disclosure of major shareholdings in EU companies whose shares are admitted to trading in a regulated market. Directive 2004/109/EC of the European Parliament and of the Council of 15 December 2004 on the Harmonization of Transparency Requirements in Relation to Information about Issuers Whose Securities Are Admitted to Trading on a Regulated Market and Amending Directive 2001/34/EC 2004 O.J. L(390) 38, Arts 9-10, 47-48. In 2013, the Transparency Directive was amended extending notification requirements to financial instruments with economic effects similar to instruments that give the holder the right to acquire voting shares, whether they are physically settled or not. Directive 2013/50/EU of the European Parliament and of the Council of 22 October 2013 amending Directive 2004/109/EC of the European Parliament and of the Council on the harmonization of transparency requirements in relation to information about issuers whose securities are admitted to trading on a regulated market, Directive 2003/71/EC of the European Parliament and of the Council on the prospectus to be published when securities are offered to the public or admitted to trading and Commission Directive 2007/14/EC laying down detailed rules for the implementation of certain provisions of Directive 2004/109/EC Text with EEA relevance 2013 O.J. L(294) 13. In contrast, US disclosure rules do not capture financial instruments that do not grant voting rights over the underlying security, such as total return swaps. Section 13(d)(1) of the Securities Exchange Act requires any person who acquires beneficial ownership of more than 5 % of voting shares to file with the SEC within ten days after the acquisition a Schedule 13D. *See* 17 C.F.R. §240.13d-l (2014). A beneficial owner is defined as any person who, directly or indirectly, through any contract, arrangement, understanding, relationship, or otherwise has the power to vote or direct the voting of the relevant securities or the power to dispose or direct the disposition of the securities. *See ibid.* §240.13d-3. Derivatives are included in the calculation of the 13D disclosure threshold only if the holder has a right to beneficial ownership over the underlying security within sixty days. *See ibid.* §240.13d-3(d)(1).

400. Financial Conduct Authority, *Hedge Fund Survey* (March 2014), 17.

derivatives, especially interest rate derivatives.[401] The top ten funds are also the most active users of repo financing.[402] What is more, some large funds appear to be taking concentrated bets on illiquid investments, most notably distressed debt.[403] The results of the March 2014 survey are largely confirmed by the FCA's June 2015 study.[404] The later survey also reports an increased exposure of hedge funds to illiquid structured/securitized products. Furthermore, the FSOC's analysis of Form PF filed by hedge fund managers in the US confirms this relationship between leverage and size.[405] A comparable survey of US hedge fund managers conducted by the FCIC reports that the largest hedge funds, as measured by AUM, are the most active users of repo financing.[406] The survey also provides evidence that prior to the financial crisis, these funds were able to bargain for low haircuts on their repo transactions.[407] Finally, the OFR in its 2020 annual report to the US Congress documents the extraordinary amount of leverage used by the largest hedge funds. According to the OFR, the average level for the ten largest hedge funds, which reached a peak of 24.6 in June 2019, stood at 15.9 in June 2020.[408]

What is more, the repercussions of the failure of Bear's internal hedge funds vividly illustrated the perils of allowing SIFIs to sponsor and invest in hedge funds. One should note that apart from Bear Stearns numerous other financial institutions suffered severe losses as a result of their exposure to hedge funds. Indeed, one of the first victims of the subprime crisis was UBS, which was forced, on 4 May 2007, to shut down its internal hedge fund unit, Dillon Read Capital Management, after suffering severe losses stemming from soured US subprime mortgage-related investments.[409] UBS subsequently took over Dillon Read's positions, whose value continued to deteriorate sharply, accounting for USD 3 billion of UBS' USD 19 billion in losses in 2007.[410] Dillon Read's bets on the US subprime market contributed substantially to the degradation of UBS' financial position, which was eventually rescued by the Swiss government and

401. *Ibid.*, 16.
402. *Ibid.*, 26.
403. *Ibid.*, 4.
404. Financial Conduct Authority, *Hedge Fund Survey* (June 2015).
405. Financial Stability Oversight Council, *Update on Review of Asset Management Products and Activities*.
406. United States Financial Crisis Inquiry Commission, *Hedge Fund Survey Selected Slides* (February 2011), 3.
407. *Ibid*, 4.
408. 'Annual Report to Congress' (Office for Financial Research, 2020), 68.
409. Stephanie Baker-Said & Elena Logutenkova, 'UBS $100 Billion Wager Prompted $24 Billion Loss in Nine Months', Bloomberg, http://www.bloomberg.com/apps/news?pid=newsarchive&sid=a3sm9FOrsWcg. Dillon Read Capital Management was a wholly owned subsidiary of UBS AG serving as the investment manager to two different hedge funds, a proprietary fund with USD 3.5 billion of capital contributed solely by UBS and an outside investor fund with more than USD 1.8 billion capital raised from third-party investors. One should note that the losses were suffered exclusive by Dillon Read's proprietary fund, which was heavily invested in subprime mortgage-backed securities. In contrast, Dillon Read's outside investor fund, which was officially launched in November 2006, was able to record gains of around USD 100 million in the first five months of 2007.
410. *Ibid.*

the Swiss Central Bank.[411] Three months after the collapse of UBS' internal hedge fund unit, on 9 August 2007, another prestigious financial institution and France's largest bank, BNP Paribas, announced that it was temporarily suspending redemptions in three funds managed by its asset management arm, BNP Paribas Investment Partners.[412] The funds, which were estimated to be worth around USD 2.2 billion, were heavily invested in US subprime MBSs.[413] The announcement by BNP Paribas that it was barring withdrawals from funds that bore its prestigious name unnerved investors, which sent its share price plummeting.[414] Furthermore, the unexpected revelation by BNP that it could not place a value on subprime securities held by its funds made market participants increasingly wary of their counterparties' potential subprime exposures, provoking a panic in short-term funding markets.[415] The panic was halted by the unprecedented injections of liquidity by central banks around the world.

In contrast, the experience of the financial crisis suggests that the distress of multiple small or medium-sized hedge funds is unlikely to pose a threat to financial stability. On the one hand, the low levels of leverage employed by small- and medium-sized funds, including leverage obtained through derivatives,[416] makes it unlikely that their simultaneous failure will jeopardize the financial health of their creditors and trading counterparties. On the other hand, hedge funds actively seek to preclude the occurrence and severity of fire sales. Most importantly, the prudent utilization of leverage by the overwhelming majority of hedge funds minimizes the magnitude of fire sales. Furthermore, empirical evidence strongly suggests that hedge funds seek to prevent catastrophic runs by their investors, short-term creditors and trading counterparties by maintaining large cash buffers and by vigorously managing the liquidity and maturity mismatch between their assets and liabilities.[417] In addition,

411. For an overview of UBS' rescue package *see* Luc Thévenoz, 'The Rescue of UBS by the Swiss Confederation', in *International Monetary and Financial Law*, ed. Mario Giovanoli and Diego Devos (Oxford University Press, 2010), 383-88.

412. 'BNP Paribas Suspends Funds Because of Subprime Problems', The New York Times, http://www.nytimes.com/2007/08/09/business/worldbusiness/09iht-09bnp.7054054.html?_r=0; Treasury Committee House of Commons, *Financial Stability and Transparency: Sixth Report of Session 2007-2008* (3 March 2008), 35.

413. *Ibid.*

414. 'Et Tu, Paribas?', The Wall Street Journal, http://online.wsj.com/articles/SB118669529375093479.

415. Financial Crisis Inquiry Commission, *The Financial Crisis Inquiry Report: Final Report of the National Commission on the Causes of the Financial and Economic Crisis in the United States*, 251-52.

416. A survey by the European Central Bank documented that information obtained by one large hedge fund prime broker suggested that approximately 60% of credit exposures were on funds with more than 1 billion of assets under management, with the remaining 40% being on smaller funds with assets under management ranging from 100 million to 1 billion. *See* European Central Bank, *Large EU Banks' Exposures to Hedge Funds* (November 2005), 20. Furthermore, in its report the FSA suggested that the average potential credit exposure of fourteen large FSA-authorized banks and branches with operations in the UK to any one hedge fund was less than USD 50 million. *See* Financial Services Authority, *Assessing the Possible Sources of Systemic Risk: A Report of the Findings of the FSA'S Hedge Fund Survey and Hedge Fund as Counterparty Survey*, 18-19.

417. In its survey, the FCA reported that the median hedge fund tends to hold a high ratio of unencumbered cash as a percentage of NAV, gross notional exposure and total borrowings. Furthermore, surveyed hedge funds report that they are able to liquidate their assets in a

the overwhelming majority of hedge funds retain the ability to enact discretionary liquidity restrictions.[418]

Despite widespread concerns regarding increasing hedge fund investments in illiquid assets, empirical studies indicate that the average hedge fund portfolio is made up mostly of fairly liquid and easily valued instruments.[419] What is more, consistent with the view that hedge fund managers exhibit superior trading skills and utilize these skills in order to preclude fire sales, Cao et al. document strong evidence of liquidity timing among hedge funds. In their study of 5,298 equity-oriented hedge funds over the period 1994-2009, the authors find that hedge fund managers are able to correctly forecast future equity market liquidity and adjust their market exposure accordingly, increasing their market exposure in anticipation of ample market liquidity and decreasing it in anticipation of poor market liquidity.[420] Finally, a number of academic researchers and policymakers have forcefully criticized hedge funds for exhibiting herding behaviour.[421] Hedge funds have been accused of crowding into the same assets, amplifying market swings during crises. In the event of a shock, investors in crowded trades may try to simultaneously unwind their positions.[422] As panicked investors rush for the exit en masse, very few will be able to get through before prices collapse.[423] Nonetheless, Reca et al., in the first direct examination of hedge fund herding in US equity markets, document that hedge funds' stock portfolios are remarkably independent, with the typical pair of hedge funds holding approximately one stock in common.[424] Contrary to conventional wisdom, which considers non-hedge fund institutional investors more diverse and less prone to herding behaviour

---

shorter period than the period after which their liabilities to investors and creditors mature. *See* Financial Conduct Authority, *Hedge Fund Survey* (March 2014), 30-33. *See also* Financial Services Authority, *Assessing the Possible Sources of Systemic Risk: A Report of the Findings of the FSA's Hedge Fund Survey and Hedge Fund as Counterparty Survey* 15-17.

418. *Ibid.*
419. Financial Conduct Authority, *Hedge Fund Survey* (March 2014), 18-19.
420. *See* Chen Yong Cao Charles, Liang Bing and Andrew W. Lo, 'Can Hedge Funds Time Market Liquidity?', *Journal of Financial Economics* 109, no. 2 (2013).
421. *See*, for instance, Andrew W. Lo, *Hedge Funds, Systemic Risk, and the Financial Crisis of 2007-2008, Written Testimony of Andrew W. Lo Prepared for the US House of Representatives Committee on Oversight and Government Reform: Hearing on Hedge Funds* (13 November 2008); Timothy F. Geithner, 'Perspectives on the US Financial System, Remarks by President Timothy F. Geithner Before the Economic Club of New York', news release, 7 May 2004. Critics routinely point out to the 2007 quant meltdown as evidence of hedge fund herding and crowded trades. The quant meltdown refers to the widespread losses that a large number of quantitative long-short equity funds, which are supposed to be market neutral, faced during the week of 6 August 2007. The losses were the result of forced liquidations of similarly constructed portfolios triggering stop-loss orders and leverage limits, thereby leading to further fire sales. *See* Amir Khandani and Andrew Lo, 'What Happened to the Quants in August 2007? (Digest Summary)', *Journal of Investment Management* 5, no. 4 (2007). Nonetheless, one should note that the losses were largely confined to a rather limited corner of the overall market, namely quantitative long-short equity funds, and were too small to jeopardize financial stability.
422. 'What Happened to the Quants in August 2007? (Digest Summary)', 9.
423. *Ibid.*
424. Richard Sias, HJ Turtle and Blerina Zykaj, 'Hedge Fund Crowds and Mispricing', *Management Science* 62 (2016): 765, 68-74.

than hedge funds, the authors find that non-hedge fund institutional investors exhibit much greater portfolio overlap than hedge funds.[425]

2.2.4 Hedge Fund Activism

Recent years have seen a tectonic shift in the power struggle between corporate insiders and shareholders. Shareholder empowerment has even led scholars to conclude that the shareholder-manager agency cost problem generated by the separation of ownership and control has been largely resolved.[426] One of the reasons behind this development is the rise of a new breed of aggressive shareholder activists: hedge funds.[427] Armed with a growing war chest reaching USD 130 billion for US funds and the support of proxy advisory firms and traditional institutional investors such as mutual funds and pension funds,[428] activist hedge funds are increasing their clout inside corporate boardrooms. Famous corporations around the world, such as Apple, Microsoft and ThyssenKrupp, have become targets of hedge fund activists, with hedge funds succeeding in changing their operational performance or corporate governance. Hedge fund activism has been widely criticized for provoking short-termism inside the corporate boardroom at the expense of long-term value. Nonetheless, the empirical evidence indicates that hedge fund activism results in substantial benefits for both investors and companies. As a result, calls for controlling activist hedge funds should be approached cautiously.

Modern shareholder activism began in the United States during the 1970s and 1980s, with individual investors such as Carl Icahn and Nelson Peltz building controlling positions and aggressively agitating for actions that would grant them short-term gains.[429] Faced with collective action problems, however, individual shareholders largely abstained from becoming involved in corporate governance.[430] With the US

425. *Ibid.*
426. Rock claims that changes in market and corporate practices have brought the problem arising out of the separation of ownership and control under control. *See generally* Edward B Rock, 'Adapting to the New Shareholder-Centric Reality', *University of Pennsylvania Law Review* 161 (2013): 1910. Berle and Means first observed that the separation of ownership and control in modern publicly held corporations gives rise to an agency problem as the interests of dispersed shareholder-principals and manager-agents diverge. Jensen and Meckling defined the costs generated by this separation as 'agency costs'. Agency costs include the costs of monitoring managers by shareholders, the bonding costs incurred by managers, and the residual loss incurred by shareholders. *See* Eugene F Fama and Michael C Jensen, 'Separation of Ownership and Control', *Journal of Law and Economics* 26, no. 2 (1983); Adolph Berle and Gardiner Means, *The Modern Corporation and Private Property* (Transaction Publishers, 1968).
427. *See* Rock, 'Adapting to the New Shareholder-Centric Reality', 1922.
428. Jessica Toonkel and Soyoung Kim, 'Activist Investors Find Allies in Mutual, Pension Funds', Reuters, http://www.reuters.com/article/2013/04/09/us-funds-activist-idUSBRE9380DU2013 0409.
429. *See generally* John C Coffee, Louis Lowenstein and Susan Rose-Ackerman, *Knights, Raiders, and Targets: The Impact of the Hostile Takeover* (Oxford University Press, 1988).
430. Two related problems make shareholders passive and rationally apathetic in widely held firms. First, while a shareholder who wishes to become involved in corporate governance must bear the costs of its efforts, including monitoring costs and the costs of launching a proxy campaign, he receives only a pro rata share of the gains if his actions are successful, allowing other

hostile takeover wave fading away in the late 1980s,[431] attention turned to the other powerful players in capital markets: institutional investors, most notably, mutual funds and pension funds.[432] Nonetheless, the promise remained unfulfilled. Nearly two decades later, researchers concluded that the impact of institutional investors on corporate governance and performance was negligible. As a legal academic concluded in 1998, '[t]he currently available evidence, taken as a whole, is consistent with the proposition that the institutions achieve the effects on firm performance that one might expect from this level of effort - namely not much'.[433]

Regulatory constraints, conflicts of interest, and a business model fundamentally incompatible with activism make institutional investor intervention 'incidental' and 'ex-post'.[434] Regulatory constraints include diversification requirements for mutual and pension funds[435] and requirements for liquidity for open-ended mutual fund

shareholders to free-ride on his efforts. Second, knowing that his or her vote will not affect the outcome, an individual shareholder does not have an incentive to carefully scrutinize a proposal submitted to a vote and vote on the proposal. *See* Daniel R Fischel and Frank Easterbrook, *The Economic Structure of Corporate Law* (Harvard University Press, 1991), 63-89; Bernard S Black, 'Shareholder Passivity Reexamined', *Michigan Law Review* 89 (1990): 526-30.

431. The US takeover boom lasted from 1984 until 1989 and was characterized by a surge in hostile takeovers and leveraged buyouts. *See* Patrick Gaughan, *Mergers, Acquisitions and Corporate Restructurings*, 5th ed. (Wiley, 2011), 57-63.

432. It was argued that institutional investors as outside blockholders had the incentives to engage in monitoring and intervene in the companies in which they invested. A large shareholder is able to spread the costs associated with monitoring and intervention over a larger share and capture higher gains from his intervention. Furthermore, his substantial voting rights allow him to pressure and potentially remove management through a proxy fight or takeover. *See* Andrei Shleifer and Robert W Vishny, 'Large Shareholders and Corporate Control', *The Journal of Political Economy* 94, no. 3 (1986): 461. Institutional investors and especially mutual funds and pension funds have come to dominate modern capital markets. In 2009, over 50% of US public equities were held by institutional investors. *See* Stephan Rabimov Matteo Tonello, 'The 2010 Institutional Investment Report: Trends in Asset Allocation and Portfolio Composition', (Conference Bd., Research Report No. R-1468-10-RR, 2010), http://ssrn.com/abstract=1707512.

433. *See* Bernard S. Black, 'Shareholder Activism and Corporate Governance in the United States', in *The New Palgrave Dictionary of Economics and the Law*, ed. John Eatwell et al. (Palgrave, 1998).

434. Traditional institutional investor activism seeks to safeguard the value of pre-existing investments. Thus, institutional investors will engage in activism only in case a company already part of the institution's portfolio is either underperforming or is in dire need of a shake-up in its corporate governance. Brian R Cheffins and John Armour, 'The Past, Present and Future of Shareholder Activism by Hedge Funds', *Journal of Corporation Law* 37, no. 1 (2011): 56.

435. For instance, the Investment Company Act of 1940 prohibits mutual funds that wish to advertise themselves as diversified from putting more than 5% of their regulated assets in the securities of any one issuer and including in the regulated part of their portfolios more than 10% of the stock of any company. *See* 15 U.S.C. §80a-5(b) (2012). Similarly, by virtue of the Employee Retirement Income Security Act of 1974 (ERISA), private pension funds are required to be diversified. *See* 29 U.S.C. §1104; Mark J. Roe, 'A Political Theory of American Corporate Finance', *Columbia Law Review* 91, no. 1 (1991): 19-21, 24-15 (summarizing the various diversification limits imposed on U.S. mutual funds and private pension funds). Similar requirements are imposed on UCITS funds by the UCITS Directive. *See* Directive 2009/65/EC of the European Parliament and of the Council of 13 July 2009 on the Coordination of Laws, Regulations and Administrative Provisions Relating to Undertakings for Collective Investment in Transferable Securities (UCITS), 2009 O.J. (L 302) 32., Art. 52 §1(a) (prohibiting mutual funds from investing more than 5% of their assets in shares of the same issuer).

investors,[436] limiting thus their ability to invest in large illiquid positions. Conflicts of interest are particularly severe for pension funds, with public pension funds subject to political pressure and private pension fund managers seeking to obtain and maintain business from their corporate clients.[437] The fundamental explanation for the reluctance of mutual and pension funds to invest in activism is their business model, which prioritizes the quest for relative returns.[438] Mutual fund and pension fund managers are judged by their performance relative to their peers. A manager engaging in activism must bear all of the costs of the effort while sharing the gains with its competitors who will typically hold shares in the same company. As a result, the manager's performance relative to its competitors will decline. Consequently, even though activism would increase the value of the company and benefit beneficiaries, managers are reluctant to engage in it.

It is this governance shortfall that hedge funds, as 'governance arbitrageurs',[439] seek to exploit. With institutional investors paralysed and unable to invest in profitable activism, activists specialize in searching for undervalued[440] and poorly governed firms and agitating for operational or governance improvements as outside blockholders. Unconstrained by restrictive regulation[441] with high-powered performance incentives and free of conflicts of interest, hedge funds are able to amass large positions falling short of control blocks and typically below 10% of target stock,[442] and engage in costly and time-consuming efforts to propose and aid in the implementation of changes in target companies. In contrast to traditional institutional investor activism, hedge funds invest in order to engage in activism. Their activism, therefore, is 'strategic' and 'ex-ante'.[443] Belonging to the group of value investors,[444] hedge fund activists conduct

436. For European regulations, *see* Directive 2009/65/EC of the European Parliament and of the Council of 13 July 2009 on the Coordination of Laws, Regulations and Administrative Provisions Relating to Undertakings for Collective Investment in Transferable Securities (UCITS), 2009 O.J. (L 302) 32., Art. 1 §2(b); for US regulations, *see* 15 U.S.C. §80a-5(a)(1).

437. For an excellent investigation of the conflicts of interests plaguing institutional investors, *see* Black, 'Shareholder Passivity Reexamined', 595-608.

438. *See* Ronald J. Gilson and Jeffrey N. Gordon, 'The Agency Costs of Agency Capitalism: Activist Investors and the Revaluation of Governance Rights', *Columbia Law Review* 113, no. 4 (2013): 889-96.

439. The term 'governance arbitrageurs' was coined by Gilson and Gordon. *See ibid.*, 896.

440. Brav, Jiang and Kim find that activists target firms with a low market relative to book value. Alon Brav, Wei Jiang, and Hyunseob Kim, 'Hedge Fund Activism: A Review', *Foundations and Trends (R) in Finance* 4, no. 3 (2010).

441. Hedge funds are not subject to any diversification requirements, allowing them to concentrate their investments in a limited number of influential positions in target companies. Furthermore, in contrast to open-ended mutual funds, hedge fund managers grant investors limited withdrawal rights. Activist funds lock up investor capital for an initial period of eighteen months to two years, with several funds adopting longer lock-ups. *See* David Nissenbaum and Maria Gabriela Bianchini, 'Activist Fund Structuring', *Schulte Roth & Zabel* (2005): 2.

442. Brav Alon, Bebchuk Lucian A, Jackson Jr. Robert J and Jiang Wei, 'Pre-Disclosure Accumulations by Activist Investors: Evidence and Policy', *Journal of Corporation Law* 39, no. 1 (2013): 12 (examining all 13D filings by activist hedge funds in the United States from 1994 until 2007 and finding that activists acquire an average stake of 8.8% and median of 6.3%).

443. *See* Marcel Kahan and Edward B Rock, 'Hedge Funds in Corporate Governance and Corporate Control', *University of Pennsylvania Law Review* 155, no. 5 (2007): 1069.

444. Activists' managers and employees are usually former investment bankers and research analysts accustomed to fundamental analysis. The crucial difference between hedge fund

diligent research with the aim of spotting targets that will benefit from intervention and identify the changes that will unlock shareholder value.[445] The most common propositions of activists are a sale of the target, return of excess cash,[446] sale or spin-offs of unrelated assets and refocusing corporate strategy,[447] improvements in firm governance, and changes in the target's long-term business plan.[448]

Gantchev models hedge fund activism as a sequential process with three different stages: demand negotiations, board representation, and proxy fight.[449] An activism campaign begins with the filing of a regulatory form announcing the crossing of a specified ownership threshold and the intentions of the activist.[450] Then follows the demand negotiations stage, where the activist communicates its demands directly to management and negotiates with it.[451] If the demands are rejected, the activist requests board representation and threatens to launch a proxy fight.[452] If management still resists, then the activist moves to the final and most aggressive stage: the commencement of a proxy fight.[453] Crucially, the activist lacking a controlling position in the target has to gather the support of other shareholders - mainly institutional investors.[454] As Gilson and Gordon note, after publicly announcing their presence, activists will start a non-public campaign seeking to convince institutional investors to support their demands.[455] Thus, the activists will move from a less to a more confrontational stage only after they make a positive assessment about the likelihood of support from

activists and value investors, such as Warren Buffett, is their willingness to adopt an aggressive stance against target management who refuse to implement their propositions. *See* William Bratton, 'Hedge Funds and Governance Targets', *Georgetown Law Journal* 95, no. 5 (2007): 1383.

445. Gilson and Gordon, 'The Agency Costs of Agency Capitalism: Activist Investors and the Revaluation of Governance Rights', 902.
446. Michael Jensen famously pointed to the agency costs generated by free cash flow, namely cash flow in excess of that required for financing all positive net present value projects. Managers will waste free cash flow in suboptimal projects or hold it on the firm's balance sheet, insulating themselves from the discipline of capital markets. *See* Jensen, 'Agency Costs of Free Cash Flow, Corporate Finance, and Takeovers'.
447. *See* Bratton, 'Hedge Funds and Governance Targets', 1390-97.
448. *Ibid.*
449. *See* Nickolay Gantchev, 'The Costs of Shareholder Activism: Evidence from a Sequential Decision Model', *Journal of Financial Economics* 107, no. 3 (2013): 613-14.
450. *Ibid.*
451. *Ibid.* Activists targeting continental European companies, which are often controlled by majority shareholders, tend to cooperate with controlling shareholders. Furthermore, the engagement is usually private, with the proxy fight stage being infrequent. Franks Julian Becht Marco, Grant Jeremy, Hannes Wagner, 'The Returns to Hedge Fund Activism: An International Study', *No. 402 European Corporate Governance Institute (ECGI)-Finance Working Paper* (2014): 3.
452. Gantchev, 'The Costs of Shareholder Activism: Evidence from a Sequential Decision Model'.
453. *Ibid.*, 614.
454. Ruth Sullivan, 'Traditional Investors Adopt Activism', The Financial Times, http://www.ft.com/intl/cms/s/0/62d5ea16-b253-11e2-a388-00144feabdc0.html. Institutional ownership in the top thousand US corporations has reached an average of 73%. *See* Matteo Tonello, 'The 2010 Institutional Investment Report: Trends in Asset Allocation and Portfolio Composition'.
455. Gilson and Gordon, 'The Agency Costs of Agency Capitalism: Activist Investors and the Revaluation of Governance Rights', 899-901.

traditional institutional investors, with the last stage – a proxy fight – being in essence an official referendum on the activists' proposals.[456]

Law and finance literature has recognized the role of large outside blockholders, and especially activist hedge funds, in improving the corporate governance and operational performance of target companies.[457] By amassing a large stake, blockholders are able to spread the costs of their activism and reap higher gains from their efforts.[458] Consequently, blockholders are sufficiently incentivized to gather costly information, engage in monitoring, and invest in activism. *Ex post*, a blockholder will discipline management for suboptimal performance. *Ex ante*, the threat of a blockholder acquiring a stake motivates management to exert greater efforts and improve performance.[459] Crucially, the gains from monitoring or successful intervention will be reaped by all shareholders of the target company.[460] What is more, in the case of corporations dominated by controlling shareholders where the agency cost shifts from being one between managers and shareholders to one between controlling and minority shareholders,[461] activist initiatives are aimed at curbing private benefit extraction by controlling shareholders.[462] Hedge fund activists seek to discipline controlling shareholders by cooperating with fellow minority shareholders and utilizing the protective tools granted by the legal regime to minority shareholders.[463]

456. Management will also make the same assessment in deciding whether to accept or reject the activist's demands. *See* 'Hedge Fund Activism, Corporate Governance and Firm Performance', 1764.
457. *See generally* Brav, Jiang and Kim, 'Hedge Fund Activism: A Review'.
458. Shleifer and Vishny, 'Large Shareholders and Corporate Control'.
459. Bebchuk Lucian A, 'Pre-Disclosure Accumulations by Activist Investors: Evidence and Policy', 12.
460. Lucian A Bebchuk and Robert J Jackson Jr, 'Law and Economics of Blockholder Disclosure', *Harvard Business Law Review* 2 (2012): 50.
461. In a concentrated ownership structure, the majority shareholder will have both the incentives and the power to discipline management and minimize the agency costs between shareholders and management. However, the controlling shareholder will have its own interests and may use its control rights in order to expropriate other shareholders. Armour John Kraakman Reinier, et al., *The Anatomy of Corporate Law: A Comparative and Functional Approach* (Oxford University Press, 2004), 22.
462. The term 'private benefits of control' refers to pecuniary and non-pecuniary benefits that are enjoyed exclusively by controlling shareholders and are not shared with other shareholders. Private benefits of control can take the form of outright theft, dilution of minority shareholder interests and social status achieved by the control of a large corporation. *See* Ronald J Gilson, 'Controlling Shareholders and Corporate Governance: Complicating the Comparative Taxonomy', *Harvard Law Review* 119, no. 6 (2006): 1663-64; Pierre-Henri Conac, Luca Enriques and Martin Gelter, 'Constraining Dominant Shareholders' Self-Dealing: The Legal Framework in France, Germany, and Italy', *European Company and Financial Law Review* 4, no. 4 (2007): 495-96.
463. For instance, Enriques and Belcredi document instances where hedge fund activists with the cooperation of minority shareholders have sought to curb the extraction of private benefits by controlling shareholders in Italian companies. *See* Luca Enriques Massimo Belcredi, 'Institutional Investor Activism in a Context of Concentrated Ownership and High Private Benefits of Control: The Case of Italy', *ECGI Law Working Paper* No. 225/2013 (2014): 22-31.

Consistent with the theory that highlights the beneficial role of activists for shareholders, academic studies have documented significant positive abnormal returns upon the announcement of the presence of an activist hedge fund.[464] The price increase reflects the market's expectation of improved firm value resulting from the activist's involvement, adjusted for the probability of success of its campaign.[465] Opponents of activism view the initial price spike as a result of inefficient market pricing that fails to incorporate the long-term costs of activism.[466] Therefore, one should expect the positive disclosure abnormal returns to be followed by negative long-term stock returns, making shareholders worse off. Nonetheless, in their comprehensive study of activist interventions in the United States from 1994 to 2007, Bebchuk, Brav, and Jiang examine stock returns in the five years after the initial stock price increase and during the three-year period following the activist's exit, documenting no such pattern of negative returns reversing the initial positive abnormal returns.[467]

The market's expectation of increased firm value resulting from the activist's intervention is largely confirmed by subsequent improvements in operational performance. The study by Bebchuk, Brav, and Jiang, using as performance metrics the ROA and Tobin's *q*, documents that activists target companies whose operating performance at the time of intervention trails that of their industry peers or their own historical levels.[468] However, target companies markedly outperform their peers during the five years following the intervention, with operating performance exceeding the intervention-year level in each year.[469] The beneficial effects of activism are corroborated by Brav, Jiang, and Kim, who use data about the performance of US manufacturing plants owned by firms targeted by hedge fund activists and find that the productivity of target firms' plants declines substantially during the three years prior to the intervention and then rebounds sharply during the three years afterwards.[470] Furthermore, underperforming plants sold after the activist intervention experience a

464. In the most comprehensive study of activist interventions in the US to date, Bebchuk, Brav, and Jiang, examining over two thousand interventions from 1994 to 2007, find large average abnormal returns of approximately 6% in a forty-day window around the filing of a Schedule 13D announcing the presence of an activist hedge funds. *See* Lucian A Bebchuk, Alon Brav and Wei Jiang, 'The Long-Term Effects of Hedge Fund Activism', *Columbia Law Review* 115, no. 5 (2015). Similar results are reached by other studies; Brav finds average abnormal returns between 7% and 8% for activist interventions in the United States, *see* Alon Brav, 'Hedge Fund Activism, Corporate Governance and Firm Performance'. Large abnormal returns have been documented for activist interventions in Europe as well. *See* Marco Becht, Julian Franks and Jeremy Grant, 'Hedge Fund Activism in Europe', *No. 283 ECGI-Finance Working Paper* (2010) (analysing a database of European activist interventions and finding average abnormal returns of 4.4% around the disclosure date).

465. Alon Brav, 'Hedge Fund Activism, Corporate Governance and Firm Performance', 1757.

466. *See* Martin Lipton, 'Bite the Apple; Poison the Apple; Paralyze the Company; Wreck the Economy', Harvard Law School Forum on Corporate Governance and Financial Regulation, http://blogs.law.harvard.edu/corpgov/2013/02/26/bite-the-apple-poison-the-apple-paralyze-the-company-wreck-the-economy/.

467. *See* Bebchuk, Brav and Jiang, 'The Long-Term Effects of Hedge Fund Activism', 1120-34.

468. *Ibid.*, 1101-18.

469. *Ibid.*

470. Alon Brav, Wei Jiang and Hyunseob Kim, 'The Real Effects of Hedge Fund Activism: Productivity, Asset Allocation, and Labor Outcomes', *The Review of Financial Studies* 28, no. 10 (1 October 2015): 2723-69.

substantial increase in productivity in the hands of the new owners.[471] These results indicate that activists are skilled at efficiently reallocating corporate assets.

Activists are also increasingly successful in pushing for governance changes in target companies. With the support of institutional investors, hedge funds in the United States are increasingly agitating for the dismantling of takeover defences or their subjection to a shareholder vote.[472] Furthermore, in their studies of activist engagements, Klein and Zur, as well as Brav, Jiang, Partnoy, and Thomas, find increases in leverage and the payout ratio in target firms following the activist intervention, indicating that hedge funds ameliorate the agency problem of free cash flow.[473] Additionally, hedge fund activism is associated with an increase in CEO turnover rate and pay-for-performance sensitivity of CEO compensation.[474]

What is more, Gantchev et al. confirming the disciplinary effects of hedge fund activism document that the threat of activism motivates firms to reduce agency costs and improve operating performance. Defining a threat as an abnormally high rate of recent activism in an industry, Gantchev, Gredil and Jotikasthira demonstrate that yet-to-be-targeted firms in an industry respond to the threat of activism by increasing leverage and payout, reducing capital expenditures and improving asset utilization.[475] In a related study, Fos finds that an increase in the likelihood of a proxy contest due to an increase in stock liquidity results in companies increasing leverage and dividend payouts, decreasing R&D and capital expenditures, reducing CEO compensation and increasing CEO turnover.[476] Interpreting his findings, Fos suggests that companies

471. *Ibid.*
472. Various studies have associated takeover defences with lower firm value. *See* Alma Cohen Lucian A. Bebchuk and Charles C.Y. Wang, 'Staggered Boards and the Wealth of Shareholders: Evidence from Two Natural Experiments', *National Bureau of Economic Research* No. w17127 (2011); Lucian A Bebchuk and Alma Cohen, 'The Costs of Entrenched Boards', *Journal of Financial Economics* 78, no. 2 (2005) (finding that staggered boards are associated with lower firm value). In their study, Bebchuk, Cohen and Ferrell construct an entrenchment index consisting of six provisions, including the adoption of a staggered board and poison pill, and conclude that the entrenching provisions are correlated with lower firm value. *See* Lucian Bebchuk, Alma Cohen and Allen Ferrell, 'What Matters in Corporate Governance?', *Review of Financial Studies* 22, no. 2 (2009). Despite the mainstream view that takeover defences lead to managerial entrenchment, various studies reach opposing results. For instance, in their study, Cremers, Litov and Sepe find that staggered boards are actually associated with an increase in firm value, while de-staggering is associated with a decrease in firm value. The authors report that the positive association between staggered boards and firm value is particularly strong for firms, which have more R&D expenses, more intangible assets, are more innovative and more complex. *See* K. J. Martijn Cremers, Lubomir P. Litov and Simone M. Sepe, 'Staggered Boards and Long-Term Firm Value, Revisited', *Journal of Financial Economics* 126, no. 2 (2017): 422-44.
473. *See* Alon Brav, 'Hedge Fund Activism, Corporate Governance and Firm Performance', 1770-73.; April Klein and Emanuel Zur, 'Entrepreneurial Shareholder Activism: Hedge Funds and Other Private Investors', *The Journal of Finance* 64, no. 1 (2009): 222-25.
474. *See* Alon Brav, 'Hedge Fund Activism, Corporate Governance and Firm Performance', 1776.
475. Nickolay Gantchev, Oleg R Gredil and Chotibhak Jotikasthira, 'Governance under the Gun: Spillover Effects of Hedge Fund Activism', *Review of Finance* 23, no. 6 (1 October 2019): 1031-68.
476. Vyacheslav Fos, 'The Disciplinary Effects of Proxy Contests', *Management Science* 63, no. 3 (2016): 655-71.

implement corporate policies usually demanded by hedge fund activists in order to decrease the likelihood of activist intervention.

The recent surge and growing success of hedge fund activism have provoked a backlash against activism from influential corporate lawyers,[477] politicians, legal academics,[478] business journalists,[479] and prominent judges.[480] Critics of hedge fund activism view hedge funds as short-term speculators who agitate for changes that will earn them a quick profit at the expense of long-term value.[481] Holding their shares for a short time period, so the argument goes, hedge funds are able to exit their investments at a profit long before the negative consequences of their actions have materialized, leaving employees and long-term shareholders worse off. As Leo Strine has observed, activists 'can easily depart and not eat their own cooking'.[482] Thus, activists exacerbate short-termism in financial markets, which are increasingly dominated by short-term investors in search of quick returns. The above-mentioned concerns have led to proposals seeking to curb the growing influence of activists.[483]

However, as noted above, in their empirical study of hedge fund interventions, Bebchuk, Brav, and Jiang find that contrary to claims that activism is harmful for long-term firm value, activists are able to create sustainable, long-term improvements in the company's share price and operational performance.[484] What is crucial to understand is that activist hedge funds are not controlling shareholders able to impose their desired changes in the company's strategy or governance, but rather large influential shareholders who invest in monitoring and proposing value-enhancing changes to other shareholders.[485] The shareholders on whose support hedge funds count to implement their agenda are traditional institutional investors – predominantly mutual funds and pension funds with long-term investment horizons that hold shares

477. *See* Lipton, 'Bite the Apple; Poison the Apple; Paralyze the Company; Wreck the Economy'.
478. Iman Anabtawi and Lynn Stout, 'Fiduciary Duties for Activist Shareholders', *Stanford Law Review* 60, no. 5 (2008): 1255-1308.
479. Andrew Ross Sorkin, 'Shareholder Democracy Can Mask Abuses', New York Times, Dealbook, http://dealbook.nytimes.com/2013/02/25/shareholder-democracy-can-mask-abuses/.
480. Leo E Strine Jr, 'One Fundamental Corporate Governance Question We Face: Can Corporations Be Managed for the Long Term Unless Their Powerful Electorates Also Act and Think Long Term?', *Business Lawyer* 66 (2010); Jack B Jacobs, '"Patient Capital": Can Delaware Corporate Law Help Revive It?', *Washington and Lee Law Review* 68, no. 4 (2011).
481. *See* Lipton, 'Bite the Apple; Poison the Apple; Paralyze the Company; Wreck the Economy'.
482. *See* Strine Jr, 'One Fundamental Corporate Governance Question We Face: Can Corporations Be Managed for the Long Term Unless Their Powerful Electorates Also Act and Think Long Term?', 8.
483. Portia Crowe, 'Bernie Sanders and Elizabeth Warren Are Going after Activist Hedge Funds', *Business Insider*, n.d., https://a.businessinsider.com/elizabeth-warren-sponsors-activist-hedge-fund-bill-2016-3?r=US&IR=T.
484. *See* Bebchuk, Brav and Jiang, 'The Long-Term Effects of Hedge Fund Activism'.
485. Indeed, Bebchuk, Brav, Jackson and Jiang document that the average activist stake reaches 8.8%, with a median of 6.3%. *See* Bebchuk Lucian A, 'Pre-Disclosure Accumulations by Activist Investors: Evidence and Policy'. Although the stake is large enough to incentivize the activist to engage in activism, it is too small to guarantee the activist's prevalence in a proxy fight or the adoption of shareholder proposals submitted by him. This is true also in cases where the activist seeks to discipline a controlling shareholder. In order to counteract the power of the controlling shareholder, the activist will often cooperate with other shareholders. *See, e.g.*, Massimo Belcredi, 'Institutional Investor Activism in a Context of Concentrated Ownership and High Private Benefits of Control: The Case of Italy', 22-31.

for a long period of time.[486] Indeed, Brav, Jiang, Partnoy, and Thomas find that activists tend to target companies with high institutional ownership.[487] Although mutual funds and pension funds are reluctant to engage in activism, they are increasingly adopting transparent voting policies and scrutinizing proposals submitted for a vote.[488]

In their study of mutual fund voting behaviour in proxy contests, Brav et al. document that mutual funds tend to vote for dissident nominees when firms have subpar performance and when the dissident shareholders are hedge fund activists.[489] Furthermore, the authors find that the support of institutional investors is crucial for an activist's success. In particular, the authors document that dissident shareholders are more likely to initiate proxy fights when the target firm's shareholder base is supportive of activism. Appel, Gormley and Keim find that activists are more likely to pursue changes to corporate control, such as board representation, compared to milder changes to corporate policies, such as shareholder proposals, when a larger share of the target's stock is held by passively managed mutual funds.[490] Furthermore, the authors document that higher ownership by passive mutual funds is associated with increased use of proxy fights and a higher likelihood that the activist obtains board representation. What is more, the popular belief that hedge fund activists are short-term investors holding stocks for a short period of time does not correspond to reality. Indeed, Brav, Jiang, Partnoy, and Thomas find an average holding period of twenty-two months for activists targeting US companies,[491] while Becht, Franks, and Grant report an average

486. Despite the popular perception of ever-increasing turnover rates and diminishing holding durations of equities, Cremers, Pareek, and Sautner find that institutional investor holding durations from 1985 until 2010 have in fact increased over time from 1.2 years in 1985 to 1.5 years in 2010, with pension funds having the longest duration, reaching approximately 1.7 years. *See* Martijn Cremers, Ankur Pareek and Zacharias Sautner, 'Short-Term Institutions, Analyst Recommendations, and Mispricing: The Role of Higher Order Beliefs', *Journal of Accounting Research* 59, no. 3 (June 2021): 911-58.
487. Wei Jiang Alon Brav, Frank Partnoy and Randall Thomas, 'Hedge Fund Activism, Corporate Governance and Firm Performance', *Journal of Finance* 63, no. 4 (2011): 1764.
488. The shift in the way that institutional investors cast their votes became evident when Lawrence Fink, the co-founder and CEO of Blackrock, the world's largest asset manager and one of the biggest shareholders of US companies, wrote a letter to all US companies in which Blackrock was a shareholder. He warned the companies that they should not assume that Blackrock was following the recommendations of proxy advisory firms blindly, but rather was reaching its voting decisions on the basis of clear guidelines and its fiduciary responsibilities to its investors. *See* Susanne Craig, 'The Giant of Shareholders, Quietly Stirring', The New York Times, http://www.nytimes.com/2013/05/19/business/blackrock-a-shareholding-giant-is-quietly-stirring.html. Indeed, major institutional investors, such as BlackRock, State Street and Vanguard, have developed specialized proxy voting departments, which are responsible for elaborating proxy voting guidelines and voting proxies. Edward Rock, 'Institutional Investors in Corporate Governance', in *The Oxford Handbook of Corporate Law and Governance*, ed. Jeffrey Gordon and Wolf-Georg Ringe (Oxford University Press, 2015).
489. Alon Brav, Wei Jiang and Tao Li, 'Picking Friends Before Picking (Proxy) Fights: How Mutual Fund Voting Shapes Proxy Contests', *ECGI Finance Working Paper* N° 601/2019 (2021), https://www.ssrn.com/abstract=3101473.
490. Ian R Appel, Todd A Gormley and Donald B Keim, 'Standing on the Shoulders of Giants: The Effect of Passive Investors on Activism', *The Review of Financial Studies* 32, no. 7 (1 July 2019): 2720-74.
491. *See* Alon Brav, 'Hedge Fund Activism, Corporate Governance and Firm Performance', 1749.

holding period of 645 days for their sample of completed activist interventions in Europe.[492]

Overall, the empirical evidence indicates that hedge fund activism results in substantial benefits for both investors and companies. Nonetheless, the limitations of hedge fund activism should be acknowledged. Hedge fund activists are more skilled at facilitating efficient capital reallocation and promoting firm policies that will increase shareholder value, such as payouts, corporate governance changes, or the sale of the company, rather than devising and implementing a long-term plan and vision for the company.[493] For instance, Greenwood and Schor document that the returns to activism are mainly driven by the activists' skills in effecting a takeover of the target. Furthermore, the course of action that an activist proposes may not always be the right one for the company and may actually result in the destruction of shareholder value. Despite the substantial evidence that target firms earn *on average* positive abnormal returns around the disclosure date of the activist's stake, numerous studies find that a significant proportion of firms actually earn negative abnormal returns.[494] It rests, therefore, upon the board of directors to convince shareholders on whose support the activist counts for the implementation of its plan of its superior long-term vision for the company.

2.3 WHAT TYPE OF HEDGE FUND REGULATION?

As our analysis in section 2.2.3 has demonstrated, the only plausible rationale for supporting hedge fund regulation is the potential systemic risk emanating from the failure of a large systemically important hedge fund or hedge funds housed within SIFIs. After having built the case for regulating hedge funds on systemic risk grounds, a natural question arises. What form should hedge fund regulation take? Two distinctions can be made, the one between self-regulation and government regulation and the other between direct and indirect regulation. Overall, we will argue that government regulation is the best choice for regulating hedge funds recognizing however the beneficial role that self-regulation has to play in tackling systemic risk. With respect to the second dilemma, namely the choice between direct and indirect regulation, we will argue that direct regulation is the best choice for tackling the systemic risk emanating from systemically important hedge funds, while indirect regulation is suited for dealing with the financial stability risks posed by hedge funds housed within SIFIs.

492. Becht Marco, 'The Returns to Hedge Fund Activism: An International Study', 13.
493. John C. Coffee and Darius Palia, 'The Impact of Hedge Fund Activism: Evidence and Implications', *Columbia Law and Economics Working Paper* 489 (2014). *See also* Cremers et al. who argue that the positive abnormal returns of target firms are explained by the superior stock-picking and trading skills of activists K J Martijn Cremers et al., 'Hedge Fund Activists: Value Creators or Stock Pickers' (2021), https://papers.ssrn.com/sol3/papers.cfm?abstract_id=3614029.
494. *See* Alon Brav, 'Hedge Fund Activism, Corporate Governance and Firm Performance' (despite documenting average abnormal returns between 7 and 8%, the authors also find that 38% of target firms earned negative abnormal returns).

2.3.1 Self-Regulation Versus Government Regulation

Self-regulation in financial markets gained traction, especially in the UK and the US, during the late 1980s.[495] According to Omarova, self-regulation can be described as 'a regime of collective rulemaking, whereby an industry-level entity develops and enforces rules and standards governing the behaviour of all industry members'.[496] Proponents of self-regulation pointed out the superior ability of industry participants to regulate their own activities and the costs of government regulation, which jeopardized the financial sector's efficiency and profitability. The growing appeal of self-regulation as a regulatory tool was supported by international organizations, including the OECD and IOSCO.[497] Nonetheless, in the aftermath of the financial crisis, there has been a notable shift towards direct government regulation of financial markets.

Self-regulation has numerous advantages over government regulation. Most notably, self-regulation is more flexible and more responsive to changing market conditions. Industry participants are able to rapidly observe changes to market conditions and adopt an adequate regulatory response. According to Black, self-regulation fosters a regulatory approach 'that is responsive, flexible, informed, targeted, which prompts greater compliance, and which at once stimulates and draws on the internal morality of the sector or organization being regulated'.[498] Furthermore, self-regulation promotes shared values among financial market participants and fosters a sense of participation in the regulatory process.[499] What is more, it can respond to the problem of regulatory arbitrage. Taking into account the global nature and complexity of financial markets, any regulatory attempt by a national government will prompt industry participants to devise ways to circumvent costly and burdensome regulation. Regulatory arbitrage can be dealt with by promoting the industry's participation in the rule-making process. Finally, in contrast to government regulation, which is traditionally limited to a single jurisdiction, self-regulatory initiatives are more likely to adopt a global approach.

495. John Braithwaite and Peter Drahos, *Global Business Regulation* (2000), 28.
496. Saule T Omarova, 'Wall Street as Community of Fate: Toward Financial Industry Self-Regulation', *University of Pennsylvania Law Review* 159, no. 2 (2011). Nonetheless, as Athanassiou correctly notes 'a conceptualization of self-regulation in the widest possible sense, including both genuinely market-driven initiatives and government-encouraged ones, appears more appropriate, not least because self-regulatory schemes are rarely entirely detached from the State, making the dichotomy between purely voluntary and government-backed arrangements artificial'. *See* Athanassiou, *Hedge Fund Regulation in the European Union: Current Trends and Future Prospects*, 220.
497. OECD, *Regulatory Policies in OECD Countries: From Interventionism to Regulatory Governance* (2002); IOSCO, *Emerging Markets Committee* (2005).
498. Julia Black, 'Decentring Regulation: Understanding the Role of Regulation and Self-Regulation in a "Post-Regulatory" World', *Current Legal Problems* 54, no. 1 (2001): 115. According to Athanassiou 'because it (self-regulation) draws on the relevant market participants' experience, expertise and superior knowledge of the regulatory issues at stake, it can be better informed, more focused and easier to adapt to new technological or economic developments'. *See* Athanassiou, *Hedge Fund Regulation in the European Union: Current Trends and Future Prospects*, 220.
499. Douglas C Michael, 'Federal Agency Use of Audited Self-Regulation as a Regulatory Technique', *Administrative Law Review* 47 (1995): 181.

As far as the hedge fund industry is concerned, self-regulatory initiatives have been prevalent in the US and the UK. The MFA in the US has adopted the 'Sound Practices for Hedge Fund Managers', currently in their fifth edition, which provide hedge fund managers 'with a framework of internal policies, practices and controls from a peer-to-peer perspective'.[500] The first edition of the standards was published in 2000 in response to the PWG's call for the adoption by hedge funds of a set of sound practices for their risk management and internal controls. In the UK, the SBAI has adopted its own 'Alternative Investments Standards', which focus on valuation, disclosure, risk management, fund governance and shareholder conduct.[501] Signatories to the 'Alternative Investments Standards' must apply them on a comply-or-explain basis. By 2020, 130 AIFMs committed to the Standards accounting for approximately USD 1 trillion in AUM. AIMA also based in the UK was the first association to publish, in 2002, a 'Guide to Sound Practices' targeted at European hedge fund managers.[502] Moreover, in April 2009, AIMA published a specialized Guide to Sound Practices for funds of hedge funds managers. AIMA has adopted additional Guides to Sound Practices for hedge fund valuation, operational risk management, hedge fund administration and business continuity management.[503]

The benefits brought by self-regulation are particularly significant in the case of hedge funds.[504] Hedge funds are designed to take advantage of regulatory gaps and evade government regulation. Self-regulation is apt to deliver a regulatory framework for hedge funds that is 'in line with financial innovation and apt to help shape the industry's conduct in detail, capturing the subtleties of the market activities of alternative investment funds in an attempt to foster the optimal degree of regulation and to induce best market practices'.[505] In addition, the global nature of the hedge fund industry necessitates a global regulatory approach, which self-regulation is better placed to offer.[506]

Despite its benefits, self-regulation entails significant costs. Private regulators have the incentive to develop rules that further their own interest rather than the public interest.[507] For instance, they may adopt anticompetitive rules erecting entry barriers to the market and industry. Furthermore, opponents of self-regulation criticize the lack of

500. Managed Funds Association, *Sound Practices for Hedge Fund Managers* (2009), 1.
501. SBAI, *The Alternative Investments Standards.*
502. AIMA, *Guide to Sound Practices for European Hedge Fund Managers* (2007); *Guide to Sound Practices for European Hedge Fund Managers* (2002).
503. AIMA, Guide to Sound Practices for Hedge Fund Valuation (Mar. London: AIMA, 2007); AIMA, Guide to Sound Practices: Business Continuity Management for Hedge Fund Managers and Funds of Hedge Funds Managers (June 2012); Guide to Sound Practices for Hedge Fund Administrators (September 2009); AIMA's Offshore Alternative Fund Directors' Guide (2015).
504. *See generally* Marco Lamandini, 'Self-Regulation – What Future in the Context of Hedge Funds?', in *Research Handbook on Hedge Funds, Private Equity and Alternative Investments*, ed. Phoebus Athanassiou (Edward Elgar, 2012).
505. *Ibid.*, 255.
506. *Ibid.*
507. According to Posner, 'Regulation is not about the public interest at all, but is a process, by which interest groups seek to promote their (private interest) ... '. Richard A Posner, 'Theories of Economic Regulation', *Bell Journal of Economics and Management Science* 5, no. 2 (1974): 341.

accountability mechanisms.[508] Moreover, self-regulatory bodies, except for those backed up by the state, lack the enforcement mechanisms necessary to ensure compliance with the adopted rules.[509] Persistent non-compliance with the rules provokes distrust towards the self-regulatory body and self-regulation as a regulatory tool. Finally, self-regulatory initiatives suffer from the so-called free rider problem. As Engert notes, 'preventing burdensome government regulation is a collective good for the industry. It follows that individual firms have an incentive to take a free ride on the self-regulation effort by others'.[510]

What is more, Doyle has noted that self-regulation is suitable for industries characterized by: (a) relatively simple firm structures, such as one person firms or partnerships; (b) intense competition; (c) well-defined goods or services; and (d) information that is widely available in the public domain.[511] In contrast, statutory regulation is ideal for industries that are geographically dispersed and complex and where information is largely in the private domain.[512] Applying Doyle's criteria to the hedge fund industry leads to the conclusion that statutory regulation is the optimal mode of regulation with respect to hedge funds. The hedge fund industry is geographically dispersed offering complex and opaque products. What is more, even after the introduction of reporting requirements towards regulators by the AIFM Directive in Europe and the Dodd-Frank Act in the US, the hedge fund industry remains secretive, with information regarding funds' investment strategy, investors and leverage resting outside the public domain.

In addition, self-regulatory initiatives are unlikely to tackle the hedge fund industry's contribution to systemic risk. The hedge fund industry should prima facie have adequate incentives to control systemic risk.[513] After all, hedge fund investors and managers will collectively suffer severe losses in the event of a systemic crisis. Both investors and managers will see their capital wiped out, while managers will also lose future fee revenue. However, the hedge fund industry will bear only a fraction of the losses, which will adversely affect a wide cross-section of economic agents.[514] Systemic risk is a negative externality imposed by the hedge fund industry on the economy as a whole.[515] The hedge fund industry does not internalize the social costs of its activity,

508. Anthony Ogus, 'Rethinking Self-Regulation', *Oxford Journal of Legal Studies* 15, no. 1 (1995): 98-99.
509. Athanassiou, *Hedge Fund Regulation in the European Union: Current Trends and Future Prospects*. Sinclair correctly observes that self-regulation 'relies substantially on the goodwill and cooperation of individual firms for their compliance'. Darren Sinclair, 'Self-Regulation Versus Command and Control? Beyond False Dichotomies', *Law & Policy* 19, no. 4 (1997): 534.
510. Andreas Engert, 'Transnational Hedge Fund Regulation', *European Business Organization Law Review* 11, no. 03 (2010): 351.
511. Marshall, 'Understanding the Asian Crisis: Systemic Risk as Coordination Failure', 36.
512. *Ibid.*
513. Engert, 'Transnational Hedge Fund Regulation', 348.
514. *Ibid.*
515. William Fung and David A Hsieh, 'A Primer on Hedge Funds', *Journal of Empirical Finance* 6, no. 3 (1999). A negative externality exists when the actions of one party negatively affect one or more third parties. The party engaging in the activity does not wholly bear the costs of its actions, which are born in part by other third parties. Thus, there is a divergence between private and social cost. James M Buchanan, 'Externality', *Economica* 29, no. 116 (1962).

which are in part borne by other market players. As a result, it lacks adequate incentives to tackle systemic risk. On the contrary, it has an incentive to take risks that are detrimental to financial stability.

However, self-regulation has an important role to play in the area of investor protection. The hedge fund industry will bear the full costs of weak investor protection since hedge fund investors will not commit new capital to hedge funds and/or withdraw their invested capital. Thus, it is in the collective interest of the hedge fund industry to develop and promote adequate safeguards for investors. It should be noted that hedge fund self-regulatory bodies have been particularly creative in devising standards and rules that guarantee a high level of investor protection. For instance, the Alternative Investment Standards promulgated by the SBAI introduce a cutting-edge and comprehensive investor protection regime imposing on signatories detailed disclosure, valuation, internal control, governance and risk management requirements.

Overall, despite the substantial costs of self-regulatory initiatives and their unsuitability for tackling systemic risk, self-regulatory initiatives in the area of systemic risk should be welcomed. Even though state regulation is the optimal mode of regulation with respect to systemic risk, self-regulation initiatives could still prove useful. Rules and standards promulgated by self-regulatory bodies applying the industry's expertise can offer government regulators a useful template for devising appropriate regulatory measures.

2.3.2 Direct Versus Indirect Regulation

A choice facing government regulators when devising a regulatory response to the financial stability risks posed by hedge funds is between direct and indirect regulation. According to Lessig, regulation of behaviour can be accomplished by law, natural constraints, social norms and markets.[516] Furthermore, Lessig distinguishes between two modes of regulation, direct and indirect. 'In its direct aspect, the law uses its traditional means to direct an object of regulation (whether the individual regulated, norms, the market, or architecture); in its indirect aspect, it regulates these other regulators so that they regulate the individual differently'.[517] In the hedge fund context, direct regulation refers to regulatory measures targeting the hedge fund industry itself.[518] Examples of direct regulatory measures include mandatory registration for hedge funds and/or their managers, limits on fund leverage and disclosure requirements. In contrast, indirect regulation is focused on the regulation of financial institutions that act as creditors, counterparties and as owners/managers of hedge funds, most notably but not exclusively prime brokers.[519] Thus, indirect regulation is

516. Lawrence Lessig, 'The New Chicago School', *The Journal of Legal Studies* 27, no. S2 (1998): 662-63.
517. *Ibid.*, 666.
518. Nabilou and Pacces, 'The Hedge Fund Regulation Dilemma: Direct Vs. Indirect Regulation', 190.
519. Paul M Jonna, 'In Search of Market Discipline: The Case for Indirect Hedge Fund Regulation', *San Diego Law Review* 45, no. 4 (2008).

accomplished 'through the direct regulation of other market participants'.[520] For instance, in order to reduce hedge fund leverage, regulators may decide to impose higher capital requirements for regulated financial institutions' exposures to hedge funds.[521] Furthermore, they may decide to impose strengthened counterparty risk management practices on financial institutions lending to hedge funds. In addition, regulators may decide to sever the ties between hedge funds and banking institutions by prohibiting SIFIs from owning or sponsoring hedge funds. An example of an indirect regulatory measure is the ban on sponsorship and ownership of hedge funds introduced by the Volcker Rule and the European Proposal on Bank Structural Reform, which was withdrawn in 2017.

Direct regulation of hedge funds and/or their managers has been criticized on various grounds.[522] First, direct regulation of the hedge fund industry, which inevitably involves a statutory definition of hedge funds, could give rise to regulatory arbitrage. Second, direct regulation may give a false sense of security to both hedge fund investors and counterparties, who may be dissuaded from performing their monitoring role. Third, one-size-fits-all rules are unsuitable for the diverse hedge fund industry, which is comprised of thousands of different funds adopting heterogeneous investment strategies. Finally, direct regulation erodes the benefits brought by hedge funds to financial markets. On the contrary, indirect regulation is praised for directly confronting the financial stability risks posed by hedge funds.[523] According to proponents of indirect regulation, systemic risk emanates solely from the relationship of hedge funds with SIFIs. As a result, indirect regulatory measures focused on hedge fund creditors, counterparties and owners or managers of hedge funds directly target the transmission channels through which systemic risk propagates. Furthermore, indirect regulation is considered easier to implement and less costly when compared to direct regulatory measures.[524]

Nonetheless, one should note that the perceived costs of a direct regulatory regime are greatly exaggerated. Regulatory arbitrage can be dealt with by introducing a sufficiently broad definition of hedge funds. A notable example is the recent AIFM Directive in Europe. In order to confront regulatory arbitrage, the AIFM introduces the concept of an AIF, which captures a wide variety of investment vehicles, including hedge funds and their managers. The definition is sufficiently broad, meaning that hedge funds are unlikely to be able to evade the requirements of the Directive. Furthermore, the argument that direct regulation gives rise to a false sense of security for investors and counterparties lacks bite. Since systemic risk is an externality, investors and counterparties do not have the correct incentives to control it. Thus, they will generally avoid making optimal investments in tackling the financial stability risks

520. *Ibid.*, 207.
521. *See*, for instance, Wulf A Kaal, 'Hedge Fund Regulation Via Basel III', *Vanderbilt Journal of Transnational Law* 44 (2011).
522. Nabilou and Pacces, 'The Hedge Fund Regulation Dilemma: Direct Vs. Indirect Regulation', 192-205.
523. Daniele Nouy, 'Indirect Supervision of Hedge Funds', *Banque de France, Financial Stability Review: Special Issue Hedge Funds* 10 (April 2007).
524. *Ibid.*

posed by hedge funds. What is more, even though direct hedge fund regulatory measures do indeed inevitably entail a one-size-fits-all approach, the same problem can be observed in other areas of financial regulation. For instance, banking regulation is applicable to a wide variety of banking institutions adopting divergent business strategies. Finally, as far as the argument that a direct regulatory regime erodes the benefits brought by hedge funds to financial markets is concerned, one should note that it is up to government regulators to adopt and implement a direct regulatory framework that strikes the right balance between controlling systemic risk and ensuring that hedge funds continue to play their beneficial role.

Furthermore, an indirect regulatory regime suffers from its own shortcomings. Most importantly, the indirect regulatory approach is premised on the hypothesis that systemic risk arises solely through the interconnectedness of hedge funds with SIFIs. Nonetheless, proponents of an indirect regulatory regime disregard another important channel through which hedge funds may contribute to financial instability, namely the market channel. Accordingly, indirect regulation is unlikely to tackle the negative consequences of a disorderly liquidation of positions by a systemically important hedge fund.[525]

What is more, the indirect approach entrusts hedge fund creditors and counterparties, most importantly prime brokers, with the crucial role of monitoring and controlling hedge fund risk-taking. Nonetheless, it should be noted that prime brokers are unlikely to have a complete overview of a fund's leverage and positions.[526] Furthermore, prime brokers, which derive a substantial part of their revenue from the services they offer to hedge funds, have an incentive to adopt a lenient approach towards their hedge fund clients and engage in regulatory arbitrage seeking to evade the limits placed by regulators on their dealings with hedge funds.[527]

Overall, an indirect regulatory approach is not a silver bullet for reducing systemic risk, with direct regulatory measures remaining the first line of defence against systemic risk emanating from systemically important hedge funds. On the one hand, the costs of a direct regulatory framework have been exaggerated by proponents of indirect regulatory measures. On the other hand, the indirect approach suffers from significant shortcomings. Nonetheless, the indirect regulatory approach remains the first and only line of defence against systemic risk posed by hedge funds housed within SIFIs. Measures targeting directly SIFIs remain the most adequate response to the financial stability risks triggered by internal hedge funds. As a result, the Volcker Rule, which prohibits banking institutions from sponsoring and investing in hedge funds, should be seen as a welcome development.

2.4 CONCLUSION

The present chapter has sought to explore the dangers posed by hedge funds, assess the rationales for their regulation and determine the appropriate regulatory response. The

525. Crockett, 'The Evolution and Regulation of Hedge Funds', 25-26.
526. *Ibid.*
527. *Ibid.*

chapter's analysis suggests that systemic risk is the sole plausible reason supporting regulatory intervention in the hedge fund industry. Financial stability risks arise through the distress of a large systemically important hedge fund and hedge funds housed within SIFIs. Financial regulators have a menu of regulatory approaches to choose from. Despite the growing number of voices advocating for a self-regulatory approach to controlling hedge fund systemic risk, the chapter's analysis has shown that government regulation is the optimal mode of regulation with respect to systemic risk. Nonetheless, self-regulatory initiatives could still prove useful, since rules and standards promulgated by self-regulatory bodies applying the industry's expertise can offer government regulators a useful template for devising appropriate regulatory measures What is more, indirect regulatory measures aimed at the creditors and counterparties to hedge funds are not a panacea to the challenge of taming financial stability risks posed by systemically important hedge funds. Nonetheless, indirect regulatory measures, such as the Volcker Rule in the US and the abandoned Proposal on Bank Structural Reform, remain the most adequate response to the systemic risk emanating from hedge funds housed within SIFIs.

CHAPTER 3

Hedge Fund Regulation in the US and the EU in the Aftermath of the Financial Crisis

3.1 INTRODUCTION

The present chapter seeks to examine hedge fund regulation in the US and the EU in the aftermath of the financial crisis. Long before the dust had settled and a consensus about the causes of the crisis had been formed, government officials and political elites, especially in the EU, attacked the industry, accusing it of being one of the architects of the crisis.[528] The opacity and complexity of hedge fund trading activities, their operation beyond the public purview and the extraordinary wealth amassed by individual hedge fund managers, even in the midst of the worst financial crisis since the Great Depression,[529] made hedge funds a target for regulators and politicians.[530] Hedge funds were viewed as the poster boys of a failed Anglo-Saxon capitalist model[531]

528. *See* Ambrose Evans-Pritchard, 'Sarkozy Turns on "Predator" Hedge Funds', The Daily Telegraph, http://www.telegraph.co.uk/finance/economics/2808197/Sarkozy-turns-on-predator-hedge-funds.html. For instance, Guilio Tremonti, the Italian Minister of Finance, described hedge funds as 'hellish' and pushed for their complete ban. *See* Tracy Corrigan, 'Hedge Funds Do Not Need Punishing They Are Suffering Enough', The Daily Telegraph, www.telegraph.co.uk/finance/comment/tracycorrigan/3212102/Hedgefunds- dont-need-punishing-they-are-suffering-enough.html.
529. A notable example was John Paulson's landmark bet against the US subprime mortgage market. His bet, which has been described as 'the greatest trade ever', earned him nearly USD 4 billion in profits in 2007 alone. For an excellent account of Paulson's bet *see* Michael Lewis, *The Big Short: Inside the Doomsday Machine* (Penguin, 2010); Gregory Zuckerman, *The Greatest Trade Ever: The Behind-the-Scenes Story of How John Paulson Defied Wall Street and Made Financial History* (Crown Business, 2010).
530. Roberta Romano, 'Against Financial Regulation Harmonization: A Comment', *No. 414 Yale Law & Economics Research Paper*, no. 414 (2010): 5.
531. The Anglo-Saxon capitalist model, mostly associated with the US and the UK (also referred to as liberal market economies), is characterized by deregulated labour and financial markets, a legal regime promoting competition in the product markets, limited or non-existent workers' participation rights in the governance of corporations, and a recognition of shareholders as

and part of a fragile and nefarious shadow banking system,[532] which served as a channel for the transmission of the initial shock within the US subprime market to the global financial system. The result was the adoption of legislation, in both the US and the EU, which radically transformed the hedge fund industry.

Section 3.2 of the present chapter will explore hedge fund regulation in the European Union in the aftermath of the financial crisis. My examination will begin with a brief overview of the history of hedge fund regulation in the EU. Furthermore, we will introduce the reader to the main provisions of the AIFM Directive, whose main objectives are the creation of a harmonized regulatory framework aimed at the protection of investors and the tackling of systemic risk and an internal market for AIFMs. The abandoned European Commission Proposal on Bank Structural Reform, which prohibited the largest EU banks from sponsoring and investing in hedge funds, will also be examined. Finally, I will delve into the developments in the area of resolution of financial institutions. After having examined the relevant EU initiatives, section 3.3 will proceed with an analysis of regulatory developments on the other side of the Atlantic. The adoption of the Dodd-Frank Act significantly altered the regulatory landscape for hedge funds in the US. The repeal of the private adviser exemption subjects hedge fund managers, for the first time, to registration with the SEC. Furthermore, the Dodd-Frank Act provides for the prudential supervision and regulation of systemically important hedge funds by the FED while hedge funds, whose failure would pose a significant risk to the financial stability of the US, may be placed into a special resolution procedure administered by the FDIC. What is more, the Volcker Rule aims to curb banks' engagement in risky non-traditional banking activities by prohibiting, *inter alia*, investments in and the sponsorship of hedge funds. In concluding my examination of regulatory developments in the US, section 3.3 will highlight the positive elements of the Dodd-Frank Act as compared to the approach taken by European regulators.

their ultimate owners. In contrast, coordinated market economies, found in much of Continental Europe, are characterized by strictly regulated labour markets, relatively underdeveloped financial markets, the dominance of banks in providing financing to corporations, widespread controlling shareholdings, strong workers' participation rights in the governance of corporations, and the adoption of a stakeholder approach to corporate governance. *See generally* Peter Hall and David Soskice, ed. *Varieties of Capitalism: The Institutional Foundations of Comparative Advantage* (Oxford University Press, 2002); Katharina Pistor, 'Legal Ground Rules in Coordinated and Liberal Market Economies', *ECGI Working Paper Series in Law* No. 30 (2005).

532. Shadow banking is defined 'as the system of credit intermediation that takes place outside the regular banking system'. Financial Stability Board, *Shadow Banking: Strengthening Oversight and Regulation; Recommendations of the Financial Stability Board* (2011). Credit intermediation consists of credit, maturity and liquidity transformation. Shadow banks are described as being 'interconnected along a vertically integrated, long intermediation chain, which intermediates credit through a range of securitization and secured funding techniques such as ABCP, asset-backed securities, collateralized debt obligations and repo'. Zoltan Pozsar et al., 'Shadow Banking', *Staff Report, Federal Reserve Bank of New York* (2010). Even though it is now widely recognized that the hedge fund industry in general is not part of the shadow banking complex, credit hedge funds, a subset of the overall hedge fund universe, are occasionally included in the list of entities classified as shadow banks. *See generally* Association, *The Role of Credit Hedge Funds in the Financial System: Asset Managers, Not Shadow Banks*.

3.2 HEDGE FUND REGULATION IN THE EUROPEAN UNION

3.2.1 The History of Hedge Fund Regulation in the EU

The tremendous growth of the AIFs industry in Europe during the 2000s forced EU policymakers to focus their attention on crafting an appropriate pan-European response to the risks posed and the opportunities offered by the burgeoning industry. In contrast to the perceived wisdom frequently expressed by EU politicians and the press that the AIF industry was completely unregulated, at least until the adoption of the AIFM Directive, one should note that AIFs, including hedge funds and private equity funds, were in fact regulated by various Member States in the EU.[533] Nonetheless, the European Commission in its 2005 Green Paper on the Enhancement of the EU Framework for Investment Funds considered that the existing patchwork of national regimes carried the risk of regulatory fragmentation hampering thus the growth of the industry.[534] As a result, it noted that there would be 'a growing need for a coherent and enlightened European approach to this sector'.[535] The Commission, adopting a pro-market stance towards the investment fund industry, established two expert groups on hedge funds and private equity funds, which issued their reports in 2006.[536] The reports focused on ways to improve the efficient organization of the hedge fund and private equity industries recommending the facilitation of cross-border marketing and distribution of funds. Following the publication of the reports, the Commission issued a White Paper, which largely echoed the industry's approach.[537]

Despite the European Commission's favourable view of the AIFs industry, the ECB and the European Parliament were more sceptical towards the industry and the risks posed by its growth. In particular, the ECB highlighted the hedge fund industry's lack of transparency, which hampered the monitoring of systemic risk.[538] Within Europe, the European Parliament was the most prominent institution to criticize the industry. The Parliament adopted various resolutions calling upon the Commission to examine hedge funds' and private equity funds' negative effects.[539] What is more, the Parliamentary Socialist Group, traditionally hostile to Anglo-Saxon capitalism, published a report in March 2007 highlighting the detrimental effects of private equity and

533. For instance, in the UK, hedge fund managers were subject to registration with the FSA, the predecessor of FCA. Regarding hedge fund regulation in the European Union prior to the adoption of the AIFM Directive, *see generally* Athanassiou, *Hedge Fund Regulation in the European Union: Current Trends and Future Prospects*, 152-64.
534. '*European Commission Green Paper on the Enhancement of the EU Framework for Investment Funds*, Com (2005) 314 Final (July 12, 2005)'.
535. *Ibid.*, 9.
536. *Report of the Alternative Investment Expert Group, Developing European Private Equity* (July 2006); *Report of the Alternative Investment Expert Group, Managing, Servicing and Marketing Hedge Funds in Europe* (July 2006).
537. '*White Paper on Enhancing the Single Market Framework for Investment Funds*, Com (2006) 686 Final (15 November 2006)'.
538. European Central Bank, *Financial Stability Review* (June 2006), 139-40.
539. 'European Parliament Resolution on Asset Management, P6_Ta-Prov(2006)0181'; 'European Parliament Resolution on the Future of Hedge Funds and Derivatives, P5_Ta(2004)0031'.

hedge funds and the need for tighter regulation.[540] The report highlighted the lack of transparency in the AIF industry and the risks that hedge funds posed to financial stability. The overall sentiment in favour of regulation was supported by public criticism of hedge funds and private equity tactics by politicians of individual Member States, most notably Germany and France.[541] However, the Commission initially refused to act on calls for stricter regulation.[542]

As previously discussed in Chapter 1, immediately after the eruption of the financial crisis, EU politicians started attacking the hedge fund industry, voicing their determination to bring it onto the regulatory radar. In September 2008, the European Parliament adopted a resolution recommending to the Commission to put forth legislative proposals regarding the regulation of hedge funds and private equity.[543] Furthermore, the European Parliament's Lehne Report adopted in July 2008 called for greater transparency of hedge funds and private equity.[544] At the international level, German Chancellor Angela Merkel, French President Nicolas Sarkozy and Italian Treasury Minister Giulio Tremonti were the main supporters of a tougher regulatory regime for hedge funds.[545] On the contrary, the US and the UK, the world's major centres for hedge fund and private equity activity, driven in part by the fear that tighter regulation would lead to an exodus of funds from their jurisdictions, fiercely resisted regulation favouring instead disclosure as the appropriate response to the risks posed by hedge funds and private equity. In preparation for the April 2009 G20 London Summit, German Chancellor Angela Merkel hosted a summit of European leaders in Berlin in order to develop a common EU policy. Germany and France were able to overcome resistance from the UK with the final press release calling for appropriate oversight and regulation of hedge funds.[546] The agreement reached at the G20 London Summit echoed German and French aspirations. The G20 leaders agreed to mandatory registration of hedge funds and/or their managers, the disclosure of appropriate information necessary for the assessment of systemic risk and risk management practices oversight.[547]

540. Socialist Group in the European Parliament, *Hedge Funds and Private Equity- a Critical Analysis* (2007).
541. Christian Reiermann, 'Controlling the Locusts; Baby Steps Against Hedge Funds', Der Spiegel, http://www.spiegel.de/international/spiegel/controlling-the-locusts-baby-steps-against-hedge-funds-a-464416.html.
542. The EU Internal Market Commissioner Charlie McCreevy stated that 'hedge funds are good for the market. They have given greater liquidity, they have added shareholder value, they have helped the rationalization and innovation of companies'. *See* Tobias Buck, 'FT Interview: Charlie McCreevy', Financial Times, http://www.ft.com/intl/cms/s/0/3a94b8c4-c043-11db-995a-000b5df10621.html#axzz3T0cY6epL.
543. 'European Parliament Resolution with Recommendations to the Commission on Hedge Funds and Private Equity, P6_Ta-Prov(2008)0425'.
544. 'European Parliament Report with Recommendations to the Commission on Transparency of Institutional Investors, A6-0296/2008'.
545. Chris Bryant, 'EU Leaders Push Sweeping Regulations', Financial Times, http://www.ft.com/intl/cms/s/0/a896e59e-011f-11de-8f6e-000077b07658.html#axzz3T0cY6epL.
546. *Ibid.*
547. According to the declaration of the G20 leaders, 'hedge funds or their managers will be registered and will be required to disclose appropriate information on an ongoing basis to supervisors or regulators, including on their leverage, necessary for assessment of the systemic

Immediately after the conclusion of the London Summit, on 29 April 2009, the European Commission put its proposal on the table. The hedge fund industry, whose lobbying power at that time was rather weak, was taken by surprise.[548] The initial Commission Proposal has been described as protectionist and ill-considered at best.[549] The most controversial aspects of the proposal were its one-size-fits-all approach, the authorization granted to the Commission to regulate the use of leverage and short selling and provisions that essentially created a fortress around Europe by severely restricting the marketing of non-EU-based funds in Europe.[550] After long and heated negotiations and a politicized clash between, on the one side, the UK and the hedge fund industry and, on the other, Germany and especially France, the final text of the Directive was adopted on 16 November 2011.

3.2.2 The AIFM Directive

The AIFM Directive represents the first piece of pan-European legislation dealing with hedge funds. The final text of the Directive was adopted after a record 1.669 amendments proposed by members of the European Parliament to the original draft directive.[551] The intensity and the duration of the negotiations indicate not only the highly political but also the technical nature of hedge fund regulation.

3.2.2.1 The AIFM Directive's Provisions

The AIFM Directive's goals are the creation of a harmonized pan-European regulatory framework for AIFMs and a genuine internal market for their activities. The rationales underpinning the adoption of the Directive are the perceived lack of adequate investor protection and the role of AIFMs, especially hedge funds, in aggravating and/or amplifying systemic risk. The requirements of the Directive are applicable to AIFMs established in the EU managing or marketing one or more AIFs irrespective of whether they are EU based or not and non-EU AIFMs managing EU AIFs or marketing AIFs in the EU, EU based or not.[552] It should be noted that the Directive does not directly target investment funds but regulates the fund manager instead. Pursuant to Article 5(1),

risks that they pose individually or collectively. Where appropriate, registration should be subject to a minimum size. They will be subject to oversight to ensure that they have adequate risk management'. *Declaration on Strengthening the Financial System, London Summit,* 2 April 2009.

548. Cornelia Woll, 'Beyond Ideological Battles: A Strategic Analysis of Hedge Fund Regulation in Europe', *Les Cahiers Europeens de Sciences Po.* 2 (2011): 12-13.
549. Ferran, 'After the Crisis: The Regulation of Hedge Funds and Private Equity in the EU'.
550. Phoebus Athanassiou and Thomas Bullman, 'The EU's AIFM Directive and Its Impact-an Overview', in *Research Handbook on Hedge Funds, Private Equity and Alternative Investments,* ed. Phoebus Athanassiou (Edward Elgar, 2012), 442, 44-51.
551. J. Baird & G. Black, 'Amendments Clog EU AIFM Directive Debate: The Political Backdrop Is also Evolving Rapidly', *The Hedge Fund Journal* (March 2010): 28.
552. Directive 2011/61/EU of the European Parliament and of the Council of 8 June 2011 on Alternative Investment Fund Managers and Amending Directives 2003/41/EC and 2009/65/EC and Regulations (EC) No. 1060/2009 and (EU) No. 1095/2010, 2011 O.J. (L 174) 1 Art. 2, at 14.

each AIF must appoint a single AIFM responsible for ensuring compliance with the requirements of the Directive.[553] Individual Member States remain responsible for regulating and supervising AIFs. One should note that numerous European countries, such as Luxembourg and Ireland, have developed specialized product-level regulation and supervision.[554]

The definition of an AIFM covers any 'legal person whose regular business is managing one or more AIFs'.[555] AIFs can be either externally managed or internally managed where the legal form of the AIF permits internal management and the AIF's management decides not to appoint an external AIFM.[556] In the latter case, the AIF itself shall be authorized as AIFM.[557] Furthermore, AIFs are defined as 'collective investment undertakings ... which raise capital from a number of investors with a view to investing it in accordance with a defined investment policy for the benefit of those investors and (which) do not require authorization pursuant to article 5 of Directive 2009/65/EC'.[558] Therefore, the application of the Directive extends to a broad array of investment vehicles, including hedge fund, private equity fund, real estate fund and commodity capital fund managers. As Jennifer Payne has noted, the target of EU regulators was primarily hedge funds but other industries, such as private equity, were swept along.[559] Certain categories of entities, such as sovereign wealth funds, pension funds, securitization special purpose entities, supranational and national institutions, central banks, holding companies and employee participation or savings schemes, are excluded from the application of the Directive.[560] An AIFM falling under the ambit of the Directive must be authorized by the competent authorities of its home Member State and comply with the requirements of the Directive.[561]

553. *Ibid.*, Art. 5(1), at 19. Curtin Edmond Duncan Angus and Crosignani Marco, 'Alternative Regulation: The Directive on Alternative Investment Fund Managers', *Capital Markets Law Journal* 6, no. 3 (2011): 333-34.
554. For a general introduction to the Luxembourgish regime *see* Isabelle Lebbe and Claude Kremer, *Les Organismes De Placement Collectif En Droit Luxembourgeois*, 3rd ed. (Larcier, 2014); Eisenhuth Michele Kremer Claude, Dusemon Gilles and Martougi Catherine, 'Luxembourg', in *Alternative Investment Funds in Europe*, ed. Lodewijk Van Setten and Danny Busch (Oxford University Press, 2014). For an overview of the Irish regime *see* generally McCann FitzGerald, 'A Guide to Investment Funds in Ireland', May 2017.
555. Directive 2011/61/EU of the European Parliament and of the Council of 8 June 2011 on Alternative Investment Fund Managers and Amending Directives 2003/41/EC and 2009/65/EC and Regulations (EC) No. 1060/2009 and (EU) No. 1095/2010, 2011 O.J. (L 174) 1 Art. 8, at 21. 'Managing AIFs' is defined as performing at least portfolio management or risk management services for one or more AIFs. *Ibid.*, Art. 4(w), at 18.
556. *Ibid.*, Art. 5(1)(a), at 19.
557. *Ibid.*, Art. 5(1)(b), at 19.
558. *Ibid.*, Art. 4(1)(a), at 16. ESMA has issued detailed guidelines elaborating on the concepts comprising the definition of an AIF. 'Guidelines on Key Concepts of the AIFMD' (ESMA, 13 August 2013).
559. Jennifer Payne, 'Private Equity and Its Regulation in Europe', *European Business Organization Law Review* 12, no. 04 (2011).
560. Directive 2011/61/EU of the European Parliament and of the Council of 8 June 2011 on Alternative Investment Fund Managers and Amending Directives 2003/41/EC and 2009/65/EC and Regulations (EC) No. 1060/2009 and (EU) No. 1095/2010, 2011 O.J. (L 174) 1 Art. 2(3), at 14-15.
561. *Ibid.*, Art. 6, at 19-20. The definition of 'Home Member State' is found in Art. 4(1)(q). 'Home Member State of the AIFM' is defined as the Member State in which the AIFM has its registered

Article 3(2) provides for a *de minimis* exemption for AIFMs managing leveraged AIFs with less than EUR 100 million AUM or less than EUR 500 million if the funds do not use leverage and do not allow investor redemptions for the first five years.[562] This exemption is premised on the insignificance of small funds to overall financial stability. Nonetheless, it should be noted that exempted funds are still subject to registration with the competent authorities of their home Member States and must provide information on their investment strategies, the main instruments in which they are trading, their principal exposures and most important concentrations.[563] Article 3(1) further exempts from the application of the Directive AIFMs, which manage an AIF(s) whose only investors are the AIFM itself or the parent undertakings or the subsidiaries of the AIFM or other subsidiaries of those parent undertakings, provided that none of those investors is itself an AIF.[564]

Provisions aimed at the protection of investors include extensive conduct of business valuation, depositary, capital, delegation and disclosure requirements. Managers of AIFs must implement organizational and administrative arrangements for identifying and managing any conflicts of interests that could adversely impact the interests of the AIFs that they manage or the funds' investors.[565] Where organizational arrangements are not sufficient to ensure, with reasonable confidence, that risks of damage to investors' interests will be prevented, the AIFM must clearly disclose the

---

office. With respect to non-EU AIFMs, 'home Member State' is defined as the Member State of reference. The rules for determining the Member State of reference are particularly complex and are found in Chapter VII of the Directive. *Ibid.*, Art. (4)(1)(q), at 17.

562. *Ibid.*, Art. 3(2), at 15. The threshold of EUR 500 million has in essence been created for private equity funds, which do not utilize leverage on a fund level and offer no redemption rights to investors until the liquidation of the fund typically after ten years. In the hedge fund context, the relevant threshold will be usually inapplicable since the overwhelming majority of hedge funds utilize leverage and offer short lock-up periods. According to Art. 4(1) of the AIFM Directive, the term 'leverage' is defined as 'any method by which the AIFM increases the exposure of an AIF it manages whether through borrowing of cash or securities, or leverage embedded in derivative positions or by any other means'. EC Delegated Regulation No. 231/2013 defines leverage as the ratio between an AIF's exposure and its net asset value. 'Commission Delegated Regulation (EU) No. 231/2013 of 19 December 2012 Supplementing Directive 2011/61/EU of the European Parliament and of the Council with Regard to Exemptions, General Operating Conditions, Depositaries, Leverage, Transparency and Supervision, Art. 6, 2013 O.J. (L 83) 1, at 21'. The exposure shall be calculated according to two different methodologies: the gross and the commitment methodology. Gross exposure is 'the sum of the absolute values of all positions' of the AIF excluding cash and cash equivalents and unused cash borrowings. Derivative instruments are valued pursuant to the methodology contained in Annex I and II of the European Commission Delegated Regulation. *Ibid.*, Art. 7, at 21-22. An AIF's exposure calculated pursuant to the commitment method is the sum of the absolute values of all the positions of an AIF, including cash and cash borrowings. Derivatives are valued in accordance to the conversion methodology contained in Annexes I and II. Furthermore, when calculating an AIF's exposure using the commitment method, AIFMs must apply netting and hedging arrangements, subject to specified conditions. *Ibid.*, Art. 8, at 22-23. Assets under management are calculated by identifying all AIFs the AIFM manages, identifying and valuing each AIF's portfolio and aggregating the values of the assets under management for all AIFs managed. *Ibid.*, Art. 2(1), at 19-20.
563. *Ibid.*, Art. 3(2), at 15.
564. *Ibid.*, Art. 3(1), at 15.
565. *Ibid.*, Art. 14(1), at 24.

general nature or sources of conflicts of interest to the investors and develop appropriate policies and procedures.[566] AIFMs must act with due care, skill, diligence and fairness in conducting their activities.[567] What is more, they must act in the interests of the AIFs managed, their investors and the integrity of the market.[568] AIFMs are required to have and employ effectively the resources and procedures that are necessary for the proper performance of their business activities and comply with all regulatory requirements relevant to the conduct of their business.[569] Most importantly, all AIF investors must be treated fairly.[570] Preferential treatment granted to particular AIF investors, through, for instance, side letters, must be disclosed in the relevant rules or instruments of incorporation of the AIF.[571]

The depositary is a key actor in the AIFM Directive's investor protection regime as a monitor of fund activities. Pursuant to Article 21, a single depositary must be appointed for each fund managed.[572] The depositary is responsible for asset custody and verification and the monitoring of cash flows, while it is also subject to oversight duties with respect to the sale, issuance, redemption and cancellation of fund units or shares, the valuation of fund units or shares and transactions involving fund assets.[573] EU credit institutions and certain EU investment firms may act as depositaries. In the case of non-EU AIFs, non-EU credit institutions and other entities of the same nature as EU eligible institutions are also eligible to act as depositaries. For EU AIFs, the depositary must be established in the home Member State of the AIF. Non-EU AIFs must appoint a depositary established in the third country where the AIF is established, the home Member State of the fund manager or the Member State of reference of the AIFM managing the AIF. In order to avoid conflicts of interest, an AIFM and a prime broker acting as counterparty to an AIF shall not act as a depositary for that AIF.[574]

The AIFM Directive creates a distinction between financial instruments that can be held in custody and other assets. Financial instruments that can be held in custody include transferable securities, money market instruments or units of collective investment undertakings that can be registered or held in an account in the name of the depositary and financial instruments that can be physically delivered to the depositary.[575] Other assets include non-financial assets, such as real estate and commodities, and financial instruments that are only directly registered with an issuer or registrar in

566. *Ibid.*, Art. 14(2), at 24.
567. *Ibid.*, Art. 12(1)(a), at 23.
568. *Ibid.*, Art. 12(1)(b), at 23.
569. *Ibid.*, Art. 12(1)(c), at 23.
570. *Ibid.*, Art. 12(1)(f), at 23.
571. *Ibid.*, Art. 12(1), at 23.
572. *Ibid.*, Art. 21(1), at 28.
573. *Ibid.*, Art. 21(7)-(9), at 29-30.
574. A prime broker may act as depositary if there is a functional and hierarchical separation of the depositary functions from its tasks as prime broker and the potential conflicts of interest are properly identified, managed and disclosed to investors. *Ibid.*, Art. 21(4), at 29.
575. 'Commission Delegated Regulation (EU) No 231/2013 of 19 December 2012 Supplementing Directive 2011/61/EU of the European Parliament and of the Council with Regard to Exemptions, General Operating Conditions, Depositaries, Leverage, Transparency and Supervision', Art. 88.

the name of the AIF, such as investments in privately held companies.[576] The Directive introduces a near strict liability regime for depositaries, making them liable for the loss of any financial instrument in their custody or held by any third party to whom custody has been delegated except if the loss can be attributed to an external event beyond the depositary's reasonable control, the consequences of which would have been unavoidable despite all reasonable efforts to the contrary.[577] External events beyond the depositary's reasonable control are force majeure type events, such as natural disasters, war, riots or other major upheavals, the adoption of local laws that impact the financial instruments held in custody and the insolvency of a third party to whom custody was delegated if the law of the country where the instrument is held in custody does not recognize the effects of segregation.[578] In respect of assets other than financial instruments held in custody, the depository will according to Article 21(12) of the AIMF Directive only be liable to the AIF or its investors for losses suffered as a result of the depositary's negligent or intentional failure to properly fulfil its obligations under the Directive.

The depositary may delegate its safekeeping function to third parties subject to stringent requirements, including, among other things, that the tasks are not delegated for the purpose of avoiding the requirements, the depositary has exercised all due skill, care and diligence in the selection and appointment of any third party and the depositary has demonstrated an objective reason for the delegation.[579] In case of a loss of financial instruments held in custody by a third party, the depositary may discharge itself of liability if all the requirements for the delegation have been fulfilled, a written contract between the depositary and the third party expressly transfers the liability of the depositary to that third party and allows the AIFM, the AIF or the depositary acting on their behalf to make a claim against the third party, and a written contract between the depositary and the AIF or the AIFM expressly provides for the discharge of the depositary's liability and establishes the objective reason to contract such a discharge.[580]

AIFMs are also required to adhere to heightened valuation standards. With respect to the valuation of assets, fund managers must ensure that AIF assets are valued and the NAV per unit or share of the AIF is calculated at least once per year either externally or, subject to certain requirements, internally.[581] If the AIFM decides to appoint an external valuer, its liability towards the AIF and its investors shall not be

576. Sebastiaan N. Hooghiemstra, 'Depositary Regulation', in *The Alternative Investment Fund Managers Directive*, 3rd ed. (Wolters Kluwer, 2020).
577. *Ibid.*, Art. 21(12), at 31. For an analysis of the depositary liability regime introduced by the AIFM Directive *see* André Prüm, 'La Directive AIFM: Nouveau Paradigme Pour La Responsabilité Des Dépositaires?', *Revue de Droit Bancaire et Financier* 1 (2011).
578. 'Commission Delegated Regulation (EU) No. 231/2013 of 19 December 2012 Supplementing Directive 2011/61/EU of the European Parliament and of the Council with Regard to Exemptions, General Operating Conditions, Depositaries, Leverage, Transparency and Supervision', Art. 101(2).
579. *Ibid.*, Art. 21(11), at 30.
580. *Ibid.*, Art. 21(13), at 31.
581. *Ibid.*, Art. 19(4), at 26-27.

affected by the fact that the AIFM has appointed an external valuer.[582] Nonetheless, the external valuer shall be liable to the AIFM for the losses suffered by the AIFM as a result of the valuer's negligence or intentional failure to carry out its tasks.[583] Finally, the Directive imposes modest initial and ongoing capital requirements for AIFMs subject to an overall cap of EUR 10 million, while, in order to cover potential professional liability risks, managers of funds must either have additional own funds appropriate to cover the potential risks or hold professional indemnity insurance.[584]

In order to curb regulatory arbitrage and protect investors from operational risk, the Directive places limits on the use of delegation arrangements. Fund managers routinely use delegation in order to perform functions and activities in a more efficient manner, such as obtain access to third-party expertise and global trading capabilities. However, the extensive use of delegation arrangements poses significant operational and supervisory risks. The extensive delegation of critical functions, such as portfolio and risk management, may result in key decisions being taken by third parties, which will also maintain the key human and technical resources. Furthermore, delegation of functions and activities, especially to third parties located outside the EU, may be used in order to circumvent the requirements of the AIFM Directive. Delegation arrangements have come under the spotlight following the UK's exit from the EU. ESMA has warned of the heightened risk of extensive use of delegation arrangements for the purpose of creating letter-box entities inside the EU.[585] UK managers, who following the UK's exit from the EU are treated as third-country AIFMs, may seek to create letter-box entities in the EU, thus availing themselves of the AIFM passport while continuing to perform critical activities and functions on a delegation basis from the UK.

Pursuant to Article 20(1), AIFMs seeking to delegate functions to third parties must notify the competent authorities of their home Member State. Furthermore, a number of conditions must be fulfilled. The delegation must take the form of a written agreement, it must be based on objective reasons, the delegate must dispose sufficient resources to perform the tasks, and the persons who conduct the business of the delegate must be of good repute and experienced. Objective reasons justifying the delegation include cost savings, optimization of business functions and processes, expertise of the delegate in administration or specific markets or investments and access of the delegate to global trading capabilities. Moreover, if the delegation concerns portfolio or risk management, the delegate must be authorized or registered for the purpose of asset management and subject to supervision or if that conditions cannot be fulfilled, subject to prior approval by the competent authorities of the home Member State. In addition, where the delegate is a third-country entity, written cooperation arrangements between the authorities of the home Member State of the AIFM and the supervisory authority of the undertaking must exist. What is more, the

582. *Ibid.*, Art. 19(10), at 27.
583. *Ibid.*
584. *Ibid.*, Art. 9, at 22.
585. Attracta Mooney and Jennifer Thompson, 'Europe's National Regulators Clash over Delegation', Financial Times, https://www.ft.com/content/44dbefcc-a9db-11e7-ab55-27219df83c97.

delegation must not prevent the effectiveness of supervision of the AIFM. Finally, the AIFM must demonstrate that the delegate has been selected with all due care and that the AIFM is able to effectively monitor and give instructions to the delegate and withdraw the delegation at any time.

Article 82 of Delegated Regulation No. 231/2013 introduces stringent rules specifically targeting letter-box entities. An AIFM shall be considered to be a letter-box entity and no longer the manager of the AIF if the AIFM: (a) is unable to supervise the delegated tasks effectively; (b) no longer has the power to take key decisions or perform senior management functions; (c) loses its contractual rights to enquire, inspect and instruct delegates or the exercise of such rights becomes practically impossible; or (d) delegates the performance of investment management functions to an extent that exceeds by a substantial margin the investment management functions performed by the AIFM itself. In assessing the extent of delegation, competent authorities must also take into account a number of qualitative criteria, such as the risk profile of the fund, the investment strategies and the importance of the assets under delegation to the risk and return profile of the fund and its investment goals. In the context of Brexit, ESMA has issued two opinions aimed at ensuring a consistent supervisory approach to requests from UK fund managers to relocate to the EU.[586] In particular, ESMA stressed the importance of ensuring that entities relocating to the EU will not use delegation in order to continue performing the bulk of portfolio and/or risk management functions in the third country but will transfer a substantial amount of portfolio and/or risk management functions to the EU. Finally, ESMA, in its letter to the European Commission regarding the impending review of the Directive, highlighted the need for additional legislative clarifications in the area of delegation.[587] The agency advocated in favour of introducing quantitative criteria when assessing the extent of delegation for the purposes of Article 82(1)(d) or a list of core functions that cannot be delegated to third parties.

Disclosure requirements towards investors are a cornerstone of the European Union's policy of enhancing the transparency of the AIF industry. Transparency requirements include the obligation of fund managers to disclose specific information to investors both prior to the investment and periodically thereafter.[588] Information that is required to be disclosed to investors prior to their investment includes the investment strategy and objectives of the AIF; the identity of the AIFM, the AIF's depositary, auditor and other service providers; a description of the AIF's valuation procedure, the AIF's liquidity risk management, the fees, charges and expenses charged to investors and the identity of the prime broker. AIFMs must also periodically disclose information regarding the percentage of AIF assets, which are subject to special arrangements arising from their illiquid nature, any new arrangements for

586. 'Opinion General Principles to Support Supervisory Convergence in the Context of the United Kingdom Withdrawing from the European Union' (ESMA, 31 May 2017); 'Opinion to Support Supervisory Convergence in the Area of Investment Management in the Context of the United Kingdom Withdrawing from the European Union' (ESMA, 13 July 2017).
587. 'Letter on the Review of the Alternative Investment Fund Managers Directive' (ESMA, 18 August 2020).
588. *Ibid.*, Art. 23, at 33-34.

managing the liquidity of the AIF, the risk profile and the risk management systems employed by the AIFM, the total amount of leverage employed, information on the main categories of assets in which the AIF is invested, including long and short market values, and the results of periodic stress tests. Furthermore, pursuant to Article 22, an audited annual report with respect to each fund managed and/or marketed in the EU must be available to investors on request.[589] The audited report shall, at the least, contain a balance sheet, an income and expenditure account, a report on the activities of the financial year and the amount of remuneration paid to senior management and members of staff whose actions have a material impact on the risk profile of the AIF.

The AIFM Directive was adopted based on the belief that AIF, and, specifically, hedge fund activities had a destabilizing effect on markets during the twin financial and sovereign debt crises. As a result, the Directive contains a wide array of provisions aimed at safeguarding financial stability. It should be stressed that the relevant provisions predominantly target the hedge fund industry since other types of AIFs, including private equity funds, do not pose systemic risk.[590]

Hedge fund managers must devise and implement appropriate risk and liquidity management systems.[591] AIFMs shall implement adequate risk management systems in order to identify, measure, manage and monitor appropriately all risks relevant to each AIF investment strategy and to which each AIF is or may be exposed. The overdependence of investors on credit ratings and the flawed business model of credit rating agencies significantly contributed to the financial crisis by fuelling the subprime mortgage bubble.[592] Reflecting the EU's push to damper over-reliance on credit ratings, the Directive prohibits AIFMs from relying solely or mechanistically on credit ratings.

589. *Ibid.*, Art. 22, at 32.

590. An important concern is the effect that a widespread failure of private equity-backed companies would have on the banking system, which finances LBO deals. However, even the European Central Bank has acknowledged that LBO activity poses little systemic risk to the banking sector. *See* European Central Bank, *Large Banks and Private Equity-Sponsored Leveraged Buyouts in the EU* (2007). Furthermore, private equity neither contributed to nor caused the recent financial crisis and there was no widespread failure of private equity-backed companies.

591. Directive 2011/61/EU of the European Parliament and of the Council of 8 June 2011 on Alternative Investment Fund Managers and Amending Directives 2003/41/EC and 2009/65/EC and Regulations (EC) No. 1060/2009 and (EU) No. 1095/2010, 2011 O.J. (L 174) 1 Arts 15 & 16, at 24-25. One should note that the particular requirements can be viewed from both an investor protection and a financial stability perspective. However, the predominant rationale behind the adoption of these particular requirements was the protection of financial stability. Heightened liquidity management requirements respond to the risk of a run by investors and creditors. *See* Ulf Klebeck, 'Liquidity Management and Side Pockets in the Alternative Investment Fund Managers Directive', in *The Alternative Investment Funds Managers Directive, European Regulation of Alternative Investment Funds* ed. Dirk Zetzsche (Kluwer Law International, 2012). On the other hand, the weaknesses of internal control, governance mechanisms and risk management that were revealed during the financial crisis have made robust risk management in financial institutions an indispensable tool for strengthening financial stability. Dirk Zetzsche and Dirk Eckner, 'Risk Management in the Alternative Investment Fund Managers Directive', in *The Alternative Investment Fund Managers Directive, European Regulation of Alternative Investment Funds*, ed. Dirk Zetzsche (Kluwer Law International, 2012).

592. *See* generally Frank Partnoy, 'Overdependence on Credit Ratings Was a Primary Cause of the Crisis', in *The Panic of 2008: Causes, Consequences, and Implications for Reform*, ed. Arthur Wilmarth, Frank Partnoy, Lawrence Mitchell (Edward Elgar, 2010).

The principle against over-reliance on credit ratings must be integrated into the AIFM's risk management systems and processes.[593]

Moreover, the risk management function must be functionally and hierarchically separate from the portfolio management function. AIFMs are additionally required to: (a) implement an appropriate, documented and regularly updated due diligence process for making investments; (b) ensure that the risks can be properly identified, measured, managed and monitored, including through the use of appropriate stress testing procedures; (c) ensure that the risk profile of the AIF corresponds to the size, portfolio structure and investment strategies and objectives of the AIF; and (d) set a maximum level of leverage, which they may employ on behalf of each AIF managed as well as the extent of the right to reuse collateral or guarantees that could be granted under the leveraging arrangement. Furthermore, AIFMs must conduct periodic appropriate stress tests and scenario analyses to address risks arising from potential changes in market conditions that may adversely affect the AIF.[594] AIFMs must also employ appropriate liquidity management systems and adopt procedures for monitoring liquidity risk. Moreover, AIFMs must ensure that the liquidity profile of the investments of the AIF complies with its underlying obligations. Furthermore, the investment strategy, liquidity profile and the redemption policy must be consistent for each AIF managed. In order to monitor liquidity risk, AIFMs are also required to conduct regular stress tests, under normal and exceptional liquidity conditions.

What is more, AIFMs must establish and apply remuneration policies that promote sound risk management and do not encourage excessive risk-taking.[595] Remuneration restrictions are also introduced for 'identified staff', whose professional activities have a material impact on the fund's risk profile.[596] 'Identified staff' includes senior management, risk-takers, control functions and any employee receiving total remuneration that takes them into the same remuneration bracket as senior management and risk-takers. In order to ensure prudent risk-taking, remuneration to the

593. 'Directive 2013/14/EU of the European Parliament and of the Council of 21 May 2013 Amending Directive 2003/41/EC on the Activities and Supervision of Institutions for Occupational Retirement Provision, Directive 2009/65/EC on the Coordination of Laws, Regulations and Administrative Provisions Relating to Undertakings for Collective Investment in Transferable Securities (UCITS) and Directive 2011/61/EU on Alternative Investment Funds Managers in Respect of over-Reliance on Credit Ratings 2013 OJ (L145). 1', Art. 3, p. 3.

594. 'Commission Delegated Regulation (EU) No 231/2013 of 19 December 2012 Supplementing Directive 2011/61/EU of the European Parliament and of the Council with Regard to Exemptions, General Operating Conditions, Depositaries, Leverage, Transparency and Supervision, Art. 6, 2013 O.J. (L 83) 1, at 21', Art. 45(3), at 34.

595. Directive 2011/61/EU of the European Parliament and of the Council of 8 June 2011 on Alternative Investment Fund Managers and Amending Directives 2003/41/EC and 2009/65/EC and Regulations (EC) No. 1060/2009 and (EU) No. 1095/2010, 2011 O.J. (L 174) 1 Art. 13, at 24. Remuneration requirements can also be viewed from both a financial stability and an investor protection perspective. Nonetheless, the provisions of the AIFM Directive have been substantially influenced by the EU's initiatives in the field of remuneration policies for credit institutions in light of the role of executive compensation in causing the financial crisis. Therefore, sound remuneration practices are considered beneficial for enhancing financial stability. Paolo Camara, 'The AIFM's Governance and Remuneration Committees', in *The Alternative Investment Funds Managers Directive, European Regulation of Alternative Investment Funds*, ed. Dirk Zetzsche (Kluwer Law International, 2012).

596. *Ibid.*, Annex II(1), at 70-71.

above-mentioned categories of staff, including carried interest, must be paid in both fixed and variable components with a minimum of 40%-60% of variable remuneration deferred and at least 50% of it paid in equity or in equity-linked instruments of the AIF(s) managed.[597] In addition, *ex post* risk adjustment of performance-related remuneration should be achieved through malus and clawback arrangements.[598] Remuneration committees staffed by non-executives must also be set up depending on the sophistication of the manager.[599] For the purpose of ensuring a uniform and consistent application of the Directive's remuneration requirements, ESMA has issued detailed remuneration guidelines. The guidelines introduce the principle of proportionality, which allows AIFMs to comply with the remuneration restrictions in a way and to the extent that is appropriate to their size, internal organization, and the nature, scope and complexity of their activities.[600]

Moreover, the Directive places limits on the reuse of AIF assets by depositaries and prime brokers, a practice widely known as 'rehypothecation'. 'Rehypothecation' is the practice that allows a prime broker or a depositary to use client assets for its own funding.[601] In a typical transaction, the prime broker or depositary will utilize client assets in order to obtain secured financing via the repo market. Rehypothecation entails several financial stability risks.[602] First, the prime broker or depositary client loses the ownership of the rehypothecated assets, which is replaced with a contractual claim to the return of equivalent assets. As a result, the client will be treated as an unsecured creditor in a prime broker or depositary bankruptcy. Moreover, rehypothecation amplifies leverage and procyclicality in the financial system since the same collateral assets can be rehypothecated multiple times. In addition, the practice of rehypothecation creates shadow chains of transactions outside the regulatory purview. Article 14(3) provides that when the AIFM uses the services of a prime broker, the terms of the prime brokerage relationship, and in particular the possibility of transfer and reuse of AIF assets, shall be set out in a written contract.[603] In addition, AIFMs are required to act with due skill, care and diligence in the selection and appointment of prime brokers. Article 21(10) curbs the ability of depositaries to reuse AIF assets.[604] The reuse of AIF assets is only possible with the prior consent of the AIF or the AIFM. If the depositary has delegated its safekeeping functions to a third party, the third party

597. *Ibid.*, Annex II(1)(m)-(n), at 70-71.
598. *Ibid.*, Annex II(1)(o), at 71.
599. *Ibid.*, Annex II(3), at 71.
600. 'Guidelines on Sound Remuneration Policies Under the AIFMD' (ESMA, 3 July 2013), 10-12.
601. Manmohan Singh and James Aitken, 'Deleveraging after Lehman-Evidence from Reduced Rehypothecation', *IMF Working Paper* WP/09/42 (2009): 3-4.
602. European Commission, 'Reporting and Transparency of Securities Financing Transactions – Frequently Asked Questions', news release, Brussels, 29 January 2014, http://europa.eu/rapid/press-release_MEMO-14-64_el.htm.
603. Directive 2011/61/EU of the European Parliament and of the Council of 8 June 2011 on Alternative Investment Fund Managers and Amending Directives 2003/41/EC and 2009/65/EC and Regulations (EC) No. 1060/2009 and (EU) No. 1095/2010, 2011 O.J. (L 174) 1 Art. 14(3), at 24.
604. *Ibid.*, Art. 21(10), at 30.

may reuse AIF assets only after obtaining the prior consent of the AIF or the AIFM and notifying the depositary.[605]

Furthermore, the AIFM Directive introduces mandatory reporting requirements that will allow national supervisors to assess the systemic risk posed by the activities of hedge funds. An AIFM must furnish to national supervisors information on, among other things, the main instruments and markets in which it is trading, the principal exposures and most important concentrations of the AIF(s) managed, any new arrangements for managing liquidity risk, the risk profile of the AIF(s) managed, the risk management systems employed, the main categories of assets in which the AIF(s) has invested and the results of stress tests.[606] What is more, for AIFs employing leverage on a substantial basis,[607] the AIFM must disclose to national supervisors detailed information about the leverage employed, including a breakdown between leverage arising from borrowing of cash or securities and leverage obtained through the use of derivatives, the identity of the five largest sources of borrowed cash or securities for each AIF managed and the amount of leverage obtained and the extent to which AIF assets have been reused.[608] The frequency of disclosure depends on the amount of AUM.[609]

The information gathered will be used by national supervisors for identifying the extent to which leverage amplifies systemic risk, risks of disorderly markets and risks to the long-term growth of the economy.[610] National supervisors are required to make all information available to competent authorities of other Member States, ESMA and

605. *Ibid.*, Art. 21(11)(d)(iv), at 31.
606. Directive 2011/61/EU of the European Parliament and of the Council of 8 June 2011 on Alternative Investment Fund Managers and Amending Directives 2003/41/EC and 2009/65/EC and Regulations (EC) No. 1060/2009 and (EU) No. 1095/2010, 2011 O.J. (L 174) 1, Art. 24(1) & (2), at 34.
607. An AIF employs leverage on a substantial basis if the ratio of the AIF's exposure calculated in accordance with the commitment method to NAV exceeds 3. 'Commission Delegated Regulation (EU) No 231/2013 of 19 December 2012 Supplementing Directive 2011/61/EU of the European Parliament and of the Council with Regard to Exemptions, General Operating Conditions, Depositaries, Leverage, Transparency and Supervision, Art. 6, 2013 O.J. (L 83) 1, at 21', Art. 111, at 63-64.
608. Directive 2011/61/EU of the European Parliament and of the Council of 8 June 2011 on Alternative Investment Fund Managers and Amending Directives 2003/41/EC and 2009/65/EC and Regulations (EC) No. 1060/2009 and (EU) No. 1095/2010, 2011 O.J. (L 174) 1, Art. 24(4), at 35.
609. 'Commission Delegated Regulation (EU) No 231/2013 of 19 December 2012 Supplementing Directive 2011/61/EU of the European Parliament and of the Council with Regard to Exemptions, General Operating Conditions, Depositaries, Leverage, Transparency and Supervision, Art. 6, 2013 O.J. (L 83) 1, at 21', Art. 110, at 62-63.
610. Directive 2011/61/EU of the European Parliament and of the Council of 8 June 2011 on Alternative Investment Fund Managers and Amending Directives 2003/41/EC and 2009/65/EC and Regulations (EC) No. 1060/2009 and (EU) No. 1095/2010, 2011 O.J. (L 174) 1 Art. 25(1), at 35. For AIFMs managing AIFs whose assets under management exceed EUR 100 million or EUR 500 million (if the funds do not use leverage and do not allow investors redemptions for the first five years) but do not exceed EUR 1 billion, the relevant information must be disclosed on a half-yearly basis. Nonetheless, reporting must be made on a quarterly basis for each AIF with more than EUR 500 million in assets under management. If the AIFM's assets under management exceed EUR 1 billion, disclosure must be made on a quarterly basis.

ESRB.[611] Furthermore, the Directive obliges AIFMs to introduce leverage limits with respect to each AIF they manage, while national supervisory authorities may impose limits to the level of leverage and other restrictions on the management of the AIF in order to safeguard financial stability.[612] Finally, national competent authorities have the power to suspend redemptions in the interest of the unitholders or the public.[613]

Moreover, if a substantial threat exists, originating or aggravated by the activities of AIFMs, to the orderly functioning and integrity of the financial market or to the stability of the whole or a part of the financial system in the European Union and there are cross-border implications and the relevant competent authorities have not taken measures to address the threat or the measures that have been taken do not sufficiently address the threat, ESMA may request the competent authorities to prohibit the marketing of units or shares of AIFs managed by non-EU AIFMs or of non-EU AIFs managed by EU AIFMs, impose restrictions on non-EU AIFMs relating to the management of an AIF in case of excess concentration of risk in a specific market on a cross-border basis or impose restrictions on non-EU AIFMs relating to the management of an AIF where its activities potentially constitute an important source of counterparty risk to a credit institution or other SIFI.[614]

The measures requested must not create regulatory arbitrage, not result in a detrimental impact on the efficiency of markets, including reduced liquidity in markets or the creation of uncertainty for market participants, and must effectively address the threat to the orderly functioning and the integrity of financial markets or to the stability of the whole or a part of the financial system in the European Union or significantly improve the ability of competent authorities to monitor the threat.[615] Pursuant to Article 47(10), the competent authorities may challenge ESMA's decision. It should be stressed that ESMA can only request and not carry out itself the above-mentioned actions. Nonetheless, as Moloney notes, 'the AIFM Directive does not envisage the national competent authorities not complying with the ESMA request'.[616]

What is more, according to Article 25(7) of the AIFM Directive, ESMA may determine that the leverage employed by an AIFM, or by a group of AIFMs, poses a substantial risk to the stability and integrity of the financial system and may issue advice to competent authorities specifying the remedial measures to be taken, including limits on the level of leverage. It should be noted that the advice that ESMA can issue pursuant to Article 25(7) is not binding upon national authorities. Nevertheless, where national supervisory authorities refuse to follow EMSA's advice, they must

611. *Ibid.*, Art. 25(2), at 35.
612. *Ibid.*, Art. 25(3), at 35. Prior to adopting any measure national supervisors must seek the advice of ESMA.
613. AIFM Directive Art. 46(2)(j). The ESRB has recommended that the Commission clarifies the role of NCAs and ESMA when using this instrument and provides guidance on the circumstances under which the NCA can suspend redemptions in the public interest. '*ESRB Response to the European Commission Consultation on the Review of AIFMD*' (2021), 17-19.
614. *Ibid.*, Art. 47(4) & (5), at 58.
615. *Ibid.*, Art 46(6), at 58-59.
616. Moloney Niamh, *EU Securities and Financial Markets Regulation* (Oxford University Press, 2014), 310-12.

provide reasons for their non-compliance.[617] ESMA may disclose the non-compliance and related reasons.

A positive aspect of the Directive is the introduction of a pan-European passporting regime for AIFM's management and marketing activities.[618] The passporting regime aims to deepen the integration of the European AIF industry. The AIFM distinguishes between the authorization of EU AIFMs and non-EU AIFMs and the management and marketing of EU AIFs and non-EU AIFs. EU-based managers are allowed, immediately after the entry of the Directive into force, to manage EU AIFs established in another Member State either directly or by establishing a branch, provided that the AIFM is authorized to manage that type of AIF.[619] An AIFM wishing to manage EU AIFs established in another Member State must disclose certain information to the competent authorities of its home Member State, which must then transmit the information to the authorities of the host Member State. National private placement regimes are inapplicable for these transactions.

Moreover, the AIFM Directive abolishes national private placement regimes governing the marketing of EU AIFs by EU AIFMs. EU AIFMs are allowed to market units or shares of EU AIFs to professional investors in the home Member State of the AIFM and any other Member State on the basis of the marketing passport provided by the AIFM Directive.[620] The passport process involves the submission of a notification to

617. Directive 2011/61/EU of the European Parliament and of the Council of 8 June 2011 on Alternative Investment Fund Managers and Amending Directives 2003/41/EC and 2009/65/EC and Regulations (EC) No. 1060/2009 and (EU) No. 1095/2010, 2011 O.J. (L 174) 1 Art. 25(7), at 35.
618. 'Marketing of AIFs' is defined as 'a direct or indirect offering or placement at the initiative of the AIFM or on behalf of the AIFM of units or shares of an AIF it manages to or with investors domiciled or with a registered office in the Union'. *Ibid.*, Art. 4(1)(x), at 18. Significant uncertainty exists due to Member States' diverging approaches to the definition of marketing. In particular, Member States adopt different approaches as regards to when marketing commences. As a result, the Commission introduced amendments to AIFM Directive creating a harmonized regulatory and supervisory approach to pre-marketing activities for AIFs managed by EU AIFMs. Pre-marketing is defined as 'the provision of information or communication, direct or indirect, on investment strategies or investment ideas by an EU AIFM or on its behalf, to potential professional investors domiciled or with a registered office in the Union in order to test their interest in an AIF or a compartment which is not yet established, or which is established, but not yet notified for marketing in accordance with Article 31 or 32, in that Member State where the potential investors are domiciled or have their registered office, and which in each case does not amount to an offer or placement to the potential investor to invest in the units or shares of that AIF or compartment'. *See* Art. 2 Directive (EU) 2019/1160 of the European Parliament and of the Council of 20 June 2019 amending Directives 2009/65/EC and 2011/61/EU with regard to cross-border distribution of collective investment undertakings 2019, O.J. (L 188) 106. Members must allow an authorized EU AIFM to engage in pre-marketing, except where the information provided to investors is sufficient to allow them to commit to acquiring units or shares of a particular AIF, amounts to subscription forms whether in draft or final form or amounts to constitutional documents, a prospectus or offering documents of an AIF which has not yet been established, in a final form. Furthermore, EU AIFMs are required to notify national competent authorities within two weeks of commencing pre-marketing.
619. *Ibid.*, Art. 33, at 41.
620. *Ibid.*, Arts 31 & 32, at 39-40. Professional investors are defined by reference to the original MiFID Directive. Pursuant to Art. 4(1)(ag) 'professional investor' means an investor which is considered to be a professional client or may, on request, be treated as a professional client

the competent authorities of the home Member State and the transmission of the notification to the competent authorities of Member States, other than the home Member State, where the AIFM intends to market AIFs. AIFMs may also manage non-EU AIFs without marketing them in the EU provided that the AIFM complies with all the requirements established in the AIFM Directive, except for Articles 21 (depositary requirements) and 22 (annual reporting to investors), and appropriate cooperation arrangements for exchange of information are in place between the competent authorities of the home Member State of the AIFM and the supervisory authorities of the third country in which the non-EU AIF is established.[621]

According to the AIFM Directive, the marketing passport for EU AIFMs managing non-EU AIFs and the management and marketing passport for non-EU AIFMs managing AIFs will not be available for two years after the entry of the Directive into force when ESMA is obliged to issue an opinion to the European Commission on the functioning of the management and marketing passports for EU AIFMs managing and/or marketing EU AIFs and the functioning of the national private placement regimes and an advice on the application of the passport and whether it should be extended to non-EU AIFs and non-EU AIFMs managing and/or marketing AIFs.[622] Upon the positive advice and an opinion from ESMA, the European Commission must within three months after receiving ESMA's positive advice and opinion adopt a delegated act providing for the extension of the passport.[623] If the European Commission decides to introduce the passport, then the passport and the national private placement regimes will coexist until three years after the entry into force of the Commission delegated act when ESMA is required to issue a further opinion on the termination of the national private placement regimes.[624] Within three months of ESMA's positive opinion, the European Commission must adopt a delegated act terminating national private placement regimes.[625]

On 30 July 2015, ESMA published its advice in relation to the extension of the passport to non-EU AIFMs and AIFs assessing six jurisdictions – Hong Kong, Jersey,

---

within the meaning of Annex II to Directive 2004/39/EC. According to Annex II MiFID, a professional client is a client who possesses the expertise, experience and knowledge to make informed investment decisions and assess the risks. MiFID introduces a list of entities that are deemed to be professional clients, including credit institutions, investment firms, insurance companies, pension funds, collective investment schemes, national and regional governments. Other clients, including private individual investors, can request to be treated as professional clients provided that certain criteria and procedure are followed. In particular, two of the following criteria must be fulfilled: (a) the client has carried out transactions, in significant size, on the relevant market at an average frequency of ten per quarter over the previous four quarters; (b) the size of the client's financial instrument portfolio, defined exceeds EUR 500.000; (c) the client works or has worked in the financial sector for at least one year in a professional position, which requires knowledge of the transactions or services envisaged. The clients must make their request in writing, the investment firms must give them a written warning of the protections they may lose and they must state in writing that they are aware of the consequences of losing the protections.

621. *Ibid.*, Art. 34, at 42.
622. *Ibid.*, Art. 67, at 64.
623. *Ibid.*
624. *Ibid.*, Art. 68, at 65.
625. *Ibid.*

Singapore, Switzerland, the US and Guernsey.[626] Following this initial advice, ESMA received a letter from the European Commission, which invited ESMA to submit by 30 June 2016 its advice on the assessment of the countries included in its first advice for which no definite views could be reached and assess another six jurisdictions, namely Australia, Bermuda, Canada, the Cayman Islands, the Isle of Man and Japan. ESMA published its advice on 18 July 2016.[627] ESMA advised positively on the extension of the marketing passport to Canada, Guernsey, Japan, Jersey and Switzerland. As far as Australia is concerned, ESMA's positive advice is conditioned on certain actions that must be taken by the Australian Securities and Investment Committee.

With regard to Hong Kong and Singapore, ESMA found no significant obstacles to the extension of the passport subject to certain caveats regarding market access. As far as the US is concerned, ESMA took the view that certain aspects of the US regulatory regime created the risk of an uneven level playing field and urged EU legislators to adopt certain mitigating actions before extending the passport to the US. ESMA was unable to reach a definite view with regard to Bermuda, the Cayman Islands and the Isle of Man. Concerning its opinion on the functioning of the EU passport and the national private placement regimes, ESMA, in its July 2015 opinion, considered that, taking into account the delay in the implementation of the AIFM Directive together with the delay in the transposition in some Member States, a definitive assessment of their functioning is difficult and therefore recommended a further opinion after a longer period.[628]

The European Commission has not yet adopted the delegated act required to activate the third-country regime. As a result, until the European Commission decides upon the positive advice of ESMA to extend the management and marketing passport, an EU AIFM managing a non-EU AIF and a non-EU AIFM managing an EU or a non-EU AIF may market an AIF(s) to professional investors in the EU on a country-by-country basis under Member States' private placement regimes. National private placement regimes are enacted at the discretion of each individual Member State and cover marketing in the domestic market. Regarding EU AIFMs managing non-EU AIFs, marketing is allowed provided that the AIFM complies with all the requirements of the Directive except for Article 21, appropriate cooperation arrangements are in place between the relevant EU and non-EU competent authorities and the third country where the non-EU AIF is established is not listed as a Non-Cooperative Country and

626. European Securities and Markets Authority, *ESMA'S Opinion to the European Parliament, Council and Commission and Responses to the Call for Evidence on the Functioning of the AIFMD EU Passport and of the National Private Placement Regimes* (30 July 2015).
627. *ESMA's Advice to the European Parliament, the Council and the Commission on the Application of the AIFMD Passport to Non-EU AIFMS and AIFS* (18 July 2016).
628. *ESMA's Opinion to the European Parliament, Council and Commission and Responses to the Call for Evidence on the Functioning of the AIFMD EU Passport and of the National Private Placement Regimes.*

Territory by FATF.[629] Individual Member States are allowed to impose stricter rules on the AIFM regarding the marketing of its units or shares in their territory.[630]

As far as non-EU AIFs are concerned, marketing is allowed provided that the non-EU AIFM complies with Articles 22, 23 and 24 (transparency requirements towards investors and national authorities) and Articles 26-30 (requirements on portfolio company disclosure and asset stripping applicable to hedge fund managers) of the AIFM Directive, appropriate cooperation arrangements for the purpose of monitoring systemic risk are in place between the relevant authorities EU and non-EU competent authorities ensuring an efficient exchange of information and the third country where the non-EU AIFM or the non-EU AIF is established is not listed as a Non-Cooperative Country and Territory by FATF.[631] Individual Member States are permitted to impose stricter rules on a non-EU AIFM marketing an AIF(s) in their territory.[632]

Assuming that the European Commission acting upon the positive advice of ESMA extends the management and marketing passport to non-EU AIFMs, non-EU AIFMs intending to manage EU AIFs and/or market AIFs managed by them in the Union must acquire prior authorization by the competent authorities of their Member State of reference and comply with all the requirements of the Directive.[633] Nonetheless, if compliance with a provision of the Directive is incompatible with compliance with the law to which the non-EU AIFM or the non-EU AIF marketed in the Union is subject, the non-EU AIFM may evade compliance with the relevant provision of the Directive.[634]

The non-EU AIFM must demonstrate that it is impossible to combine compliance with the Directive with compliance with a mandatory provision in the law to which the non-EU AIFM and/or the non-EU AIF marketed in the Union is subject, and that the law to which the non-EU AIFM and/or the non-EU AIF is subject provides for an equivalent rule having the same regulatory purpose and offering the same level of protection to the investors of the relevant AIF and the non-EU AIFM and/or the non-EU AIF complies with the equivalent rule.[635] Furthermore, the non-EU AIFM must appoint a legal representative established in its Member State of reference, which will act as the contact point of the AIFM in the European Union and ensure, together with the AIFM, compliance with the requirements of the AIFM Directive. Moreover, appropriate cooperation arrangements ensuring an efficient exchange of information must be in place between the authorities of the Member State of reference, the authorities of the home Member State of the EU AIFs concerned and the authorities of the third country where the non-EU AIFM is established. Further, the third country where the non-EU

629. Directive 2011/61/EU of the European Parliament and of the Council of 8 June 2011 on Alternative Investment Fund Managers and Amending Directives 2003/41/EC and 2009/65/EC and Regulations (EC) No. 1060/2009 and (EU) No. 1095/2010, 2011 O.J. (L 174) 1 Art. 36(1), at 44.
630. *Ibid.*, Art. 36(2), at 44.
631. *Ibid.*, Art. 42(1), at 55.
632. *Ibid.*, Art. 42(2), at 55.
633. *Ibid.*, Art. 37(1), at 44.
634. *Ibid.*, Art. 37(2), at 45.
635. *Ibid.*

AIFM is established must not be listed as a Non-Cooperative Country and Territory by FATF and the third country must have signed an agreement with the Member State of reference, which complies with the standards set by the OECD Model Tax Convention and ensures an efficient exchange of information relating to tax matters.[636]

Authorized non-EU AIFMs may benefit from the management passport and manage EU AIFs established in a Member State other than their Member State of reference either directly or by establishing a branch.[637] In order to benefit from the management passport, non-EU AIFMs must disclose certain information to the authorities of their Member State of reference, who must then transmit the information to the competent authorities of the host Member States of the AIFM.[638]

Moreover, authorized non-EU AIFMs may market units or shares of EU and non-EU AIFs in the European Union utilizing the marketing passport offered by the AIFM Directive. Article 39 of the AIFM Directive regulates the marketing of EU AIFs to EU professional investors.[639] An AIFM intending to market units or shares of EU AIFs in its Member State of reference must submit a notification to the competent authorities of its Member State of reference with respect to each EU AIF that it intends to market. In case the AIFM intends to market units or shares of an EU AIFs in Member States other than its Member State of reference, the AIFM shall submit a notification to its Member State of reference in respect of each EU AIF that it intends to market, which must then transmit the notification to the authorities of the Member States where the units or shares of the EU AIFs are intended to be marketed.

Non-EU AIFMs intending to market units or shares of non-EU AIFs must comply with additional requirements. In particular, appropriate cooperation arrangements must be in place between the authorities of the Member State of reference and the supervisory authority of the third country where the non-EU AIF is established ensuring an efficient exchange of information, the third country where the non-EU AIF is established must not be listed as a Non-Cooperative Country and Territory by FATF and the third country where the non-EU AIF is established must have signed an agreement with the Member State of reference and with each other Member States in which the non-EU AIF intends to market ensuring an effective exchange of information in tax matters and complying with the standards set by the OECD Model Tax Convention on Income and on Capital.[640] In order to start marketing non-EU AIFs, a non-EU AIF must notify the competent authorities of its Member State of reference with the authorities being obliged to transmit the notification to the authorities of the other Member States where the AIFM intends to market its funds.[641]

Finally, it should be noted that even though the AIFM Directive provides for the marketing of AIFs strictly to professional investors, Article 43 allows Member States to permit the marketing of EU and non-EU AIFs to retail investors in their territory.[642]

636. *Ibid.*, Art. 37(7), at 46-47.
637. *Ibid.*, Art. 41, at 54.
638. *Ibid.*
639. *Ibid.*, Art. 39, at 51.
640. *Ibid.*, Art. 40, at 54.
641. *Ibid.*
642. *Ibid.*, Art. 43(1), at 56.

Member States may impose stricter requirements than the requirements introduced by the AIFM Directive. Nonetheless, Member States are prohibited from imposing stricter requirements on EU AIFs established in another Member State and marketed on a cross-border basis than on AIFs marketed domestically. Numerous European countries, including Luxembourg, Germany, France and Ireland, have activated the option granted by the AIFM Directive permitting the marketing of AIFs to retail investors in their territory.[643] Where marketing to retail investors is allowed, individual countries seeking to ensure investor protection impose stricter requirements compared to the requirements of the AIFM Directive.[644]

3.2.2.2 An Assessment of the AIFM Directive

In general, the AIFM Directive has been forcefully criticized as a 'political piece of law making'.[645] Rather than responding to the specific risks posed by the activities of each different type of alternative investment vehicle falling under its ambit, the Directive adopts a one-size-fits-all approach imposing uniform requirements on a diverse population of AIFMs.[646] Indeed, scholars have argued that the adoption of the Directive is the culmination of some Member States', especially France's and Germany's,[647] long-standing desire to bring the hedge fund industry under the regulatory radar with the other types of AIFMs being swept along.[648]

Furthermore, a major concern that the provisions of the AIFM Directive seek to alleviate is the perceived lack of adequate protections for investors in hedge funds against hedge fund managers' opportunism. Nonetheless, my analysis in Chapter 2 has demonstrated that regulating hedge funds on investor protection grounds makes little sense. What is more, even if one accepts investor protection as a sound rationale for regulating hedge funds, the Directive contradicts its own stated goal by exempting small hedge funds (below EUR 100 million) from its requirements. The potential for fraud is much greater in small hedge funds with no prior track record and unsophisticated internal controls.

643. 'Report on the Operation of the Alternative Investment Fund Managers Directive (AIFMD) – Directive 2011/61/EU' (European Commission, FISMA/2016/105(02)/C, 10 December 2018), 255-56, https://ec.europa.eu/info/sites/default/files/business_economy_euro/banking_and_finance/documents/190110-aifmd-operation-report_en.pdf.
644. For instance, Luxembourg allows a manager to market Luxembourg-based AIFs to retail investors provided that the AIFs are established pursuant to the specialized product regime introduced by Part II of the UCI Law. Part II of the UCI Law contains stringent capital requirements, risk-spreading requirements and limits on leverage. Law of 12 July 2013 on Alternative Investment Fund Managers, Art. 46(1)(a).
645. Walter Henle & Allan Murry-Jones, 'Alternative Investment Fund Managers Directive', *Skadden, Arps, Meagher, Slate & Flom LLP Memo* (29 November 2010).
646. Johan Terblanche & Marie-Elisa Roussel Neil Robson, 'Preparing for Compliance with the AIFM Directive', *Financier Worldwide* (November 2012).
647. Angela Monaghan, 'U.K. Coalition Faces First Test as Germany, France Push for Tough EU Hedge Fund Rules', The Daily Telegraph, http://www.telegraph.co.uk/finance/newsbysector/banksandfinance/7721923/UK-coalition-faces-first-test-as-Germany-France-push-for-tough-EU-hedge-fund-rules.html.& Awrey, 'The Limits of EU Hedge Fund Regulation', 124.
648. Payne, 'Private Equity and Its Regulation in Europe', 582.

In contrast to investor protection, the safeguarding of financial stability against systemic risk emanating from hedge fund activities in financial markets forms a sound basis for regulating hedge funds. The AIFM Directive introduces numerous provisions applicable to both the largest systemically important funds and small- and medium-sized funds. However, pursuant to our analysis in Chapter 2, financial stability risks emanate solely from the largest hedge funds. In contrast, small- and medium-sized hedge funds are unlikely to contribute to systemic risk.

The provisions of the Directive seek to curb excessive risk-taking, ensure robust liquidity management systems in order to prevent runs by fund investors and creditors, and eliminate the perverse incentives created by excessive and misaligned compensation practices. However, the overwhelming majority of hedge fund managers were already implementing adequate safeguards against the above-mentioned risks making the provisions of the Directive rather trivial. Indeed, hedge fund managers responding to investor demand implement robust risk management systems and controls, which contribute to prudent risk-taking.[649] What is more, hedge funds are rigorously managing the liquidity and maturity mismatch between their assets and liabilities. Nevertheless, the failure of LTCM and empirical evidence strongly suggests that the provisions seeking to ensure robust risk and liquidity management are necessary to tackle the financial stability risks posed by large hedge funds.

The financial crisis revealed severe weaknesses in the design of compensation arrangements of executives in financial institutions. The structure of executive compensation created incentives for excessive risk-taking.[650] Boosting short-term profits at the expense of long-term value became the preferred strategy for executives of financial institutions who were able to walk away with generous compensation packages and shift the losses from their institutions' demise to creditors, shareholders and taxpayers.[651] Nonetheless, there is no evidence that compensation in the AIF management industry led to excessive risk-taking and jeopardized financial stability. Executive compensation problems were prevalent in mainstream financial institutions, such as commercial banks, insurance companies and investment banks.

On the contrary, the unique structure of hedge fund managers' compensation consisting of a performance-based fee of 20% of the fund's profits and a substantial co-investment by the manager ensures prudent risk-taking and an alignment of interests between investors and managers.[652] What is more, the complex provisions

649. Shadab, 'Hedge Fund Governance', 176; Awrey, 'The Limits of EU Hedge Fund Regulation', 122.
650. *See generally* Lucian A Bebchuk and Holger Spamann, 'Regulating Bankers' Pay', *Georgetown Law Journal* 98, no. 2 (2009).
651. *See* Bebchuk, Cohen and Spamann who report that during the 2000-2008 period top executives at Bear Stearns were able to cash out large amounts of performance-based compensation. The authors estimate that top executives at Bear Stearns were able to walk away with compensation reaching USD 1.4 billion while executives at Lehman Brothers derived cash flows reaching USD 1 billion. Lucian A Bebchuk, Alma Cohen and Holger Spamann, 'The Wages of Failure: Executive Compensation at Bear Stearns and Lehman 2000-2008', *Yale Journal on Regulation* 27, no. 2 (2010).
652. *See* Shadab, 'Hedge Fund Governance', 177-79; Hedge Fund Standards Board, *Response to the ESMA Consultation Paper on Guidelines on Sound Remuneration Policies under AIFMD* (September 2012), 1-2; Awrey, 'The Limits of EU Hedge Fund Regulation', 122.

introduced by the Directive are more suitable for large publicly traded institutions and not owner-managed small or midsize hedge funds which do not have sophisticated governance structures.[653] Nevertheless, the systemic risk posed by large TBTF hedge funds and the implicit government guarantees that they enjoy justify restrictions on the compensation of their managers.

Under the provisions of the AIFM Directive, AIFMs must disclose a variety of information to national supervisory authorities allowing thus national competent authorities to monitor systemic risk. Additionally, national supervisory authorities are granted the power to impose leverage limits, restrictions on the management of an AIF, and to suspend redemption in the public interest. Furthermore, ESMA may advise or request the imposition of restrictions, including bans on marketing, in order to safeguard financial stability. However, the tools introduced by the AIFM Directive to tackle the financial stability risks posed by hedge funds exhibit serious drawbacks. Restrictions on the management of an AIF represent a severe form of intrusion on a fund manager's ability to pursue its preferred investment strategy. What is more, the imposition of a ban on marketing an AIF will result in the drying up of an important source of funding, namely investor capital, possibly leading to the distress of the fund. Lastly, even though leverage limits and suspensions of redemptions are useful tools in a supervisor's toolkit, the AIFM Directive neglects other significant tools, such as liquidity ratios and mandatory stress tests conducted by supervisors.

In general, even though one should applaud the genuine desire of European regulators to tackle systemic risk emanating from hedge fund activities, the national supervisory authorities that are responsible for monitoring financial stability risks posed by individual funds, ensuring compliance with the provisions of the Directive seeking to tackle systemic risk and imposing leverage limits and other restrictions on AIFs do not have the relevant expertise in assessing systemic risk and have an overall orientation towards conduct of business supervision.[654] Taking into account that financial crises are rare events and a supervisor's success in safeguarding financial stability cannot be easily observed, supervisors charged with both a financial stability and consumer/investor protection mandate will devote their attention to consumer/investor protection. Policymakers around the world have recognized the perils of combining financial stability supervision and conduct of business supervision

653. Alternative Investment Management Association, *Response to ESMA's Consultation Paper-Guidelines on Sound Remuneration Policies under the Alternative Investment Fund Managers Directive* (September 2012), 1.

654. Council on Foreign Relations, 'A Systemic Regulator for Financial Markets', *Squam Lake Working Group on Financial Regulation Working Paper* (May 2009). For instance, the authorities responsible for the authorization of AIFMs and the monitoring of compliance with the AIFM Directive are the Dutch Authority for Financial Markets (AFM) in the Netherlands, the AMF in France, CONSOB in Italy and BAFIN in Germany. *See* Naftalis and Frankel LLP Kramer Levin, *Asset Management Update Regarding Recent Regulations Affecting Asset Managers in France* (July 2013); Gibson Dunn and Crutcher, *Germany Adopts Capital Investment Act (Kagb) to Implement the European AIFM Directive* (22 July 2013); Financial Conduct Authority, 'Implementation of the Alternative Investment Fund Managers Directive', *Policy Statement 13/5* (June 2013).

in a single agency and have moved towards the so-called twin peaks approach.[655] Interestingly though, numerous EU Members States have assigned hedge fund systemic risk supervision to national authorities predominantly charged with business conduct supervision.

Furthermore, the AIFM Directive leaves the fragmentation of hedge fund supervision across national lines intact. Home supervisors of the AIFM have the exclusive authority to monitor systemic risk, ensure compliance with the provisions of the Directive and impose leverage limits and other restrictions on AIFs. However, the cross-border nature of hedge fund activities creates systemic risk in markets other than their home one. The objective of home supervisors is to ensure financial stability in their own market.[656] As a result, they will not internalize the costs of increased systemic risk in foreign markets. Additionally, home supervisors seeking to promote their financial industry have an incentive to adopt a lenient stance towards domestic hedge funds posing risks solely to the financial stability of foreign markets. In cases where hedge funds create systemic risk to markets other than their own, host supervisors have no power to intervene, leaving them exposed to the actions of home supervisors.[657]

It should be noted that Articles 47(4) & (5) and 25(7) grant ESMA certain exceptional powers. While the exceptional powers granted to ESMA are a correct step towards addressing the forbearance of national authorities, they still suffer from significant shortcomings. Most importantly, ESMA is an agency, which is predominantly focused on securities markets and their regulation. As a result, ESMA does not have the technical resources and the expertise to monitor and address financial stability risks emanating from the hedge fund sector.

Pursuant to Article 69 of the Directive, the Commission was required by 22 July 2017 to begin a review of the application and scope of the Directive and the degree to which its objectives have been achieved and propose if necessary appropriate amendments. In this context, the Commission commissioned KPMG to conduct a general survey and carry out an evidence-based study and submitted its own report to the European Parliament and the Council.[658] The Commission report finds that the EU AIF

655. *See generally* Hélène M Vletter-van Dort, 'Some Challenges Facing European Central Banks as Supervising Authority', *European Company and Financial Law Review* 9, no. 2 (2012).
656. *See* Katharina Pistor, 'Host's Dilemma: Rethinking EU Banking Regulation in Light of the Global Crisis', in *Festschrift Für Klaus J. Hopt Zum 70. Geburtstag Am 24. August 2010, Unternehmen, Markt Und Verantwortung*, ed. Grundmann Stefan et al. (De Gruyter, 2010), 2345-56.
657. In response to the perverse incentives created by national supervision in the field of banking regulation, the European Union has moved forward with transferring supervisory authority for Eurozone countries' banking institutions to the European Central Bank, which will become a supranational supervisor. EU countries whose currency is not the euro can also decide to transfer supervisory authority to the European Central Bank. *See* Council Regulation (EU) No. 1024/2013 of 15 October 2013 conferring specific tasks on the European Central Bank concerning policies relating to the prudential supervision of credit institutions L. 2287/63 & Guido A Ferrarini and Luigi Chiarella, 'Common Banking Supervision in the Eurozone: Strengths and Weaknesses', *ECGI-Law Working Paper* No. 223 (2013).
658. 'Report from the Commission to the European Parliament and the Council Assessing the Application and the Scope of Directive 2011/61/EU of the European Parliament and of the Council on Alternative Investment Fund Managers' (European Commission, COM(2020) 232

market has grown exponentially since the introduction of the Directive. Nevertheless, the KPMG report finds that the Directive had no statistically significant effect on AIF net assets.[659] Moreover, according to the Commission report, the AIFM passport has contributed to increased cross-border distribution of AIFs. However, the Commission considers that divergent interpretations of the AIFM Directive by national regulators, divergences in national marketing rules, national gold-plating and the availability of the EU passport only for marketing to professional investors hamper the growth of the internal market for AIFs. Moreover, according to the Commission's report, the depositary regime, rules on conflicts of interest, disclosure and transparency requirements have achieved their goal of investor protection. Furthermore, supervisory reporting requirements introduced by the Directive have allowed regulators to monitor and assess systemic risk emanating from the sector. The Commission's report highlights the danger to financial stability posed by the growth of non-bank lending and considers that more information regarding leveraged loans and CLOs as well as the links between the banking sector and shadow banking sector is needed.[660]

However, the AIFM Directive has been heavily criticized by industry participants, who are concerned about the increased costs for hedge fund managers operating in Europe. Indeed, a study commissioned by the FSA regarding the original Commission Proposal concluded that one-off compliance costs could amount up to EUR 3.2 billion, whereas ongoing costs could exceed EUR 1.4 billion per year.[661] In particular, the rising compliance costs are severely impacting smaller fund managers.[662] It has been estimated that in 2014 compliance costs for funds with no more than USD 350 million of AUM rose by 31 %.[663] Indeed, it has been suggested that the typical management fee of 2 % is becoming increasingly insufficient for covering the costs of running a smaller fund. Mounting costs have forced many smaller funds to shut down with their managers joining hedge fund platforms, such as Man Group, which host multiple managers and typically offer them trading infrastructure, legal, compliance and marketing support.[664]

In a study commissioned by InvestEurope, the world's largest association of private capital providers, industry participants noted that the provisions of the

final, 10 June 2020); 'Report on the Operation of the Alternative Investment Fund Managers Directive (AIFMD) – Directive 2011/61/EU'.

659. 'Report on the Operation of the Alternative Investment Fund Managers Directive (AIFMD) – Directive 2011/61/EU', 23.

660. CLOs are asset-backed securities backed by a portfolio of leveraged loans to businesses. Leveraged loans are loans extended to risky corporate borrowers with poor credit ratings and high debt levels. Leveraged loans are usually extended in cases of extraordinary corporate transactions, such as LBOs, recapitalizations and mergers and acquisitions. *See* 'Vulnerabilities Associated with Leveraged Loans and Collateralised Loan Obligations' (Financial Stability Board, 19 December 2019), 3, https://www.fsb.org/wp-content/uploads/P191219.pdf.

661. Charles River Assocs, *Impact of the Proposed AIFM Directive across Europe* (2009), 112-13.

662. Nishant Kumar, 'Costs, Regulations Push Europe's Hedge Fund Minnows to Platforms', Reuters, http://www.reuters.com/article/2015/06/14/us-hedgefund-platform-idUSKBN0OU06I20150614.

663. *Ibid.*

664. *Ibid.*

Directive impose high costs with only modest benefits.[665] In particular, investors, who estimate that the bulk of the costs are borne by them, claim that the Directive has resulted in only a modest improvement in investor protection. In fact, hedge fund managers in the UK have suggested that restrictive regulation imposed by the EU in the aftermath of the financial crisis, most notably the AIFM Directive, was one of the main reasons for supporting Brexit.[666] Furthermore, the enactment of the AIFM Directive has driven foreign hedge fund managers, most notably US based, out of the European market, verifying fears concerning the impact of the Directive on the competitiveness of the European AIF industry.[667] Finally, the reluctance of the Commission to extend the passport to third-country AIFMs and AIFs has created an uneven level playing field between EU and non-EU managers, which have to rely on national private placement regimes.

3.2.3 Hedge Funds and Bank Structural Reform in Europe

The Proposal on Bank Structural Reform was adopted on 29 January 2014 with the objective of safeguarding financial stability in the European Union by tackling the 'too big to fail' dilemma. According to the European Commission, the Proposal 'will curtail the artificial expansion of banks' balance sheets, particularly those activities of a purely speculative nature, thereby reducing the risk that taxpayers have to step in to save failing banks, and reducing the cost and complexity of any resolution when required'.[668] The Proposal on Bank Structural Reform was a follow-up to the so-called Liikanen Report issued in 2012 by the High-Level Expert Group on reforming the structure of the EU banking sector chaired by Erkki Liikanen, Governor of the Bank of Finland.[669] The Liikanen Report recognized the pressing need for structural reform of the EU banking sector and recommended the separation of proprietary trading and other speculative activities into a separate legal entity within the same banking group if the activities to be separated amounted to a significant share of a bank's business or if the volume of these activities could be considered significant from the viewpoint of financial stability. Nonetheless, the Commission's proposal departed in a significant way from the recommendations of the Liikanen Report. In 2017 the Commission decided to withdraw the proposal citing as reasons the lack of progress and foreseeable

665. David Hellier, 'Why Are Hedge Funds Supporting Brexit?', *The Guardian*, https://www.theguardian.com/business/2015/nov/06/why-are-hedge-funds-supporting-brexit; 'European Funds Comment: The Costs (and Benefits) of the AIFMD', Debevoise and Plimpton, https://www.debevoise.com/insights/publications/2018/01/efc-the-costs-and-benefits-of-the-aifmd.
666. Paul Marshall, 'Hedge Funds Seek Refuge from Unfair European Regulations', Financial Times, https://www.ft.com/content/43ecd864-dca6-11e5-8541-00fb33bdf038.
667. Steve Johnson, 'AIFMD: US Hedge Funds Shy Away over EU Regulation', Financial Times, http://www.ft.com/intl/cms/s/0/a181b4a4-ef53-11e4-a6d2-00144feab7de.html#axzz3Zz7CIvNq.
668. 'Proposal for a Regulation of the European Parliament and of the Council on Structural Measures Improving the Resilience of EU Credit Institutions', 2.
669. *High-Level Expert Group on Reforming the Structure of the EU Banking Sector, Final Report* (October 2012).

agreement on the file.[670] Furthermore, the Commission considered that the main financial stability rationale of the proposal has been addressed by other EU regulatory initiatives, most notably the establishment of the European Banking Union.

At its core, the Proposal on Bank Structural Reform prohibited EU banks and groups above a certain size from engaging in proprietary trading and investing in AIFs, entities that sponsor AIFs and financial instruments that track the performance of such funds. It should be noted that the ban on proprietary trading and the ban on investing and sponsoring AIFs work in tandem. A financial institution could easily circumvent a prohibition on proprietary trading by, for instance, investing in hedge funds. Conversely, a ban on investing and sponsoring AIFs (e.g., hedge funds) could be evaded by engaging in proprietary trading. In addition, the proposal granted national supervisors the power to mandate the transfer of high-risk trading activities to a separate legal entity if they determined that the relevant activities pose a threat to financial stability.

According to Article 3 of the proposal, the prohibition on proprietary trading and investing in AIFs, entities that sponsor AIFs and instruments whose performance is linked to such funds would be applicable only to: (a) EU credit institutions and their EU parents (including all branches and subsidiaries) identified as globally SIFIs; and (b) EU credit institutions that are neither parent undertakings nor subsidiaries (including their branches), EU parent companies (including all their branches and subsidiaries) where one of the group entities is an EU credit institution and EU branches of credit institutions established in third countries when for a period of three consecutive years such entities have total assets of at least EUR 30 billion and have trading activities of at least EUR 10 billion or 10% of their total assets.[671] The Proposal defined proprietary trading as trading 'for the sole purpose of making a profit for own account, and without any connection to actual or anticipated client activity or for the purpose of hedging the entity's risk as a result of actual or anticipated client activity, through the use of desks, units, divisions or individual traders specifically dedicated to such position taking and profit making, including through a dedicated web-based proprietary trading platform'.[672] Most importantly, proprietary trading in sovereign debt issued by EU Member States was exempted from the proposal's ban.[673]

The ban on investing in AIFs, entities sponsoring such funds and financial instruments tracking their performance was contained in Article 6(b). The above-mentioned entities would be prohibited from using their own capital or borrowed money to acquire units or shares of AIFs, investing in financial instruments whose

670. 'ANNEX to the Communication from the Commission to the European Parliament, the Council, the European Economic and Social Committee and the Committee of the Regions 2017 COM(2017) 650 Final', 2.
671. The Proposal defined 'Credit institutions' in accordance with Art. 4(1)(1) of 'Regulation (EU) No 575/2013 of the European Parliament and of the Council of 26 June 2013 on Prudential Requirements for Credit Institutions and Investment Firms and Amending Regulation (EU) No 648/2012 Text with EEA Relevance. 2013 O.J. (L 173) 1'. Pursuant to Art. 4(1)(1), a credit institution means 'an undertaking the business of which is to take deposits or other repayable funds from the public and to grant credits for its own account'.
672. 'Proposal for a Regulation of the European Parliament and of the Council on Structural Measures Improving the Resilience of EU Credit Institutions', Art. 6(1)(a), at 26.
673. *Ibid.*, Art. 6(2)(a), at 26.

performance is linked to share or units of AIFs and holding units or shares in an entity that engages in proprietary trading or acquires units or shares in AIFs.[674] AIFs were defined in accordance with the definition set out in Article 4(1)(a) of the AIFM Directive.[675] As a result, the prohibition would cover a wide variety of AIFs, including hedge funds. An exemption was provided for closed-ended and unleveraged AIFs, namely private equity funds, established in the EU or marketed in the EU and certain other categories of alternative investment vehicles, such as venture capital funds.[676]

What is more, Article 9 of the Proposal on Bank Structural Reform would impose on national authorities the duty to review, at least annually, trading activities, in particular activities that are close to proprietary trading, such as market-making,[677] trading in derivatives, other than for hedging purposes, and investments in and acting as sponsor for securitization. The review would encompass an assessment of certain metrics, such as the size of the trading assets relative to total assets, the leverage of trading assets and the complexity of derivatives. If these metrics were exceeded and the competent national authority determined that there is a threat to financial stability of the deposit-taking entities or the stability of the EU financial system, the competent authority would have the power to require the separation of these activities.[678] Furthermore, even if the metrics were not met, the authority might still order a separation if it determined that there is a threat to the financial stability of the deposit-taking institution or to the EU financial system as a whole.[679] When the national authority ordered a split of certain activities, then these trading activities would be placed in a group entity that would be legally, economically and operationally separate from the deposit-taking institution.[680] Pursuant to Article 11, retail banks might still engage in hedging activities in order to manage their capital, liquidity and funding.[681]

Overall, the ban introduced by the Proposal on Bank Structural Reform mimicked the approach taken by US regulators. As it will be explained in Chapter 3, the Volcker Rule found in section 619 of the Dodd-Frank Act prohibits banking entities from engaging in proprietary trading and acquiring or retaining any equity, partnership or other ownership interest in or sponsoring a hedge fund or private equity fund.

674. *Ibid.*, Art. 6(1)(b), at 26.
675. *Ibid.*, Art. 6(1)(b)(i), at 26.
676. *Ibid.*, Art. 6(3), at 26.
677. According to Benos and Wetherilt, 'market makers (MMs) are intermediaries, with an inventory in a given security or financial contract, who continuously provide price quotes at which they are willing to buy and sell that security or contract. They make money by buying low (at the 'bid' price) and selling high (at the 'ask' price). In other words, MMs are rewarded for giving investors the option to trade against them on a continuous basis; that is, they are a source of liquidity'. *See* Benos Evangelos Wetherilt Anne, 'The Role of Designated Market Makers in the New Trading Landscape', *Bank of England Quarterly Bulletin* Q4 (2012): 345.
678. 'Proposal for a Regulation of the European Parliament and of the Council on Structural Measures Improving the Resilience of EU Credit Institutions', Art. 10(1), at 29.
679. *Ibid.*, Art. 10(2), at 29.
680. *Ibid.*, Art. 13, at 32.
681. *Ibid.*, Art. 11, at 30.

3.2.4 Bank Recovery and Resolution and Hedge Funds

The financial crisis revealed the lack of adequate tools to deal with the failure of European banking groups. Member States were forced to resort to costly bank rescues with the total costs of recapitalizations and asset relief measures between 2008 and 2012 amounting to 4.6% of EU 2012 GDP. Furthermore, the cross-border nature of banking in Europe led to severe collection action problems. A notable example was the bailout of Belgian-Dutch Fortis NV, a banking and insurance group with significant operations in Belgium, the Netherlands and Luxembourg.[682] Fortis suffered a severe liquidity crisis in September 2008 stemming from its involvement in the takeover of ABN AMRO by a consortium of bidders led by the Royal Bank of Scotland. The inability of Luxembourgish, Dutch and Belgian authorities to agree on a common bailout plan resulted in the break-up of the group along national lines with the Dutch state nationalizing the Dutch operations of the group and the remaining operations in Luxembourg and Belgium sold to BNP Paribas. Another acute problem witnessed during the crisis was the forbearance of national authorities from recognizing the distress of banking institutions and taking swift action.[683]

Following the costly bailouts during the financial crisis, individual Member States introduced, in an uncoordinated fashion, national resolution regimes with the UK being the first country to adopt a resolution regime designating the BOE as the lead resolution authority.[684] The European Commission, recognizing the need for harmonized domestic resolution mechanisms within the EU, called for the introduction of a minimum set of tools and powers available to national authorities, which would enable them to manage the failure of banking institutions in an orderly way. Consequently, the European Commission in June 2012 adopted a proposal for a Directive establishing a framework for the recovery and resolution of credit institutions and investment firms.[685] The final BRRD was adopted in May 2014 and establishes a common framework for the recovery and resolution of banks and investment firms.[686] The BRRD is applicable across all Member States of the EU and includes provisions concerning recovery and resolution planning, early intervention, resolution tools and powers, and financing arrangements. Furthermore, the Directive provides for the establishment of national resolution authorities, which are responsible for applying the resolution tools and powers.

682. For a short but accurate account of the Fortis debacle *see* Martin Cihák and Erlend Nier, 'The Need for Special Resolution Regimes for Financial Institutions-the Case of the European Union', *Harvard Business Law Review* 2, no. 2 (2012).
683. Jeffrey N Gordon and Wolf-Georg Ringe, 'Bank Resolution in the European Banking Union: A Transatlantic Perspective on What It Would Take', *Columbia Law Review* 115, no. 5 (2015): 1336.
684. For an overview of the different resolution regimes adopted *see ibid.*, at 417-24.
685. 'Proposal for a Directive of the European Parliament and of the Council Establishing a Framework for the Recovery and Resolution of Credit Institutions and Investment Firms and Amending Council Directives 77/91/EEC and 82/891/EC, Directives 2001/24/EC, 2002/47/EC, 2004/25/EC, 2005/56/EC, 2007/36/EC and 2011/35/EC and Regulation (EU) No 1093/2010 (Com 2012) 0280 Final (June 6, 2012)'.
686. For an analysis of the BRRD *see* André Prüm, 'Le Nouveau Cadre Européen Du Traitement Des Faillites Bancaires À Vol D'oiseau', *Revue de Droit Bancaire et Financier* 6 (2014).

The BRRD is applicable to credit institutions and investment firms established in the EU, EU-based branches of credit institutions and investment firms located outside the EU and certain financial holding companies, mixed financial holding companies, mixed-activity holding companies and parent financial holding companies and financial institutions.[687] In order to forestall the disorderly failure of financial institutions, the Directive introduces wide-ranging preventive measures. Covered institutions are required to draw up and maintain recovery plans.[688] Moreover, national competent authorities are granted a broad range of early intervention powers, such as the appointment of a temporary administrator or the ability to demand a change in business strategy.[689]

If early intervention measures fail, then resolution authorities take centre stage. Resolution proceedings can be initiated if: (a) the institution is failing or is likely to fail; (b) there is no reasonable prospect that any private sector measures or supervisory action would prevent the failure of the institution within a reasonable time frame; and (c) resolution action is necessary in the public interest.[690] Article 37(3) of the BRRD provides resolution authorities with a minimum set of resolution tools. Member States must ensure that national resolution authorities have the powers to effect a private sector acquisition of all or part of the assets and liabilities of the institutions ('sale of business tool'); establish a bridge financial company to preserve critical functions ('bridge institution tool'); transfer assets, rights or liabilities of an institution under resolution to one or more asset management vehicles ('asset separation tool'); and convert the institution's debt to equity or write down its debt in order to reduce its liabilities ('bail-in').[691] When applying resolution tools and exercising resolution powers, resolution authorities must seek to ensure the continuity of critical functions, avoid significant adverse effects on financial stability, protect public funds, protect depositors covered by deposit insurance and protect client funds and assets.[692]

---

687. Directive 2014/59/EU of the European Parliament and of the Council of 15 May 2014 Establishing a Framework for the Recovery and Resolution of Credit Institutions and Investment Firms and Amending Council Directive 82/891/EEC, and Directives 2001/24/EC, 2002/47/EC, 2004/25/EC, 2005/56/EC, 2007/36/EC, 2011/35/EU, 2012/30/EU and 2013/36/EU, and Regulations (EU) No. 1093/2010 and (EU) No. 648/2012 of the European Parliament and of the Council, 2011 O.J. (L 173) 1, Art. 1, at 211.
688. *Ibid.*, Art. 5, at 223.
689. *Ibid.*, Art. 27, at 244-45.
690. Resolution proceedings are in the public interest only if they are necessary to achieve and are proportionate to one or more of the resolution objectives, and liquidation of the institution under insolvency proceedings would not meet those resolution objectives.
691. *Ibid.*, Arts 37-44, at 256-71. The bail-in tool has been hailed as one of the most important elements of the EU's resolution regime with its advocates claiming that it is a silver bullet for making creditors and shareholders share the burden of losses in case of a bank failure and avoiding costly government bailouts. For a contrary view claiming that bail-ins can endanger financial stability *see* Goodhart Charles Avgouleas Emilios, 'Critical Reflections on Bank Bail-In', in *The Reform of International Economic Governance*, ed. Antonio Segura Serrano (Routledge, 2015).
692. Directive 2014/59/EU of the European Parliament and of the Council of 15 May 2014 Establishing a Framework for the Recovery and Resolution of Credit Institutions and Investment Firms and Amending Council Directive 82/891/EEC, and Directives 2001/24/EC, 2002/47/EC, 2004/25/EC, 2005/56/EC, 2007/36/EC, 2011/35/EU, 2012/30/EU and

Moreover, Article 71 grants resolution authorities the power to suspend the termination rights of any party to a contract, including derivatives contracts and Repos, with an institution under resolution or a subsidiary of the institution under resolution.[693] Article 68 invalidates so-called *ipso facto* clauses. A crisis prevention measure or a crisis management measure shall not be deemed to be an enforcement event or an insolvency proceeding under a contract entered into by the entity under resolution.[694] Furthermore, according to Article 70, Member States shall ensure that resolution authorities have the power to restrict secured creditors of an institution under resolution from enforcing security interests secured over property of the institution in resolution.[695] Resolution authorities may also suspend any payment or delivery obligations deriving from a contract.[696]

The suspension of termination rights, delivery and payment obligations and security interests is temporary starting from the publication of the notice of the application of resolution tools and ending at midnight at the end of the following business day.[697] Termination rights are permanently suspended if during the suspension period the liabilities covered by the contract have been transferred to another entity or the liabilities covered by the contract are subject to bail-in.[698] What is more, Member States are required to ensure that there is appropriate protection for title transfer financial collateral arrangements and set-off and netting arrangements so as to prevent the transfer of some, but not all, of the rights and liabilities that are the subject of a protected arrangement and to shield protected arrangements from modification of the governing contract.[699]

Furthermore, Article 34 of the BRRD introduces a number of principles that resolution authorities must abide by. Specifically, resolution authorities must ensure that shareholders of the institution under resolution bear losses first, creditors of the institution under resolution bear losses after shareholders in accordance with the order of the priority of their claims under normal insolvency proceedings, the management of

2013/36/EU, and Regulations (EU) No. 1093/2010 and (EU) No. 648/2012, of the European Parliament and of the Council, 2011 O.J. (L 173) 1, Art. 31(2), at 248.

693. *Ibid.*, Art. 71(1), at 299. Termination rights are defined as the right to terminate a contract, a right to accelerate, close out, set-off or net obligations or any similar provision that suspends, modifies or extinguishes an obligation of a party to the contract or a provision that prevents an obligation under the contract from arising that would otherwise arise. *Ibid.*, Art 2(1)(54), at 217.
694. *Ibid.*, Art. 68, at 297.
695. Resolution authorities are not allowed to exercise the above-mentioned power in relation to any security interest held by a central counterparty/systems/system operator over margin or collateral pledged to it by the institution. *Ibid.*, Art. 70(1) & (2), at 299.
696. *Ibid.*, Art. 69 at 298-299.
697. *See ibid.* Arts 70 & 71, at 299-300.
698. *Ibid.*, Art. 70(4), at 299.
699. *Ibid.*, Art. 77 at 304. 'Title transfer financial collateral arrangement' means a title transfer financial collateral arrangement as defined in point (b) of Art. 2(1) of Directive 2002/47/EC of the European Parliament and of the Council of 6 June 2002 on Financial Collateral Arrangements.

the institution is replaced and deposits covered by deposit insurance are fully protected.[700] What is more, creditors of the same class must be treated in an equitable manner and resolution authorities must abide by the 'no creditor worse off principle', namely that no creditor shall incur greater losses than if the institution under resolution had been liquidated under normal insolvency proceedings.[701] Finally, in order to ensure the effective application of the resolution tools, Member States are required to establish national financing arrangements having the power to raise both *ex ante* and extraordinary *ex post* contributions from institutions.[702]

Nonetheless, as Gordon and Ringe note, efforts to harmonize all domestic resolution mechanisms within the EU have been superseded by the project to create a Banking Union.[703] The sovereign debt crisis revealed a toxic link between sovereigns and banks. In order to break this link, the Euro area summit of 2012 decided to move forward with the creation of a Banking Union encompassing a common banking supervisor (SSM), a common resolution authority and fund (SRM) and a common system for deposit guarantees for the Euro area. The second pillar of the Banking Union, the SRM, comprises the SRB and the SRF.[704] The adoption of SRM went through a long process with Germany raising numerous objections regarding the legal basis of the SRM, the powers of the SRB and certain aspects of the SRF. The final SRM Regulation was adopted on 15 July 2014. Furthermore, twenty-six Member States signed in May 2014 an Intergovernmental Agreement on certain aspects of the SRF.[705]

The SRM Regulation applies to credit institutions established in a participating Member State, parent undertakings, including financial holding companies and mixed financial holding companies, established in a participating Member State, which are subject to the ECB's consolidated supervision and investment firms and financial institutions established in participating Member States, whose parent undertakings are under the ECB's consolidated supervision.[706] The SRB is the body responsible for the effective and consistent application of the SRM. The SRB is responsible for drawing up

700. Directive 2014/59/EU of the European Parliament and of the Council of 15 May 2014 Establishing a Framework for the Recovery and Resolution of Credit Institutions and Investment Firms and Amending Council Directive 82/891/EEC, and Directives 2001/24/EC, 2002/47/EC, 2004/25/EC, 2005/56/EC, 2007/36/EC, 2011/35/EU, 2012/30/EU and 2013/36/EU, and Regulations (EU) No. 1093/2010 and (EU) No. 648/2012, of the European Parliament and of the Council, 2011 O.J. (L 173) 1, Art. 34(a)-(c), at 251.
701. *Ibid.*, Art. 34(f) & (g), at 251.
702. *Ibid.*, Arts 103-104, at 326-327.
703. Gordon and Ringe, 'Bank Resolution in the European Banking Union: A Transatlantic Perspective on What It Would Take', 1305-06.
704. For an overview and a critique of the Single Resolution Mechanism *see generally* George S Zavvos and Stella Kaltsouni, 'The Single Resolution Mechanism in the European Banking Union: Legal Foundation, Governance Structure and Financing', in *Research Handbook on Crisis Management in the Banking Sector*, ed. Matthias Haentjens and Bob Wessels (Edward Elgar, 2015).
705. 'Agreement on the Transfer and Mutualization of Contributions to the Single Resolution Fund', (14 May 2014).
706. 'Regulation (EU) No. 806/2014 of the European Parliament and of the Council of 15 July 2014 Establishing Uniform Rules and a Uniform Procedure for the Resolution of Credit Institutions and Certain Investment Firms in the Framework of a Single Resolution Mechanism and a Single Resolution Fund and Amending Regulation (EU) No 1093/2010 O.J. (L 225) 1', Art. 2, at 21. A

resolution plans and the resolution of institutions referred to in Article 2 of the SRM Regulation, which are directly supervised by the ECB either because they are considered to be significant or the ECB has decided to supervise them directly (and all other cross-border groups).[707] National resolution authorities are responsible for the resolution of all other entities, unless resolution requires financing from the SRF, in which case the SRB remains the competent authority.[708]

Pursuant to Article 18 of the SRM Regulation, the SRB is responsible for triggering the resolution procedure and adopting the resolution scheme either on its own initiative or after having received a communication from the ECB.[709] Immediately after the adoption of the resolution scheme stipulating the measures to be taken, the SRB must transmit it to the European Commission, which has the power to either endorse the resolution scheme or present its objections regarding the scheme's discretionary aspects. Following the Commission's objections, the SRB must modify the resolution scheme. Moreover, in certain limited circumstances, Article 18 provides for the involvement of the Council of the European Union in the decision-making process. Upon the endorsement of the resolution scheme, the SRB must instruct the national resolution authorities to execute the scheme and exercise all the relevant resolution powers and tools. It should be stressed that the substantive provisions of the SRM Regulation mirror those of the BBRD.

The second element of the SRM is the SRF, which will be administered by the SRB.[710] The SRB has the authority to decide on the use of the SRF, which shall be used for the purpose of ensuring the effective application of the resolution tools. The target funding level of the SRF is set at 1% of the amount of covered deposits of all credit institutions within the Banking Union, approximately EUR 60 billion, to be reached within eight years. Participating Member States are required to raise *ex ante* and *ex post* contributions on the institutions covered by the SRM and located in their territories and transfer them to the Fund. During a transitional eight-year period, the funds raised at the national level will be allocated to different national compartments of the SRF, which will be progressively merged in a manner such that the national compartments will cease to exist at the end of the transitional period. Upon the SRB's decision, the fund may also borrow directly from the markets.

Finally, it should be noted that non-bank financial institutions, such as hedge funds, are outside the scope of both the BRRD and the SRM Regulation. Nonetheless, in 2012, the European Commission issued a consultation paper on a possible recovery

participating Member State is defined as an EU Member State whose currency is the euro or a non-Euro area participating Member State, which has agreed to participate in the SSM via close cooperation. *Ibid.*, Art. 4, at 24.

707. *Ibid.*, Art. 7(1) & (2), at 26.
708. *Ibid.*, Art. 7(3), at 26.
709. *Ibid.*, Art. 18, at 41-43.
710. *See generally ibid.*, Arts 67-79, at 76-81.

and resolution framework for financial institutions other than banks.[711] The consultation paper mostly dealt with financial market infrastructures, such as central counterparties and central securities depositories, and systemic insurance companies. The consultation only sparingly focused on other non-bank financial institutions, including investment funds. Nonetheless, the consultation paper recognized that the application of ordinary insolvency law, which is currently the only option available (save for a public bailout), may give rise to significant uncertainty. Subsequently, in 2013, the Committee on Economic and Monetary Affairs of the European Parliament issued a report on a recovery and resolution framework for non-bank institutions calling on the Commission to prioritize recovery and resolution of central clearing counterparties and central securities depositories exposed to credit risk, and to consider whether it is appropriate to introduce similar legislation for other financial institutions, including asset managers, and insurance companies.[712] The Parliament reiterated its call in its 2015 resolution on building a Capital Markets Union.[713] In 2016, the European Commission released a proposal for a regulation on a framework for the recovery and resolution of central counterparties, which was officially adopted in December 2020.[714] The introduction of the Regulation marks the first effort by the EU to extend resolution to non-bank financial institutions.

3.3 HEDGE FUND REGULATION IN THE UNITED STATES

3.3.1 History of Hedge Fund Regulation in the US

Hedge funds did not garner the attention of US regulators until the near collapse of LTCM in 1998. The LTCM incident prompted the first in-depth examination of the financial stability risks posed by the hedge fund industry. In its report, which was issued on 28 April 1999, the PWG considered the lessons learned from the LTCM fallout.[715] Even though the PWG recognized the potential contribution of highly leveraged financial institutions, including hedge funds, to systemic risk, it ultimately

711. Internal Market and Services DG European Commission, *Consultation on a Possible Recovery and Resolution Framework for Financial Institutions Other Than Banks* (2012).
712. 'Motion for a European Parliament Resolution on Recovery and Resolution Framework for Non-Bank Institutions 2013/2047(INI)' (European Parliament, 22 October 2013).
713. 'European Parliament Resolution of 9 July 2015 on Building a Capital Markets Union, 2015/2634(RSP)' (European Parliament, 9 July 2015).
714. *'Proposal for a Regulation of the European Parliament and of the Council on a Framework for the Recovery and Resolution of Central Counterparties and Amending Regulations (EU) No 1095/2010, (EU) No 648/2012, and (EU) 2015/2365'*, Pub. L. No. COM(2016) 856 final (2016).
715. Apart from PWG's report, a second less publicized report was issued by the US General Accounting Office at the request of the US Congress. The report focused on the gaps of the then-existing financial regulatory framework and recommended the expansion of SEC's and CFTC's regulatory authority over unregulated affiliates of securities and futures firms, which were significant providers of leverage to hedge funds, including LTCM, and major players in the OTC derivatives markets. *See* GAO, *Long-Term Capital Management: Regulators Need to Focus Greater Attention on Systemic Risk*.

advised against any form of direct hedge fund regulation.[716] The recommendations of the PWG's report largely centred upon measures to strengthen market discipline, which was considered the most effective tool to constrain excessive leverage and risk-taking.

A few years later, in 2002, the SEC, alarmed by the investor protection implications of the growth of hedge funds, launched a broad examination of the hedge fund industry. The ensuing report, prepared by the SEC staff, identified key areas of concern and offered recommendations for addressing these concerns.[717] The report focused, *inter alia,* on the lack of SEC regulatory oversight over hedge funds and their investment managers; the sweeping retailization of the hedge fund industry driven by the weakening of minimum hedge fund investment requirements; the proliferation of funds of funds and the increased investments in hedge funds by pension funds, universities, endowments, foundations and other charitable organizations; the lack of independent review over the process of valuation of fund assets; and the insufficient disclosure of potential conflicts of interest to hedge fund investors.[718] In order to alleviate the above-mentioned concerns, the report recommended several changes to the regulatory framework governing hedge funds and their managers.[719] Notably, the report urged the SEC to consider requiring hedge fund managers to register as investment advisers under the Advisers Act.

Taking up the report's recommendation to regulate hedge fund managers, the SEC, in 2004, adopted a rule, also known as the 'Hedge Fund Rule', requiring hedge fund managers to register as investment advisers with the SEC under the Advisers Act. Under section 203(b)(3) of the Advisers Act, an investment adviser was exempted from registration under the Advisers Act if it had fewer than fifteen clients in the prior twelve-month period and did not hold itself out to the public as an investment adviser. An investment manager could count an investment fund as a single client for purposes of section 203(b)(3). As a result, a hedge fund manager seeking to avoid registration under the Advisers Act could manage up to fourteen funds, irrespective of the number of investors in these funds. The SEC hedge fund rule, released on 10 December 2004, required investment advisers to count each investor of a private fund towards the threshold of fourteen clients.[720] Consequently, hedge fund managers managing a fund or funds with more than fourteen investors were required to register under the Advisers Act and comply with the Act's requirements. The SEC's decision to regulate hedge

716. Markets, *Hedge Funds, Leverage, and the Lessons of Long-Term Capital Management*, ix ('If further evidence emerges that indirect regulation of currently unregulated market participants is not effective in constraining excessive leverage, there are several matters that could be given further consideration; however, the Working Group is not recommending any of them at this time').
717. Securities and Commission, *Implications of the Growth of Hedge Funds.*
718. *Ibid.*, 79-88.
719. *Ibid.*, 88-104.
720. The rule defined a 'private fund' as 'any company (1) that would be subject to regulation under the Investment Company Act but for the exceptions provided in either section 3(c)(1) or section 3(c)(7); (2) which permitted its investors to redeem their interests within two years of purchasing them; and (3) its interests were offered based on the investment advisory skills, ability or expertise of the investment adviser'. *Ibid.*, at 72073-75.

funds was premised on the need to protect investors with the agency highlighting three noticeable developments in the hedge fund industry, namely the tremendous growth of the hedge fund industry, the increased exposure of ordinary investors to hedge funds and the growing incidence of fraudulent activity by hedge fund managers.[721] Nonetheless, the SEC's regulatory experiment with hedge funds was short-lived. On 23 June 2006, the Court of Appeals for the District of Columbia, in 'Goldstein v SEC', struck down the hedge fund rule as arbitrary.[722]

Following the SEC's unsuccessful regulatory attempt to regulate hedge funds, the PWG released, in February 2007, the 'Agreement Among PWG and U.S. Agency Principals on Principles and Guidelines Regarding Private Pools of Capital'.[723] The PWG's set of principles, which sought to offer US regulators guidance regarding their oversight of private pools of capital, including hedge funds, centred upon the tackling of systemic risk and the protection of investors. According to PWG, the exercise of market discipline by creditors, counterparties and investors remained the most effective tool to alleviate systemic risk concerns.[724] Furthermore, the PWG considered that the protection of investors could best be achieved through market discipline and regulatory barriers limiting hedge fund investing to sophisticated investors.[725] Shortly after the release of the February 2007 agreement, the PWG, in an effort to promote sound industry practices, empanelled two private sector committees, the Asset Managers' Committee, composed of representatives of the hedge fund management industry, and the Investors' Committee, composed of representatives of the hedge fund investor community.[726] The committees were tasked with the development of best practice standards for hedge fund managers and hedge fund investors based on PWG's 2007 set of principles. The committees published their draft reports in April 2008, opening them for public comment. The final best practices, which were released in January 2009, contained recommendations covering a wide range of areas, including disclosure, risk management, valuation of assets, conflicts of interest and due diligence.[727]

Nonetheless, the financial crisis and the widespread belief that hedge funds aggravated or even caused the market turbulence witnessed during 2007 and 2008

721. *Ibid.*, at 72055-59.
722. *Goldstein V. Sec, 451 F.3d 873, 884 (D.C. Cir. 2006)*. For a critique of the SEC's decision to regulate hedge funds *see* Alison S Fraser, 'Sec's Ineffective Move toward Greater Regulation of Offshore Hedge Funds: The Failure of the Hedge Fund Registration Requirement', *Cornell L. Rev.* 92 (2006).
723. *See* 'Agreement among PWG and US Agency Principals on Principles and Guidelines Regarding Private Pools of Capital', (2007).
724. *Ibid.*, 3.
725. *Ibid.*, 1.
726. Investors' Committee President's Working Group on Financial Markets, *Mission Statement*; Asset Managers' Committee President's Working Group on Financial Markets, *Mission Statement*.
727. Asset Managers' Committee, *Best Practices for the Hedge Fund Industry: Report of the Asset Managers' Committee to the President's Working Group on Financial Markets* (15 January 2009); Investors' Committee, *Principles and Best Practices for Hedge Fund Investors: Report of the Investors' Committee to the President's Working Group on Financial Markets* (15 January 2009).

significantly changed the dynamics of hedge fund regulation. The crisis led the US government and US regulatory authorities to reverse their long-standing opposition to any form of direct hedge fund regulation.[728] The comprehensive financial regulatory reform package prepared by the US Treasury in the aftermath of the financial crisis explicitly endorsed the mandatory registration of hedge fund managers and the heightened supervision and regulation of systemically important non-bank financial firms, including hedge funds.[729] What is more, the US government, an ardent opposer of international initiatives in the area of hedge fund regulation, eventually succumbed to international pressure and supported the regulatory plan agreed to by the members of the G20 in April 2009.[730]

The envisioned stricter hedge fund regulatory framework in the US became a reality with the enactment of the Dodd-Frank Act in July 2010. In contrast, to the AIFM Directive, which solely targets the AIF industry, the ambit of the Dodd-Frank Act is much broader. As Skeel notes, the Dodd-Frank Act's objectives are twofold: 'its first objective is to limit the risk of contemporary finance ... ; and the second is to limit the damage caused by the failure of large financial institutions'.[731] The provisions of the Dodd-Frank Act relating to the regulation of hedge funds and their managers can be seen as fulfilling both objectives. It should be stressed that unlike the AIFM Directive, which aims to, apart from mitigating the systemic risk emanating from the hedge fund sector, enhance investor protection, and unlike the SEC's failed regulatory effort, which was exclusively premised on the need to protect investors in hedge funds, the Dodd-Frank hedge fund regime, reflecting the Act's overall objectives, is predominantly driven by the desire to mitigate the financial stability risks posed by the hedge fund industry.

Title IV of the Dodd-Frank Act requires hedge fund managers to register as investment advisers under the Advisers Act of 1940 and disclose sensitive proprietary information to US regulators. The registration and enhanced disclosure requirements allow regulators to monitor the build-up of systemic risk in the hedge fund industry. What is more, according to the provisions of the Dodd-Frank Act, the FSOC may designate hedge funds and/or their managers as SINBFCs, which are subject to the FED's enhanced supervision and regulation. The FSOC designation process extends the regulatory perimeter to any non-bank financial company that could pose a threat to the financial stability of the US. In addition, the Volcker Rule, found in section 619 of the Dodd-Frank Act, prohibits banking entities from sponsoring or retaining any equity, partnership or other ownership interest in a hedge fund, subject to certain exceptions. Furthermore, according to the Volcker Rule, SINBFCs supervised by the FED that

728. Orfeo Fioretos, 'Capitalist Diversity and the International Regulation of Hedge Funds', *Review of International Political Economy* 17, no. 4 (2010). *See also* 'Paulson Tells G7 Let Markets Regulate Hedge Funds', Reuters, https://www.reuters.com/news/picture/paulson-tells-g7-let-markets-regulate-he-idUSDAE00054220070210.
729. Department of the US Treasury, *Financial Regulatory Reform: A New Foundation* (2009), 10-12.
730. Daniel Pimlott, 'G20 Agrees $1,100bn to Fight Crisis', Financial Times, https://next.ft.com/content/5c541a18-1eec-11de-a748-00144feabdc0.
731. Skeel, *The New Financial Deal: Understanding the Dodd-Frank Act and Its (Unintended) Consequences*, 4.

engage in the above-mentioned activities will have to comply with additional capital requirements and quantitative limits. The aim of the Volcker Rule is to reduce excessive risk-taking by SIFIs and prohibit them from benefiting from government support for their speculation at the expense of taxpayers. Finally, in an effort to mitigate the adverse consequences for financial stability resulting from the failure of large interconnected financial companies, the Dodd-Frank Act introduces a new resolution process, termed the 'OLA'.

3.3.2 The Dodd-Frank and Hedge Funds

The adoption of the Dodd-Frank Act led to a radical overhaul of hedge fund regulation in the US. Prior to the adoption of the Dodd-Frank Act, hedge funds in the US fell largely outside the regulatory perimeter. The adoption of the Dodd-Frank significantly altered the regulatory landscape for hedge funds. Hedge funds in the US are for the first time subject to a comprehensive regulatory framework.

3.3.2.1 Hedge Funds and Investment Adviser Regulation

Investment advisers, including hedge fund managers, are regulated on both a federal and state level.[732] The federal regulation of investment advisers is accomplished through the Advisers Act, which mandates the registration of investment advisers, as defined in section 202(a)(11), with the SEC.[733] Registered investment advisers must comply with the provisions of the Advisers Act, which, *inter alia*, impose reporting and record-keeping obligations, grant the SEC inspection rights, mandate the appointment of a chief compliance officer and the adoption and enforcement of a written code of ethics, limit performance-based fees, regulate the custody of client funds and securities and prohibit fraudulent conduct. In general, investment advisers are required to register with the SEC unless they are prohibited from registering pursuant to section 203A of the Advisers Act or an exemption from registration applies.

The allocation of regulatory responsibility over investment advisers between the SEC and the states depends on the size of the investment adviser as measured by its AUM.[734] Prior to the enactment of the Dodd-Frank Act, investment advisers that were

732. Except Wyoming, all US states have enacted legislation regulating investment advisers.
733. Investment Advisers Act §203(a), 15 U.S.C. §80b-3(a). Hedge fund managers fall within the section 202(a)(11) definition of investment adviser and are therefore required to register with SEC unless they are precluded from registering or an exemption from registration applies. State laws generally contain a similar definition of the term 'investment adviser'. Lederman, *Hedge Fund Regulation*, para. 12-2.
734. It should be noted that section 203A(a)(3) defines 'assets under management' as the 'securities portfolios with respect to which an investment adviser provides continuous and regular supervisory or management services'. Seeking to provide guidance on the definition and calculation of 'assets under management', the SEC in its instructions to Form ADV, which investment advisers are required to file in order to register both federally and with the states, introduces the concept of 'regulatory assets under management'. According to Item 5.F, 'regulatory assets under management' include 'securities portfolios for which the adviser provides continuous and regular supervisory and management services'. Item 5.F further

regulated by the state in which they maintained their principal office and place of business were prohibited from registering with the SEC unless they had at least USD 25 million of AUM. States were thus responsible for regulating only the smallest investment advisers with the SEC having authority over larger advisers. The Dodd-Frank retains the prohibition for advisers with less than USD 25 million and introduces a new category of 'mid-sized advisers' raising the floor for federal registration to USD 100 million.[735] Midsized investment advisers, defined as advisers that are required to be registered as investment advisers with state regulators of the state in which they maintain their principal office and place of business, are subject, if registered, to examination by state regulators and have AUM between USD 25 million to USD 100 million, are required to register with the state regulators.[736] As a result, investment advisers with at least USD 100 million of AUM are required to register with the SEC.

However, investment advisers may avoid federal registration by relying on the exemptions from registration granted under the Advisers Act that have been significantly altered with the enactment of the Dodd-Frank Act. Section 203(b)(1) of the Advisers Act, referred to as the intrastate advisers exemption, exempts from registration 'any investment adviser all of whose clients are residents of the State within such investment adviser maintains his or its principal place of business, and who does not furnish advice or issue analyses or reports with respect to securities listed or admitted to unlisted trading privileges on any national securities exchange'.[737] Nonetheless, the Dodd-Frank Act materially altered the scope of the exemption by prohibiting investment advisers to private funds, including hedge fund managers, from relying on the section 203(b)(1) exemption.[738]

By far, the most commonly used exemption by hedge fund managers prior to the enactment of the Dodd-Frank Act was the private adviser exemption found in section 203(b)(3) of the Advisers Act. The Dodd-Frank Act entirely repeals the private adviser exemption replacing it with an exemption from registration for any investment adviser that is a foreign private adviser.[739] The term 'foreign private adviser' is defined as any investment adviser, who has no place of business in the US, has, in total fewer than fifteen clients and investors in the United States in private funds advised by the

provides guidance on the definition of the term 'securities portfolios' and 'continuous and regular supervisory and management services' and the valuation of securities portfolios. *See* Item 5.f of Form PF. Regulatory assets management includes the long and short positions, on a gross basis, of the funds managed and represents a manager's gross assets under management. Most importantly, the measure captures all the leverage, both financial (repos, prime broker financing) and synthetic (leverage obtained through derivatives), employed by the funds in order to gain market exposure. In contrast, industry participants adopt a different approach towards the measurement of assets under management. The metric widely used by industry participants is AUM or NAV. Net AUM management represents the investors' capital at risk, namely the assets of the funds managed minus their liabilities.

735. Dodd-Frank Act §410, 15 U.S.C. §80b-3(a)(1) & 15 U.S.C. §80(a)(2).
736. Dodd-Frank Act §410, 15 U.S.C. §80b-3a(a)(2).
737. Investment Advisers Act §203(b)(1), 15 U.S.C. §80b-3(b)(1).
738. *Ibid.*
739. Dodd-Frank Act §403(2), 15 U.S.C. §80b-3(b)(3).

investment adviser, has aggregate AUM[740] attributable to clients in the US and investors in the US in private funds advised by the investment adviser of less than USD 25 million and neither holds itself out generally to the public in the US as an investment adviser nor acts as an investment adviser to any investment company registered under the Investment Company Act or a company that has elected to be a business development company.[741]

The Dodd-Frank Act adds several other new categories of exemptions from the registration requirement. Section 408 provides an exemption for any investment adviser of private funds if such investment adviser acts as an adviser solely to private funds and has less than USD 150 million of AUM[742] in the US.[743] Furthermore, an exemption is introduced for venture capital fund advisers.[744] Finally, another important exemption, which has been used by notable fund managers during recent years, such as George Soros and Carl Icahn,[745] is the exclusion of family offices from registration and regulation under the Advisers Act. The Dodd-Frank Act introduces section 202(a)(11)(G) of the Advisers Act that explicitly excludes family offices from the definition of investment adviser.[746]

740. Pursuant to Rule 202(a)(30)-1(c)(1) the term 'assets under management' is defined as 'regulatory assets under management'. 17 C.F.R. §275.202(a)(30)-1(c)(1).
741. Dodd-Frank Act §402(a), 15 U.S.C. §80b-2(a)(30).
742. 'Assets under management' are defined as 'regulatory assets management'. *See* 17 C.F.R. §275.203(m)-1(a)(d)(1).
743. Dodd-Frank Act §408, 15 U.S.C. §80b-3(m).
744. Dodd-Frank Act §407, 15 U.S.C. §80b-3(l)(1). A venture capital fund is defined as a private fund that represents to investors and potential investors that it is following a venture capital strategy; holds a minimum of 80% of its assets in short-term holding or qualifying investments, defined as equity securities issued by a qualifying portfolio company and acquired by the fund directly from the qualifying portfolio company, which is a company that is not subject to the reporting requirements under section 13 or 15d of the Securities Exchange Act of 1934 or does not have a security listed or traded on any exchange or organized market operating in a foreign jurisdiction, does not borrow or issue debt obligations in connection with the fund's investment and does not distribute to the fund the proceeds of such borrowing or issuance in exchange for the fund's investment and is not an investment company, private fund, a commodity pool or an issuer that would be an investment company but for the exemption provided by Rule 3a-7 under the 1940 Act; does not borrow, issue debt obligations, provide guarantees or otherwise incurs leverage in excess of 15% of the fund's aggregate capital contributions and uncalled committed capital, and any such leverage is for a non-renewable term of no longer than 120 calendar days, excluding certain guarantees by the fund of qualifying portfolio company obligations; does not provide its investors with redemption, withdrawal or repurchase rights, except in extraordinary circumstances; and is not registered under section 8 of the Investment Company Act 1940 and has not elected to be treated as a business development company under the 1940 Act. 17 C.F.R. 275.203(l)-1.
745. Russ Alan Prince, 'From Hedge Fund to Family Office', Forbes, http://www.forbes.com/sites/russalanprince/2013/11/20/from-hedge-fund-to-family-office/.
746. Dodd-Frank Act §409(a), 17 C.F.R. 275.202(a)(11)(G)-1(a). Family offices are entities established by a single family, in order to manage the family fortune. Family offices also provide additional services to family members, including tax and estate planning. Since they typically provide investment advisory services in the course of managing the wealth of a single family, they are considered to be investment advisers within the meaning of the Advisers Act. *See* Lederman, *Hedge Fund Regulation*, 12-23. The SEC has adopted Rule 202(a)(11)(G)-1 of the Advisers Act defining the term 'family office'. Under the rule, a family office is defined as a company that: (a) has no clients other than family clients; (b) is wholly owned by family clients and is exclusively controlled (directly or indirectly) by one or more family members and/or

In order to register not only with the SEC but also with state securities regulators, an investment adviser is required to file Form ADV, which is divided into two parts. Part 1 provides information about the adviser, its AUM, the private funds it manages, the adviser's business and its disciplinary history, while Part 2, also referred to as 'the brochure', contains more detailed information about the adviser's business, including the services offered, the fees charged, the investment strategies employed and potential conflicts of interest.[747] Advisers to private funds, including hedge funds, must disclose additional information regarding the structure, service providers, investors and size of each private fund managed. Investment advisers must update Form ADV annually. Furthermore, it should be noted that even though venture capital fund advisers and advisers of private funds managing less than USD 150 million are not subject to the Advisers Act registration requirement, they are mandated to file an abbreviated Form ADV.[748]

Registration under the Advisers Act subjects investment advisers to periodic disclosure and record-keeping requirements, which have been materially strengthened by the Dodd-Frank Act. The Dodd-Frank authorizes the SEC to require any federally registered investment adviser to private funds to maintain records and file reports 'as necessary and appropriate in the public interest and for the protection of investors, or for the assessment of systemic risk by the FSOC'.[749] In order to facilitate the FSOC's assessment of the systemic risk posed by the AIF industry, the SEC must share all reports and records with the FSOC.[750]

In October 2011, the SEC and the CFTC jointly adopted Form PF requiring registered investment advisers having USD 150 million or more in 'regulatory assets under management'[751] attributable to private funds to periodically disclose highly sensitive and proprietary information.[752] The level and frequency of reporting by hedge fund managers depend on the amount of 'regulatory assets under management'. Hedge fund managers managing hedge funds with less than USD 1.5 billion of 'regulatory assets under management' must file Form PF annually and report information for each hedge fund they advise regarding the fund's gross and net assets, the value of derivatives positions, the fund's borrowings, its performance, the investment strategies employed and significant counterparty exposures. Large hedge fund advisers managing at least USD 1.5 billion in 'regulatory assets under management' attributable to hedge funds are required to file Form PF quarterly and disclose, on an aggregate basis, additional detailed information regarding the exposures of the funds managed to different asset categories. With respect to hedge funds that have a NAV of at least USD

---

family entities; and (c) does not hold itself out to the public as an investment adviser. 17 C.F.R. §275.202(a)(11)(G)-1(b). Family offices meeting the above-mentioned conditions will be excluded from the definition of investment adviser.

747. *See generally* Form ADV General Instructions & Form ADV.
748. Dodd-Frank Act §407-408, 17 C.F.R. §275.204-4.
749. Dodd-Frank Act §404(2), 15 U.S.C. §80b-4(b)(1).
750. Dodd-Frank Act §404(2), 15 U.S.C. §80b-4(b)(7).
751. *See* Rule 204b-(1)(g)(1) providing that 'assets under management' means 'regulatory assets under management' as defined in the Form PF instructions. 17 C.F.R. §275.204(b)-1(g)(1).
752. *See* Commission, *Reporting by Investment Advisers to Private Funds and Certain Commodity Pool Operators and Commodity Trading Advisors on Form Pf.* & 17 C.F.R. §275.204(b)-1.

500 million, hedge fund advisers must report the relevant information about the exposures to different assets on a per fund basis. Additional information to be provided concerns the fund's portfolio liquidity, cash holdings, concentration of positions and collateral holdings. Finally, one should note that in contrast to Form ADV filings, which are publicly available, Form PF filings are strictly confidential.

Federally registered investment advisers must also comply with the extensive record-keeping requirements set forth in Rule 204-2.[753] The list of records required to be maintained is extensive and includes records concerning the adviser's organization, such as its articles of incorporation and partnership agreements, trading records and a variety of accounting records. Pursuant to section 204 of the Advisers Act, the SEC shall conduct periodic inspection of the records maintained by a registered investment adviser and may also conduct such special examinations as the SEC may prescribe.[754]

Furthermore, registration under the Advisers Act subjects investment advisers to several provisions aimed at strengthening investor protection. Most importantly, section 205(a)(1) introduces a ban on performance-based compensation, a crucial component of the hedge fund industry.[755] Nonetheless, an exemption from the prohibition applies for performance-based fees charged to 'qualified clients'.[756] In addition, the Advisers Act mandates the adoption of written compliance policies and procedures designed to prevent violation of the Advisers Act, the appointment of a chief compliance officer and the elaboration and enforcement of a written code of ethics.[757] What is more, Rule 206(4)-2 imposes heightened custodial practices on registered investment advisers that have custody of client funds or securities.[758] Investment advisers are required to maintain client assets with a 'qualified custodian'.[759] Client funds and securities of which advisers have custody must be verified by

753. 17 C.F.R. §275.204-2.
754. Investment Advisers Act §204(b)(6)(A), 15 U.S.C. §80b-4(b)(6)(A).
755. Investment Advisers Act §205(a)(1), 15 U.S.C. §80b-5(a)(1).
756. A 'qualified client' is defined as: (a) any natural person or company that has at least USD 1 million under management by the adviser, (b) any natural person or company that has a net worth of at least USD 2 million, (c) any natural person or company that is a qualified purchaser as defined in section 2(a)(51)(A) of the Investment Company Act, and (d) any executive officer, director, trustee, general partner and certain employees of the adviser. 17 C.F.R. §175.205-3.
757. *See* 17 C.F.R. §275-206(4)-7 & 17 C.F.R. §275.204A-1.
758. 17 C.F.R. §275.206(4)-2. An investment adviser is deemed to have custody of client cash or securities if it acts in any capacity, such as general partner of a limited partnership, managing member of a limited liability company or similar positions for another type of pooled investment vehicle that gives it legal ownership or access to client assets. 17 C.F.R. §275.206(4)-2(d)(2)(iii). A hedge fund manager acting as a general partner of the hedge fund limited partnership and having authority to dispose partnership assets will typically be deemed to have custody of client assets. Alan Porter, Cary Meer, Marticha Cary, *Amendments to Custody Rule under the Investment Advisers Act of 1940* (October 2003), 22.
759. 17 C.F.R. §275.206(4)-2(a)(1). The term 'qualified custodian' is defined to include banks and savings associations, registered broker-dealers, futures commission merchants and foreign financial institutions that customarily hold financial assets for their customers, provided that the foreign financial institution keeps the advisory clients' assets in customer accounts segregated from its proprietary assets. 17 C.F.R. 275-206(4)-2(d)(6). An investment adviser may act as a qualified custodian provided that it falls into one of the above-mentioned categories of financial institutions deemed qualified custodians. In this case, the adviser must obtain no less frequently than once each calendar year a written internal control report

surprise examination, at least annually, by an independent public accountant.[760] Finally, in an effort to curb fraudulent practices by investment advisers, the Advisers Act introduces broad anti-fraud provisions.[761] It should be noted that the Act's anti-fraud provisions are applicable to any investment adviser irrespective of whether or not it is registered with the SEC.

3.3.2.2 Hedge Funds as SIFIs

The financial crisis exposed crucial gaps in the US financial regulatory and supervisory framework and the weaknesses of the traditional micro-prudential approach to financial supervision and regulation, which is concerned primarily with the safety and soundness of individual banking institutions.[762] The stress across markets and institutions witnessed during 2007-2008 led to a fundamental reorientation of the US regulatory and supervisory framework towards a macro-prudential perspective. In contrast to the narrow focus of the micro-prudential approach, which seeks to address idiosyncratic risks faced by individual banks, the macro-prudential approach focuses 'on the stability of the financial system as a whole'.[763] The Dodd-Frank Act firmly endorses the systemic orientation of the macro-prudential approach, most notably by creating the FSOC and giving it a clear statutory mandate to identify risks to the financial stability of the United States, promote market discipline and respond to emerging risks in the US financial system.[764] What is more, in an effort to extend the regulatory and supervisory perimeter to all financial institutions that may contribute to systemic risk, the FSOC is granted the authority to designate a 'nonbank financial company' as systemically important and subject it to supervision and regulation by the FED, if the Council determines that its material distress or the nature, scope, size, scale, concentration, interconnectedness or mix of its activities could pose a threat to the financial stability of the US.[765] The Council designated four non-bank financial companies as systemically important: AIG, General Electric Capital Corporation,

prepared by an independent public accountant that includes an opinion on whether controls are in place regarding the custody of client assets. 17 C.F.R. 275.206(4)-2(a)(6)(ii).

760. 17 C.F.R. §275-206(4)-2(a)(4).
761. Investment Advisers Act §206, 15 U.S.C. §80b-6.
762. *See generally* Karl Whelan, 'The ECB's Role in Financial Supervision', *Working Paper, UCD Centre for Economic Research* WP09/15 (2009); European Central Bank, *Financial Stability Review* (May 2014), 135-41.
763. Crockett Andrew, Brunnermeier Markus K, Goodhart Charles A, Persaud Avinash and Shin Hyun Song, *The Fundamental Principles of Financial Regulation* (Princeton University Press, 2009).
764. Dodd-Frank Act §112, 12 U.S.C. §5322. The FSOC consists of ten voting members and five non-voting members. The voting members are the Secretary of the Treasury, which is also the chairperson of the FSOC; the Chairman of the FED; the Chairman of the SEC; the Chairperson of the CFTC; the Chairman of the FDIC; the Director of the Federal Housing Finance Agency; the Chairman of the National Credit Union Administration; the Comptroller of the Currency, an individual with insurance industry expertise appointed by the US President and the Director of the CFPB. The five non-voting members comprise the director of the OFR, the director of the Federal Insurance Office, a state insurance regulator, a state banking supervisor and a state securities commissioner.
765. Dodd-Frank Act §§113, 115, 12 U.S.C. §§5323, 5325.

MetLife and Prudential Financial. The designation of MetLife was subsequently rescinded by a federal district court,[766] while the Council voted to rescind the designations of AIG, Prudential Financial and General Electric Capital Global Holdings.

Pursuant to section 102 of the Dodd-Frank Act, the term 'nonbank financial company' encompasses both a 'US nonbank financial company' and a 'foreign nonbank financial company'.[767] The term 'US nonbank financial company' is defined as a company that is incorporated or organized under the laws of the United States or any state and is 'predominantly engaged in financial activities'.[768] Furthermore, a foreign non-bank financial company is a company that is incorporated or organized in a country other than the United States and is 'predominantly engaged in, including through a branch in the United States, financial activities'.[769] A company is 'predominantly engaged in financial activities' either if the company derives in either of its two most recently ended fiscal years 85% or more of its annual gross revenues from 'activities that are financial in nature' or if 85% or more of its assets as of the end of either of its two most recently completed fiscal years relate to 'activities that are financial in nature'.[770] The definition of 'activities that are financial in nature' is found in section 4(k)(4) of the BHCA and includes providing financial, investment, or economic advisory services and lending, exchanging, transferring, investing for others, and safeguarding money or securities.[771] Thus, hedge funds and their managers, along with other categories of non-bank financial institutions such as insurance companies, private equity funds and their managers, are captured by the definition of non-bank financial company and may be placed under the FED's supervision and regulation if the FSOC determines that the material distress or activities of the non-bank financial company could pose risks to the financial stability of the US.

Section 113(a)(2) of the Dodd-Frank Act enumerates the factors that the FSOC must take into account in determining whether a non-bank financial company's material distress or activities could jeopardize US financial stability and, therefore, whether a non-bank financial institution should be designated as systemically important.[772] In particular, the FSOC must consider the degree of leverage of the company; the amount and nature of the financial assets of the company; the amount and type of

766. MetLife is a traditional life insurance group headquartered in New York, which is not affiliated with any insured depositary institution. MetLife successfully mounted a legal challenge against the FSOC's designation arguing that it does not pose any risks to the US financial system and that the metrics used by the FSOC in arriving at its determination were flawed. The court held that the FSOC's decision to designate MetLife as systemically important was arbitrary and capricious. The court held that the FSOC's analysis did not lead to a finding that MetLife's distress would cause severe impairment of financial intermediation or of financial market functioning. In addition, the court criticized the FSOC's analysis for failing to consider the costs imposed by the MetLife's designation as a systemically important financial institution. *See* Ryan Tracy and Erik Holm, 'MetLife Wins Bid to Shed 'Systemically Important' Label', The Wall Street Journal, http://www.wsj.com/articles/federal-judge-rescinds-federal-government-determination-that-metlife-is-systemically-important-1459349828.
767. Dodd-Frank Act §102(a)(4)(C), 12 U.S.C. §5311(a)(4)(C).
768. Dodd-Frank Act §102(a)(4)(A), 12 U.S.C. §5311(a)(4)(A).
769. Dodd-Frank Act §102(a)(4)(B), 12 U.S.C. §5311(a)(4)(B).
770. Dodd-Frank Act §102(a)(6), 12 U.S.C. §5311(a)(6), 12 C.F.R. §242.3.
771. Bank Holding Company Act §4(k)(4), 12 U.S.C. §1843(k)(4) & 12 C.F.R. §242, Appendix A.
772. Dodd-Frank Act §113(a)(2), 12 U.S.C. §5323(a)(2).

its liabilities, most notably its reliance on short-term financing; the extent and types of off-balance-sheet exposures; the extent and types of transactions and relationships of the company with other non-bank financial companies; the importance of the company as a source of credit and liquidity for the US economy; the importance of the company as a source of credit for low-income, minority or underserved communities; the recommendation, if any, of a member of the FSOC; the operation by the non-bank financial company or its ownership interest in any clearing settlement, or payment business; the extent to which assets are managed rather than owned; the extent to which ownership of AUM is diffuse; and any other risk-related factors that the FSOC deems appropriate.[773]

On 11 April 2012, the FSOC issued its final rule and interpretative guidance detailing the manner in which it will apply the statutory standards and considerations and the process for assessing whether a non-bank financial company is systemically important in that its material distress or activities could pose a threat to financial stability.[774] In 2019, the Council issued its final interpretative guidance, which replaced the 2012 interpretative guidance and introduced significant amendments to the designation process.[775] In contrast to the 2012 interpretative guidance, the final guidance prioritizes an activities-based approach and considers entity-specific designation as a last resort measure. The Council's activities-based approach consists of a two-step process. In the first step, the Council will monitor financial markets and market developments, in consultation with financial regulatory agencies, in order to identify products, activities or practices that could pose risks to financial stability.[776] If the Council identifies a potential risk to financial stability, then, as the second step, the Council will work with financial regulatory agencies at both the federal and state levels to seek the implementation of actions to address the identified risk.[777] Finally, if through its engagement with regulatory authorities, the Council considers that the actions taken by regulators are insufficient to address the identified risk to US financial stability, then the Council retains the authority under section 120 of the Dodd-Frank Act to publicly issue non-binding recommendations to primary financial regulators to apply new or heightened standards and safeguards.[778] Numerous scholars have criticized the FSOC's shift towards an activities-based approach, arguing that the Council lacks the power to implement activities-based regulation directly and the fragmented US regulatory structure will hamper the effectiveness of activities-based rules.[779]

According to the final guidance, the Council will proceed with entity-specific designations only if the activities-based approach does not adequately address an

773. *Ibid.*
774. Financial Stability Oversight Council, *Authority to Require Supervision and Regulation of Certain Nonbank Financial Companies*, *77 Fed. Reg* (11 April 2012), 21637.
775. 12 C.F.R. Part 1310 Appendix A.
776. 12 C.F.R. Part 1310 Appendix A(I)(a).
777. 12 C.F.R. Part 1310 Appendix A(I)(b).
778. *Ibid.*
779. Daniel Schwarcz, Patricia A McCoy and Jeremy Kress, 'Comment of Legal Scholars on Authority To Require Supervision and Regulation of Certain Nonbank Financial Companies, Financial Stability Oversight Council RIN 4030-AA00', 13 May 2019.

identified potential risk. More specifically, the Council will pursue an entity-specific determination only if: (a) the Council's engagement with the relevant financial regulatory agencies using an activities-based approach does not adequately address the potential risk or if the potential risk to US financial stability is outside the jurisdiction or authority of regulatory agencies and (b) the potential threat identified is one that can be addressed by an entity-specific designation. In evaluating a non-bank financial company, the FSOC will focus, apart from the statutory considerations set forth in section 113(a)(2) of the Dodd-Frank Act, on three distinct transmission channels through which a non-bank financial company's material financial distress or activities could affect other financial firms and markets, thereby jeopardizing financial stability: (a) exposure channel; (b) asset liquidation; and (c) critical function or service channel.[780] Moreover, pursuant to the Final Guidance, before proceeding with any designation, the Council must conduct a cost-benefit analysis and determine that the expected benefits justify the expected costs that the designation would impose.[781]

The FSOC's review process consists of two stages.[782] The first stage involves the preliminary evaluation of non-bank financial companies identified as potentially posing risks to US financial stability. During Stage 1, the Council will notify non-bank financial companies identified and engage extensively with both the company and its financial regulators. The Council will conduct its preliminary analysis relying on public information and information provided to supervisory and regulatory authorities. Following the preliminary assessment, the Council may decide to advance the company to Stage 2 if it determines that the non-bank financial company merits further review. During Stage 2, the FSOC will conduct an in-depth evaluation of the company. At the end of Stage 2, the Council may propose the designation of the firm as SIFI. The company has the right to request a hearing before the Council. Following the hearing, the Council may vote to make a final determination.

As far as hedge funds and their managers are concerned, the FSOC, in its 2012 interpretative guidance, left open the possibility of designating hedge funds and their managers as systemically important.[783] Nonetheless, the FSOC did not offer any guidance on how it intended to apply the designation process to hedge funds and their managers. In particular, it was unclear which of the following four levels of focus the Council would apply for assessing the systemic importance of hedge fund entities: (a) individual investment funds; (b) family of funds following the same or similar investment strategies that are managed by the same hedge fund manager; (c) hedge fund managers as stand-alone entities; and (d) hedge fund managers and their funds collectively. The FSOC noted that its determinations were applicable to individual

780. 12 C.F.R. Part 1310 Appendix A(III)(b).
781. 12 C.F.R. Part 1310 Appendix A(III)(e).
782. 12 C.F.R. Part 1310 Appendix A(IV)(a) & (b).
783. For instance, the FSOC considered establishing a tailored set of metrics or thresholds in order to evaluate hedge funds and their managers relying on the information provided in Form PF. Financial Stability Oversight Council, *Authority to Require Supervision and Regulation of Certain Nonbank Financial Companies, 77 Fed. Reg* (11 April 2012), 21643-44.

entities, while it also stressed that it understood the distinction between an asset manager's own assets and the distinct nature of AUM.[784]

In order to better inform its assessment of the financial stability implications of the asset management industry, the FSOC asked the OFR to analyse the extent to which asset management companies pose risks to US financial stability and whether such risks can be mitigated by subjecting asset managers to supervision by the FED and enhanced prudential standards.[785] In response to the FSOC's request, the OFR prepared a report analysing the potential of asset management firms and their activities to contribute to systemic risk. The resulting OFR study on Asset Management and Financial Stability, issued in September 2013, noted an increase in industry concentration and concluded that 'the failure of a large asset management firm could be a source of risk, depending on its size, complexity, and the interaction among its various investment management strategies and activities'.[786] Despite the findings of the OFR study, the FSOC announced that it would develop an activities-based approach to evaluating the risks emanating from the asset management industry, rather than focusing on particular asset management firms.[787]

Subsequently, the Council, in December 2014, issued a notice seeking public comments on whether asset management products and activities may pose potential risks to US financial stability.[788] In particular, the Council's notice sought public comments on the financial stability implications of liquidity and redemption practices, leverage, operational risk and resolution, i.e., the potential systemic fallout of the failure or closure of an asset manager or fund. Furthermore, the FED openly argued against singling out specific asset managers or funds as SIFIs considering that risks in asset management can be addressed with market-wide regulation. In April 2016, the FSOC reversed course and announced the creation of an interagency working group to assess the financial stability implications of hedge fund activities.[789] The Council's analysis found that a small number of large hedge funds exhibit a high level of leverage, while it considered that Form PF does not provide a complete picture of the risk profiles of hedge funds. The working group identified two main channels through which hedge fund leverage can destabilize financial markets: (a) fire sales by leveraged funds, which have the potential to significantly disrupt financial markets and (b) counterparties'

784. *Ibid.*, 21645.
785. *Ibid.*, 21644.
786. Office for Financial Research, *Asset Management and Financial Stability* (September 2013), 18. It should be emphasized that the OFR study does not focus specifically on the hedge fund industry. Furthermore, the large asset managers identified in the OFR study are mainly insurance companies, mutual fund complexes and asset management arms of financial institutions with no single hedge fund management firm mentioned in the study.
787. Gina Chon & Stephen Foley, 'Asset Managers May Escape Systemic Label', Financial Times, http://www.ft.com/intl/cms/s/0/d2739c66-182c-11e4-a6e4-00144feabdc0.html#axzz3Qpc CPZ3L.
788. Financial Stability Oversight Council, *Notice Seeking Comment on Asset Management Products and Activities* (December 2014).
789. *Update on Review of Asset Management Products and Activities*, 20-21.

exposures to hedge funds, which may transmit stress to SIFIs.[790] The working group was subsequently abandoned by the Treasury Secretary, Steven Mnuchin, during the Trump presidency.[791] Nonetheless, the fallout from the recent Archegos debacle forced the FSOC to reconvene the hedge fund working group in order to assess financial stability risks emanating from the hedge fund sector.[792]

Designation as systemically important subjects a non-bank financial company to FRB supervision and heightened prudential standards. The Dodd-Frank Act directs the FRB to impose on SINBFCs capital requirements, leverage limits, liquidity requirements, resolution plans and credit exposure report requirements, concentration limits and risk management requirements.[793] What is more, the FRB is authorized to impose additional contingent capital requirements, enhanced public disclosures, short-term debt limits and such other prudential standards as the FRB on its own, or pursuant to FSOC recommendations, determines are necessary.[794] In order to mitigate the systemic risk posed by systemically important non-bank financial institutions, the FRB is empowered to adopt more stringent standards than the ones applicable to other non-bank financial companies that do not present similar risks to US financial markets.[795] Section 166 also directs the FRB to implement a regulatory framework for the early remediation of weaknesses of non-bank financial companies.

For each non-bank financial company designated as systemically important, the FRB shall establish enhanced prudential standards taking into account the nature, scope, size, scale, concentration, interconnectedness and mix of activities of the relevant company, in case the company is a US one, the degree to which it is already regulated by one or more primary financial regulatory agencies, in the case of a foreign company, the extent to which the company is subject to prudential standards in its home country and any other risk-related factor that the Board may consider appropriate.[796] The FRB has promulgated enhanced prudential standards for BHCs and foreign bank organizations.[797] The Board has recognized that non-bank financial companies designated as systemically important may have different businesses, structures, and activities, thus posing varying types of risks to the financial system. As a result, it

790. Jonah Crane, 'Remarks by Deputy Assistant Secretary Jonah Crane at a Meeting of the Financial Stability Oversight Council', US Department of the Treasury, 16 October 2016, https://www.treasury.gov/press-center/press-releases/Pages/jl0612.aspx.
791. David Lawder, 'Pressure for Hedge Fund Scrutiny Builds as Yellen Leads Her First U.S. Financial Stability Meeting', Reuters, https://www.reuters.com/article/us-usa-markets-treasury-idINKBN2BN2AA.
792. 'Readout of Financial Stability Oversight Council Meeting on March 31, 2021', US Department of the Treasury, 31 March 2021.
793. Dodd-Frank Act §165(b)(1)(A), 12 U.S.C. §5365(b)(1)(A).
794. Dodd-Frank Act §165(b)(1)(B), 12 U.S.C. §5365(b)(1)(B).
795. Dodd-Frank Act §165(a)(1), 12 U.S.C. §5365(a)(1). What is more, the FED may increase the stringency of the prudential standards applied on the basis of the factors utilized by the FSOC in assessing the systemic importance of a non-bank financial company. *Ibid.* Section 165(a)(2)(A) further authorizes the FED to differentiate prudential standards among non-bank financial institutions on an individual basis or by category after taking into account factors such as their capital structure, riskiness, complexity, financial activities and size. Dodd-Frank Act §165(a)(2)(A), 12 U.S.C. §5365(a)(2)(A).
796. 12 C.F.R. §252.4.
797. 12 C.F.R. Part 252.

considers that the enhanced prudential standards applicable to banking institutions may not be appropriate for non-bank financial companies. The FRB has noted that the application of prudential standards for non-bank financial companies will be made after a careful assessment of the business model, risk profile and capital structure of the designated firm. It is still not clear what type of prudential standards the FED will apply to hedge funds and/or their managers if the Council eventually decides to move forward with their designation as systemically important.

3.3.2.3 Hedge Funds and the Volcker Rule

The Volcker Rule finds its historical precedent in the Banking Act of 1933 (also known as the 'Glass-Steagall Act'),[798] which forced the dismantling of the universal banking model. The Act's adoption was prompted by the widespread bank failures during the Great Depression. The architects of the Glass-Steagall Act claimed that banks' involvement in the securities markets resulted in aggressive risk-taking and conflicts of interest.[799] The Act prohibited commercial banks from underwriting and dealing in securities, while investment banks were precluded from engaging in the business of deposit-taking.[800] Thus, the Act imposed a strict separation between commercial banking and investment banking functions. Furthermore, the BHC Act of 1956 separated banking from the insurance business.[801] Numerous academic researchers have argued that these restrictions contributed to a period of financial resilience and stability.[802] During the 1980s and 1990s, regulators progressively relaxed the prohibitions imposed by the Glass-Steagall Act and the BHCA of 1956. The 1998 merger between Citicorp (a banking institution) and the Travelers Group (a financial conglomerate with an insurance business and an investment banking arm, Salomon Smith Barney), creating Citigroup, forced the US Congress to repeal the prohibitions.[803] The Gramm-Leach-Bliley Financial Services Modernization Act of 1999 overturned the separation of commercial banking, investment banking and insurance activities with its adoption followed by another high-profile merger between JP Morgan and Chase Manhattan in 2000.[804]

The repeal of the Glass-Steagall Act ushered in the ascent of megabanks. Nonetheless, the severe losses suffered by US universal banks during the financial

798. *Banking Act of 1933, 48 Stat. 162, Now Repealed.*
799. *75 Cong. Rec. 9912 (1932) (Remarks of Senator Bulkley, Stating That 'the Banker Who Has Nothing to Sell to His Depositors Is Much Better Qualified to Advise Disinterestedly … Than the Banker Who Uses the List of Depositors … To Distribute Circulars Concerning This, That or the Other Investment on Which the Bank Is to Receive … Profit … ').*
800. For an overview of the restrictions imposed by the Glass-Steagall Act *see generally* Arthur E Wilmarth, 'The Transformation of the US Financial Services Industry, 1975-2000: Competition, Consolidation, and Increased Risks', *University of Illinois Law Review* (2002).
801. *Bank Holding Company Act of 1956, Pub. L. No. 511, 70 Stat.133.*
802. Richardson Matthew, 'Large Banks and the Volcker Rule', 186.
803. The merger between Citicorp and the Travelers Group violated both the letter and the spirit of the Glass-Steagall Act and was based on a temporary exemption under the Bank Holding Company Act of 1956 approved by the FED. *See Ibid.*, 221.
804. *Gramm-Leach-Bliley Financial Services Modernization Act, Pub. L. No. 106-102, 113 Stat. 1338 (1999).*

crisis, most notably Citigroup,[805] led to calls for the reinstatement of Glass-Steagall type restrictions. According to Whitehead, the adoption of the Volcker Rule was, in effect, an effort 'to return to a traditional banking model-to create a regulatory divide, much like the Glass-Steagall Act had before its repeal'.[806]

Section 619 of the Dodd-Frank Act, commonly referred to as the 'Volcker Rule', named after its creator and former Chairman of the FED Paul Volcker, prohibits banking entities from engaging in proprietary trading and from acquiring or retaining any equity, partnership or other ownership interest in or sponsoring a hedge fund or private equity fund.[807] Furthermore, according to the Volcker Rule, non-bank financial companies designated by the FSOC as systemically important that engage in the above-mentioned activities are required to comply with additional capital and quantitative limits.[808] As Armour notes, the basic rationale behind the Volcker Rule is the protection of the financial system against the systemic risk emanating from the failure of a banking institution or a systemically important non-bank financial institution by curbing their involvement in activities considered too risky by policymakers.[809] Moreover, the prohibitions introduced by the Volcker Rule seek to mitigate the moral hazard created by explicit and implicit government guarantees enjoyed by financial institutions whose soundness is essential for the orderly functioning of financial markets.[810] Explicit and implicit guarantees are thus restricted to core functions, such as the provision of retail banking services. It should be noted that even though the academic literature primarily emphasizes the financial stability concerns that the adoption of the Volcker Rule seeks to alleviate, the main impetus for the rule, according to its creator Paul Volcker, is the elimination of conflicts of interests between bankers and their clients.[811]

On 31 January 2014, five agencies, the SEC, the CFTC, the FDIC, the FED and the OCC, adopted regulations implementing the Volcker Rule. In 2019 and 2020, the agencies introduced amendments to the covered fund restrictions of the implementing regulations. The Volcker Rule, as implemented by the final regulations, prohibits a banking entity, acting as principal, from directly or indirectly acquiring or retaining any ownership interest in, or sponsoring, a covered fund.[812] The definition of a 'banking entity' is wide, encompassing any FDIC-insured depository institution; any company that controls an FDIC-insured depository institution; any company that is treated as a

805. For an overview of Citigroup's debacle and its eventual demise *see* Arthur E Wilmarth, 'Citigroup: A Case Study in Managerial and Regulatory Failures', *Indiana Law Review* 47, no. 1 (2014).
806. Charles K Whitehead, 'The Volcker Rule and Evolving Financial Markets', *Harvard Business Law Review* 1, no. 1 (2011): 42.
807. Dodd-Frank Act §619, 12 U.S.C. §1851(a)(1).
808. Dodd-Frank Act §619, 12 U.S.C. §1851(a)(2).
809. Awrey Dan Armour John et al., *Principles of Financial Regulation* (Oxford University Press, 2016).
810. *Ibid.*
811. Phil Mattingly, 'Volcker Says Proprietary Trading Poses Conflicts of Interest', Bloomberg, http://www.bloomberg.com/news/articles/2012-05-09/volcker-says-prop-trading-poses-conflicts-of-interest-for-banks.
812. 12 C.F.R. §248.10(a)(1).

BHC for purposes of section 8 of the International Banking Act; and any affiliate or subsidiary of any such entity.[813]

What is more, a 'covered fund' is defined to include any issuer of securities that would be an investment company, as defined by the Investment Company Act, but for section 3(c)(1) or 3(c)(7).[814] As previously mentioned, hedge funds routinely rely on the exemptions contained in section 3(c)(1) and 3(c)(7) in order to evade registration under the Investment Company Act. With respect to a banking entity that is a US banking entity or is controlled by a US banking entity, the definition of a 'covered fund' also includes a foreign fund that is organized or established outside the US and the ownership interests of which are offered and sold solely outside the US; is or holds itself out as being an entity or arrangement that raises money from investors primarily for the purpose of investing in securities for resale or other disposition or otherwise trading in securities; and is sponsored by the banking entity or the ownership interests of which are owned by such banking entity.[815] The definition also includes any commodity pool under the Commodity Exchange Act for which either the commodity pool operated has claimed an exemption under 17 CFR 4.7 or the commodity pool operator is registered with the CFTC and participation units are substantially owned by qualified eligible persons and there has been no public offering to persons other than qualified eligible persons.[816] Several entities are excluded from the definition of covered fund, including joint ventures and acquisition vehicles, loan securitization vehicles, venture capital funds, family wealth management vehicles, credit funds, and foreign public funds.[817]

813. 12 C.F.R. §248.2(c).
814. 12 C.F.R. §248.10(b)(i).
815. A foreign fund that, if organized or offered in US, would not rely on section 3(c)(1) or 3(c)(7) in order to evade registration under the Investment Company Act will not be considered a covered fund. 12 C.F.R. §248.10(b)(iii).
816. The Commodity Exchange Act regulates the trading of commodity futures in the US and gives the CFTC authority to regulate commodity pool operators, commodity trading advisers and commodity exchanges. The CFTC imposes on commodity pool operators a variety of disclosure, reporting, documentation and record-keeping requirements. Pursuant to the Commodity Exchange Act, commodity pools are defined as investment trusts, syndicates, or similar forms of enterprise trading in commodity interests, such as commodities for future delivery, security futures products or swaps. 7 U.S.C. §1a(10)(A). A commodity pool operator is any person, who engages in a business of a nature of a commodity pool, investment trust, syndicate or similar form of enterprise and solicits investments for the purpose of trading in commodity interests and is registered with the CFTC as a commodity pool operator. 7 U.S.C. §1a(11). 17 C.F.R. §4.7 provides relief from certain disclosure and record-keeping requirements for commodity pools operators offering participation units only to qualified eligible persons. The definition of the term 'qualified eligible persons' includes among others investment companies, banks, insurance companies, accredited investors and certain investment advisers. 17 C.F.R. §4.7(a)(2) & (3).
817. 12 C.F.R. §248.10(c). Foreign public funds are defined as any issuer that is organized or established outside the US; is authorized to offer and sell interests, and such interests are offered and sold through one or more public offerings; and with respect to a fund that is sponsored by a banking entity, or is controlled directly or indirectly by US banking entity, the fund's interests must be sold predominantly to persons other than such sponsoring banking entity, its affiliates, the fund itself and its directors and senior executive officers. 12 C.F.R. §248.10(c)(1). Credit funds are defined as funds that invest solely in loans, debt instruments, rights and other related assets and interest rate or foreign exchange derivatives that directly relate to the loans, debt instruments or other rights or assets and directly reduce the interest rate and foreign exchange risks related to such loans, debt instruments or other rights or assets.

Prohibited sponsorship of a covered fund includes serving as a general partner, managing member, or trustee of a fund; selecting or controlling a majority of the fund's directors, trustees, or management of a covered fund; or sharing with the covered fund the same name or a variation of the same name.[818] Ownership interests, whose acquisition and retention is banned, are defined as any equity, partnership or other similar interest.[819]

The Volcker Rule is 'designed to address the risks attendant to principal activity and not those that are borne by customers of the banking entity or for which the banking entity lacks design or intent to take a proprietary interest as principal'.[820] As a result, the prohibition against the acquisition and retention of ownership interests in covered funds applies to banking entities acting as principal. The ban does not apply to banking entities acting solely as agent, broker, custodian, trustee or in a similar fiduciary capacity for the account of or on behalf of a customer, provided that the banking entity does not have or retain beneficial ownership of any ownership

12 C.F.R. §248.10(c)(15). A family wealth management vehicle is any entity that is not, and does not hold itself out as being, an entity or arrangement that raises money from investors primarily for the purpose of investing in securities for resale or other disposition or otherwise trading in securities; for family wealth management vehicles that are trusts, the grantors of the entire entity are all family customers; and for non-trust family wealth management vehicles, family customers must own a majority of voting interests as well as a majority of equity interests and ownership of the entity is limited to family customers and up to five closely related persons. 12 C.F.R. §248.10(c)(17). Venture capital funds are defined by reference to 17 C.F.R. 275.203(l)-1.

818. 12 C.F.R. §248.10(d)(9).

819. 12 C.F.R. §248.10(d)(6). The term 'other similar interest' means an interest that has rights to participate in the selection or removal of a covered fund's general partner, managing member, member of the board of directors or trustees, investment manager, investment adviser or commodity trading advisor, excluding the rights of a creditor to exercise remedies upon the occurrence of an event of default and the right to participate in the removal of an investment manager for cause or participate in the selection of a replacement manager; rights to receive a share of covered fund's income, profits or gains; rights to a covered fund's residual underlying assets; interest that receives income on a pass-through basis or has a rate of return that depends on the performance of the underlying assets of the covered fund; rights to receive a spread between the interest received from the underlying assets of the fund and the interest paid out by the fund; rights to payment by the covered fund that are reduced by loss offsets; synthetic rights similar to the above-mentioned rights. The definition of ownership interest does not include any senior loan or senior debt interest provided that holders of such interest do not have the right to receive a share of the gains or profits of the fund but are only entitled to receive interest at a stated rate and repayment of a fixed principal amount; the entitlement to payments is absolute; and the holders of the interest do not have rights to a covered fund's residual underlying assets. Furthermore, restricted profit interests are excluded from the definition of ownership interest. Restricted profit interests are interests held by an entity, employee or former employee that acts as investment manager, investment adviser, commodity trading advisor or other service provider of the covered fund provided that the sole purpose of the interest is to allow the sharing in the profits of the fund as performance compensation for investment management, advisory, commodity trading advisory or other services to the fund; all such profit once allocated is distributed to the entity, employee or former employee thereof promptly after being earned or if not so distributed is retained by the covered fund for establishing a reserve amount to satisfy contractual obligations regarding subsequent losses of the fund; and the interest is not transferable with certain exceptions for transfers to immediate family members and affiliates.

820. *Ibid.*, Preamble at 5668.

interest.[821] In addition, a banking entity may acquire ownership interests as trustee in connection with a deferred compensation or similar plan or in the ordinary course of collecting a debt.[822] What is more, despite the ban on fund sponsorship and investments, banking entities are still allowed to advise covered funds. Finally, the Volcker Rule does not limit the ability of the banking entity to invest alongside covered funds. Co-investments are allowed provided that they are made in compliance with applicable laws and regulations.[823]

Furthermore, the Volcker Rule creates an exemption, allowing a banking entity to invest in and sponsor a covered fund subject to certain conditions.[824] The banking entity must provide bona fide trust, fiduciary, investment advisory services or commodity trading advisory services to such fund and organize and offer the fund solely to its customers who use such services. An investment in the fund is permitted provided that it does not exceed 3 % of the outstanding ownership interests in the fund one year after its establishment. The total investments of a banking entity in such funds should be limited to 3 % of its Tier 1 capital. In addition, the banking entity is prohibited from guaranteeing, assuming or insuring the obligations or performance of the covered fund. Moreover, the fund must not share the same name or a similar name with the entity and may not use the word 'bank' in its name. Directors and employees are prohibited from retaining any ownership interest in the fund, except for any director or employee of the banking entity who is directly providing investment advisory or other services to the covered fund. Furthermore, specified disclosures must be made to prospective and actual fund investors. The banking entity must also comply with the so-called Super 23A restrictions, which place limits on transactions between the banking entity and its affiliates and the covered fund.[825]

The Volcker Rule introduces an additional exemption for underwriting and market-making activities in ownership interests of covered funds.[826] Moreover, banking entities are allowed to acquire ownership interests in covered funds in connection with certain risk-mitigating hedging activities.[827] Nevertheless, sponsorship and investment activities may be prohibited if they pose a threat to the financial stability of the banking entity or the US, involve material conflicts of interest, or would result in a

821. 12 C.F.R. §248.10(a)(2).
822. *Ibid.*
823. 12 C.F.R. §248.12(a)(5).
824. 12 C.F.R. §248.11(a).
825. 12 C.F.R. §248.14.
826. 12 C.F.R. §248.11(c). If the banking entity sponsors or advises the covered fund or invests in the covered fund under the organizing and offering exemption, then the ownership interests acquired in connection to the underwriting and market-making activities must not exceed 3 % of the outstanding ownership interests in the fund total investments of a banking entity in such funds should be limited to 3 % of its Tier 1 capital.
827. 12 C.F.R. §248.13(a). The ownership interest must be acquired for the purpose of hedging specific risks in connection with a compensation agreement with an employee or former employee providing investment advisory or other services to the covered fund or a position taken by the banking entity acting as an intermediary for a customer seeking exposure to the profits and losses of a covered fund. 12 C.F.R. §248.13(a)(1).

material exposure of the banking organization to high-risk assets or trading strategies.[828]

The Volcker Rule does not prohibit non-bank financial companies designated as systemically important by the FSOC from engaging in proprietary trading and investing in and sponsoring covered funds. However, a non-bank financial company supervised by the FED, which engages in proprietary trading or invests in and sponsors hedge funds and private equity funds, will be subject to additional capital requirements and quantitative limits set by the FED.[829] It should be noted that, at present, there is no non-bank financial company designated as systemically important.

3.3.2.4 Orderly Liquidation Authority

When the financial crisis hit, US government officials were left with two options to resolve distress at a systemically important non-bank financial institution: either allow the institution to enter into bankruptcy or engineer some kind of government bailout. The mainstream view holds that the bankruptcy of Lehman Brothers in September 2008 exposed the perils of the bankruptcy process with its bankruptcy filing unleashing the financial crisis. In response to the inadequacies of the bankruptcy process, the Dodd-Frank Act introduced a special resolution regime, administered by the FDIC, for ailing non-bank financial institutions, whose failure could destabilize the US financial system, also known as the OLA.[830]

Under OLA, the FDIC is appointed as a receiver to carry out the liquidation and winding up of 'covered financial companies'. A 'covered financial company' is a 'financial company' to which a 'systemic risk determination' has been made.[831] A 'financial company' is defined as any company that is incorporated or organized under any provision of federal or state law and is: (a) a BHC as defined in section 2(a) of the BHCA of 1956; (b) a non-bank financial company supervised by the FED; (c) any company that is predominantly engaged in activities that the FED has determined are financial in nature or incidental thereto; and (d) any subsidiary of the above that is predominately engaged in activities that the FED has determined are financial in nature or incidental thereto.[832] On their own initiative or at the request of the Secretary of the Treasury, the FDIC and the FED must make a written recommendation as to whether

828. 12 C.F.R. §248.15.
829. Dodd-Frank Act §619, 12 U.S.C. §1851(a)(2). Two of the companies previously designated as systemically important, GE Capital and AIG, were affiliated with insured depository institutions. As a result, they were captured by the prohibition on sponsorship and investments in covered funds applicable to banking entities.
830. Dodd-Frank Act §§201-217, 12 U.S.C. §§5381-5394. For an excellent overview and critique of OLA *see generally* Stephen J Lubben, 'Resolution, Orderly and Otherwise: B of a in Ola', *University of Cincinnati Law Review* 81, no. 2 (2013). In 2018, the US Treasury under the Trump administration released a report recommending the reform of OLA. In particular, the Treasury recommended introducing a new specialized bankruptcy procedure for distressed financial companies, while retaining a reformed OLA as an emergency tool in exceptional circumstances.
831. Dodd-Frank Act §201(a)(8), 12 U.S.C. §5381(a)(8)(A).
832. Dodd-Frank Act §201(a)(11)(B), 12 U.S.C. §5381(11). It should be stressed that government-insured deposit-taking banks have long been subject to special resolution procedures again

the FDIC should be appointed as a receiver for a financial company. Upon receipt of the above-mentioned recommendation, the Treasury Secretary, in consultation with the President of the United States, must seek appointment of the FDIC as receiver if the Secretary determines that: (a) the financial company is in default or in danger of default;[833] (b) the failure of the financial company and its resolution under otherwise applicable federal or state law would have serious adverse effects on the financial stability of the US;[834] (c) no viable private sector alternative is available to prevent the default of the company; (d) the effect on the claims or interests of creditors, counterparties, and shareholders of the financial company and other market participants as a result of actions to be taken under the receivership proceedings is appropriate, given the impact that any action so taken would have on US financial stability; and (e) an orderly liquidation would avoid or mitigate the potential adverse effects.[835]

If a determination has been made, the Secretary of the Treasury must notify both the company and the FDIC.[836] If the board of directors of the company accepts the appointment of the FDIC as a receiver, the Secretary of the Treasury will appoint the FDIC as a receiver.[837] If the board of directors objects to the FDIC's appointment, then the Secretary of the Treasury must file a petition with the United States Court for the District of Columbia requesting an order authorizing the appointment of the FDIC as a receiver.[838] The court's examination will be limited to whether the Secretary's determination that the company is in default or in danger of default and satisfies the definition of a financial company is not 'arbitrary and capricious', a highly deferential standard.[839]

When acting as a receiver, the FDIC has broad powers assuming virtually complete control over the liquidation process. Upon the appointment of the FDIC as a receiver, an automatic stay is imposed on all actions against the company. The FDIC succeeds to all rights, titles, powers and privileges of the financial company and its assets, has the authority to take over the assets and operations of the financial company, collect all obligations and money owed to the company, resolve claims to creditors and repudiate or assign contracts entered into by the financial company.[840]

---

administered by the FDIC. *See generally* Stanley V. Ragalevsky and Sarah J. Ricardi, 'Anatomy of a Bank Failure', *The Banking Law Journal* (December 2009).

833. A company is in default or in danger of default if: (a) a bankruptcy case has been, or likely will be, commenced with respect to the financial company; (b) the financial company has incurred, or is likely to incur, losses that will deplete all or substantially all of its capital, and there is no reasonable prospect for the company to avoid such depletion; (c) the assets of the financial company are, or are likely to be, less than its obligations to creditors and others; or (d) the financial company is, or is likely to be, unable to pay its obligations in the ordinary course of business. Dodd-Frank Act §203(c)(4), 12 U.S.C. §5383(c)(4).
834. It should be noted that OLA does not displace bankruptcy but rather serves as an alternative to it, if policymakers determine that the entry of the firm in bankruptcy proceedings would have adverse financial stability consequences.
835. Dodd-Frank Act §203(b), 12 U.S.C. §5383(b).
836. Dodd-Frank Act §202(a)(1)(A)(i), 12 U.S.C. §5382(a)(1)(A)(i).
837. *Ibid.*
838. *Ibid.*
839. Dodd-Frank Act §202(a)(1)(A)(iv), 12 U.S.C. §5382(a)(1)(A)(iv).
840. Dodd-Frank Act §§210(c)(1), 210(a)(2), 210(a)(1)(B)(ii), 210(a)(1)(B)(i), 210(a)(1)(A)(i), 12 U.S.C. §§5390(c)(1), 5390(a)(2), 5390(a)(1)(B)(i), 5390(a)(1)(A)(i).

Furthermore, the FDIC may arrange for the acquisition of selected assets and liabilities of a financial company by private acquirers without a court, creditor, contract counterparty or shareholder approval.[841] In addition, the FDIC may arrange for the sale of the company to private acquirers.[842] The FDIC also has the authority to transfer selected assets and liabilities to a bridge financial company.[843] The bridge financial company can be created without court, creditor, contract counterparty or shareholder approval.[844]

Despite the FDIC's broad resolution powers, the Dodd-Frank Act introduces limits to its authority. For instance, in exercising its authority to dispose of the financial company's assets, the FDIC must conduct its operations in a manner that maximizes returns, minimizes losses and preserves financial stability.[845] Furthermore, any action taken by the FDIC must be necessary for purposes of the financial stability of the US and not for the purpose of preserving the company, while the agency must also ensure that the shareholders of the financial company do not receive payment until after all other claims are fully paid and that unsecured creditors bear losses in accordance with the priority-of-claim provisions.[846] In addition, the FDIC may not take an equity interest in or become a shareholder of the financial company.[847] Even though in principle similarly situated creditors must be treated equally, the FDIC has the power to treat such creditors differently by transferring claims to a bridge company or making additional payments for the purpose of maximizing the value of the assets, maximizing returns, facilitating the receivership or the operation of the bridge financial company or minimizing losses.[848] However, creditors are entitled to receive at least what they would have received in a liquidation under the US Bankruptcy Code or similar state insolvency proceeding.[849] Furthermore, the Dodd-Frank Act contains anti-cherry picking rules, requiring all 'qualified financial contracts' with a particular counterparty to be transferred to a single third-party financial institution or bridge financial company.[850]

Most importantly, unlike the Bankruptcy Code, OLA places restrictions on the ability of counterparties to 'qualified financial contracts' to terminate, liquidate or accelerate their contracts. A counterparty to a qualified financial contract may not terminate, liquidate, or net such contract solely by reason of the appointment of the FDIC as receiver or the insolvency or financial condition of the company for which the

841. Dodd-Frank Act §210(a)(G)(i)(I), 12 U.S.C. §5390(a)(G)(i)(I).
842. Dodd-Frank Act §210(a)(G)(i)(II), 12 U.S.C. §5390(a)(G)(i)(II).
843. Dodd-Frank Act §210(h)(1)(A), 12 U.S.C. §5390(h)(1)(A).
844. Dodd-Frank Act §210(h)(2)(E)(ii), 12 U.S.C. §5390(h)(2)(E)(ii). The bridge financial company is granted a charter for two years that can be extended for no more than three additional one-year periods. Dodd-Frank Act §210(h)(12), 12 U.S.C. §5390(h)(12).
845. Dodd-Frank Act §210(a)(9)(E), 12 U.S.C. §5390(a)(9)(E).
846. Dodd-Frank Act §206, 12 U.S.C. §5386.
847. *Ibid.*
848. Dodd-Frank Act §210(b)(4), 12 U.S.C. §5390(b)(4).
849. *Ibid.*
850. Dodd-Frank Act §210(c)(9)(A), 12 U.S.C. §5390(c)(9)(A). 'Qualified financial contracts' are defined as any contract for the purchase, sale, or loan of securities, 'commodity contract, forward contract, repurchase agreement, or swap agreement'. Dodd-Frank Act §210(c)(8)(D)(i), 12 U.S.C. §5390(c)(8)(D)(i).

FDIC has been appointed as receiver until 5:00 pm on the business day following the date of appointment of the FDIC.[851] Furthermore, a counterparty is barred from exercising its contractual rights after it has received notice that its qualified financial contract has been transferred to another financial institution, including a bridge financial company.[852]

The resolution process will be funded by the newly created 'Orderly Liquidation Fund', which is established in the US Treasury and managed by the FDIC.[853] To finance the receivership, the FDIC is authorized to issue obligations to the US Treasury up to a maximum amount of: (a) 10% of the book value of the covered financial company's total consolidated assets during the first thirty days after the appointment of the FDIC as receiver; and (b) 90% of the fair value of the financial company's total consolidated assets after the first thirty days.[854] Prior to the drawing of any borrowings, the FDIC and the Treasury must agree to a liquidation and repayment plan.[855] If the funds recouped by the disposition of the liquidated assets are insufficient to repay the debt to the US Treasury, the FDIC is required to impose risk-based assessments on the financial sector.[856]

Overall, it remains to be seen how the FDIC will utilize its authority to deal with the failure of a systemically important hedge fund. In the aftermath of the unprecedented bailouts of mainstream financial institutions during the financial crisis, the FDIC has focused its efforts on devising resolution strategies for dealing with the distress of systemically important institutions other than investment funds.[857] Nonetheless, the FDIC's resolution powers will be of utmost importance when dealing with the failure of a systemically important hedge fund. As it will be explained in Chapter 4, the bankruptcy process is ill-suited for grappling with the systemic effects of a hedge fund failure. Certain provisions included in OLA and the resolution tools in the FDIC's disposal kit may prove crucial for resolving a hedge fund failure. For instance, the one-day stay imposed on derivatives counterparties allows the FDIC to transfer a fund's derivatives portfolio to a third-party acquirer or a bridge financial company.[858]

3.4 CONCLUSION

The financial crisis led to a complete overhaul of the regulatory landscape with hedge funds being one of the first targets of US and European regulators. The regulatory

851. Dodd-Frank Act §210(c)(10)(B)(i)(I), 12 U.S.C. §5390(c)(10)(B)(i)(I).
852. Dodd-Frank Act §210(c)(10)(B)(i)(II), 12 U.S.C. §5390(c)(10)(B)(i)(II).
853. Dodd-Frank Act §210(n)(1), 12 U.S.C. §5390(n)(1).
854. Dodd-Frank Act §210(n)(5), 12 U.S.C. §5390(n)(5).
855. Dodd-Frank Act §210(n)(9), 12 U.S.C. §5390(n)(9).
856. Dodd-Frank Act §210(o), 12 U.S.C. §5390(o).
857. For instance, the FDIC has devised a new strategy for resolving large financial institution groups, termed 'Single Point of Entry'. Under the 'Single Point of Entry' strategy, only the top-tier holding company of a SIFI will be placed under resolution with all of its operating subsidiaries continuing business as usual. *See generally* David A Skeel, 'Single Point of Entry and the Bankruptcy Alternative', in *Across the Great Divide: New Perspectives on the Financial Crisis*, ed. Martin Neil Bailey and John B Taylor (Hoover Press, 2014).
858. *See* discussion *infra*. Ch. 4.

initiatives in the hedge fund field have already significantly impacted the hedge fund industry with numerous industry insiders raising alarms regarding the increased costs for hedge funds operating in the US and Europe. Nonetheless, the Dodd-Frank Act, as compared with the European regulatory developments, adopts a measured approach towards the systemic risks posed by the hedge fund industry offering a useful template for ameliorating the EU's regulatory architecture with regard to the hedge fund industry.[859] Certain aspects of the US regime, such as the authority granted to the FSOC to designate hedge funds as SIFIs, the Volcker Rule and the FDIC's authority to resolve systemically important hedge funds elaborately tackle the systemic risk posed by large systemically important hedge funds and hedge funds housed within SIFIs. In contrast, the regulatory regime introduced by European Union legislators suffers from severe weaknesses when it comes to addressing the systemic risk posed by large systemically important hedge funds and hedge funds housed within systemically important institutions. First, the AIFM Directive leaves the fragmentation of hedge fund supervision along national lines largely intact. Second, the recovery and resolution regime introduced in Europe does not extend to hedge funds whose disorderly failure could pose risks to financial stability. Third, the Commission decided to withdraw the Proposal on Bank Structural Reform, which adequately tackled the systemic risk posed by hedge funds housed within SIFIs.

859. Indeed, Kaal in his study finds that the hedge fund industry has been moderately affected by the registration and increased disclosure requirements introduced by the Dodd-Frank Act. *See* Wulf A Kaal, 'Hedge Fund Manager Registration under the Dodd-Frank Act', *San Diego Law Review* 50, no. 2 (2013). In a related study, the same author documents that the registration and disclosure requirements mandated by the Dodd-Frank Act have had a positive effect on hedge fund performance. Wulf A Kaal, Barbara Luppi and Sandra Paterlini, 'Did the Dodd-Frank Act Impact Hedge Fund Performance?', *No. 14-09, University of St. Thomas (Minnesota) Legal Studies Research Paper* No. 14-09 (2014).

CHAPTER 4

A Modest Proposal for Improving the Current EU Supervisory and Regulatory Regime

4.1 INTRODUCTION

The present chapter will offer a modest proposal for improving the current EU supervisory and regulatory regime with respect to hedge funds. Section 4.2 will highlight the perils of housing hedge funds within SIFIs and deal with the necessity of introducing a European equivalent of the Volcker Rule. Therefore, the stance of European legislators, which have withdrawn the proposal for Bank Structural Reform, will be criticized.

Section 4.3 will propose a single supervisory framework for systemically important hedge funds in the Eurozone. In particular, I will argue that the current system of the AIFM Directive whereby hedge fund systemic risk supervision remains at the national level is jeopardizing financial stability. As a result, I will propose a new systemic risk architecture for hedge fund supervision in the Eurozone. The model of hedge fund regulation on systemic risk grounds should move closer to the one introduced in the US, where the FSOC has the authority to designate funds as SIFIs and subject them to the FED's supervision. Indeed, this approach was also accepted by the FSB and IOSCO, which proposed assessment methodologies for identifying globally systemically important hedge funds and hedge fund managers.[860] Although a truly

860. At the Cannes Summit in November 2011, the G20 leaders of the major economies tasked the FSB, in consultation with IOSCO, with developing assessment methodologies for identifying non-bank, non-insurer global systemically important financial institutions. In response to the G20 request, the FSB and IOSCO, on 8 January 2014, published a consultative document, which sets out a proposed high-level framework and specific assessment methodologies for identifying non-bank, non-insurer global systemically important financial institutions. IOSCO & FSB, *Assessment Methodologies for Identifying Non-Bank Non-Insurer Global Systemically Important Financial Institutions, Consultative Document* (January 2014). In March 2015, the FSB and

pan-European supervisor would be the optimal approach, the best approach taking into account the difficulties and costs associated with allocating supervisory responsibility to a new or existing EU supervisory agency, the stiff resistance that such an initiative would encounter from the non-euro area Member States and the expertise of the ECB in issues of financial stability, would be to allocate supervisory powers to the ECB and bring hedge funds designated as systemically important by the ESRB within the scope of the SSM.

Finally, section 4.4 will deal with the necessity of introducing a resolution framework for hedge funds. The BRRD and the SRM's scope should be extended to deal with the failure of large systemically important hedge funds. This section will also highlight certain resolution tools, which can be used in the case of a hedge fund failure. Although, it may seem a first glance that hedge funds share some unique characteristics that make them unfit for resolution tools applied to banks, such as asset management companies, the section will argue that some of these resolution tools can actually be used in case of a hedge fund failure.

4.2 INTRODUCING THE VOLCKER RULE IN EUROPE

4.2.1 The Case for Prohibiting the Sponsorship and Ownership of Hedge Funds by SIFIs

SIFIs, also called LCFIs, 'can be defined as financial intermediaries engaged in some combination of commercial banking, investment banking, asset management, insurance, and/or the payments system, whose failure poses a systemic risk to the financial system as a whole'.[861] SIFIs engage in multiple business lines across geographical borders and exhibit complex capital structures. They include household names such as Citigroup, Morgan Stanley, Deutsche Bank and BNP Paribas. It should be noted that apart from banking institutions, SIFIs may also include other types of financial institutions, such as insurance companies and finance subsidiaries of industrial companies.

The creation of these financial conglomerates was the result of deregulation, globalization, consolidation and expansion of banks in multiple business lines. The

IOSCO issued a second consultative document with a revised proposal for a high-level framework and specific assessment methodologies for identifying non-bank, non-insurer global systemically important financial institutions. IOSCO & FSB, *Assessment Methodologies for Identifying Non-Bank Non-Insurer Global Systemically Important Financial Institutions, Consultative Document* (March 2015). It should be noted that after criticism from the FED, the FCA and the asset management industry, the FSB has decided to predominantly focus on potential financial stability risks stemming from structural vulnerabilities associated with asset management activities instead of designating individual firms as systemically important. *See* Financial Stability Board, *Proposed Policy Recommendations to Address Structural Vulnerabilities from Asset Management Activities* (June 2016). However, as noted by Thomas Vartanian, partner at the law firm Dechert, 'Once the FSB staff gets invested in an issue, it is very difficult for it to go away. It can change direction and momentum. But it is hard for it to be eradicated'. Stephen Foley Barney Jopson and Caroline Binham, 'Fund Managers to Escape Systemic Label', Financial Times, https://next.ft.com/content/4e9d566e-2999-11e5-8613-e7aedbb7bdb7.

861. Richardson Matthew, 'Large Banks and the Volcker Rule', 182.

first step was made in 1970 when the New York Stock Exchange abolished the prohibition against the public listing of its members, which were constituted as partnerships or closely held corporations.[862] Wall Street investment banks were for decades organized as partnerships.[863] The partnership form made senior bankers-partners not only entitled to all of the firms' profits but also liable for all of its losses. The partnership model ensured prudent risk-taking and restrained their expansion since partners were personally liable for the firms' losses. Furthermore, their illiquid stakes forced them to adopt a long-term approach to managing their firms. Following the end of the ban on public listing, major Wall Street firms decided to go public, abandoning the partnership form. A major reason for this shift was the opportunity for partners to cash out their stakes in an initial public offering. Other crucial reasons were the ability of firms to tap capital markets in order to fund their trading activities and technological innovations in both information technology and finance.[864] The last firm to float was Goldman Sachs in 1999.

In the aftermath of the financial crisis and the demise of major financial institutions, numerous commentators have argued in favour of a return to the partnership model.[865] More specifically, it has been argued that the partnership structure would have prevented the excessive risk-taking and build-up of leverage that ultimately led to the near collapse of the financial system. Flawed compensation arrangements and job retention and promotion concerns motivated management to pursue risky strategies.[866] Public ownership allowed senior executives to take these huge gambles at the expense of their shareholders, creditors and taxpayers. Had these executives owned illiquid partnership stakes in their firms, so the argument goes, they would never have jeopardized their personal fortune by aggressively using leverage and exotic financial instruments. The partnership structure in essence makes the owners the managers of the firm. As a result, it tackles the agency problem, which characterizes public companies. In a public company setting, dispersed shareholders are unable and unwilling to monitor management. Consequently, managers may take actions that are contrary to their shareholders' interests. Numerous academics, most notably Larry Ribstein,[867] have stressed the benefits of the unincorporated firms, such as general and limited partnerships and LLCs, a significant form of business organization in numerous countries around the world.

862. Alan D. Morrison and William J. Wilhelm Jr., 'The Demise of Investment Banking Partnerships: Theory and Evidence', *Journal of Finance* 63, no. 1 (2008): 311-350, 311.
863. For the historical evolution of investment banks *see* Alan D. Morrison and William J. Wilhelm, *Investment Banking: Institutions, Politics, and Law* (Oxford University Press, 2008).
864. 'The Demise of Investment-Banking Partnerships: Theory and Evidence', *Oxford Financial Research Center Working Paper*, http://papers.ssrn.com/sol3/papers.cfm?abstract_id=569 109.
865. 'A Partnership Solution for Investment Banks', DEALBOOK, http://dealbook.nytimes.com/20 08/08/20/a-partnership-solution-for-investment-banks/.
866. *See* Emilios Avgouleas and Jay Cullen, 'Excessive Leverage and Bankers' Pay: Governance and Financial Stability Costs of a Symbiotic Relationship', *Columbia Journal of European Law* 21, no. 1 (2015): 1-46.
867. Larry Ribstein, *The Rise of the Unincorporation* (Oxford University Press, 2009).

Moreover, the repeal of the Glass-Steagall Act in 1999, which separated commercial banks from the securities industry, and the abolition of barriers to intrastate and interstate bank mergers and branching fostered consolidation within the US bank industry.[868] During the period of 1990 to 2005, the US banking industry witnessed a spectacular merger wave involving more than 5,400 mergers.[869] By 2005, the share of total banking assets held by the ten largest US banking institutions reached 55%.[870] A similar merger wave occurred in Europe.[871] The merger wave was in part driven by regulatory reforms. For instance, the Big Bang reforms in the UK engineered by the Thatcher government radically changed the structure of the UK financial markets and unleashed a wave of consolidation within the financial services industry.[872] The Big Bang reforms refer to a series of reforms seeking to improve the competitive position of the City of London and put an end to anticompetitive practices at the London Stock Exchange. The reforms included the abolition of fixed minimum commissions, the opening of exchange membership to foreign firms and the abolition of the 'single capacity' rule, which prohibited brokers from trading for their own account and jobbers (market makers) from acting for customers, permitting thus firms to act as both brokers and dealers.[873] Moreover, the EU actively encouraged the creation of universal banks.[874] A notable example was the Second Banking Directive, which permitted deposit-taking institutions to become engaged in securities markets and investment banking activities.

The rise of LCFIs coincided with the emergence of financial innovations, such as derivatives products, which led to the erosion of the boundaries between commercial and investment banking, and the tremendous growth of the financial services industry in most developed economies. For instance, between 1980 and 2007, the industry's

868. The Glass-Steagall Act, which was passed in 1933, prohibited banks from engaging in capital market activities, such as purchasing securities for their own account, selling, underwriting and distributing securities. Banks were also prohibited from affiliating with securities firms. Furthermore, non-banking firms were prohibited from accepting deposits. The Act has been credited with enhancing the stability of the US banking system. The restrictions of the Glass-Steagall Act were progressively eroded. The merger between Citicorp, a banking entity, and the Travelers Group, an insurance and securities conglomerate, which created Citigroup, the first universal bank in the US since 1933, pressured Congress to repeal the Glass-Steagall Act. *See* generally Arthur E. Wilmarth, 'The Dark Side of Universal Banking: Financial Conglomerates and the Origins of the Subprime Financial Crisis', *Connecticut Law Review* 41, no. 4 (2009).
869. Kenneth D Jones and Robert C Oshinsky, 'The Effect of Industry Consolidation and Deposit Insurance Reform on the Resiliency of the US Bank Insurance Fund', *Journal of Financial Stability* 5, no. 1 (2009): 58.
870. *Ibid.*
871. Barnes Colleen Amel Dean, Panetta Fabio and Salleo Carmelo, 'Consolidation and Efficiency in the Financial Sector: A Review of the International Evidence', *Journal of Banking & Finance* 28, no. 10 (2004).
872. *See generally* Emilios Avgouleas, 'Large Systemic Banks and Fractional Reserve Banking, Intractable Dilemmas in Search of Effective Solutions', in *Reconceptualizing Global Finance and Its Regulation*, ed. Arner Douglas, Avgouleas Emilios and Buckley Ross (Cambridge University Press), 664-66.
873. Norman S. Poser, 'Automation of Securities Markets and the European Community's Proposed Investment Services Directive', *Law and Contemporary Problems* 55, no. 4 (1992): 31.
874. Avgouleas, 'Large Systemic Banks and Fractional Reserve Banking, Intractable Dilemmas in Search of Effective Solutions', 666-72.

share of total US domestic corporate profits rose from 10% to 40% with its stock market value reaching 19% of the total stock market capitalization.[875] LCFIs came to dominate the markets for underwriting, syndicated lending, derivatives and securitization.[876] LCFIs also came to dominate cross-border finance, creating interconnections within and across borders.[877] LCFIs' large-scale securitization of credit based on an 'originate to distribute' strategy fuelled the credit bubble that set the stage for the global financial crisis.[878] It should be noted that in the run-up to the financial crisis securitizers, apart from acting as underwriters, were also heavily invested in MBSs suffering devastating losses on their holdings.[879] For instance, in 2007, Bank of America held over USD 24 billion of MBSs. The deterioration in the value of MBSs, following the outbreak of the financial crisis, forced it to report approximately USD 15 billion in losses on mortgage-related assets.

Owing to their size, interconnectedness and complexity, these institutions are perceived to be too important to fail. They operate with the benefit of explicit and implicit government guarantees. Explicit government guarantees include deposit insurance and lender of last resort facilities, while implicit government guarantees stem from the expectation that the government will step in to save an ailing financial institution whose distress could jeopardize financial stability. The resulting state subsidy has been well documented in academic literature. Haldane estimates that the amount of the implied annual subsidy to the world's largest banks reached USD 70 billion over the period from 2002 to 2007.[880] In a separate study, Acharya et al. find that expectations of government bailouts are embedded in credit spreads on bonds issued by the largest financial institutions.[881] According to the authors, bond premiums do not fully reflect the institutions' risk-taking.

The combination of government guarantees, shareholder short-termism, limited liability of managers and high-powered performance-based compensation led to excessive risk-taking in the years leading up to the financial crisis.[882] The distress of

875. 'The Financial System: What Went Wrong', The Economist, http://www.economist.com/node/10881318.
876. Wilmarth, 'The Dark Side of Universal Banking: Financial Conglomerates and the Origins of the Subprime Financial Crisis', 994-95.
877. IMF, *Impact of Regulatory Reforms on Large and Complex Financial Institutions, Staff Discussion Note, SPN/10/16* (3 November 2010), 7.
878. *See generally* Wilmarth, 'The Dark Side of Universal Banking: Financial Conglomerates and the Origins of the Subprime Financial Crisis'.
879. Prasad Krishnamurthy and Ryan Bubb, 'Regulating Against Bubbles', *University of Pennsylvania Law Review* 163, no. 6 (2015): 1582.
880. Andrew G Haldane and Philip Booth, 'On Being the Right Size', *Journal of Financial Perspectives* 2, no. 1 (2014).
881. Anginer Deniz, Acharya Viral and Warburton Joseph, 'The End of Market Discipline? Investor Expectations of Implicit State Guarantees', *http://papers.ssrn.com/sol3/papers.cfm?abstract_id=1961656* (2013). Furthermore, Balasubramanian and Cyree examine whether or not yield spread levels and yield spread changes on subordinated notes and debentures increase for too-big-too fail banking institutions after the adoption of the Dodd-Frank Act. The authors find that the TBTF discount is reduced by 94% after the passage of the Dodd-Frank Act. Ken B Cyree and Bhanu Balasubramanian, 'The Determinants of Yield Spreads and the Market Discipline of Banks', *Available at SSRN 1350951* (2009).
882. Julian TS Chow and Jay Surti, 'Making Banks Safer: Can Volcker and Vickers Do It?', *WP/11/236 IMF Working Papers* (2011): 3-4.

several of these conglomerates, most notably UBS, Bear Stearns, Fortis, Lehman Brothers, AIG and the Royal Bank of Scotland, threatened to paralyse the financial system. From the beginning of the subprime crisis in 2007 until 2009, banks and insurers suffered USD 1.1 trillion of losses with the seventeen largest LCFIs accounting for more than half of these losses.[883] For instance, the Royal Bank of Scotland reported a loss of GBP 28 billion in 2008, the biggest in British corporate history, while AIG suffered a spectacular net loss of more than USD 99.3 billion in 2008 alone.[884]

Two main arguments have been put forward in favour of the LCFI model: (a) synergies through economies of scope and scale and (b) reduction in idiosyncratic risk. Economies of scale arise by spreading fixed costs, such as market infrastructure and IT technology, over a large customer base, while economies of scope are accomplished through diversifying business activities across products, services and/or geographies.[885] For instance, economies of scope may arise from cross-selling underwriting and lending services.[886] In addition, diversification of business lines protects a financial institution against idiosyncratic shocks that adversely impact individual business lines.[887] Despite the perceived benefits of the LCFI model, empirical studies point in the opposite direction. In their review of the empirical studies on efficiency gains achieved by economies of scale and scope, Gambacorta and Van Rixtel conclude that 'academic studies have difficulties in establishing significant and substantial positive economies of scale and especially of scope'.[888] Consistent with the view that diversification does not lead to wide-scale synergies, Laeven and Levine report evidence of a diversification discount.[889] The market valuations of financial conglomerates are lower than if those firms were broken into individual firms specializing in individual activities. In short, the whole is worth less than the sum of the parts. In a separate study, Schmid and Walter report a similar financial conglomerate discount.[890] Finally, in his study of diversifying versus focusing US bank mergers in 1988-1995, DeLong finds that focused mergers in terms of activities and geography significantly enhance shareholder value

883. Wilmarth, 'The Dark Side of Universal Banking: Financial Conglomerates and the Origins of the Subprime Financial Crisis', 968.
884. Gordon Rayner, 'Banking Bailout: The Rise and Fall of RBS', The Daily Telegraph, http://www.telegraph.co.uk/finance/newsbysector/banksandfinance/4291807/Banking-bailout-The-rise-and-fall-of-RBS.html; Matthew Karnitschnig et al., 'U.S. to Take over AIG in $85 Billion Bailout; Central Banks Inject Cash as Credit Dries Up', http://www.wsj.com/articles/SB122156561931242905.
885. Leonardo Gambacorta and Adrian van Rixtel, 'Structural Bank Regulation Initiatives: Approaches and Implications', *BIS Working Papers* No .412 (April 2013) 8-9.
886. Christian Laux and Uwe Walz, 'Cross-Selling Lending and Underwriting: Scope Economies and Incentives*', *Review of Finance* 13, no. 2 (2009).
887. Pazarbasioglu Ceyla Viñals José, Surti Jay, Narain Aditya, Erbenova Michaela and Chow Julian, 'Creating a Safer Financial System: Will the Volcker, Vickers and Liikanen Structural Measures Help?', *IMF Discussion Note* SDN/13/4 (14 May 2013) 21-22.
888. Gambacorta and Rixtel, 'Structural Bank Regulation Initiatives: Approaches and Implications', 9.
889. Luc Laeven and Ross Levine, 'Is There a Diversification Discount in Financial Conglomerates?', *Journal of Financial Economics* 85, no. 2 (2007).
890. Markus M Schmid and Ingo Walter, 'Do Financial Conglomerates Create or Destroy Economic Value?', *Journal of Financial Intermediation* 18, no. 2 (2009).

upon the announcement of the merger, while diversifying mergers do not create value.[891]

As far as the reduction in idiosyncratic risk is concerned, one should note that there are two types of risk: idiosyncratic and systematic or market-wide risk.[892] Idiosyncratic risk is diversifiable, while market-wide risk is not. Even though the operation of multiple business lines may result in a reduction of the volatility of a financial firm's overall portfolio, the most important aspect, from a societal point of view, is whether financial conglomerates can withstand market-wide risk.[893] Indeed, empirical studies find that even though diversification reduces the likelihood of individual bank failure, it results in the aggravation of systemic risk. For instance, De Jonghe's study concludes that the diversification of financial activities leads to an increase in financial firms' tail betas.[894] While diversification lowers the probability of individual bank failure, it actually exposes banks to the same risks increasing the likelihood of joint failure. In a related study, DeYoung and Roland find that diversification increases the market risk of financial firms.[895] What is more, diversification and the concomitant growth of intra-firm exposures raise the likelihood of intra-firm contagion.[896] Losses could spread quickly inside the group, impacting crucial, from a social welfare perspective, parts, such as retail banking operations. A similar conclusion is reached by Tasca and Battiston, who find that full risk diversification jeopardizes financial stability.[897]

Following the financial crisis, regulators in the US and Europe have sought to constrain the activities of LCFIs. Restricting the scope of LCFIs' activities maximizes social welfare by limiting reputation-driven or exposure-driven contagion inside and across firms, safeguarding the provision of retail banking services, limiting government guarantees to depositary institutions offering vital financial services and facilitating resolution.[898] Furthermore, as Viñals et al. note, 'activity restrictions can be useful in managing risks that are difficult to measure and address using price-based tools'.[899] Despite the strengthening of regulatory tools seeking to improve bank capital and liquidity standards, such as capital buffers, limits on leverage and tight liquidity

891. Gayle L. DeLong, 'Stockholder Gains from Focusing Versus Diversifying Bank Mergers', *Journal of Financial Economics* 59, no. 2 (1 February 2001): 221-52.
892. According to Higgins, 'systematic risk reflects exposure to economywide, or market wide events, such as interest rate changes and business cycles, and cannot be reduced by diversification. Unsystematic risk or idiosyncratic risk, on the other hand, reflects investment-specific events, such as fires and lawsuits, which can be eliminated through diversification'. Robert C. Higgins, *Analysis for Financial Management* (McGraw-Hill, 2012), 300-01.
893. Richardson Matthew, 'Large Banks and the Volcker Rule', 184.
894. Olivier De Jonghe, 'Back to the Basics in Banking? A Micro-Analysis of Banking System Stability', *Journal of Financial Intermediation* 19, no. 3 (2010).
895. Robert DeYoung and Karin P. Roland, 'Product Mix and Earnings Volatility at Commercial Banks: Evidence from a Degree of Total Leverage Model', *Journal of Financial Intermediation* 10, no. 1 (1 January 2001): 54-84.
896. Chow and Surti, 'Making Banks Safer: Can Volcker and Vickers Do It?', 3.
897. Tascan Paolo and Battiston Stefano, 'Diversification and Financial Stability', *SRC Discussion Paper No. 10* (February 2014).
898. *Ibid.*, 3-4.
899. Viñals José 'Creating a Safer Financial System: Will the Volcker, Vickers and Liikanen Structural Measures Help?', 12.

standards,[900] certain business lines may be too complex for effective supervision and imposition of price-based tools seeking to address tail risk.[901] As Avgouleas notes, the inherent complexity of LCFIs makes their regulation a Herculean task.[902]

Hedge fund sponsorship and investments became a profitable business for financial institutions in the early 1990s, when major investment banks spotted the opportunities offered by in-house hedge funds.[903] The outsized returns offered by hedge funds as well as the rise of traders up the hierarchy within financial institutions, in contrast to the traditionally more conservative investment bankers, can be seen as the main factors that caused this shift. Before the introduction of the Volcker Rule, major US financial institutions, such as Goldman Sachs, Citigroup and Morgan Stanley, used to run major hedge fund arms.[904] The adoption of the Volcker Rule has forced these institutions to largely shed their hedge fund arms and lose some of their star traders.[905] In contrast, European financial institutions are still allowed to run internal hedge funds. For instance, a significant hedge fund arm is run by Deutsche Bank, one of Europe's biggest financial institutions.[906] Nevertheless, following the financial crisis,

900. Basel III adopted by the Basel Committee on Banking Supervision introduces a new set of stringent capital buffers, leverage and liquidity standards. Basel III seeks to improve both the quantity and quality of bank capital, reduce bank leverage, address procyclicality and strengthen bank liquidity. For an overview of Basel III *see* Emily Lee, 'Basel III: Post-Financial Crisis International Financial Regulatory Reform', *Journal of International Banking Law and Regulation* 28 (2013). The Basel Committee on Banking Supervision was established in 1974 in response to the financial market turbulence caused by the breakdown of the Bretton Woods system of managed exchange rates. The Committee acts as a forum for cooperation between its member countries on issues related to banking supervision setting standards for the regulation and supervision of banks. It should be noted that the standards have no legal force and that it is the responsibility of individual national authorities to implement these standards. *See generally* Charles Goodhart, *The Basel Committee on Banking Supervision: A History of the Early Years, 1974-1997* (Cambridge University Press, 2011).
901. Viñals José 'Creating a Safer Financial System: Will the Volcker, Vickers and Liikanen Structural Measures Help?', 12.
902. Avgouleas, 'Large Systemic Banks and Fractional Reserve Banking, Intractable Dilemmas in Search of Effective Solutions'.
903. Connor and Woo, 'An Introduction to Hedge Funds', 1-39. It should be noted that financial institutions expanded their business lines to not only hedge funds but also private equity and venture capital.
904. Scott Patterson and Ryan Tracy, 'Fed Gives Banks More Time to Sell Private Equity, Hedge Fund Stakes', The Wall Street Journal, http://www.wsj.com/articles/fed-gives-banks-more-time-to-sell-private-equity-hedge-fund-stakes-1418933398.
905. *Ibid.* Furthermore, the introduction of the Volcker Rule, which has forced banks to axe their proprietary trading desks, has fundamentally changed the recruiting model of hedge funds. Hedge funds, which used to recruit employees from the vast pool of seasoned bank proprietary traders, are now forced to fundamentally rethink the way they recruit their employees. Indeed, hedge funds are starting to increasingly rely on in-house training introducing, for instance, graduate training programmes for junior staff. Miles Johnson, 'Beyond Banking: Traditional Talent Pool Dries up for Hedge Funds', Financial Times, https://next.ft.com/content/7880dc7a-77d8-11e5-a95a-27d368e1ddf7.
906. Deutsche Bank's asset management arm, called Deutsche Asset Management, offered alternative investment funds, including hedge funds, private equity and real estate funds. In 2018, Deutsche Asset Management rebranded to DWS and was spun off as a separate company through an IPO with Deutsche Bank holding the majority of the shares in the new company. Olaf Storbeck, 'Deutsche Bank's DWS Puts IPO Price at €32.50 a Share', Financial Times, https://www.ft.com/content/de81fc28-2dfe-11e8-a34a-7e7563b0b0f4.

numerous European financial institutions, such as UBS, were forced to axe their hedge fund arms.[907] The adoption of the Proposal on Bank Structural Reform, which would have introduced an outright ban, would have resulted in a further retreat of European banking institutions from the hedge fund business, similar to the one observed in the US.

With respect to hedge funds, one should make a distinction between hedge funds supported by an LCFI's own capital and hedge funds sponsored by an LCFI using solely outside investor capital. As far as hedge funds supported by a banking firm's own capital are concerned, banning LCFIs' involvement in the hedge fund business promotes financial stability. Although hedge funds in general employ a modest level of leverage, certain hedge funds can be highly leveraged and can thus easily fail during a crisis. A notable example was the failure of Bear Stearns' hedge funds, which led to its ultimate demise. Apart from the direct losses suffered by Bear Stearns due to its direct investments in the funds' capital, Bear also suffered irreversible reputational damage.

Furthermore, internal hedge funds, supported by the LCFI's own capital, are able to engage in excessive risk-taking and finance themselves at below-market rates by taking advantage of the explicit or implicit government guarantees of their parent companies.[908] Indeed, in their empirical study of private equity investments sponsored by the private equity arms of large banks between 1983 and 2009, Fang et al. find that bank-affiliated deals, defined as deals where banks become involved as an equity investor, have worse financing terms and worse *ex post* outcomes, namely more debt downgrades and a higher likelihood of experiencing bankruptcy, compared to stand-alone deals.[909] According to the authors, the above-mentioned evidence indicates that banks are not superior equity investors, and their investments do not provide any positive signal for the quality of the deal.[910] The evidence lends support to the view that bank managers taking advantage of government guarantees seek to maximize revenues by increasing the volatility of their investments.[911] As far as parent-financed deals, defined as deals where the bank acts as both an equity and a debt investor, are concerned, the authors document that they enjoy significantly better financing terms compared to stand-alone deals, benefiting thus from the government guarantees of their parents.[912] Applying the above-mentioned evidence in the hedge fund context leads one to conclude that hedge funds supported by the banking firm's own capital increase systemic risk by benefiting from the government guarantees of their parents. A ban on investing in hedge funds will end this market distortion at the expense of stand-alone hedge funds and ensure a healthy degree of competition.

What is more, an interesting question arises with respect to the systemic risk posed by hedge funds sponsored by LCFIs using exclusively outside investors' capital.

---

907. Peter Thal Larsen, 'UBS Forced to Axe Hedge Fund', Financial Times, http://www.ft.com/intl/cms/s/0/df424920-f948-11db-9b6b-000b5df10621.html#axzz3kj273vS6.
908. Richardson Matthew, 'Large Banks and the Volcker Rule'.
909. Viral V. Acharya, Philipp Schnabl and Gustavo Suarez, 'Securitization Without Risk Transfer', *Journal of Financial Economics* 107, no. 3 (1 March 2013): 515-36.
910. *Ibid.*, 2139-44.
911. *Ibid.*
912. *Ibid.*

Certain researchers have argued that funds run by LCFIs without using the firms' own capital do not jeopardize financial stability.[913] Nonetheless, even the sponsorship of hedge funds by LCFIs without any direct investment by the parent company can contribute to systemic risk. Market confidence in the whole group can evaporate after the failure of a sponsored fund jeopardizing its own financial stability. Additionally, in the case of managing AIFs, the LCFI income generated from running these funds represents a proportion of its AUM. According to Richardson et al., 'if the stream of revenues from these businesses is capitalized by the equity market and the firm can borrow against this capitalization, then a loss in the present value of revenues can have an effect similar to investing one's own capital'.[914]

In addition, the sponsorship of and investment in hedge funds by LCFIs may result in serious conflicts of interest.[915] The Group of Thirty Working Group on Financial Reform in its 2009 report recognized that the risks, market volatilities and conflicts of interests arising from LCFIs' involvement in proprietary trading and hedge fund sponsorship and investments are difficult to measure and control.[916] Conflicts of interest may arise in the commingling of LCFIs' investment and commercial banking activities with their hedge fund activities.[917] Commercial banking activities, which involve deposit-taking and the granting of loan and investment banking activities, which include advisory services on corporate financing and mergers and acquisitions, allow LCFIs to have access to significant non-public information regarding their customers. Consequently, internal hedge funds may take advantage of the non-public information acquired in the course of the LCFIs' investment and commercial banking activities at the expense of their customers. As a result, information asymmetries and conflicts of interest are amplified. Informational asymmetries and conflicts of interest can be particularly severe in activities involving complex and opaque financial products and transactions, such as investments in and sponsorship of hedge funds.

Nonetheless, it has been argued that structural measures, such as the ban on proprietary trading and hedge fund sponsorship and investment, may push certain activities to unregulated entities, such as stand-alone hedge funds, where they can still contribute to financial instability. For instance, Gong and Page argue that in the presence of unregulated shadow banks imposing bank regulations increases systemic risk.[918] According to the IMF, 'structural measures may push certain activities to unregulated entities where they can still exert systemic risk. A widespread collapse of such units could adversely affect confidence and liquidity in the financial system,

913. Richardson Matthew, 'Large Banks and the Volcker Rule', 192-93.
914. *Ibid.*, 193.
915. Acharya and Richardson, 'Causes of the Financial Crisis'.
916. Working Group on Financial Reform The Group of Thirty, *Financial Reform: A Framework for Financial Stability* (2009), 27.
917. Hossein Nabilou, 'Bank Proprietary Trading and Investment in Private Funds: Is the Volcker Rule a Panacea or Yet Another Maginot Line?', *Banking & Finance Law Review* 32, no. 2 (1 April 2017): 306-07.
918. Gong Rui and Page Frank, 'Shadow Banks and Systemic Risks', *SRC Discussion Paper No. 55* (February 2016).

thereby involving the real economy and retail banks'.[919] However, it should be noted that after the adoption of the AIFM Directive in Europe and the Dodd-Frank Act in the US, hedge funds are not the unregulated and opaque vehicles their critics portray them to be.

What is more, the analysis in Chapter 2 has shown that the overwhelming majority of hedge funds, that is small- and medium-sized funds, do not pose a risk to financial stability. In contrast to traditional financial institutions, which were the main perpetrators of the recent financial crisis, hedge funds were the victims of it. In fact, hedge funds were able to weather the financial crisis far better than traditional financial institutions. As a result, structural measures banning the sponsorship and investment in hedge funds will result in the diversification of risks to the entities best able to handle them. As far as large systemically important hedge funds are concerned, a framework providing for the designation of hedge funds as systemically important and their ongoing supervision and regulation are the appropriate response to their contribution to systemic risk.

4.2.2 Introducing the Volcker Rule in Europe

The present section will seek to make the case for the introduction of a Volcker-style ban in Europe. Consequently, the stance of European regulators with the withdrawal of the Proposal on Bank Structural Reform will be criticized. Despite the criticism levelled against the Proposal on Bank Structural Reform, our analysis suggests that the Proposal on Bank Structural Reform is a sensible response to the risks posed by banks' speculative activities. Nonetheless, a major flaw of the Proposal was that the ban on proprietary trading and the prohibition of hedge fund sponsorship and investments did not extend to non-bank systemically important institutions, such as insurance companies.

In response to the financial crisis and the demise of the LCFI model, various jurisdictions around the world adopted bank structural reforms seeking to shield essential banking activities from riskier activities, such as sponsoring and investing in hedge funds and private equity funds and proprietary trading.[920] The US was the first jurisdiction to introduce bank structural reform measures with the adoption of the Volcker Rule, which imposes an outright ban on speculative activities. The rule prohibits banking entities from engaging in proprietary trading, sponsoring and investing in hedge funds and private equity funds. Furthermore, non-bank systemically

919. SDN 13/4 IMF Staff Discussion Note (2013). In addition, as Whitehead observes 'In short, even if proprietary trading is no longer located in banks, it may now be conducted by less-regulated entities that affect banks and banking activities'. *See* Whitehead, 'The Volcker Rule and Evolving Financial Markets', 46.

920. *See generally* Randall D. Guynn and Patrick Kenadjian, 'Structural Solutions: Blinded by Volcker, Vickers, Liikanen, Glass Steagall and Narrow Banking', in *Too Big to Fail III: Structural Reform Proposals – Should We Break up the Banks?*, ed. Patrick S. Kenadjian and Andreas Dombret (De Gruyter, 2014); Matthias Lehmann Bonn, 'Volcker Rule, Ring-Fencing or Separation of Bank Activities – Comparison of Structural Reform Acts around the World', *LSE Legal Studies Working Paper* No. 25 (2014).

important institutions designated by the FSOC for supervision by the FED will be subject to enhanced capital requirements and quantitative limits with respect to the above-mentioned activities. Nonetheless, the Volcker Rule introduces certain exceptions from the prohibition of proprietary trading and hedge fund sponsorship and investments.

The Volcker Rule has been sharply criticized for its definitional ambiguity and the exemptions permitting banking entities to continue their market-making and hedging activities and, under limited circumstances, to sponsor and invest a *de minimis* amount in hedge funds.[921] Banking institutions can potentially exploit these exemptions and jeopardize their financial stability. For instance, banking entities may mask hedge fund-like investments as hedging or market-making activities. Furthermore, sponsoring and investing in hedge funds, even under limited circumstances and for a *de minimis* amount, exposes banking institutions to systemic risk. Even a small amount of direct investment in an ailing hedge fund may cause irreversible reputational damage to a banking institution. Most importantly, it should be noted that even though the Volcker Rule imposes a ban on proprietary trading and hedge fund sponsorship and investments on banking institutions, it does not introduce such a blanket prohibition for non-bank SIFIs. Housing these activities within non-bank SIFIs poses exactly the same financial stability risks as housing these activities within banking institutions.

The UK quickly followed the US' example establishing the Vickers Commission. The Commission's mandate was the formulation of recommendations for reform of the UK banking sector with the aim of mitigating systemic risk, minimizing moral hazard, reducing the occurrence and impact of bank failures and promoting resolvability. The Commission published its final recommendations in September 2011.[922] In contrast to the US, which chose to impose an outright ban on speculative activities, the Vickers Commission adopted the so-called ring-fencing approach to bank reorganization recommending the ring-fencing of UK banks' retail operations. Schwarz defines ring-fencing as 'legally deconstructing a firm to reallocate and reduce risk more optimally, such as by protecting the firm's assets and operations and minimizing its internal and affiliate risks'.[923]

According to the recommendations of the Vickers Commission, banks' retail and commercial banking activities in the UK should be transferred to a separate legal entity within their corporate group. Pursuant to the Commission's final report, the taking of deposits from and the provision of overdrafts to individuals and SMEs in the UK should be provided inside the ring-fenced bank.[924] What is more, certain activities, such as the taking of deposits from and the provision of payment services to customers within the

921. *See*, for instance, Whitehead, 'The Volcker Rule and Evolving Financial Markets', 50-51.and Darell Duffie, *Drawing Boundaries Around and Through the Banking System, World Economic Forum, Financial Development Report* (31 October 2012), 43-44.
922. Independent Commission on Banking, *Final Report* (September 2011). For a detailed discussion of the UK's approach *see* Kern Alexander, 'Regulating the Structure of the EU Banking Sector', *European Business Organization Law Review* 16, no. 2 (2015): 231-42.
923. Steven L. Schwarcz, 'Ring-Fencing', *Southern California Law Review* 87 (2013): 82. The definition of ring-fencing offered by Schwarz is broad capturing not only the UK ring-fencing regime but also the Volcker Rule and the Glass-Steagall Act.
924. *Ibid.*, 38-39.

EEA and certain services to individuals and non-financial companies within the EEA, including trade finance and mortgages, may also be provided inside the ring-fenced bank.[925] Nonetheless, the Commission's report included a wide range of prohibited activities, which may be provided inside the group but outside the ring-fence. Prohibited activities include market-making, proprietary trading and hedge fund and private equity investments.[926]

Following the release of the Vickers Report, the UK adopted the Financial Services Act 2013, which received Royal Assent on 18 December 2013.[927] The Act implements the recommendations of the Vickers Report and introduces a ring-fencing regime for the largest UK banks applicable from January 2019. What is more, the PRA is mandated to make policy to implement the ring-fencing regime. Core banking services consisting of accepting deposits or other payments, facilities for withdrawing money, and overdrafts are required to be placed into a separate legal entity. Ring-fenced bodies are prohibited from engaging in excluded activities, including securities underwriting, dealing in investments as principal and commodities trading. The provisions are applicable to deposit-taking institutions, which are incorporated in the UK, except for building societies, credit unions or banks that hold 'core deposits' consisting of retail and small- and medium-sized business deposits below GBP 25 billion.

Pursuant to the PRA's rules, ring-fenced bodies are required to hold an extra systemic risk buffer.[928] The PRA has set systemic risk buffer rates ranging from 1% of risk-weighted assets for Barclays, Santander and HSBC to 2% for Lloyds Banking Group. In addition, the ring-fenced body must be legally, economically and operationally independent. At least half of its board members must be independent from the group. It may enter into transactions with other members of its group provided that the transactions are done on an arm's-length basis, the ring-fenced body holds capital against the credit risk related to its exposures and limits its exposures to any single entity to 25% of its capital.[929] The rules also include restrictions on the ability of the ring-fenced body to make distributions to other members of the group.[930]

Overall, the ring-fencing regime has been heavily criticized by the largest banking groups, which have been forced to radically restructure their operations.[931] The wholesale divisions of banks, which after the introduction of the ring-fencing regime, are unable to finance their operations with retail deposits, have seen a rise in their

925. *Ibid.*, 54.
926. *Ibid.*, 51-52.
927. *Financial Services (Banking Reform) Act 2013 (UK)*.
928. 'Systemic Risk Buffer Rates for Ring-Fenced Banks and Large Building Societies', HM Treasury, 2 February 2021, https://www.bankofengland.co.uk/prudential-regulation/publication/2019/systemic-risk-buffer-rates-for-ring-fenced-banks-and-large-building-societies.
929. Prudential Regulation Authority, The Implementation of ring-fencing: Prudential Requirements, intragroup arrangements and use of financial market infrastructures, July 2016, Policy Statement PS20/16, 14-15, 17-18.
930. *Ibid.*, 14.
931. 'New Rules Force UK Banks to Restructure, Hold Extra Capital', The Wall Street Journal, http://www.wsj.com/articles/ringfenced-british-banks-will-need-permission-to-pay-dividends-says-bank-of-england-1444899418.

funding costs.[932] Moreover, the implementation of the rules has proven to be costly, particularly for smaller banks.[933] Executives of the banking groups covered by the ring-fencing regime are also particularly concerned about the lack of control over the ring-fenced bodies, which will have separate boards of directors and management.[934] Furthermore, concerns have been raised regarding the impact of ring-fencing on the competitiveness of UK banks and its impact on the UK economy.[935] The UK government has commissioned an independent review of the operation of the ring-fencing regime, which will assess its impact on competition in the banking sector, the international competitiveness of UK banks and the provision of financial services to the real economy.[936] Moreover, the review will consider any unintended consequences of the ring-fencing regime. According to its critics, the introduction of the ring-fencing regime represents a rejection of the model of universal banking and the benefits brought by it.[937] Nonetheless, as the analysis in section 4.2.1 of Chapter 4 has shown, the benefits brought by the universal banking model are rather illusory, with the empirical evidence strongly indicating that financial conglomeration poses risks to financial stability. As a result, structural measures, such as the ring-fencing regime, represent a welcome development.

However, the ring-fencing model suffers from significant shortcomings. Most importantly, the regime does not adequately tackle reputational risk.[938] Market confidence in the whole group may evaporate due to problems in subsidiaries housing speculative activities, such as hedge fund investments or sponsorship. Furthermore, the ring-fencing regime does not totally prohibit intragroup exposures, thereby allowing losses from one part of the group to spread to other parts. Finally, it should be noted that ring-fencing facilitates resolution only at the retail bank level and not at the group level.[939] The relevant provisions do not include any activity restrictions on the non-ring-fenced parts of the group.

The EU was a late mover in introducing bank structural reform measures. In response to the massive bank failures witnessed during the financial crisis, the European Commission established, in February 2012, a High-Level Expert Group, in order to examine possible reforms to the structure of the EU banking sector. The High-Level Group concluded that no specific business model fared particularly well, or particularly poorly, in the financial crisis.[940] The Group considered that the main cause

932. Laura Noonan and Stephen Morris, 'Banks Set for Clash with UK Regulator over Ringfencing Rules', Financial Times, https://www.ft.com/content/e19ef658-992a-497d-b73b-bf051aabf674.
933. *Ibid.*
934. Emma Dunkley & Martin Arnold, 'Global Banks Fret over UK Ringfencing Rules', Financial Times, https://next.ft.com/content/a1ac7434-15c6-11e5-be54-00144feabdc0.
935. Steven L Schwarcz, 'Ring-Fencing', *Southern California Law Review* 87, no. 1 (2013): 103.
936. 'Systemic Risk Buffer Rates for Ring-Fenced Banks and Large Building Societies'.
937. James Titcomb, 'HSBC: "The UK Has Rejected the Concept of Universal Banking"', The Daily Telegraph, http://www.telegraph.co.uk/finance/newsbysector/banksandfinance/11582516/HSBC-shares-jump-after-profits-smash-forecasts.html.
938. Viñals José, 'Creating a Safer Financial System: Will the Volcker, Vickers and Liikanen Structural Measures Help?', 17.
939. *Ibid.*, 17-18.
940. *High-Level Expert Group on Reforming the Structure of the EU Banking Sector, Final Report*, iv.

of the financial crisis was excessive risk-taking, most notably excessive real estate related lending and trading in highly complex instruments.[941] The recommendations of the High-Level Expert Group largely mirrored the Vickers recommendations. The Group recommended the separation of the trading and the banking activities of large financial institutions into two legally separate entities ('trading bank' and 'commercial bank'), both operating within a BHC structure.

Following the release of the Liikanen Report and inspired by its recommendations, France and Germany enacted, in 2013, bank structural reform measures seeking to curb bank speculative activities and protect bank deposit-taking and customer-oriented activities.[942] The approach taken by German and French legislators follows the spirit of the UK ring-fencing regime. Nevertheless, the approach of German and French legislators differs from the UK regime in that the ring-fence applies to the trading entity and not the deposit-taking bank.[943] The ring-fencing measures have a limited scope covering only systemically important banks.[944] Under the German and French reforms, deposit-taking institutions must either transfer their speculative activities, such as proprietary trading and certain relations with hedge funds, to a separate trading subsidiary or stop them altogether.[945] The subsidiary must be a separate legal entity and is prohibited from accepting deposits or offering retail payment services.[946] French reforms additionally prohibit the trading entity from engaging in certain activities, such as high-frequency trading.[947] Deposit-taking institutions may continue to conduct certain activities, including hedging activities, underwriting activities and market-making, subject to certain limits.[948] French measures also allow the deposit-taking institutions to enter into transactions with hedge funds and other highly leveraged funds provided that sufficient security has been given.[949] Overall, as Howarth and James note, the French and German reforms are weaker than the UK ring-fencing

941. *Ibid.*, at iv.
942. Financial Stability Board, *Structural Banking Reforms, Cross-Border Consistencies and Global Financial Stability Implications* (2014), 10. Loi no. 2013-672 du 26 juillet 2013 de séparation et de régulation des activités bancaires, J.O. n°173 du 27 juillet 2013, p. 12530 & Gesetz zur Abschirmung von Risiken und zur Planung der Sanierung und Abwicklung von Kreditinstituten und Finanzgruppen v. 7.8.2013, BGBl. 2013 I p. 3090.
943. For a detailed analysis of the French and German regimes *see* Élisabeth Coulomb, 'La Loi Bancaire: La France Précède L'europe', *Revue-Banque* 765 (2013); Jens-Hinrich Binder, 'To Ring-Fence or Not, and How? Strategic Questions for Post-Crisis Banking Reform in Europe', http://papers.ssrn.com/sol3/papers.cfm?abstract_id=2543860 (2014).
944. Article 511-47-I Code monétaire et financier (French Financial Services Act) & §3(2) 1 Kreditwesengesetz - KWG (German Banking Act).
945. Matthias Lehmann, 'Volcker Rule, Ring-Fencing or Separation of Bank Activities: Comparison of Structural Reform Acts Around the World', *LSE Law, Society and Economy Working Papers* 25/2014 (2014): 9.
946. Article 511-48-I Code monétaire et financier (French Financial Services Act); §25f(6) Kreditwesengesetz - KWG (German Banking Act).
947. Article 511-48-II Code monétaire et financier (French Financial Services Act).
948. Shearman and Sterling, *Comparison of New EU Proposals on Proprietary Trading and Ring-Fencing against US, UK, French and German Rules* (26 February 2014), 12.
949. Article 511-47-I 2 para. 7 Code monétaire et financier (French Financial Services Act).

regime.[950] The authors argue that in contrast to France and Germany, the decision of the UK to appoint an independent commission to examine bank structural reform insulated the process from industry lobbying and allowed non-business actors to participate in it.

Despite the recommendations of the Liikanen Report and the bank structural reform measures adopted by major EU jurisdictions, such as France and Germany, the EU decided to adopt a model closer to the US one. The Proposal on Bank Structural Reform adopted in January 2014 prohibited EU banks and groups above a certain size from engaging in proprietary trading and investing in AIFs, entities that sponsor AIFs and financial instruments that track the performance of such funds.[951] The ban on investing in and sponsoring AIFs covered hedge funds, but the proposal provided an exemption for private equity funds and venture capital funds. In addition, the Proposal granted national authorities the power to require the separation of high-risk trading activities, such as trading in derivatives and market-making. Separated activities were required to be placed in a ring-fenced subsidiary. Retail banks could nonetheless continue to engage in hedging activities, such as interest rate trading, in order to manage their capital, liquidity and funding.

It should be noted that taking into account the various structural measures adopted by different Member States, such as the ring-fencing regimes introduced in the UK, France and Germany, the Proposal allowed the European Commission to grant a derogation from the separation requirement provided that the Member State had adopted legislation that had an equivalent effect to the Proposal.[952] Nevertheless, as Lehmann notes, only the UK ring-fencing regime would fulfil the criteria allowing it thus to continue applying.[953] Furthermore, the Proposal empowered the European Commission to grant derogations to credit institutions and parent companies of a third country that had introduced equivalent structural measures.[954] Nonetheless, there was widespread scepticism on whether the European Commission would actually apply such derogations.[955]

In general, considering the shortcomings of the ring-fencing regime, the stance of the European Commission, which clearly favoured an outright ban on proprietary trading and hedge fund sponsorship and investments, should be largely applauded. In addition, the Proposal is, in certain areas, a marked improvement over the US Volcker Rule. For instance, unlike the Volcker Rule, which allows hedge fund sponsorship and investments in limited circumstances, the Proposal introduced a strict ban without granting any exemptions.

950. David Howarth and Scott James, 'The Politics of Bank Structural Reform: Business Power and Agenda Setting in the United Kingdom, France, and Germany', *Business and Politics* 22, no. 1 (2020): 25-51.
951. 'Proposal for a Regulation of the European Parliament and of the Council on Structural Measures Improving the Resilience of EU Credit Institutions'.
952. *Ibid.*, Art. 21, at 37, 38.
953. Lehmann, 'Volcker Rule, Ring-Fencing or Separation of Bank Activities: Comparison of Structural Reform Acts Around the World', 14.
954. *Ibid.*, Art. 27, at 41.
955. Sterling, *Comparison of New EU Proposals on Proprietary Trading and Ring-Fencing against US, UK, French and German Rules*, 2.

Nevertheless, the Proposal on Bank Structural Reform suffered from a significant drawback. Due to the absence of a European framework for designating non-bank financial institutions that have the potential to threaten financial stability as systemically important, it captured solely banking groups leaving other financial institutions that may pose systemic risk, such as insurance companies, outside its scope. However, financial stability risk may also emanate from proprietary desks and hedge funds housed within non-bank SIFIs. A notable example was the failure of Bear Stearns, an investment bank, which was triggered by losses suffered by its internal hedge funds.[956] On the contrary, the Volcker Rule recognizing the systemic risk posed by the involvement of non-bank systemically important institutions in hedge fund sponsorship and investments and proprietary trading mandates enhanced capital requirements and quantitative limits with respect to the above-mentioned activities. Even though the rationale behind imposing these measures is sound, capital requirements and quantitative limits are unlikely to be sufficient to adequately tackle the systemic risk posed by housing these activities within non-bank financial institutions. Therefore, an outright ban would be the optimal solution.

Another significant shortcoming of the Proposal was the exclusion of market-making and hedging from the definition of proprietary trading. As a result, banks and entities within the same group might effectively evade the ban on proprietary trading by masking their proprietary trades as market-making or hedging transactions. Distinguishing between legitimate market-making or hedging transactions and proprietary trading is a complex and delicate exercise, which involves an examination of the motivation behind the trade.[957] Even though the Proposal granted national authorities the power to separate trading activities, including market-making, these activities, which would be transferred to a separate ring-fenced subsidiary, might still pose financial stability risks. Losses suffered by the subsidiary might spread to the other parts of the group, including the retail operations. Furthermore, reputational damage might lead to erosion of confidence in the whole group. Moreover, even if national authorities decided to separate certain high-risk activities, retail banks might continue to engage in hedging transactions. Even though market-making and hedging transaction pose considerable risks, an outright ban on them would be counterproductive. Despite the gradual entry of non-bank financial institutions into the market-making business, banks are still dominant market makers in a variety of assets.[958] Banks'

956. It should be noted that the financial crisis of 2008 brought the end of independent investment banks, which converted to banks, collapsed or were acquired by bigger banking institutions. Lehman Brothers declared bankruptcy, Merill Lynch was acquired by Bank of America, Bear Stearns was sold to JP Morgan Chase and Goldman Sachs and Morgan Stanley converted to bank holding companies. 'As Goldman and Morgan Shift, a Wall St. Era Ends', Dealbook, http://dealbook.nytimes.com/2008/09/21/goldman-morgan-to-become-bank-holding-companies/?_r=0.

957. Ryan Bubb and Marcel Kahan, 'Regulating Motivation: A New Perspective on the Volcker Rule', *Texas Law Review* 96 (2018): 1020-21.

958. For instance, high-frequency traders have emerged as important market makers in numerous markets and most notably the US Treasury market. *See* Foucault Thierry, 'Where Are the Risks in High-Frequency Trading', *Banque de France, Financial Stability Review* 20 (April 2016); Stanislav Dolgopolov, 'Regulating Merchants of Liquidity: Market Making from Crowded Floors to High-Frequency Trading', *University of Pennsylvania Journal of Business Law* 18,

complete retreat from the market-making business would result in a breakdown of market liquidity and a sharp rise in price volatility.[959] What is more, hedging transactions are essential for mitigating the risks associated with banks' retail operations, such as foreign exchange risk.

Overall, the Proposal on Bank Structural Reform adopted a measured and targeted approach towards the financial stability risks posed by internal hedge funds. Nevertheless, in order to better safeguard financial stability, an extension of the ban on proprietary trading and hedge fund sponsorship and investments to non-bank SIFIs is warranted.

4.3 TOWARDS A NEW HEDGE FUND SYSTEMIC RISK ARCHITECTURE

4.3.1 Centralizing Hedge Fund Supervision in the Eurozone

The financial and sovereign debt crises exposed critical gaps in the financial stability architecture of the European Union. Despite the exponential growth of EU cross-border banking, supervision, resolution and deposit protection remained at the national level. The financial trilemma theory advanced by Dirk Schoenmaker states that financial stability, financial integration, and national financial policies are incompatible.[960] The actions of national authorities, which are focused on protecting domestic interests, jeopardize financial stability. Consequently, pursuing national financial policies will result in the under-provision of financial stability as a public good. The effects of the trilemma are amplified in the context of a monetary union, where the degree of financial integration is high. The lessons of the trilemma are that financial stability can be ensured with the replacement of national financial policies by supranational ones. Indeed, during the twin crises, the actions of national supervisors were occasionally aimed at protecting their national interests at the expense of financial stability.[961] This 'home bias' of national authorities was evident even before the twin crises with supervisors seeking to promote their national champions and bolster local banking systems.[962]

no. 3 (2015). Nonetheless, high-frequency trading firms are unlikely to replace banks lacking their balance sheet to hold the substantial positions required for making markets. Joe Rennison, 'High-Frequency Traders: Bond Market Scourge or Saviour?', Financial Times, https://next.ft.com/content/ab70bdf2-4507-11e5-b3b2-1672f710807b.

959. Tough regulation enacted in the aftermath of the financial crisis has forced banks to steadily retreat from the market-making business resulting in a liquidity squeeze in important markets, such as the corporate and government bond market. Anchalee Worrachate, 'Bond Liquidity Seen Worsening by BofA as Regulations Tighten', Bloomberg, http://www.bloomberg.com/news/articles/2015-11-04/bond-liquidity-seen-worsening-by-bank-of-america-merrill-lynch.
960. Dirk Schoenmaker, 'The Financial Trilemma', *Economics Letters* 111, no. 1 (2011).
961. Danièle Nouy, 'The Banking Union and Financial Integration, Speech at the Joint Conference of the European Commission and European Central Bank on "European Financial Integration and Stability"', news release, 27 April 2015, https://www.bankingsupervision.europa.eu/press/speeches/date/2015/html/se150427.en.html.
962. *Ibid.*

Furthermore, the Eurozone sovereign debt crisis witnessed the fragmentation of financial markets. At the height of the crisis, depositors in Southern European countries, who were worried about the solvency of national banks exposed to sovereign debt, were massively transferring funds to the stronger Northern European countries.[963] Additionally, cross-border banking flows declined with banks withdrawing funds to their domestic markets and cutting back on foreign lending. Indeed, regulators of Northern European countries started ring-fencing their national banking systems, protecting them against infection by the sovereign debt crisis. A prominent example was UniCredit's transfer of funds from its healthy German subsidiary to its Italian parent company at a time when the ban was facing a liquidity squeeze. The move provoked the intervention of the German banking regulator with Italian regulators pushing back, thus sparking a clash.[964] The fragmentation of financial markets in the Eurozone impaired the transmission mechanism of monetary policy.[965]

Most importantly, the sovereign debt crisis revealed the 'diabolic loop' between sovereign and bank credit risk.[966] On the one hand, the distress of sovereigns can spread to the countries' banks. Banks in Southern European countries held large amounts of sovereign bonds. The deterioration of the countries' creditworthiness led to a severe deterioration of the creditworthiness of banks. A notable example was Greece where the government's distress and eventual debt default resulted in an acute banking crisis. On the other hand, a banking crisis can lead to the worsening of the sovereign's credit standing. During the crisis, sovereigns were forced to resort to government bailouts of ailing banks, thus increasing sovereign distress. For instance, the collapse of the Irish banking system forced the Irish government to guarantee bank debt. The bailout strained government finances forcing Ireland to resort to financial assistance by the EU and the IMF.

In response to the flaws of the Eurozone's institutional set-up, EU leaders decided to move forward with the creation of a Banking Union for the Eurozone as an essential complement to monetary union.[967] The three main pillars of the envisioned Banking Union were joint supervision, joint resolution and joint deposit insurance. Nonetheless, numerous commentators have noted that according to the lessons of the financial

963. Schaefer Sara Enrich David and Forelle Charles, 'European Banks Fear a Flight', The Wall Street Journal, http://www.wsj.com/articles/SB10001424052702304019404577416200222787714.
964. David Enrich and Alessandra Galloni, 'Turmoil Frays Ties across Continent', The Wall Street Journal, http://www.wsj.com/articles/SB10001424052702304065704577426560281463958.
965. For instance, while the ECB's policy rate was the same for all countries, borrowers in Southern European countries faced significantly higher borrowing costs compared to borrowers in stronger Northern countries. Vítor Constâncio, 'Towards the Banking Union, Speech at the 2nd FIN-FSA Conference on EU Regulation and Supervision "Banking and Supervision under Transformation" Organised by the Financial Supervisory Authority, Helsinki', news release, 12 February 2013.
966. Jens Dammann, 'The Banking Union: Flawed by Design', *Georgetown Journal of International Law* 45, no. 4 (2013); Luis Garicano Brunnermeier Markus et al., 'Breaking the Sovereign-Bank Diabolic Loop: A Case for Esbies' (paper presented at the American Economic Review Papers and Proceedings, 2015).
967. For an excellent narrative of the events that led to an agreement for the creation of the Banking Union *see generally* Niamh Moloney, 'European Banking Union: Assessing Its Risks and Resilience', *Common Market Law Review* 51, no. 6 (2014).

stability trilemma, the Banking Union should be applicable to the whole EU.[968] According to this view, the maintenance of financial stability in an interconnected EU financial market and the preservation of the EU single market for financial services can be achieved only by extending the geographic scope of the Banking Union to the entire EU-27.[969] However, in light of the serious obstacles that the extension of the Banking Union to all of the then twenty-eight EU Member States would encounter, the project of the Banking Union was eventually confined to euro area Member States. Most notably, the impetus for the creation of the Banking Union was the intensifying sovereign debt crisis and the fundamental flaws in the construction of the monetary union that the sovereign debt crisis forcefully revealed. Furthermore, an extension of the Banking Union would encounter severe political opposition, most notably from the UK.[970] Finally, there were reservations about how the Banking Union would be implemented to non-euro area Member States, which have their own currencies, their own national central banks applying divergent interest rate policies and domestic banks without access to Euro system liquidity provision.[971]

On 15 October 2013, the European leaders took the first step towards the completion of the Banking Union with the adoption of the SSM Regulation,[972] which

968. *See*, for instance, Dirk Schoenmaker, 'Firmer Foundations for a Stronger Banking Union', *No. 2015/13 Bruegel Working Paper* (November 2015).
969. Bernhard Speyer, 'EU Banking Union: Do It Right, Not Hastily!', *Deutsche Bank Research EU Monitor* (July 2012).
970. On 23 June 2016, in a historic referendum, the British citizens voted to leave the EU. Even though the referendum was not legally binding, senior political figures, including then British Prime Minister David Cameron, announced their intention to respect its result. The UK officially exited the EU on 31 January 2020. The UK and the EU agreed on a transition period until 31 December 2020 during which the UK continued to participate in the customs union and the Single Market. On 30 December 2020, just before the end of the transition period, the UK and the EU signed the EU-UK Trade and Cooperation Agreement, which governs the relationship between the two parties after Brexit in areas such as trade in goods and services, digital trade, intellectual property, fisheries, transport and law enforcement. Furthermore, on 26 March 2021, the UK and the EU agreed on a memorandum of understanding creating a framework for voluntary regulatory cooperation in financial services. For an analysis of the procedure for exiting the EU *see* Gavin Barrett, 'The Era of Article 50: How the UK Will Leave the EU If It Opts for Brexit in Its 23 June 2016 Vote', *UCD Working Papers in Law, Criminology and Socio-Legal Studies Research Paper* No. 2/2016 (2016); Phoebus Athanassiou, 'Withdrawal and Expulsion from the EU and EMU: Some Reflections', *European Central Bank Legal Working Paper Series* No. 10 (2009). For an analysis of the potential economic impact of the UK's exit from the EU *see* HM Government, *HM Treasury Analysis: The Long-Term Economic Impact of EU Membership and the Alternatives* (April 2016). For an analysis of the possible impact of the exit on the UK's financial services sector *see* John Springford, 'Brexit and EU Regulation: A Bonfire of the Vanities?', *Centre for European Reform* (February 2016). Finally, for an analysis of the implications of the Trade and Cooperation Agreement for financial services *see* Niamh Moloney, 'Financial Services under the Trade and Cooperation Agreement: Reflections on Unfinished Business for the EU and UK', *Brexit Institute Working Paper Series* No. 3/2021 (2021), https://papers.ssrn.com/sol3/papers.cfm?abstract_id=3783135.
971. Eilis Ferran, 'European Banking Union and the EU Single Financial Market: More Differentiated Integration, or Disintegration?', *University of Cambridge Faculty of Law Research Paper* No. 29 (2014); Douglas J Elliott, 'Key Issues on European Banking Union: Trade-Offs and Some Recommendations', *Global Economy and Development Working Paper* 52 (November 2012).
972. 'Council Regulation (EU) No. 1024/2013 of 15 October 2013 Conferring Specific Tasks on the European Central Bank Concerning Policies Relating to the Prudential Supervision of Credit Institutions, 2013 O.J. (L 287), 63'.

established the SSM transferring thus the responsibility for the prudential supervision of euro area banks, or more precisely credit institutions,[973] to the ECB.[974] The allocation of supervisory authority to the ECB was legally based on Article 127(6) of the TFEU[975] and Article 25(2) of the ESCB Statute,[976] according to which 'the Council, acting by means of regulations in accordance with a special legislative procedure, may unanimously, and after consulting the European Parliament and the European Central Bank, confer specific tasks upon the European Central Bank concerning policies relating to the prudential supervision of credit institutions and other financial institutions with the exception of insurance undertakings'.

The SSM Regulation introduces a mechanism, the so-called SSM, comprised of the ECB and national authorities.[977] The ECB is responsible for the effective and consistent functioning of the SSM. The SSM is predominantly focused on micro-prudential supervision. Nonetheless, the SSM was established with a macro-prudential focus in mind too. Pursuant to the SSM Regulation, the aim of the SSM is 'to contribute to the safety and soundness of credit institutions and the stability of the financial system within the Union and each Member State'.[978] The mechanism is applicable to euro area Member States. In contrast, non-euro area Member States do not take part in the SSM, but they may decide to opt in by entering into a close cooperation agreement.[979] Two non-euro area Member States, Croatia and Bulgaria, have decided to accede to the Banking Union.[980]

---

973. According to Art. 2(3) of the SSM Regulation a credit institution means a credit institution as defined in point 1 of Art. 4(1) of Regulation (EU) No. 575/2013. *Ibid.*, Art. 2(3), at 73. Pursuant to Art. 4(1) of Regulation (EU) No. 572/2013, credit institution means an undertaking the business of which is to take deposits or other repayable funds from the public and to grant credits for its own account.
974. It should be stressed that the establishment of the SSM was a precondition for the direct recapitalization of banks by the ESM. *See* European Stability Mechanism, 'FAQ on the Main Features of the Future ESM Direct Recapitalization Instrument'.
975. 'Consolidated Version of the Treaty on the Functioning of the European Union', Art. 127(6), at 03.
976. *Protocol on the Statute of the European System of Central Banks and of the European Central Bank, 2012 O.J. (C 326) 230*, Art. 25(2), at 240.
977. For an excellent analysis of the SSM *see generally* Eddy Wymeersch, 'The Single Supervisory Mechanism or 'SSM', Part One of the Banking Union', *No. 255 National Bank of Belgium Working Paper* (2014); Eilis Ferran and Valia SG Babis, 'The European Single Supervisory Mechanism', *Journal of Corporate Law Studies* 13, no. 2 (2013); Kern Alexander, 'European Banking Union: A Legal and Institutional Analysis of the Single Supervisory Mechanism and the Single Resolution Mechanism', *European Law Review* 40, no. 2 (2015). For an excellent analysis of the relationship between the ECB and the national supervisory authorities *see* André Prüm, 'L'union Bancaire Européenne Et Les Autorités De Surveillance Nationales', *Revue de Droit Bancaire et Financier* 4 (2014).
978. 'Council Regulation (EU) No 1024/2013 of 15 October 2013 Conferring Specific Tasks on the European Central Bank Concerning Policies Relating to the Prudential Supervision of Credit Institutions, 2013 O.J. (L 287), 63', Art. 1, at 72. The macro-prudential focus is also evident from the conferral of certain macro-prudential tasks to the ECB by virtue of Art. 5 of the SSM Regulation. *Ibid.*, Art. 5, at 75.
979. *Ibid.*, Art. 7, at 77-78.
980. 'ECB Establishes Close Cooperation with Bulgaria's Central Bank', ECB (10 July 2020), https://www.bankingsupervision.europa.eu/press/pr/date/2020/html/ssm.pr200710~ae2abe1f23.en.htm.

The SSM Regulation confers upon the ECB the exclusive competence for carrying out key supervisory tasks, including the authorization and licensing of credit institutions, the assessment of acquisitions and disposals of holdings in credit institutions, ensuring compliance with EU banking micro-prudential regulations, including capital, liquidity and related requirements, overseeing internal governance, internal assessment and risk management arrangements and procedures, carrying out stress tests, conducting consolidated supervision and carrying out supervisory tasks in relation to early intervention.[981] With respect to the macro-prudential tools granted to the ECB, Article 5 of the SSM Regulation grants to the ECB the authority to impose, if necessary, higher requirements for capital buffers, including countercyclical buffer rates and more stringent measures for addressing systemic or macro-prudential risks than those applied by national authorities.[982] Pursuant to the SSM Regulation, the ECB is the direct supervisor of the most significant banks, while less significant banks will continue to be supervised by national authorities.[983] Nonetheless, the ECB shall issue regulations, guidelines and general instructions to national authorities and exercise oversight over the system.[984] Furthermore, the ECB may decide to take over supervision from a national authority.[985]

The combination of monetary policy and prudential supervision under one roof may lead to potential conflicts of interest.[986] The ECB might be tempted to lower interest rates in order to support a weak financial sector, fuelling thus inflation and contravening its primary mandate of price stability.[987] Indeed, there is a concern that the central bank may continue to pump liquidity into an ailing financial sector out of fear that the failure of financial institutions would destabilize markets. Furthermore, the failure of a financial institution may lead to the loss of the ECB's credibility, which would in turn result in damaging the credibility of its monetary policy.

In order to avoid conflicts of interest between the ECB's supervisory and monetary policy tasks, a central principle underlying the SSM is the principle of

981. *Ibid.*, Arts 4-5, at 74.
982. *Ibid.*, Art. 5, at 75. National authorities are competent to apply capital buffers, including countercyclical buffer rates and any other measures aimed at addressing systemic or macro-prudential risks provided in relevant European banking law.
983. *Ibid.*, Art. 6(4), at 76. Whether a credit institution is significant or not is generally determined on the basis of: (a) the total value of its assets; (b) the importance of the credit institution to the economy of the country in which it is located or to the EU as a whole; (c) the significance of the credit institution's cross-border activities; and whether the credit institution has requested or received public financial assistance from the ESM or its predecessor, the EFSF.
984. *Ibid.*, Art. 6(5)(a), at 76.
985. *Ibid.*, Art. 6(5)(c), at 76.
986. The literature is not conclusive as to whether the combination of monetary policy and prudential supervision results in conflicts of interest. *See*, for instance, Charles Goodhart and Dirk Schoenmaker, 'Should the Functions of Monetary Policy and Banking Supervision Be Separated?', *Oxford Economic Papers* 47, no. 4 (1995); Carmine Di Noia and Giorgio Di Giorgio, 'Should Banking Supervision and Monetary Policy Tasks Be Given to Different Agencies?', *International Finance* 2, no. 3 (1999). In a recent study, Rutkowski and Schnabel find that the allocation of supervisory responsibilities to the central bank leads to higher inflation without having any effect on the occurrence of crises. *See* Rutkowski Felix and Schnabel Isabelle, 'Should Monetary Policy and Banking Supervision Be Separated?' (15 February 2016).
987. Kenichi Ueda and Fabian Valencia, 'Central Bank Independence and Macro-Prudential Regulation', *Economics Letters* 125, no. 2 (2014).

separation of monetary policy and supervision introduced by Article 25 of the SSM Regulation.[988] Additionally, one should note that the conventional central banker's view regarding the trade-off between price stability and financial stability is sceptical towards the existence of such a trade-off.[989] On the one hand, price stability is a precondition for financial stability. On the other hand, financial stability ensures the orderly functioning of the transmission mechanism of monetary policy. Furthermore, it should be stressed that in performing its monetary policy tasks, the primary mandate of the ECB remains the safeguarding of price stability.[990] The quantitative definition of price stability adopted by the ECB provides a clear and measurable yardstick against which the ECB can be held accountable.[991] What is more, the SSM Regulation establishes an internal functional separation of the ECB's tasks. The planning and execution of ECB's supervisory tasks are undertaken by a newly created internal body, the Supervisory Board.[992] The Supervisory Board is responsible for carrying out preparatory works regarding the ECB's supervisory tasks and proposing draft decisions to the ECB's Governing Council, which is the supreme decision-making body of the ECB.[993]

The lessons of the financial stability trilemma, namely that financial stability, financial integration and national financial policies are incompatible, are also applicable with respect to the hedge fund industry. In a world of highly integrated financial markets, national hedge fund supervision is unlikely to be able to guarantee financial stability. As a result, the optimal solution would be to move towards a system of pan-European hedge fund supervision. Under the current system of hedge fund supervision as introduced by the AIFM Directive, the home authorities of the AIFM are responsible for the prudential supervision of the AIFM, including monitoring the systemic risk posed by leveraged AIFs, namely hedge funds, ensuring compliance with limits on remuneration, risk management and liquidity management requirements and the imposition of leverage limits and other restrictions on the management of a

988. 'Council Regulation (EU) No 1024/2013 of 15 October 2013 Conferring Specific Tasks on the European Central Bank Concerning Policies Relating to the Prudential Supervision of Credit Institutions, 2013 O.J. (L 287), 63', Art. 25, at 85.
989. Professor Otmar Issing, 'Monetary and Financial Stability: Is There a Trade-Off?, Speech at the Conference on "Monetary Stability, Financial Stability and The Business Cycle", Bank for International Settlements, Basle', news release, 28-29 March 2003.
990. *See* Ferran and Babis, 'The European Single Supervisory Mechanism', 266-67. Ferran and Babis note that the financial stability mandate granted to the ECB with respect to supervision does not contradict the primary objective of ensuring price stability in performing its monetary policy tasks, since 'a new function is being conferred on the ECB, new objectives can be set as conditions for the exercise of this function'. For a contrary view, *see* Dammann, 'The Banking Union: Flawed by Design', 1076-77, claiming that the prime objective of maintaining price stability is also applicable to the ECB's role as supervisor.
991. The ECB Governing Council has defined price stability as 'a year-on-year increase in the Harmonized Index of Consumer Prices (HICP) for the euro area of below 2%. Price stability is to be maintained over the medium term'. The Governing Council has also clarified that, in the pursuit of price stability, it aims to maintain inflation rates below, but close to, 2% over the medium term.
992. 'Council Regulation (EU) No 1024/2013 of 15 October 2013 Conferring Specific Tasks on the European Central Bank Concerning Policies Relating to the Prudential Supervision of Credit Institutions, 2013 O.J. (L 287), 63', Art. 26(1), at 85.
993. *Ibid.*, Art. 26(8), at 86.

leveraged AIF. Moreover, AIFs, including hedge funds, continue to be regulated and supervised at national level.

Nevertheless, national supervisory policies are unlikely to be able to safeguard financial stability. The objective of home supervisors is to ensure financial stability in their own market. Home supervisors are accountable to the national government of their home country. As a result, they will not internalize the costs of increased systemic risk in foreign markets. For instance, a national supervisor may decide to adopt a lenient stance towards a systemically important domestic or foreign hedge fund if it poses systemic risk solely in markets other than its home market. Losses from the failure of a systemically important hedge fund will thus spread to jurisdictions other than the Member State charged with supervision. Moreover, a jurisdiction may decide to engage in a race to the bottom[994] offering a lax supervisory environment in order to attract hedge fund business.[995]

A pan-European response, namely the creation of a supranational pan-European supervisor for the hedge fund industry on systemic risk grounds, would be the optimal solution to the financial stability trilemma. The UK's exit from the EU has paved the way for deeper centralization in the field of financial regulation and supervision. Prior to Brexit, such an endeavour would encounter several obstacles. Most notably, there would be a lack of political consensus for such an initiative, in part due to the UK's stiff resistance to hand over its power to supervise the hedge fund sector, a crucial industry for the UK economy. London is Europe's leading centre for hedge fund management, offering a pool of specialized service providers, talented employees and developed supervisory practices and culture. Indeed, UK-based hedge fund managers have been ardent opponents of EU regulatory initiatives, which in their view, stifle innovation and unfairly penalize the hedge fund industry.[996]

The opposition of the UK to EU-wide regulatory and supervisory initiatives, including the project of the Banking Union, is a reflection of the structure of its economy. Hall and Soskice distinguish between two different types of market economies, LMEs and CMEs.[997] LMEs, which include the UK and the US, allow economic agents to coordinate their activities most efficiently through competitive market arrangements and are characterized by a market-enhancing approach to supervision and regulation. In contrast, CMEs, which include Germany and numerous other

994. The race to the bottom theory was developed by scholars in the field of corporate law. Cary was the first to articulate this theory. He claimed that the thirst of Delaware for revenues generated by incorporations has led it to develop a lax corporate regime. In turn, this has influenced other states, which compete with each other in a race to the bottom. *See* generally William L Cary, 'Federalism and Corporate Law: Reflections Upon Delaware', *The Yale Law Journal* 83, no. 4 (1974). But *see* Roberta Romano, 'The States as a Laboratory: Legal Innovation and State Competition for Corporate Charters', *Yale Journal on Regulation* 23, no. 2 (2006) (arguing that competition allows for the proliferation of innovative and efficient state corporate law rules).
995. Andrew Johnston, 'Regulating Hedge Funds for Systemic Stability: The EU'S Approach', *European Law Journal* 21, no. 6 (2015).
996. Paul Marshall, 'Hedge Funds Seek Refuge from Unfair European Regulations', Financial Times, http://www.ft.com/intl/cms/s/0/43ecd864-dca6-11e5-8541-00fb33bdf038.html#axzz41p9Qh800.
997. Hall and Soskice, *Varieties of Capitalism: The Institutional Foundations of Comparative Advantage* (Oxford University Press, 2002).

Continental European countries, facilitate non-market modes of coordination, such as relational or incomplete contracting and greater reliance on collaborative, as opposed to competitive, relationships. In CME systems, the state adopts a more intrusive approach to supervision and regulation.

Nevertheless, even after the UK's exit from the EU, an initiative for centralizing hedge fund supervision would still face significant challenges. As Moloney notes, the political, sovereign debt market, and fiscal conditions, which were a prerequisite for the reallocation of supervisory responsibilities, brought by the Banking Union, are absent.[998] Furthermore, complex legal issues would arise in relation to the transfer of supervisory powers to a new or existing EU agency, such as ESMA. Pursuant to the Meroni doctrine, EU institutions may not delegate powers to an EU agency, in so far as these powers are discretionary to such an extent that the wide margin of discretion might enable the execution of actual economic policy.[999] Any delegation of powers should involve only clearly defined executive powers subject to strict review in light of objective criteria determined by the delegating authority. Supervision, which includes the application of rules by the supervising authority, necessarily involves the exercise of discretion. Restraining supervisory powers, in order to ensure compliance with the Meroni doctrine, is unlikely to be conducive to effective supervision.[1000]

The European Court of Justice, in its landmark 22 January 2014 ruling on ESMA's powers under the Short Selling Regulation, adopted a rather liberal approach to the application of the Meroni doctrine. The UK government challenged ESMA's powers under Article 28 of the Short Selling Regulation to prohibit or impose conditions on short selling or similar transactions or require notification or public disclosure of net short positions. In particular, the UK government alleged that ESMA's powers were contrary to Meroni since they entailed a wide margin of discretion. Further, ESMA was given a wide range of choices as to what measures to impose, with these choices having very significant policy implications. In addition, the factors ESMA had to take into account before acting were highly subjective. In its seminal ruling, the Court of Justice held that ESMA's powers were limited by a number of conditions and procedural

998. Niamh Moloney, 'Banking Union and the Implications for Financial Market Governance in the EU', in *European Banking Union*, ed. Danny Busch and Guido Ferrarini (Oxford University Press, 2014), 535.

999. *See Case 10/56, Meroni & Co., Industrie Metallurgiche S.A.S, 1958 E.C.R. 139.*On the Meroni doctrine and its evolution *see generally* Miroslava Scholten and Marloes van Rijsbergen, 'The ESMA-Short Selling Case: Erecting a New Delegation Doctrine in the EU Upon the Meroni-Romano Remnants', *Legal Issues of Economic Integration* 41, no. 4 (2014); Stefan Griller and Andreas Orator, 'Everything under Control? The "Way Forward" for European Agencies in the Footsteps of the Meroni Doctrine', *European Law Review* 35, no. 1 (2010); Merijn Chamon, 'The Empowerment of Agencies under the Meroni Doctrine and Article 114 TFEU: Comment on United Kingdom V. Parliament and Council (Short-Selling) and the Proposed Single Resolution Mechanism', *ibid.*, 39, no. 3 (2014); 'EU Agencies: Does the Meroni Doctrine Make Sense', *Maastricht Journal of European and Comparative Law* 17, no. 3 (2010).

1000. *See generally* Elizabeth Howell, 'The European Court of Justice: Selling US Short?', *European Company and Financial Law Review* 11, no. 3 (2014); Valia SG Babis, 'The Power to Ban Short-Selling: The Beginning of a New Era for EU Agencies?', *University of Cambridge Faculty of Law Research Paper* No. 27 (2014).

requirements and therefore complied with the Meroni doctrine.[1001] However, even after the favourable ruling of the European Court of Justice, significant legal uncertainty regarding the limits of the Meroni doctrine remains. Moreover, the restrictions imposed by the Meroni doctrine would not allow ESMA to be conferred with the wide-ranging powers necessary to effectively supervise the hedge fund sector.[1002]

Nonetheless, the above-mentioned obstacles are not insurmountable. Even though the political, sovereign debt market, and fiscal conditions, which were a prerequisite for the reallocation of supervisory responsibilities, brought by the Banking Union, are absent, the creation of the Banking Union and the conferral of bank supervisory powers upon the ECB have clearly demonstrated the willingness of euro area Member States to embrace deeper centralization as far as financial market governance is concerned. Moreover, the establishment of the Banking Union has already laid the necessary political and technical groundwork for the centralization of hedge fund supervision. Consequently, despite the fact that the optimal level of centralization of hedge fund supervision on systemic risk grounds would be the European one, centralization could take place at the euro area level with Member States emulating the example of the Banking Union and conferring supervisory powers on the ECB. The expertise of the ECB in issues of financial stability, the close link between financial stability and monetary policy, the ECB's well-guarded independence and its evolution into a banking supervisor strongly advocate in favour of its designation as hedge fund systemic risk supervisor for the euro area.

Furthermore, one could argue that a common hedge fund supervisory regime without the participation of the biggest hedge fund centre in Europe, namely the UK, makes little sense. Nevertheless, it should be noted that the investment fund sector in the Eurozone has been experiencing a boom in recent years with the growth of total

1001. In particular, short selling measures must address a threat to the orderly functioning and integrity of financial markets or to the stability of the whole or part of the financial system of the Union and there are cross-border implications. Moreover, ESMA can take the measures only if no competent authority has taken measures to address the threat or one or more of those authorities have taken measures which have proven not to address the threat adequately. Furthermore, ESMA must take into account the extent to which the measure significantly addresses the threat to the orderly functioning and integrity of financial markets and the stability of the financial system, does not create the risk of regulatory arbitrage and does not have a detrimental effect on the efficiency of financial markets. ESMA shall review the measures at appropriate intervals and at least every three months. Additionally, before imposing the measures, ESMA must consult the ESRB and notify the relevant competent authorities. Finally, the Commission has adopted a delegated regulation specifying criteria and factors to be taken into account by ESMA in determining in which cases threats to the orderly functioning and integrity of financial markets or to the stability of the whole or part of the financial system arise. 'Regulation (EU) No 236/2012 of the European Parliament and of the Council of 14 March 2012 on Short Selling and Certain Aspects of Credit Default Swaps 2012 OJ (L 86), 1', Arts 28, 19.

1002. For instance, Busch and van Rijn note that the Meroni doctrine prohibits the conferral of regulatory powers to an agency. As a result, an agency would not be allowed to adopt tailored prudential requirements for non-bank SIFIs, such as hedge funds. Danny Busch and Mirik B. J. van Rijn, 'Towards Single Supervision and Resolution of Systemically Important Non-Bank Financial Institutions in the European Union', *European Business Organization Law Review* 19, no. 2 (2018): 356.

euro area financial sector assets being driven primarily by investment funds.[1003] The growth of the investment funds sector is a pillar of the EU's broader plan to create a genuine capital markets union to complement bank financing for the real economy.[1004]

Indeed, Article 127(6) of the TFEU and Article 25(2) of the ESCB Statute, used as a legal basis for the conferral of bank supervisory powers on the ECB and the establishment of the SSM, allows for the extension of the ECB's supervisory powers to other financial market participants, including hedge funds.[1005] Pursuant to the wording of Article 127(6) of the TFEU and Article 25(2) the ESCB Statute, the ECB may be conferred with specific tasks concerning policies relating to the prudential supervision of credit institutions and other financial institutions with the exception of insurance undertakings. The TFEU and the ESCB Statute do not provide a definition for the term 'financial institution'. Instead, EU banking legislation contains inconsistent definitions of the term.[1006] According to René Smits, the term is to be defined broadly and interpreted without regard to the definitions existing in EU banking legislation with the only limit being the specific exclusion of insurance undertakings.[1007] Indeed, as the

1003. Hermans Lieven Doyle Nicola, Molitor Philippe and Weistroffer Christian, 'Shadow Banking in the Euro Area: Risks and Vulnerabilities in the Investment Fund Sector', *European Central Bank Occasional Paper Series* No. 174 (June 2016).

1004. In contrast to the UK, which boosts deep and liquid capital markets, Continental European countries predominantly rely on the banking system for the channelling of savings to productive investments. Recognizing the benefits that deep capital markets offer to savers, investors, businesses and the financial system in general, the European Commission announced in September 2015 an action plan on building a capital markets union. The aim of the plan is to mobilize capital investments in Europe, deepen financial integration and promote competition, enhance the stability of the financial system and better connect financing to investment projects across the EU. The Commission's action plan comprises of numerous steps, including the support of venture capital and equity markets, the promotion of new form of financing, such as crowd-funding and loan-origination funds, the revival of securitization markets, the strengthening of cross-border investments in investment funds and the increase of cross-border competition in Europe's asset management industry. *See generally* Wolf-George Ringe, 'Capital Markets Union for Europe – a Political Message to the UK', *Law and Financial Markets Review* 9, no. 1 (2015); Andreas Dombret and Patrick S. Kenadjian (eds), *The European Capital Markets Union: A Viable Concept and a Real Goal?* (De Gruyter, 2015). For studies on the relative merits, from an economic point of view, of bank-based and market-based financial systems *see* Ross Levine, 'Bank-Based or Market-Based Financial Systems: Which Is Better?', *Journal of Financial Intermediation* 11, no. 4 (2002); Aslı Demirgüç-Kunt and Vojislav Maksimovic, 'Funding Growth in Bank-Based and Market-Based Financial Systems: Evidence from Firm-Level Data', *Journal of Financial Economics* 65, no. 3 (2002); Thorsten Beck and Ross Levine, 'Industry Growth and Capital Allocation: Does Having a Market-or Bank-Based System Matter?', *ibid.*, 64, no. 2.

1005. Moloney, 'Banking Union and the Implications for Financial Market Governance in the EU', 535.

1006. René Smits, *The European Central Bank, Institutional Aspects* (Kluwer Law International, 1997), 358. *See*, for instance, the different definitions of the term contained in 'Regulation (EU) No 575/2013 of the European Parliament and of the Council of 26 June 2013 on Prudential Requirements for Credit Institutions and Investment Firms and Amending Regulation (EU) No 648/2012 Text with EEA Relevance. 2013 O.J. (L 173) 1'; 'Directive (EU) 2015/849 of the European Parliament and of the Council of 20 May 2015 on the Prevention of the Use of the Financial System for the Purposes of Money Laundering or Terrorist Financing, Amending Regulation (EU) No 648/2012 of the European Parliament and of the Council, and Repealing Directive 2005/60/EC of the European Parliament and of the Council and Commission Directive 2006/70/EC, 2015 O.J. (L 141) 1'.

1007. *The European Central Bank, Institutional Aspects*, 359.

author further notes, the 'Community legislator, when activating article 25.2 of the ESCB Statute (article 127(6) of the TFEU), can give a suitable definition of the term "financial institution" without being confined to the various meanings attributed to it in secondary legislation'.[1008] As a result, hedge funds may be considered covered by Article 127(6) of the TFEU and Article 25.2 of the ESCB Statute, allowing euro area Member States to confer prudential supervisory powers upon the ECB and bringing systemically important hedge funds located in the Eurozone within the scope of the SSM.[1009]

Another potential candidate for serving as a hedge fund systemic risk supervisor is the ESRB, an EU agency established in 2010.[1010] The ESRB is part and parcel of the EU's post-crisis new supervisory architecture. Its mission is to monitor and assess systemic risk in the EU financial system. The ESRB has the power to collect and analyse information in order to identify systemic risk signals, determine the priorities of these risks and issue appropriate warnings and recommendations in view of these risks. The ESRB is housed within the ECB, with the ECB providing its secretariat. It is directed by a General Board, whose members include the President and Vice President of the ECB, the governors of all EU national central banks and one representative of the competent national supervisory authorities of each Member State. Despite the initial appeal of the ESRB as a potential supervisor, allocating supervisory responsibilities to the ESRB suffers from significant shortcomings. Most notably, in its present form, the ESRB is a soft law body lacking legally binding powers. Conferral of significant supervisory powers on the ESRB, necessary, in order to ensure effective supervision of the hedge fund sector, would run afoul of the Meroni doctrine. Moreover, the ESRB lacks the resources and expertise to properly supervise financial market participants.

Nevertheless, the ESRB's macro-prudential mandate and expertise in assessing systemic risk make it an ideal candidate for monitoring systemic risk in the hedge fund sector, assessing the risk posed by individual hedge funds and designating funds which pose a risk to financial stability as systemically important. Emulating the example of the FSOC in the US, the ESRB could be tasked with designating hedge funds as systemically important. Designation would subject systemically important hedge funds based in the Eurozone to the ECB's supervision. Furthermore, as Busch and van Rijn argue, since the ESRB's designation power would be circumscribed by various conditions and criteria, the conferral of the power of designation on the ESRB would be compliant with the Meroni doctrine in line with the *Short Selling* case.[1011] In particular,

1008. *Ibid.*
1009. E-mail exchange with Rene Smits (on file with the author).
1010. 'Regulation (EU) No 1092/2010 of the European Parliament and of the Council of 24 November 2010 on European Union Macro-Prudential Oversight of the Financial System and Establishing a European Systemic Risk Board, 2010 O.J. (L 331) 1'. For an overview of ESRB's history, mission and powers *see* Eilís Ferran, 'Can Soft Law Bodies Be Effective? The Special Case of the European Systemic Risk Board', *European Law Review* 35 (2010); Mads Andenas and Iris HY Chiu, 'Financial Stability and Legal Integration in Financial Regulation', *European Law Review* 38 (2013).
1011. Busch and van Rijn, 'Towards Single Supervision and Resolution of Systemically Important Non-Bank Financial Institutions in the European Union', 352.

designation would hinge on an assessment of whether a fund poses a threat to financial stability. The assessment would be subject to predetermined criteria and conditions.

As far as the criteria for determining whether a fund is a threat to financial stability are concerned, it should be stressed that both theory and empirical research indicate that the largest hedge funds are systemically important. As the FSB and IOSCO noted, 'in theory, the larger the size of a fund, the greater its potential impact on counterparties (counterparty channel) and markets (market channel)'. Furthermore, numerous surveys document that the largest funds aggressively use leverage, are the most active users of repo financing and are taking investments in illiquid securities. Nevertheless, there is a remote possibility that a large fund does not pose any risks to financial stability. For instance, despite its size, a large fund may utilize a trivial amount of leverage without obtaining any repo financing and invest solely in liquid and exchange-traded securities.

As a result, following the approach of the Dodd-Frank Act and the FSB and IOSCO, hedge funds above a certain size would be subject to closer examination by the ESRB, which will take into account certain impact factors for determining whether these funds pose a threat to financial stability. As far as the materiality threshold for determining whether a large hedge fund should be scrutinized further and the impact factors that the ESRB would use in determining whether it is systemically important are concerned, the proposed assessment methodologies for identifying globally systemically important investment funds, including hedge funds, promulgated by the FSB and IOSCO serve as a useful guide. In particular, pursuant to the proposed indicators for assessing the systemic importance of hedge funds developed by the FSB and IOSCO, hedge funds that exceed USD 400 billion of gross notional exposure would be assessed further against five different impact factors, namely size, interconnectedness with counterparties, complexity, substitutability[1012] and cross-border jurisdictional activities.

Size is measured as the gross notional exposure of a fund, thus allowing supervisors to take into account the amount of leverage used by the fund. The interconnectedness of the fund with counterparties is captured by using several

1012. The main channels through which hedge funds may contribute to systemic risk are the credit and market channel. Nevertheless, the FSB and IOSCO, in their March 2015 consultative document, recognized that investment funds, including hedge funds, may also contribute to systemic risk via the critical services/substitutability channel. The critical services/ substitutability channel refers 'to the impact of distress or liquidation of an investment fund that provides a function or service to the markets upon which market participants heavily rely'. *See* IOSCO & FSB, *Assessment Methodologies for Identifying Non-Bank Non-Insurer Global Systemically Important Financial Institutions, Consultative Document* (March 2015): 34-35. For instance, the failure of a hedge fund acting as a significant liquidity provider in a particular market may result in the breakdown of the relevant market. Nevertheless, no single hedge fund is currently an important player in a particular market, such that its failure could jeopardize financial stability. Furthermore, the hedge fund industry exhibits a high degree of substitutability with numerous substitutes available for most strategies. Indeed, the January 2014 FSB and IOSCO consultative document considered that investment funds are unlikely to contribute to systemic risk via the critical services/substitutability channel. *Assessment Methodologies for Identifying Non-Bank Non-Insurer Global Systemically Important Financial Institutions, Consultative Document* (2015), 35.

indicators, including the balance sheet financial leverage of the fund, its leverage ratio, the ratio of gross notional exposure to NAV, the nature of investors in the fund, net current credit exposure of globally SIFIs to the fund, the counterparty credit exposure to the fund and the ratio of collateral posted by the fund to its NAV. Furthermore, the criteria for assessing the substitutability of the fund are the NAV of the fund compared to the size of the underlying market, the daily trading volume of certain asset classes of the fund compared to the overall daily trading volume of the same market segment and the fund holdings per certain asset classes compared to the overall daily trading volume of the same asset class. Complexity is measured by using several indicators among which are the non-centrally cleared derivatives trade volumes of the fund versus the total trade volumes of the fund, the ratio of collateral posted by counterparties that has been reused by the fund, the investment fund liquidity profile, the amount of less liquid assets and the proportion of an investment fund's portfolio using high-frequency trading strategies. Finally, cross-jurisdictional activities are assessed by taking into account the number of jurisdictions in which a fund invests, the number of jurisdictions in which a fund is sold/listed and the number of jurisdictions where the fund has counterparties.

Under my proposal, the focus would be on individual funds rather than their managers. Nonetheless, it should be noted that the FSB and IOSCO have also proposed specific methodologies for identifying systemically important investment managers.[1013] The FSB and IOSCO considered that investment fund managers may pose risks to financial stability via the exposures, market and critical services/substitutability channel. However, one should be vigilant in extending the regulatory perimeter to hedge fund managers. Hedge fund managers and hedge funds are distinct entities. The assets held by the managers are separated from the underlying asset portfolio of the funds. Hedge fund managers typically carry small balance sheets. The economic exposures, which pose a threat to financial stability, are created at the fund level.[1014] Furthermore, the practice of providing indemnification or guarantees by hedge fund managers in favour of the funds managed is virtually non-existent in the hedge fund industry. Moreover, runs by investors occur predominantly at the fund level and not at the manager level. Finally, crucial data for assessing the systemic importance of hedge funds, such as Form PF in the US, are available to supervisors in a per entity format.[1015]

According to my proposal, if the ESRB's analysis leads to the conclusion that a large hedge fund poses risks to financial stability, the ESRB would have the authority to designate the fund as systemically important and bring it within the scope of the SSM. Large systemically important hedge funds would be supervised by the ECB, which would have the authority to impose tailored prudential standards, including

1013. *Assessment Methodologies for Identifying Non-Bank Non-Insurer Global Systemically Important Financial Institutions, Consultative Document* (2015), 47. In contrast, the FSB and IOSCO, in their January 2014 consultative document, adopted a fund-level approach. *Assessment Methodologies for Identifying Non-Bank Non-Insurer Global Systemically Important Financial Institutions, Consultative Document* (2014).

1014. *Assessment Methodologies for Identifying Non-Bank Non-Insurer Global Systemically Important Financial Institutions, Consultative Document* (2014), 30.

1015. *Ibid.*

leverage limits, liquidity ratios, suspension of redemptions and mandatory stress tests. Leverage limits will allow the ECB to curb the excessive use of leverage, which contributes to the build-up of systemic risk via the market and the credit channel. The distress of an overleveraged fund will result in severe losses for its counterparties, which have extended credit to it, possibly leading to their own distress. If these counterparties are SIFIs, their distress will jeopardize the stability of the financial system. Furthermore, the extensive use of leverage aggravates both the probability and magnitude of fire sales.[1016]

What is more, macro-prudential liquidity tools, such as liquidity requirements and suspension of redemptions, are essential for tackling liquidity risk in investment funds.[1017] Massive redemptions by panicked investors may force funds to engage in fire sales causing severe market dislocations. The risk of investor runs is higher for funds with significant liquidity mismatches. Fire sales may also result from runs by creditors and derivatives counterparties. For instance, in times of market stress funds may be forced to sell off assets, in order to satisfy margin calls by derivatives counterparties.

Liquidity ratios have become a centrepiece of bank regulation in the aftermath of the financial crisis. During the crisis, many banks, despite being solvent, were unable to roll over their short-term financing, suffering thereby a severe liquidity squeeze. The crisis revealed the perils of structural mismatches between assets and liabilities and short-term funding. As a result, the BCBS has introduced two new ratios, which seek to shield banks against liquidity shocks. The two ratios, the NSFR and the LCR, aim to tackle mismatches between assets and liabilities and promote more resilient forms of funding, namely medium and long-term financing of assets. On the one hand, the NSFR seeks to ensure that banks hold adequate stable financing and finance their assets with long-term liabilities.[1018] On the other hand, the LCR requires banks to hold sufficient high-quality liquid assets, namely cash, government bonds and other liquid securities, such as corporate debt securities, in order to be able to meet their liquidity needs for a thirty-calendar day liquidity stress scenario.[1019] Similar liquidity ratios, such as liquidity buffers requiring funds to hold sufficient high-quality assets in order to meet

1016. Brunnermeier Markus Konrad et al., *The Fundamental Principles of Financial Regulation*, 16-22.
1017. 'Macroprudential Policy Beyond Banking: An ESRB Strategy Paper' (ESRB, July 2016), 18.
1018. According to the BCBS, 'The NSFR is defined as the amount of available stable funding relative to the amount of required stable funding. This ratio should be equal to at least 100% on an ongoing basis'. 'Available stable funding' is defined as the portion of capital and liabilities expected to be reliable over the time horizon considered by the NSFR, which extends to one year. The amount of such stable funding required ('Required stable funding') of a specific institution is a function of the liquidity characteristics and residual maturities of the various assets held by that institution as well as those of its off-balance sheet (OBS) exposures. Basel Committee on Banking Supervision, *Basel III: The Net Stable Funding Ratio* (October 2014). *See also* Christian McNamara and Andrew Metrick, 'Basel III G: Shadow Banking and Project Finance', *Yale Program on Financial Stability Case Study* 2014-1G-V1 (2014).
1019. Basel Committee on Banking Supervision, *Basel III: The Liquidity Coverage Ratio and Liquidity Risk Monitoring Tools* (January 2013). For a criticism of the LCR *see* Andrew W Hartlage, 'The Basel III Liquidity Coverage Ratio and Financial Stability', *Michigan Law Review* 111, no. 3 (2012) (arguing that the LCR may push banks to engage in regulatory arbitrage undermining financial stability).

outflows, should be at the disposal of the ECB in order to deal with runs by creditors and investors at systemically important hedge funds.

Moreover, the suspension of investor redemptions by the ECB is a useful complementary macro-prudential liquidity tool. The implementation of suspensions is a simple exercise for supervisory authorities, which contributes to financial stability by halting investor runs. Hedge funds managers often reserve the right to impose the suspension of redemptions in extreme market circumstances. However, funds have a duty to act in the best interest of investors, which may differ from those of the market as a whole.[1020] Consequently, hedge fund managers may be reluctant to enact these discretionary liquidity restrictions. Furthermore, fund managers are unable to assess the systemic risk implications of investor redemptions and fire sales of assets.

Finally, even though AIFs are required to conduct appropriate stress tests and scenario analyses to address risks arising from potential changes in market conditions that might adversely impact the fund and conduct stress tests specifically aimed at monitoring liquidity risk, these internally managed stress tests are prone to manipulation by fund managers. For instance, in order to increase their profits and consequently their compensation, fund managers have an incentive to make aggressive investments in illiquid securities financed with short-term borrowing. Nevertheless, in the event of a market meltdown, the fund will be faced with a severe liquidity squeeze forcing it to sell these illiquid securities at fire sale prices in order to repay its creditors. Taking into account that investors may react negatively to the increase in risk-taking, fund managers may seek to manipulate stress tests, in order to present a more favourable picture of the fund's risk and liquidity profile. In contrast to internal stress tests, stress tests conducted by the ECB would present a more impartial view of a fund's risks.[1021] Indeed, even the IMF has supported the use of stress testing in gauging the risks posed by asset management companies.[1022]

4.4 HEDGE FUNDS AND RESOLUTION

4.4.1 Bankruptcy, Bailouts or Resolution?

The response of US and EU governments to the distress of financial institutions during the financial and sovereign debt crises was marked by a preference to avoid bankruptcy filings, due to the destabilizing effects of bankruptcy on financial stability. Instead, authorities preferred to inject vast amounts of taxpayer money into troubled financial firms. The bankruptcy process may offer substantial benefits when dealing with the distress of SIFIs. The bankruptcy process offers transparency and firm priority rules.[1023]

1020. Cominetta et al., 'Macroprudential Liquidity Tools for Investment Funds – A Preliminary Discussion'.
1021. In the aftermath of the financial crisis, stress tests have become an essential part of banking supervision in both the US and the EU. Supervisory stress tests of banking institutions were first conducted in the US during the heights of the financial crisis. *See generally* Beverly Hirtle and Andreas Lehnert, 'Supervisory Stress Tests', *FRB of New York Staff Report*, no. 696 (2014).
1022. IMF, *Global Financial Stability Report* (April 2015), 96-97.
1023. Jackson and Skeel Jr, 'Dynamic Resolution of Large Financial Institutions', 447.

Furthermore, judicial review allows creditors to challenge treatment that does not respect their entitlements.[1024] Moreover, the threat of losses, which the bankruptcy process imposes on creditors and shareholders, curbs moral hazard.[1025] In addition, the involvement of the parties themselves, which have a direct financial stake in the outcome of the process, in key decisions in bankruptcy, results in a more efficient resolution of financial distress.[1026]

Nevertheless, the bankruptcy process exhibits significant shortcomings. Most notably, the goal of the bankruptcy process is to maximize the value of a particular firm. Consequently, the bankruptcy process is not designed to deal with financial stability risks arising from the failure of a SIFI. For instance, bankruptcy judges have no particular expertise in financial markets. In addition, the bankruptcy process is lengthy, with the payouts to creditors made at a later stage of the process. This has the potential to cause a crisis of confidence and a temporary liquidity squeeze for creditors, who are usually other financial institutions.[1027] Moreover, a massive liquidation of the firm's assets during the bankruptcy process can result in fire sales causing dislocations in financial markets.[1028] Furthermore, US and EU bankruptcy laws provide special protections to repo and derivatives counterparties, allowing them to enforce their contracts outside the bankruptcy process. Contrary to ordinary creditors, counterparties are able to immediately terminate all outstanding contracts, calculate the gains and losses on each contract, set them off against each other ('close-out netting') and immediately liquidate any assets held as collateral. Even though these special privileges have been justified by the need to safeguard financial stability, the exercise of these rights can actually aggravate financial instability. Finally, in contrast to financial regulatory and supervisory authorities, the principal players in a bankruptcy process do not take into account the effects of their actions on the stability of the financial system.[1029]

Despite the unsuitability of bankruptcy for resolving SIFIs, the approach taken by authorities during the financial and the sovereign debt crises, namely government bailouts, suffers from its own drawbacks. Government bailouts can impose enormous costs on taxpayers and in extreme circumstances, as witnessed during the sovereign debt crisis, bring the sovereign to the verge of insolvency. Furthermore, rescue financing by governments increases moral hazard.[1030] Knowing that the firm will be rescued *ex post* by the government, investors, executives and creditors have an incentive to engage in excessive risk-taking. Investors, executives and creditors will reap the returns of their risky behaviour while exposing taxpayers to significant risk. Moreover, government bailouts provoke distortions in the internal governance of the

1024. *Ibid.*
1025. *Ibid.*, 448.
1026. *Ibid.*
1027. John Armour, 'Making Bank Resolution Credible', *No. 244 ECGI Law Working Paper* (2014).
1028. *Ibid.*, 7.
1029. Jackson and Skeel Jr, 'Dynamic Resolution of Large Financial Institutions', 449.
1030. Kenneth Ayotte and David A Skeel, 'Bankruptcy or Bailouts', *Journal of Corporation Law* 35, no. 3 (2009): 485-86.

firm.[1031] In exchange for committing taxpayer money, the government will usually demand a strong involvement in the firm's decision-making. Moreover, government rescues are usually engineered and implemented in a very short time frame leaving authorities little time to devise an appropriate strategy, conduct adequate due diligence on the distressed firm or benefit from an increase in value of the failing institution's assets.[1032] Finally, unpredictable ad hoc government rescues may increase uncertainty in financial markets, triggering widespread panic.[1033]

In response to the shortcomings of the bankruptcy process and taxpayer-funded bailouts, politicians, regulators and academic researchers promoted the idea of special resolution regimes as a silver bullet for dealing with the failure of SIFIs.[1034] In the US, the Dodd-Frank Act introduced a special resolution regime, also known as OLA, for handling the distress of non-bank financial institutions, whose failure could pose risks to the US financial system. As far as the EU is concerned, European legislators adopted the BRRD establishing a common framework for the recovery and resolution of banks and investment firms and moved forward with the creation of a Eurozone-wide SRM applicable to banking institutions established in countries that have decided to join the Banking Union. The objectives of effective resolution regimes are to reduce moral hazard by imposing losses on shareholders and creditors, minimize taxpayer support to failing firms, grant authorities considerable control over the resolution process so as to minimize systemic risk, confer upon authorities the power to take control of the failing institution at an early stage of its distress and equip them with adequate tools in order to deal with a financial firm's distress.[1035]

4.4.2 Hedge Funds and Resolution in the EU

In contrast to OLA, which captures non-bank SIFIs, including systemically important hedge funds, the BRRD and the SRM are applicable to banking institutions, investment firms and (mixed) financial holdings. Consequently, they do not capture a variety of non-bank financial institutions whose failure may threaten financial stability, including systemically important hedge funds. In addition, in contrast to banks, investment firms and insurance companies, hedge funds are not subject to any specific type of

1031. *Ibid.*, 486-87.
1032. Rodgin Cohen and Morris Goldstein, 'The Case for an Orderly Resolution Regime for Systemically-Important Financial Institutions', *The Pew Financial Reform Project Briefing Paper* 13 (2009): 3.
1033. Skeel, *The New Financial Deal: Understanding the Dodd-Frank Act and Its (Unintended) Consequences*, 25-26.
1034. *See*, for instance, Financial Stability Board, *Key Attributes of Effective Resolution Regimes for Financial Institutions, Basel* (October 2011); Andrew Bailey, 'The UK Bank Resolution Regime, Speech at the ICAEW Financial Services Faculty Breakfast, London', news release, 26 November 2009.
1035. Cohen and Goldstein, 'The Case for an Orderly Resolution Regime for Systemically-Important Financial Institutions', 4; Cihák and Nier, 'The Need for Special Resolution Regimes for Financial Institutions-the Case of the European Union', 403.

EU-wide framework governing their insolvency.[1036] Nonetheless, the LTCM debacle serves as a reminder that the failure of systemically important hedge funds may jeopardize financial stability. In the absence of a special resolution regime, governments will be forced to resort to costly taxpayer-funded bailouts in order to rescue a systemically important hedge fund and prevent the opening of bankruptcy proceedings. Indeed, the main reason behind the government-engineered rescue of LTCM was the adverse consequences of LTCM's bankruptcy on the financial system. Despite the hesitation of European legislators to proceed with a radical extension of the scope of application of the BRRD and the SRM, such an extension is warranted by the ineffectiveness of government bailouts and the bankruptcy process in dealing with the failure of a systemically important hedge fund and the necessity of centralizing hedge fund resolution at the supranational level.[1037]

At first glance, it may seem that special resolution regimes are unsuitable for dealing with the failure of a systemically important hedge fund. The BRRD and the SRM are predominantly focused on the resolution of banking institutions, whose investor base, business model and capital structure differ markedly from those of hedge funds. Banking institutions' core business model is accepting deposits and extending loans. Their capital structure consists of a mix of debt and equity. Debt takes the form of deposits, short-term borrowings, such as repos, and long-term debt, including loans extended by other banks in the interbank market. Furthermore, banks are highly leveraged institutions with the average leverage ratio of EU globally systemically important banks standing at 3.9% in 2013.[1038] Their investor base consists of both unsophisticated investors, such as retail depositors and sophisticated investors, including other financial institutions. In contrast, hedge funds are pooled investment vehicles administered by professional investment managers. The hedge fund manager is responsible for investing the fund's capital. The losses and gains from investments accrue directly to investors and not the hedge fund manager. The capital structure of hedge funds consists of funds allocated by sophisticated investors and debt. Even though some individual hedge funds may be highly leveraged, hedge funds exhibit on average a reasonable level of leverage. Furthermore, hedge funds routinely utilize derivatives in order to achieve synthetic leverage.

Nonetheless, a closer look at the BRRD will reveal that the Directive contains crucial provisions for dealing in an orderly fashion with the failure of a systemically important hedge fund. The BRRD includes provisions, which suspend the termination rights of parties to derivatives contracts and Repo, invalidate 'ipso facto' clauses, restrict secured creditors of an institution under resolution from enforcing security interests secured over property of the institution in resolution and suspend any

1036. European Commission, *Consultation on a Possible Recovery and Resolution Framework for Financial Institutions Other Than Banks*, 41.
1037. For a similar proposal advocating the introduction of a special resolution procedure for hedge funds whose failure could pose a risk to financial stability *see* Jon Danielsson, Ashley Taylor and Jean-Pierre Zigrand, 'Highwaymen or Heroes: Should Hedge Funds Be Regulated?: A Survey', *Journal of Financial Stability* 1, no. 4 (2005).
1038. Marco Pagano, 'Lessons from the European Financial Crisis', in *Financial Regulation: A Transatlantic Perspective*, ed. Ester Faia et al. (Cambridge University Press, 2015), 45.

payment or delivery obligations deriving from a contract.[1039] The suspension starts from the publication of the notice of the application of resolution tools and ends at midnight at the end of the following business day.[1040] Furthermore, the suspension of termination rights is permanent if during the suspension period the liabilities covered by the contract have been transferred to another entity, such as a bridge institution, third-party acquirer or an asset separation vehicle, or the liabilities covered by the contract are subject to bail-in.[1041] As a result, the provisions of the BRRD adequately tackle the financial stability risks posed by the special privileges granted to derivatives and repo counterparties. The perils of the special privileges have been widely discussed in academic literature, with researchers forcefully advocating their repeal.[1042] Furthermore, the BRRD equips resolution authorities with useful tools for dealing with the failure of a financial institution, such as the sale of business tool, the bail-in tool, the establishment of a bridge financial institution and the establishment of an asset management company.

Indeed, systemically important hedge funds typically carry a large derivatives portfolio since derivatives allow them to gain exposure to a variety of assets and obtain synthetic leverage. In addition, repos constitute an important source of debt financing for hedge funds. The application of the BRRD and the concomitant repeal of the special privileges that its provisions introduce would grant national resolution authorities the necessary time to arrange the sale of a derivatives portfolio to a private purchaser, namely another financial institution, or its transfer to an asset management company.

Consider the case of LTCM. LTCM's potential bankruptcy threatened financial stability due to the massive liquidation of its derivatives positions that would follow. Nevertheless, LTCM's arbitrage strategy was profitable in the long-run.[1043] Indeed, the consortium of financial institutions that injected capital into LTCM and assumed the management of its portfolio was able to eventually make a profit.[1044] The roots of LTCM's distress were the heightened volatility and flight to liquidity prevailing in world financial markets, which according to Mehrling 'caused all the price discrepancies that LTCM was betting would narrow over time to widen instead'.[1045] In essence, the government-engineered bailout of LTCM was an out-of-court restructuring with LTCM's creditors agreeing to infuse the firm with and wind down its portfolio in an orderly fashion. Even though the government-sponsored bailout was successful, ad

1039. *See* Directive 2014/59/EU of the European Parliament and of the Council of 15 May 2014 Establishing a Framework for the Recovery and Resolution of Credit Institutions and Investment Firms and Amending Council Directive 82/891/EEC, and Directives 2001/24/EC, 2002/47/EC, 2004/25/EC, 2005/56/EC, 2007/36/EC, 2011/35/EU, 2012/30/EU and 2013/36/EU, and Regulations (EU) No. 1093/2010 and (EU) No. 648/2012, of the European Parliament and of the Council, 2011 O.J. (L 173) 1, Arts 69-71, at 299-301.

1040. *Ibid.*, Art. 71(2), at 300.

1041. *Ibid.*, Art. 71(2)(4), at 300.

1042. *See*, for instance, Stephen J Lubben, 'Repeal the Safe Harbors', *American Bankruptcy Institute Law Review* 18 (2010); 'Derivatives and Bankruptcy: The Flawed Case for Special Treatment', *University of Pennsylvania Journal of Business Law* 12, no. 1 (2009).

1043. Mehrling Perry, 'Minsky and Modern Finance', *The Journal of Portfolio Management* 26, no. 2 (2000): 85.

1044. *Ibid.*

1045. *Ibid.*

hoc rescues, which have to be devised and implemented in a very short period of time, are unlikely to effectively deal with a systemically important hedge fund failure in the future with sound resolution regimes remaining the optimal solution to tackling financial institutions', including systemically important hedge funds', distress.

The introduction of an effective resolution regime, such as the regime established by the BRRD, would allow resolution authorities to, in an orderly fashion, handle an LTCM-type hedge fund failure caused by temporary adverse market movements. The stay on termination rights would allow national resolution authorities to seek a private purchaser for the fund's derivatives portfolio. In case private parties were unwilling to purchase the troubled fund's portfolio, due to a generalized panic in financial markets and the simultaneous distress of other financial institutions, such as banking institutions, which would otherwise be interested in snapping up the portfolio, resolution authorities would have the power to transfer the distressed derivatives portfolio to a newly created asset management company under their ownership and direction. The use of an asset management vehicle allows for the distressed derivatives portfolio to be separated and managed in such a way as to maximize its value either through an eventual sale or an orderly wind down.[1046] Pursuant to the BRRD resolution, authorities may exercise the power to transfer assets, rights or liabilities only if the situation of the particular market for those assets is of such a nature that the liquidation of those assets under normal insolvency proceedings could have an adverse effect on one or more financial markets,[1047] such a transfer is necessary to ensure the proper functioning of the institution under resolution[1048] or bridge institution or such a transfer is necessary to maximize liquidation proceeds.[1049] Finally, the bail-in tool would be at the disposal of national resolution authorities, allowing them to reduce the principal amount of debt instruments, such as credit lines extended to the fund and repos.

The benefits of centralized supervision would be illusionary if national authorities were responsible for the resolution of systemically important hedge funds.

1046. The asset separation tool bears resemblance to another tool introduced by the BRRD, the bridge institution tool. When using the bridge institution tool, national resolution authorities have the power to transfer shares or other instruments of ownership or all or any assets, rights and liabilities of one or more institutions under resolution to a limited-life bridge institution. The bridge institution is an entity owned and controlled by the authorities, which may only operate for a maximum period of two years. The institution is authorized to conduct essential financial services pending an onward sale or entity wind down. In contrast to asset management vehicles, the bridge financial institution's aim is to preserve the failing institution's critical functions, such as payment and infrastructure services provided by the failing firm. *See* Cihák and Nier, 'The Need for Special Resolution Regimes for Financial Institutions-the Case of the European Union', 409.

1047. Directive 2014/59/EU of the European Parliament and of the Council of 15 May 2014 Establishing a Framework for the Recovery and Resolution of Credit Institutions and Investment Firms and Amending Council Directive 82/891/EEC, and Directives 2001/24/EC, 2002/47/EC, 2004/25/EC, 2005/56/EC, 2007/36/EC, 2011/35/EU, 2012/30/EU and 2013/36/EU, and Regulations (EU) No. 1093/2010 and (EU) No. 648/2012, of the European Parliament and of the Council, 2011 O.J. (L 173) 1, Art. 42(5)(a), at 265. Since the disorderly unwinding of a distressed derivatives portfolio in the midst of a generalized crisis could adversely affect financial markets, resolution authorities would be able to use the asset separation tool by invoking Art. 42(5)(a).

1048. *Ibid.*, Art. 42(5)(b), at 265.

1049. *Ibid.*, Art. 42(5)(c), at 265.

National resolution authorities would prioritize domestic interests at the expense of euro area financial stability.[1050] The potential centralization of hedge fund supervision at the euro area level would necessitate the centralization of resolution. Emulating the example of OLA, which provides for the resolution of non-bank financial institutions that can jeopardize financial stability, the SRM's scope could be expanded to capture non-bank financial institutions whose failure may pose systemic risk, such as systemically important hedge funds. As Busch and van Rijn note, the expansion of the scope of SRM can be based on Article 114 of the TFEU, which is the SRM's legal basis.[1051] Article 114 TFEU allows the adoption of measures for the approximation of national provisions aiming at the establishment and functioning of the Single Market. Centralized resolution promotes the functioning of the internal market by improving the level playing field and enhancing financial stability.[1052] Furthermore, it has been argued that complex legal issues would arise in case of an extension of the scope of the SRB.[1053] The SRB is the central body of the SRM established as an EU agency and therefore operating under the constraints of the Meroni doctrine. Nonetheless, the SRM Regulation deftly tackles the legal risks related to the application of the Meroni doctrine by conferring upon the SRB discretionary powers of a purely preparatory nature concerning the drafting of a resolution plan and recommending the use of resolution tools with the ultimate decision resting with the European Commission and the European Council.[1054] As a result, the same procedure may be utilized in case of an extension of the scope of the SRB, in order to ensure compliance with the Meroni doctrine.

What is more, further challenges would be posed by the need to create resolution funding arrangements for the purpose of supporting the resolution process. The SRF, at the disposal of the SRB, provides funding support for the resolution of the institutions currently covered by the SRM and is financed by *ex ante* and extraordinary *ex post* contributions raised at the national level and contributed to the fund. The extension of the scope of the BRRD and the SRM to include other financial institutions whose failure could threaten financial stability, such as hedge funds, would require either the creation of a new fund financed by *ex ante* and *ex post* contributions raised at the national level or alternatively the broadening of the ambit of the SRF to encompass *ex ante* and *ex post* contributions by other SIFIs allowing thus the SRF's use in their resolution.[1055]

1050. *See* Nicolas Véron and Guntram B. Wolff, 'From Supervision to Resolution: Next Steps on the Road to European Banking Union', *No. PB13-5 Policy Brief, Peterson Institute For International Economics* (February 2013).
1051. Busch and van Rijn, 'Towards Single Supervision and Resolution of Systemically Important Non-Bank Financial Institutions in the European Union', 356.
1052. *Ibid.*
1053. Moloney, 'Banking Union and the Implications for Financial Market Governance in the EU', 535.
1054. *See* Alexander, 'European Banking Union: A Legal and Institutional Analysis of the Single Supervisory Mechanism and the Single Resolution Mechanism', 180 (offering also a critique of the adopted scheme).
1055. One should highlight the legal challenges associated with the creation of the SRF. The structure and functioning of the SRF are regulated by the SRM Regulation and an Intergovernmental Agreement between the Member States participating in the Banking Union. The Intergovernmental Agreement regulates the transfer of funds raised at the national level to the

4.5 CONCLUSION

The present chapter has sought to explore and highlight the shortcomings of the current hedge fund supervisory and regulatory regime in the EU and offer realistic suggestions for its overhaul. The current regime exhibits fundamental flaws, which contribute to systemic risk. The failure of Bear Stearns exposed the perils of housing hedge funds within SIFIs and stressed the necessity of limiting the interconnectedness of hedge funds with SIFIs. Consequently, my analysis suggests that the EU Proposal on Bank Structural Reform was a sensible response to the risks posed by banks' sponsorship of and investments in hedge funds. In addition, my analysis has highlighted the perils of a national approach to the prudential supervision of hedge funds, advocating a new systemic risk architecture for hedge fund supervision in the Eurozone. Finally, the absence of a resolution framework for hedge funds in the EU leaves the EU financial system vulnerable to systemic shocks caused by the failure of systemically important hedge funds. As a result, the chapter has argued in favour of the extension of the scope of the BRRD and SRM.

SRF and the gradual mutualization of the contributions. The method of concluding an Intergovernmental Agreement was adopted due to the strong disagreement among participating Member States about whether the duty to transfer the contributions levied at the national level to the SRF could be based on EU law. In particular, Germany forcefully argued that Art. 144 of the TFEU, which served as a legal basis for the adoption of the SRM Regulation, could not serve as a legal basis for the obligation to mutualize resolution contributions raised at the national level. *See* Moloney, 'European Banking Union: Assessing Its Risks and Resilience', 1658.

Concluding Remarks

The present book has sought to introduce the reader to the world of hedge funds, assess the rationales for regulatory intervention in the hedge fund industry, analyse the optimal regulatory response to the risks posed by hedge funds, examine the US and EU hedge fund regulatory regimes and offer proposals for the improvement of the current EU supervisory and regulatory regime.

Having examined the rationales in support of hedge fund regulation offered in academic literature, the book concludes that systemic risk posed by the largest hedge funds and hedge funds housed within SIFIs is the only plausible rationale for hedge fund regulation. Furthermore, the analysis suggests that direct government regulation is the optimal response to the financial stability risks posed by hedge funds. Nevertheless, indirect regulatory measures and self-regulatory initiatives are significant supplementary measures for dealing with systemic risk.

The book has also sought to provide a comparative examination of hedge fund regulation in Europe and the US. The AIFM Directive represents a landmark piece of legislation with European regulators adopting a particularly stringent regulatory regime. As far as the US regulatory initiatives in the field of hedge funds are concerned, the Dodd-Frank Act provides for a comprehensive regulatory framework, which adequately addresses systemic risk. Apart from requiring the registration of hedge fund managers, the Act introduces a systemic designation mechanism, which grants to the FSOC the authority to designate a non-bank financial institution, including a hedge fund, as systemically important and subject it to the FED's supervision and regulation. Additionally, the Act introduces a resolution procedure for dealing with the failure of systemically important non-bank financial institutions. Overall, the examination has highlighted the superiority of the US regime urging European legislators to emulate the approach taken by their US counterparts.

Most notably, the book has endeavoured to offer concrete proposals for improving the current EU supervisory and regulatory framework. It has advocated the introduction of a US-style Volcker Rule in Europe, which came close to becoming a reality with the adoption of the Proposal on Bank Structural Reform. Moreover, I have argued in favour of reforming the system of hedge fund supervision. The book urges European legislators to proceed with the centralization of hedge fund supervision at the euro area level with the allocation of supervisory responsibilities to the ECB. According to the book's proposal, the ECB would assume prudential supervision of hedge funds designated as systemically important by the ESRB, which would be brought under the remit of the SSM. The book has additionally analysed whether the transfer of prudential supervision to the ECB is legally and practicably possible. Finally, it has proposed the extension of the scope of the BRRD and the SRM to include hedge funds.

Overall, the book has sought to offer only a general framework for centralizing hedge fund supervision at the euro area level and extending the scope of the BRRD and the SRM to hedge funds. Most notably, the aim of the book was to convince our readers that the transition to a new hedge fund supervisory and regulatory regime is legally and practicably possible. I hope that future researchers, legislators and supervisors will find it worthwhile to develop the proposals into a concrete supervisory and regulatory regime.

Bibliography

Andreas, Dombret, and Patrick S. Kenadjian (eds). *The European Capital Markets Union: A Viable Concept and a Real Goal?*. De Gruyter, 2015.

Abreu, Dilip, and Markus K Brunnermeier. 'Bubbles and Crashes'. *Econometrica* 71, no. 1 (2003): 173-204.

Acharya, Viral V, and Matthew Richardson. 'Causes of the Financial Crisis'. *Critical Review* 21, no. 2-3 (2009): 195-210.

Acharya Viral V., Schnabl Philipp and Suarez Gustavo. 'Securitization without Risk Transfer'. *Journal of Financial Economics* 107, no. 3 (2013): 515-36.

Acharya Viral, Deniz Anginer and Joseph Warburton. 'The End of Market Discipline? Investor Expectations of Implicit State Guarantees'. http://papers.ssrn.com/sol3/papers.cfm?abstract_id=1961656 (2013).

Adair, Turner. *The Turner Review: A Regulatory Response to the Global Banking Crisis*. 2009.

Adam L. Aiken, Christopher P. Clifford and Jesse A. Ellis. 'Hedge Funds and Discretionary Liquidity Restrictions'. (2013). http://papers.ssrn.com/sol3/papers.cfm?abstract_id=2185999.

Admati, Anat, and Martin Hellwig. *The Bankers' New Clothes: What's Wrong with Banking and What to Do About It*. Princeton University Press, 2014.

Agarwal, Vikas, Nicole M Boyson, and Narayan Y Naik. 'Hedge Funds for Retail Investors? An Examination of Hedged Mutual Funds'. *Journal of Financial and Quantitative Analysis* 44, no. 02 (2009): 273-305.

Agarwal, Vikas, Naveen D Daniel, and Narayan Y Naik. 'Role of Managerial Incentives and Discretion in Hedge Fund Performance'. *The Journal of Finance* 64, no. 5 (2009): 2221-56.

Agarwal, Vikas, and Sugata Ray. 'Determinants and Implications of Fee Changes in the Hedge Fund Industry'. SSRN 1784545.

'Agreement among PWG and US Agency Principals on Principles and Guidelines Regarding Private Pools of Capital'. (2007).

'Agreement on the Transfer and Mutualization of Contributions to the Single Resolution Fund'. 14 May 2014.

Aguilar, Luis A. 'Speech by Sec Commissioner: Hedge Fund Regulation on the Horizon - Don't Shoot the Messenger'. News release, 18 June 2009.

Aitken, Manmohan Singh and James. 'Deleveraging after Lehman-Evidence from Reduced Rehypothecation'. *IMF Working Paper WP/09/42* (2009).

Aiken L. Adam, Christopher P. Clifford, and Jesse A. Ellis. 'Hedge Funds and Discretionary Liquidity Restrictions'. *Journal of Financial Economics* 116, no. 1 (April 2015): 197–218.

Alan Porter, Cary Meer, Marticha Cary. *Amendments to Custody Rule under the Investment Advisers Act of 1940*. October 2003.

Alberto, Manconia, Massimo Massab, Ayako Yasuda. 'The Role of Institutional Investors in Propagating the Crisis of 2007–2008'. *Journal of Financial Economics* 104, no. 3 (2012): 491-518.

Alessandro, Beber, Daniela Fabbri and Marco Pagano. 'Short-Selling Bans and Bank Stability'. http://papers.ssrn.com/sol3/papers.cfm?abstract_id=2710371.

Alexander, Kern. 'European Banking Union: A Legal and Institutional Analysis of the Single Supervisory Mechanism and the Single Resolution Mechanism'. *European law review* 40, no. 2 (2015): 154-87.

Alexander, Kern. 'Regulating the Structure of the EU Banking Sector'. *European Business Organization Law Review* 16, no. 2 (2015): 227-53.

AIMA. *Guide to Sound Practices for Hedge Fund Valuation*. Mar. London: AIMA, 2007.

Alon Brav, Wei Jiang, Frank Partnoy, and Randall Thomas. 'Hedge Fund Activism, Corporate Governance and Firm Performance'. *Journal of Finance* 63, no. 4 (2011).

Amel Dean, Barnes Colleen, Panetta Fabio, and Salleo Carmelo. 'Consolidation and Efficiency in the Financial Sector: A Review of the International Evidence'. *Journal of Banking & Finance* 28, no. 10 (2004): 2493.

Anabtawi, Iman, and Lynn Stout. 'Fiduciary Duties for Activist Shareholders'. *Stanford Law Review* 60 (2008): 1255-308.

Andenas, Mads. 'Who Is Going to Supervise Europe's Financial Markets'. In *Financial Markets in Europe: Towards a Single Regulator*, edited by Mads Andenas and Yannis Avgerinos: Kluwer Law International, 2003.

Andenas, Mads, and Iris HY Chiu. 'Financial Stability and Legal Integration in Financial Regulation'. *European Law Review* 38 (2013): 335-59.

Ang, Andrew, Sergiy Gorovyy, and Gregory B Van Inwegen. 'Hedge Fund Leverage'. *Journal of Financial Economics* 102, no. 1 (2011): 102-26.

Ann Davis, Henny Sender and Gregory Zuckerman. 'Amid Amaranth's Crisis, Other Players Profited'. The Wall Street Journal, http://online.wsj.com/news/articles/SB117012628156391989.

Ann Davis, Henny Sender, and Gregory Zuckerman. 'What Went Wrong at Amaranth'. The Wall Street Journal, http://online.wsj.com/news/articles/SB115871715733268470.

'Annual Report to Congress'. Office for Financial Research, 2020.

Appel, Ian R, Todd A Gormley, and Donald B Keim. 'Standing on the Shoulders of Giants: The Effect of Passive Investors on Activism'. *The Review of Financial Studies* 32, no. 7 (1 July 2019): 2720–74.

Aragon, George O, and Philip E Strahan. 'Hedge Funds as Liquidity Providers: Evidence from the Lehman Bankruptcy'. *Journal of Financial Economics* 103, no. 3 (2012): 570-87.

Aragon, George, and Philip E Strahan. 'Hedge Funds as Liquidity Providers'. *Journal of Financial Economics* 103, no. 3 (2012): 570-87.

Armour, Brian R Cheffins and John. 'The Past, Present and Future of Shareholder Activism by Hedge Funds'. *Journal of Corporation Law* 37, no. 1 (2011).

Armour, John. 'Making Bank Resolution Credible'. *No. 244 ECGI Law Working Paper* (2014).

Armour John, Awrey Dan, Davies Paul, Enriques Luca, Gordon Jeffrey N., Mayer Colin, and Payne Jennifer. *Principles of Financial Regulation*. Oxford University Press, 2016.

Arnold, Emma Dunkley, and Martin. 'Global Banks Fret over UK Ringfencing Rules'. The Financial Times, https://next.ft.com/content/a1ac7434-15c6-11e5-be54-00144feabdc0.

'As Goldman and Morgan Shift, A Wall St. Era Ends'. Dealbook, http://dealbook.nytimes.com/2008/09/21/goldman-morgan-to-become-bank-holding-companies/?_r=0.

Association, Alternative Investment Management. *A Guide to Institutional Investors' Views and Preferences Regarding Hedge Fund Operational Infrastructures*. May 2011.

Association, Alternative Investment Management. *Response to ESMA'S Consultation Paper-Guidelines on Sound Remuneration Policies under the Alternative Investment Fund Managers Directive*. September 2012.

Association, Alternative Investment Management. *The Role of Credit Hedge Funds in the Financial System: Asset Managers, Not Shadow Banks*. March 2012.

Association, Managed Funds. *Sound Practices for Hedge Fund Managers*. 2009.

Assocs, Charles River. *Impact of the Proposed AIFM Directive across Europe*. 2009.

Athanassiou, Phoebus. 'The Conceptual Underpinnings of Onshore Hedge Fund Regulation: A Global and European Perspective'. *Journal of Corporate Law Studies* 8, no. 2 (2008): 251-88.

Athanassiou, Phoebus. *Hedge Fund Regulation in the European Union: Current Trends and Future Prospects*. Kluwer Law International, 2009.

Athanassiou, Phoebus. 'Withdrawal and Expulsion from the EU and EMU: Some Reflections'. *European Central Bank Legal Working Paper Series* No. 10 (2009).

Avgouleas Emilios. 'A New Framework for the Global Regulation of Short Sales: Why Prohibition Is Inefficient and Disclosure Insufficient'. *Stanford Journal of Law, Business and Finance* 15, no. 2 (2010): 376-425.

Avgouleas Emilios. 'Large Systemic Banks and Fractional Reserve Banking, Intractable Dilemmas in Search of Effective Solutions'. In *Reconceptualizing Global Finance and Its Regulation*, edited by Arner Douglas, Avgouleas Emilios and Buckley Ross, 659-92: Cambridge University Press.

Avgouleas Emilios, and Jay Cullen. 'Excessive Leverage and Bankers' Pay: Governance and Financial Stability Costs of a Symbiotic Relationship'. *Columbia Journal of European Law* 21, no. 1 (2015): 1–46.

Avgouleas Emilios, and Goodhart Charles. 'Critical Reflections on Bank Bail-In'. In *The Reform of International Economic Governance*, edited by Antonio Segura Serrano: Routledge, 2015.

Aviram, Amitai. 'Placebo Effect of Law: Law's Role in Manipulating Perceptions, The'. *George Washington Law Review* 75, no. 1 (2006): 54.

Awrey, Dan. 'The Limits of EU Hedge Fund Regulation'. *Law and Financial Markets Review* 5, no. 2 (2011): 119-28.

Ayotte, Kenneth, and David A Skeel. 'Bankruptcy or Bailouts'. *Journal of Corporation Law* 35, no. 3 (2009): 469.

Babis, Valia SG. 'The Power to Ban Short-Selling: The Beginning of a New Era for EU Agencies?'. *University of Cambridge Faculty of Law Research Paper* No. 27 (2014).

Bailey, Andrew. 'The UK Bank Resolution Regime, Speech at the ICAEW Financial Services Faculty Breakfast, London'. News release, 26 November 2009.

Bailey Andrew, Breeden Sarah, and Stevens Gregory. 'The Prudential Regulation Authority'. *Bank of England Quarterly Bulletin* Q4 (2012).

Bank of England, Prudential Regulation Authority. *The Implementation of Ring-Fencing: Prudential Requirements, Intragroup Arrangements and Use of Financial Market Infrastructures, Consultation Paper, Cp37/15.* October 2015.

Banzaca, Jennifer. 'Key Considerations for Hedge Fund Managers in Organizing and Operating Valuation Committees'. *Hedge Fund Law Report* 5, No. 32 (August 2012).

Barberis, Nicholas, and Richard Thaler. 'A Survey of Behavioral Finance'. *National Bureau of Economic Research* No. w9222 (2002).

Barney Jopson, Stephen Foley, and Caroline Binham 'Fund Managers to Escape Systemic Label'. Financial Times, https://next.ft.com/content/4e9d566e-2999-11e5-8613-e7aedbb7bdb7.

Barth, Daniel, Juha Joenvaara, Mikko Kauppila, and Russell R. Wermers. 'The Hedge Fund Industry Is Bigger (And Has Performed Better) Than You Think'. OFR Working Paper 20-01, March 2021.

Bebchuk Lucian A, Brav Alon, Jackson Robert J, and Jiang Wei. 'Pre-Disclosure Accumulations by Activist Investors: Evidence and Policy'. *Journal of Corporation Law* 39, no. 1 (2013): 1-34.

Bebchuk, Lucian A, Alon Brav, and Wei Jiang. 'The Long-Term Effects of Hedge Fund Activism'. *Columbia Law Review* 115, no. 5 (2015): 1085-155.

Bebchuk, Lucian A, and Alma Cohen. 'The Costs of Entrenched Boards'. *Journal of Financial Economics* 78, no. 2 (2005): 409-33.

Bebchuk, Lucian A, Alma Cohen, and Holger Spamann. 'The Wages of Failure: Executive Compensation at Bear Stearns and Lehman 2000-2008'. *Yale Journal on Regulation*, no. 2 (2010): 257.

Bebchuk, Lucian A, and Robert J Jackson Jr. 'Law and Economics of Blockholder Disclosure'. *Harvard Business Law Review*2 (2012): 39.

Bebchuk, Lucian A, and Holger Spamann. 'Regulating Bankers' Pay'. *Georgetown Law Journal* 98, no. 2 (2009): 247.

Bebchuk, Lucian, Alma Cohen, and Allen Ferrell. 'What Matters in Corporate Governance?'. *Review of Financial studies* 22, no. 2 (2009): 783-827.

Beber, Alessandro, and Marco Pagano. 'Short-Selling Bans Around the World: Evidence from the 2007-09 Crisis'. *The Journal of Finance* 68, no. 1 (2013): 343-81.

Becht, Marco, Julian Franks, and Jeremy Grant. 'Hedge Fund Activism in Europe'. *No. 283 ECGI-Finance Working Paper* (2010).

Becht Marco, Franks Julian, Grant Jeremy, and Hannes Wagner. 'The Returns to Hedge Fund Activism: An International Study'. *No. 402 European Corporate Governance Institute (ECGI)-Finance Working Paper* (2014).

Beck, Thorsten, and Ross Levine. 'Industry Growth and Capital Allocation: Does Having a Market-or Bank-Based System Matter?'. *Journal of Financial Economics* 64, no. 2 (2002): 147-80.

Ben-David, Itzhak, Justin Birru, and Andrea Rossi. 'The Performance of Hedge Fund Performance Fees'. Charles A. Dice Center for Research in Financial Economics Working Paper 2020-14, 2020.

Beny, Laura Nyantung. 'Insider Trading Laws and Stock Markets around the World: An Empirical Contribution to the Theoretical Law and Economics Debate'. *Journal of Corporation Law* 32, no. 2 (2006): 237.

Berger, Philip G, and Eli Ofek. 'Diversification's Effect on Firm Value'. *Journal of Financial Economics* 37, no. 1 (1995): 39-65.

Berle, Adolph, and Gardiner Means. *The Modern Corporation and Private Property*. Transaction Publishers, 1968.

Bhattacharya, Utpal, and Hazem Daouk. 'The World Price of Insider Trading'. *The Journal of Finance* 57, no. 1 (2002): 75-108.

Bianchini, David Nissenbaum, and Maria Gabriela. 'Activist Fund Structuring'. *Schulte Roth & Zabel* (2005).

Biais, Bruno, Bisiere Christophe, and Jean Paul Decamps. 'Short Sales Constraints, Liquidity and Price Discovery: An Empirical Analysis on the Paris Bourse'. *European Financial Management* 5 (1999): 395–409.

Binder, Jens-Hinrich. 'To Ring-Fence or Not, and How? Strategic Questions for Post-Crisis Banking Reform in Europe'. *http://papers.ssrn.com/sol3/papers.cfm?abstract_id=2543860* (2014).

Black, Bernard S. 'Shareholder Passivity Reexamined'. *Michigan Law Review* 89 (1990): 520-608.

Black, Bernard S. 'Shareholder Activism and Corporate Governance in the United States'. In *The New Palgrave Dictionary of Economics and the Law*, edited by John Eatwell et al., Palgrave, 1998, 459-65.

Black, G. Baird & J. Baird. 'Amendments Clog EU AIFM Directive Debate: The Political Backdrop Is Also Evolving Rapidly'. *The Hedge Fund Journal* (March 2010).

Black, Julia. 'Decentring Regulation: Understanding the Role of Regulation and Self-Regulation in a "Post-Regulatory" World'. *Current Legal Problems* 54, no. 1 (2001): 103-46.

Bland, Ben. 'Bear Stearns Hedge Funds Wiped Out'. The Telegraph, http://www.telegraph.co.uk/finance/markets/2812344/Bear-Stearns-hedge-funds-wiped-out.html.

Block, Stanley B. 'Merger Arbitrage Hedge Funds'. *Journal of Applied Finance* 16, no. 1 (2006).

'BNP Paribas Suspends Funds Because of Subprime Problems'. The New York Times, http://www.nytimes.com/2007/08/09/business/worldbusiness/09iht-09bnp.7054054.html?_r=0.

Board, Hedge Fund Standards. *Hedge Fund Standards*. 2012.

Board, Hedge Fund Standards. *Response to the ESMA Consultation Paper on Guidelines on Sound Remuneration Policies under AIFMD.* September 2012.

Boehmer, Ekkehart, Charles M Jones, and Xiaoyan Zhang. 'Shackling Short Sellers: The 2008 Shorting Ban'. *Review of Financial Studies* 26, no. 6 (2013).

Boehmer, Ekkehart, Charles M Jones, Juan (Julie) Wu, and Xiaoyan Zhang. 'What Do Short Sellers Know?'. *Review of Finance* 24, no. 6 (1 November 2020): 1203–35.

Boesky, Ivan F. *Merger Mania, Arbitrage: Wall Street's Best Kept Money-Making Secret*. Holt Reinhart and Winston, 1985.

Bollen, Nicolas PB, and Veronika K Pool. 'Do Hedge Fund Managers Misreport Returns? Evidence from the Pooled Distribution'. *The Journal of Finance* 64, no. 5 (2009): 2257-88.

Bonn, Matthias Lehmann. 'Volcker Rule, Ring-Fencing or Separation of Bank Activities – Comparison of Structural Reform Acts around the World'. *LSE Legal Studies Working Paper* No. 25 (2014).

Braithwaite, John, and Peter Drahos. *Global Business Regulation*. 2000.

Bratton, William. 'Hedge Funds and Governance Targets'. *Georgetown Law Journal* 95, no. 5 (2007): 1375-2017.

Brav, Alon, Wei Jiang, and Hyunseob Kim. 'Hedge Fund Activism: A Review'. *Foundations and Trends (R) in Finance* 4, no. 3 (2010): 185-246.

Brav, Alon, Wei Jiang, and Hyunseob Kim. 'The Real Effects of Hedge Fund Activism: Productivity, Asset Allocation, and Labor Outcomes'. *The Review of Financial Studies* 28, no. 10 (1 October 2015): 2723–69.

Brav, Alon, Wei Jiang, and Tao Li. 'Picking Friends Before Picking (Proxy) Fights: How Mutual Fund Voting Shapes Proxy Contests'. ECGI Finance Working Paper N° 601/2019, 2021. https://www.ssrn.com/abstract=3101473.

Bray, Susan Pulliam, and Chad. 'Trader Draws Record Sentence'. The Wall Street Journal. http://online.wsj.com/news/articles/SB10001424052970203914304576627191081876286.

Berman, Bradley et al. *General Solicitation and General Advertising*. Harvard Law School Forum on Corporate Governance. https://corpgov.law.harvard.edu/2021/06/21/general-solicitation-and-general-advertising/

Brown, Gregory W, Jeremiah Green, and John RM Hand. 'Are Hedge Funds Systemically Important?'. *The Journal of Derivatives* 20, no. 2 (2012): 8-25.

Brown, Stephen J, William N Goetzmann, and James Park. 'Hedge Funds and the Asian Currency Crisis of 1997'. *National Bureau of Economic Research* No. w6427. (1998).

Bruck, Connie. *Predator's Ball*. Penguin, 2013.

Brunnermeier, Markus K. 'Deciphering the Liquidity and Credit Crunch 2007-2008'. *Journal of Economic Perspectives* 23, no. 1 (2009): 77-100.

Brunnermeier Markus K, Crockett Andrew, Goodhart Charles A, Persaud Avinash, Shin Hyun Song. *The Fundamental Principles of Financial Regulation*. Princeton University Press, 2009.

Brunnermeier, Markus K, and Stefan Nagel. 'Hedge Funds and the Technology Bubble'. *The Journal of Finance* 59, no. 5 (2004): 2013-40.

Brunnermeier Markus, Luis Garicano et al. 'Breaking the Sovereign-Bank Diabolic Loop: A Case for Esbies'. Paper Presented at the American Economic Review Papers and Proceedings, 2015.

Bryant, Chris. 'EU Leaders Push Sweeping Regulations'. Financial Times. http://www.ft.com/intl/cms/s/0/a896e59e-011f-11de-8f6e-000077b07658.html#axzz3T0cY6epL.

Bubb, Ryan, and Marcel Kahan. 'Regulating Motivation: A New Perspective on the Volcker Rule'. *Texas Law Review* 96 (2018): 1019–52.

Buchanan, James M. 'Externality'. *Economica* 29, no. 116 (1962): 371-84.

Buchanan John, Heesang Chai Dominic, and Deakin Simon. *Hedge Fund Activism in Japan: The Limits of Shareholder Primacy*. Cambridge University Press, 2012.

Buck, Tobias. 'FT Interview: Charlie McCreevy'. http://www.ft.com/intl/cms/s/0/3a94b8c4-c043-11db-995a-000b5df10621.html#axzz3T0cY6epL.

Buffett, Warren. 'Letter to the Editor'. *Financial History* 86 (Summer 2006).

Bullman, Phoebus Athanassiou, and Thomas. 'The EU'S AIFM Directive and Its Impact-an Overview'. In *Research Handbook on Hedge Funds, Private Equity and Alternative Investments*, edited by Phoebus Athanassiou: Edward Elgar, 2012.

Bundesbank, Deutsche. *Financial Stability Review*. November 2006.

Bundesbank, Deutsche. 'Hedge Funds and Their Role in the Financial Markets'. *Monthly Report* (March 1999).

Bundesbank, Deutsche. *Monthly Report*. December 2010.

Burton, Steven J. 'Ronald Dworkin and Legal Positivism'. *Iowa Law Review*. 73 (1987): 109.

Busch, Danny, and Mirik B. J. van Rijn. 'Towards Single Supervision and Resolution of Systemically Important Non-Bank Financial Institutions in the European Union'. *European Business Organization Law Review* 19, no. 2 (n.d.): 301–63.

Caldwell, Ted. 'Introduction: The Model for Superior Performance'. In *Hedge Funds: Investment and Portfolio Strategies for the Institutional Investor*, edited by Jess Lederman & Robert A. Klein, 1-17. Burr Ridge, Ill.: Irwin Professional Publishing, 1995.

Camara, Paolo. 'The AIFM'S Governance and Remuneration Committees'. In *The Alternative Investment Funds Managers Directive, European Regulation of Alternative Investment Funds*, edited by Dirk Zetzsche, 237-52: Kluwer Law International, 2012.

Cao Charles, Chen Yong, Liang Bing, and Andrew W. Lo. 'Can Hedge Funds Time Market Liquidity?'. *Journal of Financial Economics* 109, no. 2 (2013): 493-516.

Cao Charles, Liang Bing, Lo Andrew, and Petrasek Lubomir. 'Hedge Fund Holdings and Stock Market Efficiency'. *Finance and Economics Discussion Series, Federal Reserve Board, Washington D.C.* (May 2014).

Capdeville, J.P. Kovar, and J. Lasserre. ' L'autorité De Contrôle Prudentiel '. In *Les Annales De La Régulation*, edited by Th. Revet et L. Vidal, 2013.

Carnell Richard Scott, Macey Jonathan, and Miller Geoffrey. *The Law of Financial Institutions*. 4th ed.: Wolters Kluwer, 2013.

Carruthers, Bruce G. 'Diverging Derivatives: Law, Governance and Modern Financial Markets'. *Journal of Comparative Economics* 41, no. 2 (2013): 386-400.

Cary, William L. 'Federalism and Corporate Law: Reflections Upon Delaware'. *The Yale Law Journal* 83, no. 4 (1974): 663-705.

Cassar, Gavin, and Joseph Gerakos. 'Hedge Funds: Pricing Controls and the Smoothing of Self-Reported Returns'. *Review of Financial Studies* 24, no. 5 (2011): 1698-734.

Center For Hedge Fund Research, Imperial College, London. *The Value of the Hedge Fund Industry to Investors, Markets and the Broader Economy*. 2012.

Chamon, Merijn. 'The Empowerment of Agencies under the Meroni Doctrine and Article 114 TFEU: Comment on United Kingdom V. Parliament and Council (Short-Selling) and the Proposed Single Resolution Mechanism'. *European Law Review* 39, no. 3 (2014): 380-403.

Chamon, Merijn. 'EU Agencies: Does the Meroni Doctrine Make Sense'. *Maastricht Journal of European and Comparative Law* 17, no. 3 (2010): 281.

Chang, Sue. '2011 Was a Year of Horrors for Hedge Funds'. The Wall Street Journal. http://www.marketwatch.com/story/2011-was-a-year-of-horrors-for-hedge-funds-2011-12-23.

Charles Forelle, Alkman Granitsas. 'Greece Asks for $60 Billion Bailout'. The Wall Street Journal. http://online.wsj.com/news/articles/SB10001424052748703709804575201330937572258?mg=reno64-wsj.

Chasan, Emily. 'Hedge Funds Offered Weak Returns in 2010'. Reuters, http://www.reuters.com/article/2010/12/31/us-hedgefunds-yearend-idUSTRE6BU1W720101231.

Chen, Yong. 'Derivatives Use and Risk Taking: Evidence from the Hedge Fund Industry'. *Journal of Financial and Quantitative Analysis* 46, no. 04 (2011): 1073-106.

Childs, John Authers, and Mary. 'Hedge Funds: Overpriced, Underperforming'. The Financial Times, https://next.ft.com/content/9bd1150e-1b76-11e6-b286-cddde55ca122.

Chincarini, Ludwig. 'A Case Study on Risk Management: Lessons from the Collapse of Amaranth Advisors LLC'. *Journal of Applied Finance* 18, no. 1 (2008): 152.

Chincarini, Ludwig. 'Hedge Funds – an Introduction'. In *Research Handbook on Hedge Funds, Private Equity and Alternative Investments*, edited by Phoebus Athanassiou, 13: Edward Elgar, 2012.

Choi, Stephen Jung, and Adam C Pritchard. *Securities Regulation*. Foundation Press, 2008.

Chow, Julian TS, and Jay Surti. 'Making Banks Safer: Can Volcker and Vickers Do It?'. *WP/11/236 IMF Working Papers* (2011): 1-34.

Chung, Juliet. 'Falcone Admits Wrongdoing, Agrees to Five-Year Ban'. The Wall Street Journal, http://online.wsj.com/news/articles/SB10001424127887323608504579023123351192450.

Chung, Juliet. 'Hedge Funds again Prove a Laggard'. The Wall Street Journal, http://online.wsj.com/news/articles/SB10001424127887323723104578188022542455136.

Cihák, Martin, and Erlend Nier. 'The Need for Special Resolution Regimes for Financial Institutions-the Case of the European Union'. *Harvard Business Law Review* 2, no. 2 (2012): 395.

Code monétaire et financier (French Financial Services Act).

Coffee, John C., and Darius Palia. 'The Impact of Hedge Fund Activism: Evidence and Implications'. Columbia Law and Economics Working Paper 489, 2014.

Coffee, John C, Louis Lowenstein, and Susan Rose-Ackerman. *Knights, Raiders, and Targets: The Impact of the Hostile Takeover.* Oxford University Press, 1988.

Coggan, Philip. *The Economist Guide to Hedge Funds.* The Economist Books, 2010.

Cohan, William D. *House of Cards: A Tale of Hubris and Wretched Excess on Wall Street.* Anchor, 2010.

Cohen, Rodgin, and Morris Goldstein. 'The Case for an Orderly Resolution Regime for Systemically-Important Financial Institutions'. *The Pew Financial Reform Project Briefing Paper* 13 (2009).

Cominetta, Matteo, Claudia Lambert, Anouk Levels, Anders Ryden, and Christian Weistroffer. 'Macroprudential Liquidity Tools for Investment Funds – A Preliminary Discussion'. European Central Bank, n.d. https://www.ecb.europa.eu/pub/financial-stability/macroprudential-bulletin/html/ecb.mpbu201810_03.en.html.

Conac, Pierre-Henri, Luca Enriques, and Martin Gelter. 'Constraining Dominant Shareholders' Self-Dealing: The Legal Framework in France, Germany, and Italy'. *European Company and Financial Law Review* 4, no. 4 (2007): 491-528.

Congress, US, Senate Permanent Subcommittee on Investigations. *Excessive Speculation in the Natural Gas Market.* 2007.

Connor, Gregory, and Mason Woo. 'An Introduction to Hedge Funds'. *Discussion paper, 477. Financial Markets Group, London School of Economics and Political Science* (2004).

'Consolidated Version of the Treaty on the Functioning of the European Union'. News release.

Constâncio, Vítor. 'Towards the Banking Union, Speech at the 2nd FIN-FSA Conference on EU Regulation and Supervision 'Banking and Supervision under Transformation' Organised by the Financial Supervisory Authority, Helsinki'. News release, 12 February 2013.

Copeland, Rob. 'Hedge Funds Drive to Another Record'. The Wall Street Journal, http://online.wsj.com/news/articles/SB1000142405270230404990457951613245854 6194.

Copeland, Rob. 'Returns from Activist Hedge Funds Are Causing a Stir'. The Wall Street Journal, http://online.wsj.com/articles/returns-from-activist-hedge-funds-are-causing-a-stir-1404773120.

'Corporate Governance: Shareholders at the Gates'. The Economist, http://www.economist.com/news/business/21573134-americas-proxy-season-will-pit-management-against-owners-never-shareholders.

Corrigan, Tracy. 'Attacking Speculators Is a Good Bet for Troubled Politicians'. The Daily Telegraph, http://www.telegraph.co.uk/finance/financialcrisis/7423145/Attacking-speculators-is-a-good-bet-for-troubled-politicians.html.

Corrigan, Tracy. 'Hedge Funds Do Not Need Punishing They Are Suffering Enough'. The Daily Telegraph, www.telegraph.co.uk/finance/comment/tracycorrigan/3212102/Hedgefunds-dont-need punishing-they-are-suffering-enough.html.

Corsetti, Giancarlo, Paolo Pesenti, and Nouriel Roubini. 'What Caused the Asian Currency and Financial Crisis? Part I: A Macroeconomic Overview'. *National Bureau of Economic Research Working Paper* No. w6834 (1998).

Cortey, Linda. 'Gagner Un Coup D' Avance'. Luxembourger Wort, https://www.wort.lu/de/business/place-financiere-gagner-un-coup-d-avance-57270aec1bea9dff8fa770a6.

Coulomb, Élisabeth. 'La Loi Bancaire: La France Précède L'europe'. *Revue-Banque* 765 (2013).

Craig, Susanne. 'The Giant of Shareholders, Quietly Stirring'. The New York Times, http://www.nytimes.com/2013/05/19/business/blackrock-a-shareholding-giant-is-quietly-stirring.html.

Crane, Jonah. 'Remarks by Deputy Assistant Secretary Jonah Crane at a Meeting of the Financial Stability Oversight Council'. US Treasury, 16 October 2016. https://www.treasury.gov/press-center/press-releases/Pages/jl0612.aspx.

Crawford, Alan. 'Germany to Temporarily Ban Naked Short Selling, Some Swaps of Euro Bonds'. Bloomberg, http://www.bloomberg.com/news/2010-05-18/germany-to-start-temporary-ban-on-naked-short-selling-of-euro-bonds-banks.html.

Cremers, K. J. Martijn, Lubomir P. Litov, and Simone M. Sepe. 'Staggered Boards and Long-Term Firm Value, Revisited'. *Journal of Financial Economics* 126, no. 2 (2017): 422–44.

Cremers, Martijn, Ankur Pareek, and Zacharias Sautner. 'Short-Term Institutions, Analyst Recommendations, and Mispricing: The Role of Higher Order Beliefs'. *Journal of Accounting Research* 59, no. 3 (June 2021): 911–58.

Criado Sarai, Degabriel Laurent, Lewandowska Magdalena, Lindén Staffan, and Ritter Peer. *Report on Sovereign CDS*. 2010.

Crockett, Andrew. 'The Evolution and Regulation of Hedge Funds'. *Banque de France, Financial Stability Review: Special Issue Hedge Funds* 10 (April 2007): 19-26.

Crockett, Andrew. 'Marrying the Micro-and Macro-Prudential Dimensions of Financial Stability'. *BIS Speeches* 21 (2000).

Crowe, Portia. 'Bernie Sanders and Elizabeth Warren Are Going after Activist Hedge Funds'. Business Insider, https://www.businessinsider.com/elizabeth-warren-sponsors-activist-hedge-fund-bill-2016-3?r = US&IR = T.

Crutcher, Gibson Dunn. *Germany Adopts Capital Investment Act (KAGB) to Implement the European AIFM Directive.* 22 July 2013.

Cyree, Ken B, and Bhanu Balasubramanian. 'The Determinants of Yield Spreads and the Market Discipline of Banks'. *Available at SSRN 1350951* (2009).

Dahlman, Carl J. 'The Problem of Externality'. *The Journal of Law & Economics* 22, no. 1 (1979): 141-62.

Dai Rui, Massoud Nadia, Nandy Debarshi, and Saunders Anthony. 'Hedge Funds in M&A Deals: Is There Exploitation of Private Information?' Working Paper, 2010.

Dammann, Jens. 'The Banking Union: Flawed by Design'. *Georgetown Journal of International Law* 45, no. 4 (2013): 1057.

Danielsson, Jon, Ashley Taylor, and Jean-Pierre Zigrand. 'Highwaymen or Heroes: Should Hedge Funds Be Regulated?: A Survey'. *Journal of Financial Stability* 1, no. 4 (2005): 522-43.

Davidoff, Steven. 'Black Market Capital'. *Columbia Business Law Review* 2008, no. 1 (2008): 173-268.

Davis, Sarah Dunn. 'Market Manipulation Annotated Bibliography'. 2010.

De Jonghe, Olivier. 'Back to the Basics in Banking? A Micro-Analysis of Banking System Stability'. *Journal of Financial Intermediation* 19, no. 3 (2010): 387-417.

de Lhoneux Etienne, Simoes Lopes Elisabeth, Cadilhac Eric, and Götz Ulrike. 'La Banque Centrale Du Luxembourg- Développements Législatifs 2004-2013'. *Droit Bancaire et Financier au Luxembourg* 1 (2014).

De Long Bradford, Shleifer Andrei, Summers Lawrence, and Waldmann Robert. 'Noise Trader Risk in Financial Markets'. *Journal of Political Economy* 98, no. 4 (1990): 703-38.

Debevoise and Plimpton. 'European Funds Comment: The Costs (and Benefits) of the AIFMD', https://www.debevoise.com/insights/publications/2018/01/efc-the-costs-and-benefits-of-the-aifmd.

Dechert. *International Short Selling Regulation: Recent Developments*. 2008.

Declaration on Strengthening the Financial System, London Summit. 2 April 2009.

Deloitte. *Alternative Investment Fund Managers Directive: Meeting the Challenge*. 2013.

DeLong Gayle L., 'Stockholder Gains from Focusing versus Diversifying Bank Mergers', *Journal of Financial Economics* 59, no. 2 (1 February 2001): 221–52.

Demaria, Cyril. *Introduction to Private Equity: Venture, Growth, LBO and Turn-around Capital.* Wiley, 2013.

Demirgüç-Kunt, Aslı, and Vojislav Maksimovic. 'Funding Growth in Bank-Based and Market-Based Financial Systems: Evidence from Firm-Level Data'. *Journal of Financial Economics* 65, no. 3 (2002): 337-63.

DeYoung, Robert, and Karin P Roland. 'Product Mix and Earnings Volatility at Commercial Banks: Evidence from a Degree of Total Leverage Model'. *Journal of Financial Intermediation* 10, no. 1 (2001): 54-84.

Di Noia, Carmine, and Giorgio Di Giorgio. 'Should Banking Supervision and Monetary Policy Tasks Be Given to Different Agencies?'. *International Finance* 2, no. 3 (1999): 361-78.

Dodd, Peter. 'Merger Proposals, Management Discretion and Stockholder Wealth'. *Journal of Financial Economics* 8, no. 2 (1980): 105-37.

Dolgopolov, Stanislav. 'Regulating Merchants of Liquidity: Market Making from Crowded Floors to High-Frequency Trading'. *University of Pennsylvania Journal of Business Law* 18, no. 3 (2015).

Doyle Nicola, Hermans Lieven, Molitor Philippe, and Weistroffer Christian. 'Shadow Banking in the Euro Area: Risks and Vulnerabilities in the Investment Fund Sector'. *European Central Bank Occasional Paper Series* No. 174 (June 2016).

Dreyfuss, Barbara. *Hedge Hogs: The Cowboy Traders Behind Wall Street's Largest Hedge Fund Disaster*. Random House, 2013.

Duffie, Darell. *Drawing Boundaries Around and Through the Banking System, World Economic Forum, Financial Development Report*. 31 October 2012.

Duffie, Darrell, Ada Li, and Theo Lubke. 'Policy Perspectives on OTC Derivatives Market Infrastructure'. *Staff Report, Federal Reserve Bank of New York* (2010).

Dunbar, Nick. 'An Imaginary Wolf-Pack'. Nick Dunbar, http://www.nickdunbar.net/articles-and-reviews/an-imaginary-wolf-pack/.

Duncan Angus, Curtin Edmond, and Crosignani Marco. 'Alternative Regulation: The Directive on Alternative Investment Fund Managers'. *Capital Markets Law Journal* 6, no. 3 (2011).

Eckner, Dirk Zetzsche, and Dirk. 'Risk Management in the Alternative Investment Fund Managers Directive'. In *The Alternative Investment Fund Managers Directive, European Regulation of Alternative Investment Funds,* edited by Dirk Zetzsche, 265-332: Kluwer Law International, 2012.

Edwards, Franklin R. 'Hedge Funds and Investor Protection Regulation'. *Economic Review-Federal Reserve Bank Of Atlanta* 91, no. 4 (2006): 35.

Edwards, Franklin R. 'Hedge Funds and the Collapse of Long-Term Capital Management'. *The Journal of Economic Perspectives* 13, no. 2 (1999): 189-210.

Edwards, Franklin R, and Edward R Morrison. 'Derivatives and the Bankruptcy Code: Why the Special Treatment'. *Yale Journal on Regulation* 22, no. 1 (2005): 91.

Eichengreen, Barry. 'Understanding Asia's Financial Crisis'. *Clemens Lecture Series* no. *10* (1998).

Eichengreen, Barry and Donald Mathieson. 'Hedge Funds, What Do We Really Know?'. *IMF Economic Issues* 19 (1999).

Elineau, Rodolphe B. 'Regulating Short Selling in Europe after the Crisis'. *International Law and Management Review* 8, no. 2 (2011): 61.

Elliott, Douglas J. 'Key Issues on European Banking Union: Trade-Offs and Some Recommendations'. *Global Economy and Development Working Paper* 52 (November 2012).

Engert, Andreas. 'Transnational Hedge Fund Regulation'. *European Business Organization Law Review* 11, no. 03 (2010): 329-78.

Enrich David, Schaefer Sara, and Forelle Charles. 'European Banks Fear a Flight'. Wall Street Journal, http://www.wsj.com/articles/SB10001424052702304019404577416200222787714.

Epstein, Gerald A. *Financialization and the World Economy*. Edward Elgar, 2005.

Estrella, Arturo, and Mary R Trubin. 'The Yield Curve as a Leading Indicator: Some Practical Issues'. *Current Issues in Economics and Finance* 12, no. 5 (2006): 1-7.

'Et Tu, Paribas?'. The Wall Street Journal http://online.wsj.com/articles/SB118669529375093479.

Eurekahedge. *The Eurekahedge Report*. 11 January 2009.

European Central Bank. *Financial Stability Review*. May 2014.

European Central Bank. *Financial Stability Review*. June 2006.

European Central Bank. *Large Banks and Private Equity-Sponsored Leveraged Buyouts in the EU*. 2007.

European Central Bank. *Large EU Banks' Exposures to Hedge Funds*. November 2005.

European Central Bank. *Recent Developments in Supervisory Structures in EU Member States (2007-2010)*. October 2010.

European Central Bank. ECB Establishes Close Cooperation with Bulgaria's Central Bank'. 10 July 2020, https://www.bankingsupervision.europa.eu/press/pr/date/2020/html/ssm.pr200710~ae2abe1f23.en.htm.

Evans-Pritchard, Ambrose. 'Sarkozy Turns on "Predator" Hedge Funds'. The Daily Telegraph, http://www.telegraph.co.uk/finance/economics/2808197/Sarkozy-turns-on-predator-hedge-funds.html.

Fama, Eugene F, and Michael C Jensen. 'Separation of Ownership and Control'. *Journal of Law and Economics* 26, no. 2 (1983): 301-25.

Fayot, Franz. 'Luxembourg'. In *The Banking Regulation Review*, edited by Jan Putnis, 565-86: Law Business Research, 2015.

Feldstein, Martin. 'Why Greece Will Default'. Project Syndicate, http://www.project-syndicate.org/commentary/why-greece-will-default.

Felsenthal, David. 'Regulation of OTC Derivatives Markets - EU vs US Initiatives'. Harvard Law School Forum on Corporate Governance and Financial Regulation, http://blogs.law.harvard.edu/corpgov/2012/09/23/regulation-of-otc-derivatives-markets-eu-vs-us-initiatives/.

Fenn, George W, Nellie Liang, and Stephen Prowse. *The Economics of the Private Equity Market*. Staff Series. Board of Governors of the Federal Reserve System (US), 1995.

Ferguson, Roger, and David Laster. 'Hedge Funds and Systemic Risk'. *Banque de France, Financial Stability Review: Special Issue Hedge Funds*, no. 10 (2007): 45-54.

Ferran, Eilis. 'After the Crisis: The Regulation of Hedge Funds and Private Equity in the EU'. *European Business Organization Law Review* 12, no. 3 (2011): 379-414.

Ferran, Eilis. 'European Banking Union and the EU Single Financial Market: More Differentiated Integration, or Disintegration?'. *University of Cambridge Faculty of Law Research Paper* No. 29 (2014).

Ferran, Eilis. 'Examining the UK'S Experience in Adopting the Single Financial Regulator Model'. *Brooklyn Journal of International Law* 28, no. 2 (2003): 257.

Ferran, Eilís. 'Can Soft Law Bodies Be Effective? The Special Case of the European Systemic Risk Board'. *European Law Review* 35 (2010): 751-76.

Ferran, Eilis, and Valia SG Babis. 'The European Single Supervisory Mechanism'. *Journal of Corporate Law Studies* 13, no. 2 (2013): 255-85.

Ferrarini, Guido A, and Luigi Chiarella. 'Common Banking Supervision in the Eurozone: Strengths and Weaknesses'. *ECGI-Law Working Paper* No. 223 (2013).

'Final Rule: Prohibitions and Restrictions on Proprietary Trading and Certain Interests in, and Relationships with, Hedge Funds and Private Equity Funds'.

Finance, Deutsche Bank Markets Prime. *Eleventh Annual Alternative Investment Survey*. 2013.

Financial Stability Board. Vulnerabilities Associated with Leveraged Loans and Collateralised Loan Obligations (19 December 2019), https://www.fsb.org/wp-content/uploads/P191219.pdf.

Financial Stability Board. *2015 Update of List of Global Systemically Important Insurers*. 3 November 2015.

Financial Stability Board. *Key Attributes of Effective Resolution Regimes for Financial Institutions, Basel*. October 2011.

Financial Stability Board. *Proposed Policy Recommendations to Address Structural Vulnerabilities from Asset Management Activities*. June 2016.

Financial Stability Board. *Regulatory Framework for Haircuts on Non-Centrally Cleared Securities Financing Transactions*. 14 October 2014.

Financial Stability Board. *Regulatory Framework for Haircuts on Non-Centrally Cleared Securities Financing Transactions*. 12 November 2015.

Financial Stability Board. *Shadow Banking: Strengthening Oversight and Regulation; Recommendations of the Financial Stability Board*. 2011.

Financial Stability Board. *Structural Banking Reforms, Cross-Border Consistencies and Global Financial Stability Implications*. 2014.

Financial Crisis Inquiry Commission, United States. *The Financial Crisis Inquiry Report: Final Report of the National Commission on the Causes of the Financial and Economic Crisis in the United States*. 2011.

Financial Crisis Inquiry Commission, United States. *Hedge Fund Survey Selected Slides*. February 2011.

Financial Services (Banking Reform) Act 2013 (UK).

'The Financial System: What Went Wrong'. The Economist, http://www.economist.com/node/10881318.

Fioretos, Orfeo. 'Capitalist Diversity and the International Regulation of Hedge Funds'. *Review of International Political Economy* 17, no. 4 (2010): 696-723.

Fisch, Jill, and Eric Roiter. 'A Floating NAV for Money Market Funds: Fix or Fantasy'. *University of Illinois Law Review* (2012): 1003.

Fischel, Daniel R, and Frank Easterbrook. *The Economic Structure of Corporate Law*. Harvard University Press, 1991.

Flannery, Rusell. 'Former Shanghai Ghetto District Moves to Turn Itself into China's Hedge Fund Hub'. Forbes, http://www.forbes.com/sites/russellflannery/2013/10/19/former-shanghai-ghetto-moves-to-turn-itself-into-china-hedge-fund-hub/.

Fleming, Michael J, and Kenneth Garbade. 'The Repurchase Agreement Refined: GCF Repo'. *Current Issues in Economics and Finance* 9, no. 6 (2003).

Foley, Gina Chon & Stephen. 'Asset Managers May Escape Systemic Label'. Financial Times, http://www.ft.com/intl/cms/s/0/d2739c66-182c-11e4-a6e4-00144feabdc0.html#axzz3QpcCPZ3L.

Foley, Stephen. 'Hedge Holdings Soar Despite Returns Trailing Behind Equities'. Financial Times, http://www.ft.com/intl/cms/s/0/5ed8bd60-61a5-11e3-916e-00144feabdc0.html#axzz3BWm0pIlK.

Forelle, David Gauthier-Villars, and Charles. 'Downgrades Fan Fresh Euro Fears'. The Wall Street Journal, http://online.wsj.com/news/articles/SB10001424052970203735304577162832015883536?mg=reno64-wsj.

'The Forum: Insider Trading: Hedge Funds in the Crosshairs, Nyu School of Law Forum'. Youtube, 2013.

Fos, Vyacheslav. 'The Disciplinary Effects of Proxy Contests'. *Management Science* 63, no. 3 (2016): 655–71.

Foucault Thierry, Pagano Marco, and Roell Ailsa. *Market Liquidity: Theory, Evidence, and Policy*. Oxford University Press, 2013.

Frank, Gong Rui, and Page. 'Shadow Banks and Systemic Risks'. *SRC Discussion Paper No. 55* (February 2016).

Fraser, Alison S. 'Sec's Ineffective Move Toward Greater Regulation of Offshore Hedge Funds: The Failure of the Hedge Fund Registration Requirement'. *The Cornell Law Review* 92 (2006): 795.

Fung, William, and David A Hsieh. 'Empirical Characteristics of Dynamic Trading Strategies: The Case of Hedge Funds'. *Review of Financial Studies* 10, no. 2 (1997): 275-302.

Fung, William, and David A Hsieh. 'A Primer on Hedge Funds'. *Journal of Empirical Finance* 6, no. 3 (1999): 309-31.

Fung, William, David A Hsieh, and Konstantinos Tsatsaronis. 'Do Hedge Funds Disrupt Emerging Markets?'. *Brookings-Wharton Papers on Financial Services*, no. 1 (2000): 377-401.

Gadinis, Stavros. 'Market Structure for Institutional Investors; Comparing the US and EU Regimes'. *Virginia Law and Business Review* 3, no. 2 (2008): 311.

Galbraith, John Kenneth. *The Great Crash, 1929*. Mariner Books, 1955.

Galloni, David Enrich, and Alessandra. 'Turmoil Frays Ties across Continent'. Wall Street Journal, http://www.wsj.com/articles/SB10001424052702304065704577426560281463958.

Gantchev, Nickolay. 'The Costs of Shareholder Activism: Evidence from a Sequential Decision Model'. *Journal of Financial Economics* 107, no. 3 (2013): 610-31.

Gantchev, Nickolay, Oleg R Gredil, and Chotibhak Jotikasthira. 'Governance under the Gun: Spillover Effects of Hedge Fund Activism*'. *Review of Finance* 23, no. 6 (1 October 2019): 1031–68.

GAO. *Long-Term Capital Management: Regulators Need to Focus Greater Attention on Systemic Risk*. October 1999.

Garel Alexandre, Vermeille Sophie, and Deniaud Cyrile. 'Reflexions Sur Le Court-Termisme De Certains Dirigeants Et Actionnaires De Societes Cotees. La Generalisation Des Droit De Vote Bouble Ans Les Societes Cotees Est-Elle Une Reponse Adaptee?'. *Revue Trimestrielle De Droit Financier*, no. 2 (June 2014).

Gaughan, Patrick. *Mergers, Acquisitions and Corporate Restructurings*. 5th ed.: Wiley, 2011.

Geithner, Timothy F. 'Perspectives on the US Financial System, Remarks by President Timothy F. Geithner Before the Economic Club of New York'. News release, 7 May 2004.

Georgia Bullitt, Thomas Harman, Christopher Menconi, Bill Zimmerman, and Christopher Jackson. 'Legal Considerations for Registered Investment Companies Investing in Derivatives: Part I'. *The Investment Lawyer* 17, no. 8 (August 2010): 14-16.

Gesetz zur Abschirmung von Risiken und zur Planung der Sanierung und Abwicklung von Kreditinstituten und Finanzgruppen v. 7.8.2013, BGBl. 2013 I.

Getmansky Mila, Lee Peter, and Lo Andrew. 'Hedge Funds a Dynamic Industry in Transition'. *National Bureau of Economic Research Working Paper* No. w21449 (August 2015).

Getmansky, Mila, Andrew W Lo, and Igor Makarov. 'An Econometric Model of Serial Correlation and Illiquidity in Hedge Fund Returns'. *Journal of Financial Economics* 74, no. 3 (2004): 529-609.

Gilson, Ronald J. 'Controlling Shareholders and Corporate Governance: Complicating the Comparative Taxonomy'. *Harvard Law Review* 119, no. 6 (2006): 1641-79.

Gilson, Ronald J., and Jeffrey N. Gordon. 'The Agency Costs of Agency Capitalism: Activist Investors and the Revaluation of Governance Rights'. *Columbia Law Review* 113, no. 4 (2013): 863-927.

Goergen, Marc Limpach, and Francois. 'Les Compétences, Pouvoirs Et Moyens D'intervention De La CSSF'. *Droit Bancaire et Financier au Luxembourg* 1 (2014).

Goetzmann, William N, Jonathan Ingersoll Jr, and Stephen A Ross. 'High Water Marks'. *National Bureau of Economic Research* No. w6413 (February 1998).

Goldstein, Itay, Emre Ozdenoren, and Kathy Yuan. 'Trading Frenzies and Their Impact on Real Investment'. *Journal of Financial Economics* 109, no. 2 (2013): 566-82.

Goldstein, Matthew. 'Bear Stearns to the Rescue-Sort of "BusinessWeek"', http://www.businessweek.com/stories/2007-06-22/bear-stearns-to-the-rescue-sort-ofbusinessweek-business-news-stock-market-and-financial-advice.

Goodhart, Charles. *The Basel Committee on Banking Supervision: A History of the Early Years, 1974-1997*. Cambridge University Press, 2011.

Goodhart, Charles, and Dirk Schoenmaker. 'Should the Functions of Monetary Policy and Banking Supervision Be Separated?'. *Oxford Economic Papers* 47, no. 4 (1995): 539-60.

Gordon, Jeffrey N, and Wolf-Georg Ringe. 'Bank Resolution in the European Banking Union: A Transatlantic Perspective on What It Would Take'. *Columbia Law Review* 115, no. 5 (2015): 1297-369.

Gorton, Gary. 'Are Naked Credit Default Swaps Too Revealing'. *Investment Dealers' Digest* 76 (2010): 21-22.

Government, HM. *HM Treasury Analysis: The Long-Term Economic Impact of EU Membership and the Alternatives.* April 2016.

Gregory Zuckerman, Juliet Chung, and Michael Corkery. 'Hedge Funds Cut Back on Fees'. The Wall Street Journal, http://www.wsj.com/articles/SB10001424127887323893004579054952807556352.

Griller, Stefan, and Andreas Orator. 'Everything under Control? The "Way Forward" for European Agencies in the Footsteps of the Meroni Doctrine'. *European Law Review* 35, no. 1 (2010): 3-35.

Gross, Thomas C Baxter Jr, and David. 'The Federal Reserve's Response to the Crisis: Doing Whatever It Takes within Its Legal Authority'. In *International Monetary and Financial Law: The Global Crisis*, edited by Mario Giovanoli and Diego Devos, 293-304: Oxford University Press, 2010.

Grosshandler, Seth. 'Statement Before the House Subcommittee on Regulatory Reform, Commercial & Antitrust Law of the House Committee of the Judiciary'. News release, 26 March 2014.

Group, Counterparty Credit Risk Management Policy. *Toward Greater Financial Stability: A Private Sector Perspective*. July 2005.

Group, Counterparty Risk Management Policy. *Improving Counterparty Risk Management Practices*. June 1999.

Groves, Theodore, and John Ledyard. 'Optimal Allocation of Public Goods: A Solution to the "Free Rider" Problem'. *Econometrica* 45, no. 4 (1977): 783-809.

Guillaumie, Cyrille, Giuseppe Loiacono, Christian Winkler, and Steffen Kern. 'Market Impacts of Circuit Breakers – Evidence from EU Trading Venues'. ESMA Working Paper No. 1, 2020.

Guizot, Armelle. *The Hedge Fund Compliance and Risk Management Guide*. John Wiley and Sons, 2006.

Haight, Randy. 'Community of Support: Moving Toward Indirect Regulation of the Hedge Fund Industry'. *Marshall Global Markets Law Journal* 3, no. 1 (2014).

Haldane, Andrew G, and Philip Booth. 'On Being the Right Size'. *Journal of Financial Perspectives* 2, no. 1 (2014): 13-25.

Hale, Galina. 'Could We Have Learned from the Asian Financial Crisis of 1997–98?'. *FRBSF Economic Letter* 2011 (2011): 6.

Harner, Michelle M. 'Corporate Governance and Public Policy Implications of Activist Distressed Debt Investing'. *The Fordham Law Review* 77, no. 2 (2008): 703.

Harrison, Diane. 'A Battle Cry for Hedge Funds: Separate but Not Equal'. *FINAlternatives* (3 April 2012).

Hartlage, Andrew W. 'The Basel III Liquidity Coverage Ratio and Financial Stability'. *Michigan Law Review* 111, no. 3 (2012): 453-83.

Hau, Harald, and Sandy Lai, 'The Role of Equity Funds in the Financial Crisis Propagation'. *Review of Finance* 21, no. 1 (1 March 2017): 77–108.

'Hedge Funds: Going Nowhere Fast'. The Economist, http://www.economist.com/news/finance-and-economics/21568741-hedge-funds-have-had-another-lousy-year-cap-disappointing-decade-going.

Higgins, Robert C. *Analysis for Financial Management*. McGraw-Hill, 2012.

High-Level Expert Group on Reforming the Structure of the EU Banking Sector, Final Report. October 2012.

Hirtle, Beverly, and Andreas Lehnert. 'Supervisory Stress Tests'. *FRB of New York Staff Report*, no. 696 (2014).

HM Treasury. 'Systemic Risk Buffer Rates for Ring-Fenced Banks and Large Building Societies', 2 February 2021. https://www.bankofengland.co.uk/prudential-regulation/publication/2019/systemic-risk-buffer-rates-for-ring-fenced-banks-and-large-building-societies.

Hogan Thomas L., Meredith Neil, and Pan Xuhao. 'Evaluating Risk-Based Capital Regulation'. *Mercatus Working Paper, Arlington, VA: Mercatus Center at George Mason University* (January 2013).

Holm, Ryan Tracy, and Erik. 'MetLife Wins Bid to Shed 'Systemically Important' Label'. The Wall Street Journal, http://www.wsj.com/articles/federal-judge-rescinds-federal-government-determination-that-metlife-is-systemically-important-1459349828.

Hooghiemstra, Sebastiaan N. 'Depositary Regulation'. In *The Alternative Investment Fund Managers Directive*, 3rd edition: Wolters Kluwer, 2020.

House of Commons, Treasury Committee. *Financial Stability and Transparency: Sixth Report of Session 2007-2008*. 3 March 2008.

House of Lords, European Union Committee. *Directive on Alternative Investment Fund Managers, Volume 1: Report*. 10 February 2010.

Hovenkamp, Herbert. 'Positivism in Law & Economics'. *California Law Review* 78, no. 4 (1990): 815-52.

Howard, Davies, and Green David. *Global Financial Regulation*: The Essential Guide. Polity Press, 2013.

Howarth, David, and Scott James. 'The Politics of Bank Structural Reform: Business Power and Agenda Setting in the United Kingdom, France, and Germany'. *Business and Politics* 22, no. 1 (2020): 25–51.

Howell, Elizabeth. 'The European Court of Justice: Selling US Short?'. *European Company and Financial Law Review* 11, no. 3 (2014).

Hu, Henry T. C., and Bernard Black. 'Debt, Equity and Hybrid Decoupling: Governance and Systemic Risk Implications'. *European Financial Management* 14, no. 4 (September 2008): 663–709.

Hu, Henry T C, and Bernard Black. 'The New Vote Buying: Empty Voting and Hidden (Morphable) Ownership'. *Southern California Law Review* 79 (2006): 811–908.

Huang, Peter H, Kimberly D Krawiec, and Frank Partnoy. 'Derivatives on TV: A Tale of Two Derivatives Debacles in Prime-Time'. *Green Bag 2d* 4 (2001): 257-453.

Hull, John. *Risk Management and Financial Institutions*. Wiley, 2012.

IAIS. *Globally Systemically Important Insurers: Initial Assessment Methodology*. 18 July 2013.

Ian Appel, Todd Gormley, and Donald Keim. 'Standing on the Shoulders of Giants: The Effects of Passive Investors on Activism'. *http://papers.ssrn.com/sol3/papers.cfm?abstract_id=2693145* (March 2016).

Ibbotson, Roger G, Peng Chen, and Kevin X Zhu. 'The ABCs of Hedge Funds: Alphas, Betas, and Costs'. *Financial Analysts Journal* 67, no. 1 (2011): 15-25.

Iftekhar Hasan, Nadia Massoud, Anthony Saunders, and Keke Song. 'Which Financial Stocks Did Short Sellers Target in the Subprime Crisis?'. *Journal of Banking & Finance* 54 (2015): 87-103.

IMF. *Global Financial Stability Report: Financial Market Turbulence: Causes, Consequences and Policies*. 2007.

IMF. *European Union: Publication of Financial Sector Assessment Program, Technical Note on European Securities and Markets Authority*. March 2013.

IMF. *Global Financial Stability Report*. April 2015.

IMF. *Impact of Regulatory Reforms on Large and Complex Financial Institutions, Staff Discussion Note, SPN/10/16*. 3 November 2010.

IMF. *International Capital Markets: Part I. Exchange Rate Management and International Capital Flows, World Economic and Financial Surveys*. 1993.

IMF. *International Capital Markets: Part II, Systemic Issues in International Finance, World Economic and Financial Surveys*. 1993.

IMF. Staff Discussion Note, SDN 13/4. 2013.

Index, Credit Suisse/Tremont Hedge Fund. *One for the History Books: Hedge Fund Performance in 2008*. January 2009.

Index, Credit Suisse/Tremont Hedge Fund. *Hedge Funds Hit a High Note 2009 Industry Review*. 2010.

IOSCO. *Emerging Markets Committee*. 2005.

IOSCO & FSB. *Assessment Methodologies for Identifying Non-Bank Non-Insurer Global Systemically Important Financial Institutions, Consultative Document*. March 2015.

IOSCO & FSB. *Assessment Methodologies for Identifying Non-Bank Non-Insurer Global Systemically Important Financial Institutions, Consultative Document*. January 2014.

Schnabel Isabel, and Rutkowski Felix. 'Should Monetary Policy and Banking Supervision Be Separated?'. (15 February 2016).

ISDA, Clifford Chance. *Regulation of OTC Derivatives Markets*. September 2012.

Issing, Professor Otmar. 'Monetary and Financial Stability: Is There a Trade-Off?, Speech at the Conference on "Monetary Stability, Financial Stability and The Business Cycle", Bank for International Settlements, Basle'. News release, 28–29 March 2003.

Itzhak Ben-David, Franzoni Francesco, Landier Augustin, and Moussawi Rabih. 'Do Hedge Funds Manipulate Stock Prices?'. *The Journal of Finance* 68, no. 6 (2013): 2383-434.

Itzhak Ben-David, Franzoni Fransesco, and Moussawi Rabih. 'Hedge Fund Stock Trading in the Financial Crisis of 2007–2009'. *Review of Financial Studies* 25, no. 1 (2012): 1-54.

Jackson, Thomas H, and David A Skeel Jr. 'Dynamic Resolution' of Large Financial Institutions'. *Harvard Business Law Review* 2 (2012): 435.

Jacobs, Jack B. '"Patient Capital": Can Delaware Corporate Law Help Revive It?'. *Washington and Lee Law Review* 68, no. 4 (2011): 1645.

James Chanos, President, and Kynikos Associates. *Prepared Statement for the U.S. Securities and Exchange Commission Roundtable on Hedge Funds.* 15 May 2003.

Jensen, Michael C. 'Agency Costs of Free Cash Flow, Corporate Finance, and Takeovers'. *The American economic review* 76, no. 2 (1986): 323-29.

Jickling, Mark. 'Lessons of Long-Term Capital Management and Amaranth Advisors'. In *Research Handbook on Hedge Funds, Private Equity and Alternative Investments*, edited by Phoebus Athanassiou, 293-308: Edward Elgar Publishing, Inc., 2012.

Johannsen, Kevin R. 'Jumping the Gun: Hedge Funds in Search of Capital under UCITS IV'. *Brooklyn Journal of Corporate Financial and Commercial Law* 5, no. 2 (2010): 473.

Johnson, Christian A. 'Exigent and Unusual Circumstances: The Federal Reserve and the Us Financial Crisis'. In *Law Reform and Financial Markets*, edited by Alexander Kern & Niamh Moloney: Edward Elgar, 2010.

Johnson, Miles. 'Beyond Banking: Traditional Talent Pool Dries up for Hedge Funds'. Financial Times, https://next.ft.com/content/7880dc7a-77d8-11e5-a95a-27d368e1ddf7.

Johnson, Steve. 'AIFMD: US Hedge Funds Shy Away over EU Regulation'. Financial Times, http://www.ft.com/intl/cms/s/0/a181b4a4-ef53-11e4-a6d2-00144feab7de.html#axzz3Zz7ClvNq.

Johnston, Andrew. 'Regulating Hedge Funds for Systemic Stability: The EU's Approach'. *European Law Journal* 21, no. 6 (2015): 758-86.

Jones, Charles M, and Owen A Lamont. 'Short-Sale Constraints and Stock Returns'. *Journal of Financial Economics* 66, no. 2 (1 November 2002): 207–39.

Jones, Kenneth D, and Robert C Oshinsky. 'The Effect of Industry Consolidation and Deposit Insurance Reform on the Resiliency of the US Bank Insurance Fund'. *Journal of Financial Stability* 5, no. 1 (2009): 57-88.

Jonna, Paul M. 'In Search of Market Discipline: The Case for Indirect Hedge Fund Regulation'. *San Diego Law Review* 45, no. 4 (2008): 989.

Jordan, Cally, and Pamela S Hughes. 'Which Way for Market Institutions? The Fundamental Question of Self-Regulation'. *Berkeley Business Law Journal* 4, no. 2 (2007).

Jorion, Philippe. 'Risk Management Lessons from Long-Term Capital Management'. *European Financial Management* 6, no. 3 (2000): 277-300.

Jr., Richard A. Opper. 'Not Such a Bad Year for Hedge Funds'. *New York Times*, 31 January 1999.

Kaal, Wulf A. 'Hedge Fund Manager Registration under the Dodd-Frank Act'. *San Diego Law Review* 50, no. 2 (2013): 243-469.

Kaal, Wulf A. 'Hedge Fund Regulation Via Basel III'. *Vanderbilt Journal of Transnational Law* 44 (2011): 389.

Kaal, Wulf A, Barbara Luppi, and Sandra Paterlini. 'Did the Dodd-Frank Act Impact Hedge Fund Performance?'. *No. 14-09, University of St. Thomas (Minnesota) Legal Studies Research Paper*, no. 14-09 (2014).

Kahan, Marcel, and Edward Rock. 'How to Prevent Hard Cases from Making Bad Law: Bear Stearns, Delaware, and the Strategic Use of Comity'. *Emory Law Journal* 58 (2008): 713.

Kahan, Marcel, and Edward B Rock. 'Hedge Funds in Corporate Governance and Corporate Control'. *University of Pennsylvania Law Review* 155, no. 5 (2007): 1021-93.

Kelly, Kate. 'Bear Stearns Hedge Fund Managers May Face Indictments'. The Wall Street Journal, http://online.wsj.com/news/articles/SB121358606462876535?mg=reno64-wsj.

Kenadjian, Randall D. Guynn, and Patrick. 'Structural Solutions: Blinded by Volcker, Vickers, Liikanen, Glass Steagall and Narrow Banking'. In *Too Big to Fail III: Structural Reform Proposals – Should We Break up the Banks?*, edited by Patrick S. Kenadjian and Andreas Dombret: De Gruyter, 2014.

Kennard, Alan L. 'The Hedge Fund Versus the Mutual Fund'. *The Tax Lawyer* 57, no. 1 (2003): 133-61.

Khandani, Amir, and Andrew Lo. 'What Happened to the Quants in August 2007? (Digest Summary)'. *Journal of Investment Management* 5, no. 4 (2007): 29-78.

Kim, Jessica Toonkel, and Soyoung. 'Activist Investors Find Allies in Mutual, Pension Funds'. Reuters, http://www.reuters.com/article/2013/04/09/us-funds-activist-idUSBRE9380DU20130409.

Klebeck, Ulf. 'Liquidity Management and Side Pockets in the Alternative Investment Fund Managers Directive'. In *The Alternative Investment Funds Managers Directive, European Regulation of Alternative Investment Funds* edited by Dirk Zetzsche, 253-64: Kluwer Law International, 2012.

Klein, April, and Emanuel Zur. 'Entrepreneurial Shareholder Activism: Hedge Funds and Other Private Investors'. *The Journal of Finance* 64, no. 1 (2009): 187-229.

Kowsmann, Patricia. 'Portugal Bailout Plan Detailed'. http://online.wsj.com/news/articles/SB10001424052748703937104576302883922114642?mg=reno64-wsj.

KPMG/AIMA. *KPMG/AIMA Global Hedge Fund Survey: The Evolution of an Industry*. 2012.

Kraakman Reinier et al. *The Anatomy of Corporate Law: A Comparative and Functional Approach*. Oxford University Press, 2004.

Kraakman, Ronald J Gilson, and Reinier. 'Market Efficiency after the Financial Crisis: It's Still a Matter of Information Costs'. *ECGI Law Working Paper No. 242/2012* (February 2014).

Kramer Levin, Naftalis, and Frankel LLP. *Asset Management Update Regarding Recent Regulations Affecting Asset Managers in France*. July 2013.

Kreditwesengesetz - KWG (German Banking Act).

Kremer Claude, Eisenhuth Michele, Dusemon Gilles, and Martougi Catherine. 'Luxembourg'. In *Alternative Investment Funds in Europe*, edited by Lodewijk Van Setten and Danny Busch: Oxford University Press, 2014.

Kremer, Isabelle Lebbe, and Claude. *Les Organismes De Placement Collectif En Droit Luxembourgeois*. 3rd ed.: Larcier, 2014.

Krishnamurthy, Prasad, and Ryan Bubb. 'Regulating Against Bubbles'. *University of Pennsylvania Law Review* 163, no. 6 (2015).

Krugman, Paul. 'What Happened to Asia?', http://web.mit.edu/krugman/www/DISINTER.html.

Kumar, Nishant. 'Costs, Regulations Push Europe's Hedge Fund Minnows to Platforms'. The Reuters, http://www.reuters.com/article/2015/06/14/us-hedgefund-platform-idUSKBN0OU06I20150614.

Lack, Simon A. *The Hedge Fund Mirage: The Illusion of Big Money and Why It's Too Good to Be True*. Wiley, 2011.

Laeven, Luc, and Ross Levine. 'Is There a Diversification Discount in Financial Conglomerates?'. *Journal of Financial Economics* 85, no. 2 (2007): 331-67.

Lamandini, Marco. 'Self-Regulation - What Future in the Context of Hedge Funds?'. Ch. 244 In *Research Handbook on Hedge Funds, Private Equity and Alternative Investments*, edited by Phoebus Athanassiou, 244: Edward Elgar, 2012.

Lamar, Mia. 'Hedge Funds Multiply in Asia, Pursuing Flood of Cash'. http://online.wsj.com/news/articles/SB10001424052702303704304579382243771070218.

Lange, Kathleen E. 'New Antifraud Rule: Is Sec Enforcement the Most Effective Way to Protect Investors from Hedge Fund Fraud'. *The Fordham Law Review* 77, no. 2 (2008): 851.

Larsen, Peter Thal. 'UBS Forced to Axe Hedge Fund', http://www.ft.com/intl/cms/s/0/df424920-f948-11db-9b6b-000b5df10621.html#axzz3kj273vS6.

Laux, Christian, and Uwe Walz. 'Cross-Selling Lending and Underwriting: Scope Economies and Incentives*'. *Review of Finance* 13, no. 2 (2009): 341-67.

Lawder, David. 'Pressure for Hedge Fund Scrutiny Builds as Yellen Leads Her First U.S. Financial Stability Meeting'. Reuters, https://www.reuters.com/article/us-usa-markets-treasury-idINKBN2BN2AA.

Lavelle, Kathryn C. *Money and Banks in the American Political System*. Cambridge University Press, 2013.

Lederman, Scott J. *Hedge Fund Regulation*. 2nd ed.: Practicing Law Institute, May 2016.

Lee, Emily. 'Basel III: Post-Financial Crisis International Financial Regulatory Reform'. *Journal of International Banking Law and Regulation* 28 (2013).

Lehmann, Matthias. 'Volcker Rule, Ring-Fencing or Separation of Bank Activities: Comparison of Structural Reform Acts Around the World'. LSE Law, Society and Economy Working Papers 25/2014, 2014.

Lehmann, Matthias, and Christian Tietje 'The Role and Prospects of International Law in Financial Regulation and Supervision'. In *International Law in Financial Regulation and Monetary Affairs*, edited by Thomas Cottier et al.: Oxford University Press, 2012.

Lessig, Lawrence. 'The New Chicago School'. *The Journal of Legal Studies* 27, no. S2 (1998): 661-91.

Levine, Ross. 'Bank-Based or Market-Based Financial Systems: Which Is Better?'. *Journal of Financial Intermediation* 11, no. 4 (2002): 398-428.

Lewis, Michael. *The Big Short: Inside the Doomsday Machine*. Penguin, 2010.

Lewis, Winnifred A. 'Waiving Fiduciary Duties in Delaware Limited Partnerships and Limited Liability Companies'. *Fordham Law Review* 82, no. 2 (2013).

Lhabitant, François-Serge. *Hedge Funds: Myths and Limits*. Wiley, 2002.

Lipton, Martin. 'Bite the Apple; Poison the Apple; Paralyze the Company; Wreck the Economy'. Harvard Law School Forum on Corporate Governance and Financial Regulation, http://blogs.law.harvard.edu/corpgov/2013/02/26/bite-the-apple-poison-the-apple-paralyze-the-company-wreck-the-economy/.

Liz Alderman, and Matthew Saltmarsh. 'Worries Rise over Spain and Italy Debt'. http://www.nytimes.com/2011/08/03/business/global/pressure-builds-on-italy-and-spain-over-finances.html?pagewanted = all&_r = 0.

Lloyd Dixon, Noreen Clancy, and Krishna B. Kumar. *Rand Corporation, Hedge Funds and Systemic Risk*. Rand Corporation, 2012.

Lo, Andrew W. *Hedge Funds: An Analytic Perspective*. Princeton University Press, 2010.

Lo, Andrew W. *Hedge Funds, Systemic Risk, and the Financial Crisis of 2007-2008, Written Testimony of Andrew W. Lo Prepared for the US House of Representatives Committee on Oversight and Government Reform: Hearing on Hedge Funds*. 13 November 2008.

'Locust, Pocus – German Capitalism'. The Economist, http://www.economist.com/node/3935994.

Logutenkova, Stephanie Baker-Said, and Elena. 'UBS $100 Billion Wager Prompted $24 Billion Loss in Nine Months'. Bloomberg http://www.bloomberg.com/apps/news?pid = newsarchive&sid = a3sm9FOrsWcg.

Lowenstein, Roger. *When Genius Failed: The Rise and Fall of Long-Term Capital Management*. Random House, 2000.

Lubben, Stephen J. 'Derivatives and Bankruptcy: The Flawed Case for Special Treatment'. *University of Pennsylvania Journal of Business Law* 12, no. 1 (2009): 61.

Lubben, Stephen J. 'Repeal the Safe Harbors'. *American Bankruptcy Institute Law Review* 18 (2010): 319.

Lubben, Stephen J. 'Resolution, Orderly and Otherwise: B of a in Ola'. *University of Cincinnati Law Review* 81, no. 2 (2013): 4.

Lucian A. Bebchuk, Alma Cohen, and Charles C.Y. Wang. 'Staggered Boards and the Wealth of Shareholders: Evidence from Two Natural Experiments'. *National Bureau of Economic Research* No. w17127 (2011).

Lysandrou, Photis. 'The Primacy of Hedge Funds in the Subprime Crisis'. *Journal of Post Keynesian Economics* 34, no. 2 (2011): 225-54.

Macey, Jonathan R. *Corporate Governance: Promises Kept, Promises Broken*. Princeton University Press, 2010.

Malkiel, Burton G. *A Random Walk Down Wall Street: The Time-Tested Strategy for Successful Investing (Revised and Updated)*. Norton, 2012.

Mallaby, Sebastian. *More Money Than God: Hedge Funds and the Making of a New Elite*. Penguin Books, 2010.

Management, J.P. Morgan Asset. *Investment Insights: Spotlight on Market Neutral Investing*. 2012.

Markets, The President's Working Group on Financial. *Hedge Funds, Leverage, and the Lessons of Long-Term Capital Management*. April 1999.

Marsh, Sarah. 'Short-Sellers Make VW the World's Priciest Company'. Reuters, http://www.reuters.com/article/2008/10/28/us-volkswagen-idUSTRE49R3I920081028.

Marshall, David. 'Understanding the Asian Crisis: Systemic Risk as Coordination Failure'. *Federal Reserve Bank of Chicago, Economic Perspectives* 22 (1998): 13-28.

Marshall, Paul. 'Hedge Funds Seek Refuge from Unfair European Regulations'. Financial Times, http://www.ft.com/intl/cms/s/0/43ecd864-dca6-11e5-8541-00fb33bdf038.html#axzz41p9Qh800.

Martin, Katie, Lawrence Fletcher, and Robin Wigglesworth. 'They Can Do What They Want': Archegos and the $6tn World of the Family Office'. *Financial Times*, https://www.ft.com/content/c319839d-d185-4e8a-bbc7-659bebe58031.

Martynova, Marina, and Luc Renneboog. 'A Century of Corporate Takeovers: What Have We Learned and Where Do We Stand?'. *Journal of Banking & Finance* 32, no. 10 (2008): 2148-77.

Masciandaro, Donato, and Marc Quintyn. 'Reforming Financial Supervision and the Role of the Central Banks: A Review of Global Trends, Causes and Effects (1998-2008)'. *CEPR Policy Insight* 30, no. 1 (2009): 11.

Masciandaro, Donato, and Marc Quintyn. 'Regulating the Regulators: The Changing Face of Financial Supervision Architectures before and after the Crisis'. *European Company Law* 6, no. 5 (2009): 187-96.

Massa, Massimo, Bohui Zhang, and Hong Zhang. 'Governance through Threat: Does Short Selling Improve Internal Governance?'. *INSEAD Working Paper No. 2013/83/FIN* (July 9 2013).

Massa, Massimo, Bohui Zhang, and Hong Zhang. 'The Invisible Hand of Short Selling: Does Short Selling Discipline Earnings Management?'. *Review of Financial Studies* 28, no. 6 (2015): 1701-36.

Massimo Belcredi, Luca Enriques. 'Institutional Investor Activism in a Context of Concentrated Ownership and High Private Benefits of Control: The Case of Italy'. *ECGI Law Working Paper No. 225/2013* (2014).

Massoudi, Tracy Alloway, and Arash. 'Hedge Funds Step into the Shadows'. Financial Times, http://www.ft.com/intl/cms/s/0/b7e2de34-29e4-11e3-9bc6-00144feab7de.html?siteedition=intl#axzz37SMH17Yl.

Masters, Brooke. 'European Short-Selling Ban Comes under Attack'. Financial Times, http://www.ft.com/intl/cms/s/0/763a185e-c4e1-11e0-9c4d-00144feabdc0.html.

Matthew Karnitschnig et al. 'U.S. To Take over AIG in $85 Billion Bailout; Central Banks Inject Cash as Credit Dries Up'. http://www.wsj.com/articles/SB122156561931242905.

Matteo, Tonello. 'Poison Pills in 2011'. Harvard Law School Forum on Corporate Governance and Financial Regulation, http://blogs.law.harvard.edu/corpgov/2011/04/03/poison-pills-in-2011/.

Matteo Tonello, Stephan Rabimov. 'The 2010 Institutional Investment Report: Trends in Asset Allocation and Portfolio Composition'. (Conference Bd., Research Report No. R-1468-10-RR, 2010), http://ssrn.com/abstract=1707512.

Mattingly, Phil. 'Volcker Says Proprietary Trading Poses Conflicts of Interest'. Bloomberg, http://www.bloomberg.com/news/articles/2012-05-09/volcker-says-prop-trading-poses-conflicts-of-interest-for-banks.

McCahery, Joseph A, and Erik PM Vermeulen. *Corporate Governance of Non-Listed Companies*. Oxford University Press, 2010.

McCahery, Joseph A., and Alexander de Roode. 'The Lost Decade for Hedge Funds: Three Threats'. European Corporate Governance Institute Working Paper No. 486, 2019.

McCann FitzGerald, 'A Guide to Investment Funds in Ireland'. May 2017.

McDonough, William J. 'Statement Before the Committee on Banking and Financial Services US House of Representatives'. News release, 1 October 1998.

Mechanism, European Stability. 'FAQ on the Main Features of the Future ESM Direct Recapitalization Instrument'.

Meissner, Gunter. *Credit Derivatives: Application, Pricing, and Risk Management*. Wiley, 2009.

Mellon, Cassey Quirk and Bank of New York. *The Hedge Fund of Tomorrow*. April 2009.

Metrick, Christian McNamara, and Andrew. 'Basel III G: Shadow Banking and Project Finance'. *Yale Program on Financial Stability Case Study* 2014-1G-V1 (2014).

Michael, Douglas C. 'Federal Agency Use of Audited Self-Regulation as a Regulatory Technique'. *Administrative Law Review* 47 (1995): 171-253.

Mohammad, Mahathir. 'Highwaymen of the Global Economy'. *The Wall Street Journal*, September 23 1997.

Moloney, Niamh. 'Banking Union and the Implications for Financial Market Governance in the EU'. In *European Banking Union*, edited by Danny Busch and Guido Ferrarini: Oxford University Press, 2014.

Moloney, Niamh. 'European Banking Union: Assessing Its Risks and Resilience'. *Common Market Law Review* 51, no. 6 (2014): 1609-70.

Moloney, Niamh. 'Financial Services under the Trade and Cooperation Agreement: Reflections on Unfinished Business for the EU and UK'. Brexit Institute Working Paper Series, No. 3/2021, 2021.

Monaghan, Angela. 'U.K. Coalition Faces First Test as Germany, France Push for Tough EU Hedge Fund Rules'. The Daily Telegraph, http://www.telegraph.co.uk/finance/newsbysector/banksandfinance/7721923/UK-coalition-faces-first-test-as-Germany-France-push-for-tough-EU-hedge-fund-rules.html.

Monaghan, Angela. 'UK Coalition Faces First Test as Germany, France Push for Tough EU Hedge Fund Rules'. The Daily Telegraph, http://www.telegraph.co.uk/finance/newsbysector/banksandfinance/7721923/UK-coalition-faces-first-test-as-Germany-France-push-for-tough-EU-hedge-fund-rules.html.

Mooney Attracta, and Jennifer Thompson, 'Europe's National Regulators Clash over Delegation', Financial Times, https://www.ft.com/content/44dbefcc-a9db-11e7-ab55-27219df83c97.

Morley, John. 'The Separation of Funds and Managers: A Theory of Investment Fund Structure and Regulation'. *Yale Law Journal* 123, no. 5 (2014): 1228-607.

Morrison, Edward R, Mark J Roe, and Christopher S Sontchi. 'Rolling Back the Repo Safe Harbors'. *Business Lawyer* 69, no. 4 (2014).

Mueller, Dennis C. 'A Theory of Conglomerate Mergers'. *The Quarterly Journal of Economics* 83, no. 4 (1969): 643-59.

Murrell, Peter Grajzl, and Peter. 'Allocating Lawmaking Powers: Self-Regulation Versus Government Regulation'. *Journal of Comparative Economics* 35, no. 3 (2007).

Murry-Jones Allan, and Walter Henle. 'Alternative Investment Fund Managers Directive '. *Skadden, Arps, Meagher, Slate & Flom LLP Memo* (29 November 2010).

Neil Robson, Johan Terblanche, and Marie-Elisa Roussel. 'Preparing for Compliance with the AIFM Directive'. *Financier Worldwide* (November 2012).

Nabilou, Hossein. 'Bank Proprietary Trading and Investment in Private Funds: Is the Volcker Rule a Panacea or Yet Another Maginot Line?'. *Banking & Finance Law Review* 32, no. 2 (1 April 2017): 297–341.

Nabilou, Hossein. 'Addressing Interconnectedness of Hedge Funds with Large Complex Financial Institutions: Is the Volcker Rule Panacea?'. *Available at SSRN 2329335* (2013).

Nabilou, Hossein, and Alessio M Pacces. 'Hedge Fund Regulation Dilemma: Direct Vs. Indirect Regulation'. *William and Mary Business Law Review* 6, no. 1 (2015): 183.

Naik, Narayan. 'Hedge Funds: Transparency and Conflicts of Interest'. *Policy Department Economics and Scientific Policy, European Parliament* (2007).

Narayan, Vikas Agarwal Kevin A Mullally, and Y Naik. 'Hedge Funds: A Survey of the Academic Literature'. *Foundations and Trends in Finance* (2015).

'New Rules Force UK Banks to Restructure, Hold Extra Capital'. The Wall Street Journal, http://www.wsj.com/articles/ringfenced-british-banks-will-need-permission-to-pay-dividends-says-bank-of-england-1444899418.

Ng, Kate Kelly, and Serena. 'Bear Stearns Bails out Fund with Big Loan', http://online.wsj.com/articles/SB118252387194844899.

Niamh, Moloney. *EU Securities and Financial Markets Regulation*. Oxford University Press, 2014.

Nier, Erlend Walter. 'Financial Stability Frameworks and the Role of Central Banks: Lessons from the Crisis'. *IMF Working Paper WP/09/42* (2009).

Nikolaou, Kleopatra. 'Liquidity (Risk) Concepts Definition and Interactions'. *European Central Bank Working Paper Series* No. 1008 (February 2009).

Nouy, Daniele. 'Indirect Supervision of Hedge Funds'. *Banque de France, Financial Stability Review: Special Issue Hedge Funds* 10 (April 2007).

Nouy, Danièle. 'The Banking Union and Financial Integration, Speech at the Joint Conference of the European Commission and European Central Bank on "European Financial Integration and Stability"'. News release, 27 April 2015, https://www.bankingsupervision.europa.eu/press/speeches/date/2015/html/se150427.en.html.

Noyer, Christian. 'Hedge Funds: What Are the Main Issues'. *Banque de France, Financial Stability Review: Special Issue Hedge Funds*, no. 10 (2007): 105-11.

OECD. *Annual Survey of Investment Regulation of Pension Funds*. 2013.

OECD. *Regulatory Policies in OECD Countries: From Interventionism to Regulatory Governance*. 2002.

Ogus, Anthony. 'Rethinking Self-Regulation'. *Oxford Journal of Legal Studies* 15, no. 1 (1995): 97-108.

Omarova, Saule T. 'Wall Street as Community of Fate: Toward Financial Industry Self-Regulation'. *University of Pennsylvania Law Review* 159, no. 2 (2011): 411-92.

Ortenca, Aliaj. 'Hedge Fund Industry Assets Surge to Record $3.6tn'. Financial Times, https://www.ft.com/content/6d757883-2800-469a-a719-af085568b53d.

Pagano, Marco. 'Lessons from the European Financial Crisis'. In *Financial Regulation: A Transatlantic Perspective*, edited by Ester Faia et al.: Cambridge University Press, 2015.

Pais, Amelia, and Philip A Stork. 'Short-Selling, Leverage, and Systemic Risk'. http://papers.ssrn.com/sol3/papers.cfm?abstract_id = 2350125.

Papademos, Lucas. 'Opening Remarks at the Press Briefing on the Occasion of the Publication of the December 2006 ECB Financial Stability Review'. News release, 11 December 2006.

Paredes, Troy A. 'On the Decision to Regulate Hedge Funds: The Sec's Regulatory Philosophy, Style, and Mission'. *University of Illinois Law Review* (2006): 975.

Paribas, BNP. 'BNP Paribas Investment Partners Temporarily Suspends the Calculation of the Net Asset Value of the Following Funds: Parvest Dynamic ABS, BNP Paribas ABS Euribor and BNP Paribas ABS Eonia'. http://www.bnpparibas.com/en/news/press-release/bnp-paribas-investment-partners-temporaly-suspends-calculation-net-asset-value-fo.

Parisi, Francesco, and Jonathan Klick. 'Functional Law and Economics: The Search for Value-Neutral Principles of Lawmaking'. *Chi.-Kent Law Review* 79, no. 2 (2004): 431.

Parliament, Socialist Group in the European. *Hedge Funds and Private Equity- a Critical Analysis*. 2007.

'A Partnership Solution for Investment Banks'. Dealbook, http://dealbook.nytimes.com/2008/08/20/a-partnership-solution-for-investment-banks/.

Partnoy, Frank. 'Overdependence on Credit Ratings Was a Primary Cause of the Crisis'. In *The Panic of 2008: Causes, Consequences, and Implications for Reform*, edited by Wilmarth, Arthur, Partnoy, Frank, and Mitchell, Lawrence: Edward Elgar, 2010.

Partnoy, Frank. 'US Hedge Fund Activism'. In *Research Handbook on Shareholder Power*, edited by Jennifer G. Hill and Randall S. Thomas, 99: Edward Elgar, 2015.

Partnoy, Frank, and David A Skeel Jr. 'Promise and Perils of Credit Derivatives'. *The University of Cincinnati Law Review* 75 (2006): 1019.

'Paulson Tells G7 Let Markets Regulate Hedge Funds'. https://www.reuters.com/news/picture/paulson-tells-g7-let-markets-regulate-he-idUSDAE00054220070210.

Payne, Jennifer. 'Private Equity and Its Regulation in Europe'. *European Business Organization Law Review* 12, no. 4 (2011): 559-85.

Payne, Jennifer. 'The Regulation of Short Selling and Its Reform in Europe'. *European Business Organization Law Review* 13, no. 3 (2012): 413-40.

Perry, Mehrling. 'Minsky and Modern Finance'. *The Journal of Portfolio Management* 26, no. 2 (2000): 81-88.

Petrasic, Kevin. 'The Volcker Rule Proposal-Many Questions, Few Answers'. *Paul Hastings Memorandum* (November 2011).

Pimlott, Daniel. 'G20 Agrees $1,100bn to Fight Crisis'. The Financial Times, https://next.ft.com/content/5c541a18-1eec-11de-a748-00144feabdc0.

Pistor, Katharina. 'Host's Dilemma: Rethinking EU Banking Regulation in Light of the Global Crisis'. In *Festschrift Für Klaus J. Hopt Zum 70. Geburtstag Am 24. August 2010, Unternehmen, Markt Und Verantwortung*, edited by Grundmann Stefan et al.: De Gruyter, 2010.

Pistor, Katharina. 'Legal Ground Rules in Coordinated and Liberal Market Economies'. *ECGI Working Paper Series in Law* No. 30 (2005).

Plender, John. 'Markets Insight: Bank Deregulation Part of Thatcher Legacy'. The Financial Times, http://www.ft.com/intl/cms/s/0/7f8aaf08-a122-11e2-bae1-00144feabdc0.html#axzz3kyMqvlBo.

Poser S Norman, 'Automation of Securities Markets and the European Community's Proposed Investment Services Directive'. *Law and Contemporary Problems* 55, no. 4 (1992): 29-51.

Posner, Richard A. 'Theories of Economic Regulation'. *Bell Journal of Economics and Management Science* 5, no. 2 (1974): 335.

Pozsar, Zoltan, Tobias Adrian, Adam Ashcraft, and Hayley Boesky. 'Shadow Banking'. *Staff Report, Federal Reserve Bank of New York* (2010).

Preqin. *Global Hedge Fund Report*. 2014.

Preqin. *Preqin Special Report: Asia-Pacific Hedge Funds Potential for Record Growth*. September 2013.

President's Working Group on Financial Markets, Asset Managers' Committee. *Mission Statement*.

President's Working Group on Financial Markets, Investors' Committee. *Mission Statement*.

PriceWaterHouseCoopers. *Transparency Versus Returns: The Institutional Investor View of Alternative Assets*. March 2008.

Prince, Russ Alan. 'From Hedge Fund to Family Office'. http://www.forbes.com/sites/russalanprince/2013/11/20/from-hedge-fund-to-family-office/.

Prüm, André. 'L'union Bancaire Européenne Et Les Autorités De Surveillance Nationales'. *Revue de Droit Bancaire et Financier* 4 (2014).

Prüm, André. 'La Directive AIFM: Nouveau Paradigme Pour La Responsabilité Des Dépositaires?'. *Revue de Droit Bancaire et Financier* 1 (2011).

Prüm, André. 'Le Nouveau Cadre Européen Du Traitement Des Faillites Bancaires À Vol D'oiseau'. *Revue de Droit Bancaire et Financier* 6 (2014).

Prussen, Elvinger Hoss. *Specialised Investment Funds*. February 2015.

Radelet, Steven, and Jeffrey Sachs. 'The Onset of the East Asian Financial Crisis'. *National Bureau of Economic Research* No. w6680 (1998).

Ramon, Moreno. 'What Caused East Asia's Financial Crisis'. *Federal Reserve Bank of San Fransisco Economic Letters* (August 7, 1998).

Rayner, Gordon. 'Banking Bailout: The Rise and Fall of RBS'. http://www.telegraph.co.uk/finance/newsbysector/banksandfinance/4291807/Banking-bailout-The-rise-and-fall-of-RBS.html.

Reiermann, Christian. 'Controlling the Locusts; Baby Steps Against Hedge Funds'. http://www.spiegel.de/international/spiegel/controlling-the-locusts-baby-steps-against-hedge-funds-a-464416.html.

Relations, Council on Foreign. 'A Systemic Regulator for Financial Markets'. *Squam Lake Working Group on Financial Regulation Working Paper* (May 2009).

Rennison, Joe. 'High-Frequency Traders: Bond Market Scourge or Saviour?' The Financial Times, https://next.ft.com/content/ab70bdf2-4507-11e5-b3b2-1672f710807b.

Research, Hedge Fund. *Record Number of Hedge Funds Liquidate in 2008*.

Research, Office for Financial. *Asset Management and Financial Stability*. September 2013.

Riassetto, Isabelle. 'Dépositaires – Quelles Différences Entre La Directive OPCVM V Et La Directive AIFM?'. *Revue de Droit Bancaire et Financier* 4 (2014).

Ribstein, Larry. *The Rise of the Unincorporation*. Oxford University Press, 2009.

Ribstein, Larry E. 'Uncorporation and Corporate Indeterminacy'. *University of Illinois Law Review* (2009).

Ricardi, Stanley V. Ragalevsky, and Sarah J. 'Anatomy of a Bank Failure'. *The Banking Law Journal* (December 2009).

Richard A, Brealy, Myers Stewart C., and Allen Franklin. *Corporate Finance*. 8th ed.: McGraw-Hill, 2006.

Richard, Christine S. *Confidence Game: How Hedge Fund Manager Bill Ackman Called Wall Street's Bluff*. Bloomberg Press, 2010.

Richardson Matthew, Smith Roy, and Walter Ingo. 'Large Banks and the Volcker Rule'. In *Regulating Wall Street: The Dodd-Frank Act and the New Architecture of Global Finance*, edited by Viral Acharya et al., 181-212: Wiley, 2010.

Ringe, Wolf-George. 'Capital Markets Union for Europe – a Political Message to the UK'. *Law and Financial Markets Review* 9, no. 1 (2015).

Rixtel, Leonardo Gambacorta, and Adrian van. 'Structural Bank Regulation Initiatives: Approaches and Implications'. *BIS Working Papers* No. 412 (April 2013).

Robinson, Stephen. 'The AIFMD Unveiled'. In *Hedge Funds: Jurisdictional Comparisons*, edited by Stephen Ball, Sweet and Maxwell, 2, 2013.

Rock, Edward. 'Institutional Investors in Corporate Governance'. In *The Oxford Handbook of Corporate Law and Governance*, edited by Jeffrey Gordon and Wolf-Georg Ringe, Oxford University Press, 2015.

Rock, Edward B. 'Adapting to the New Shareholder-Centric Reality'. *University of Pennsylvania Law Review* 161 (2013): 1907.

Roe, Mark J. 'A Political Theory of American Corporate Finance'. *Columbia Law Review* 91, no. 1 (1991): 10-67.

Rohrer, Julie. 'The Red-Hot World of Julian Robertson'. *Institutional Investor*, May 1986, 86.

Roll, Richard. 'The Hubris Hypothesis of Corporate Takeovers'. *Journal of business* 59, no. 2 (1986): 197-216.

Romano, Roberta. 'Against Financial Regulation Harmonization: A Comment'. *No. 414 Yale Law & Economics Research Paper*, no. 414 (2010).

Romano, Roberta. 'States as a Laboratory: Legal Innovation and State Competition for Corporate Charters'. *Yale Journal on Regulation* 23, no. 2 (2006): 209.

Roubini, Nouriel, and Brad Setser. *Bailouts or Bail-Ins*. Peterson Institute for International Economics, 2004.

Russolillo, Steven. 'Hedge Funds Severely Underperforming This Year'. The Wall Street Journal, http://blogs.wsj.com/moneybeat/2013/08/21/hedge-funds-severely-underperforming-this-year/.

Saguato, Guido Ferrarini and Paolo. 'Regulating Financial Market Infrastructures'. In *The Oxford Handbook on Financial Regulation*, edited by Moloney et al. Niamh, 568-96: Oxford University Press, 2015.

Samuel Hanson et al. 'A Macroprudential Approach to Financial Regulation'. *The Journal of Economic Perspectives* 25 (2011): 3-28.

Saporito, Bill. 'Are Short Sellers to Blame for the Financial Crisis'. Tim, http://content.time.com/time/business/article/0,8599,1842499,00.html.

Scherbina, Anna. 'Asset Price Bubbles: A Selective Survey'. *IMF WP/13/45* (February 2013).

Schlefer, Niall Ferguson, and Jonathan. 'Who Broke the Bank of England?'. *Harvard Business School BGIE Unit Case No. 709-026* (September 9 2009).

Schmid, Markus M, and Ingo Walter. 'Do Financial Conglomerates Create or Destroy Economic Value?'. *Journal of Financial Intermediation* 18, no. 2 (2009): 193-216.

Schoenmaker, Dirk. 'The Financial Trilemma'. *Economics Letters* 111, no. 1 (2011): 57-59.

Schoenmaker, Dirk. 'Firmer Foundations for a Stronger Banking Union'. *No. 2015/13 Bruegel Working Paper* (November 2015).

Scholes, Myron S. 'The Future of Hedge Funds'. *Journal of Financial Transformation* 10 (1997).

Scholten, Miroslava, and Marloes van Rijsbergen. 'The ESMA-Short Selling Case: Erecting a New Delegation Doctrine in the EU Upon the Meroni-Romano Remnants'. *Legal Issues of Economic Integration* 41, no. 4 (2014): 389-405.

Schwarcz Daniel, Patricia A McCoy, and Jeremy Kress, 'Comment of Legal Scholars on Authority To Require Supervision and Regulation of Certain Nonbank Financial Companies, Financial Stability Oversight Council RIN 4030-AA00', 13 May 2019.

Schwarcz, Steven L. 'Ring-Fencing'. *Southern California Law Review* 87, no. 1 (2013): 69-110.

Schwarcz, Steven L. 'Systemic Risk'. *Georgetown Law Journal* 97, no. 1 (2008): 193.

Scott, Hal. 'Interconnectedness and Contagion'. *Committee on Capital Market Regulation* (2012).

Scott, Hal. *Written Testimony of Hal Scott before the Committee on Financial Services, United States House of Representatives*. Vol. 1, June 2011.

Sergent, Fanny. 'Luxembourg: A Hedge Fund Center "Par Excellence"'. *HFM Week Special Report: Luxembourg 2015* (2015).

Servaes, Henri. 'The Value of Diversification During the Conglomerate Merger Wave'. *The Journal of Finance* 51, no. 4 (1996): 1201-25.

Services, Citi Prime Finance Business Advisory. *Institutional Investment in Hedge Funds: Evolving Investor Portfolio Construction Drives Product Convergence*. June 2012.

Settlements, Bank for International. *69th Annual Report*. 7 June 1999.

Shadab, Houman. 'Houman Shadab Testifies Before Congress on Hedge Funds and the Financial Crisis'. Youtube, 2009.

Shadab, Houman B. 'The Challenge of Hedge Fund Regulation'. *Regulation* 30, no. 1 (2007): 36-41.

Shadab, Houman B. 'Fending for Themselves: Creating a US Hedge Fund Market for Retail Investors'. *New York University Journal of Legislation and Public Policy* 11, no. 2 (2007): 251.

Shadab, Houman B. 'Hedge Fund Governance'. *Stanford Journal of Law, Business, and Finance* 19, no. 1 (2013): 1.

Shadab, Houman B. 'Hedge Funds and the Financial Market'. *Committee on Oversight and Government Reform, Hedge Funds and the Financial Markets* (2008).

Shadab, Houman B. 'The Law and Economics of Hedge Funds: Financial Innovation and Investor Protection'. *Berkeley Business Law Journal* 6 (2009): 240-97.

Shadab, Houman B. 'Coming Together after the Crisis: Global Convergence of Private Equity and Hedge Funds'. *Northwestern Journal of International Law and Business* 29, no. 3 (2009): 603.

Sharpe, William, Gordon Alexander and Jeffery V Bailey. 'Investments, Englewood'. NJ: Prentice Hall, 1990.

Shiller, Robert J. *Irrational Exuberance.* Princeton University Press, 2005.

Shleifer, Andrei. *Inefficient Markets: An Introduction to Behavioral Finance.* Oxford university press, 2000.

Shleifer, Andrei, and Lawrence H Summers. 'The Noise Trader Approach to Finance'. *The Journal of Economic Perspectives* 4, no. 2 (1990): 19-33.

Shleifer, Andrei, and Robert Vishny. 'Fire Sales in Finance and Macroeconomics'. *Journal of Economic Perspectives* 25, no. 1 (2011): 29-48.

Shleifer, Andrei, and Robert W Vishny. 'Large Shareholders and Corporate Control'. *The Journal of Political Economy* 94, no. 3 (1986): 461-88.

Shleifer, Andrei, and Robert W Vishny. 'The Limits of Arbitrage'. *The Journal of Finance* 52, no. 1 (1997): 35-55.

Shleifer, Andrei, and Robert W Vishny. 'Liquidation Values and Debt Capacity: A Market Equilibrium Approach'. *The Journal of Finance* 47, no. 4 (1992): 1343-66.

Shleifer, Andrei. *Inefficient Markets: An Introduction to Behavioral Finance.* Oxford University Press, 2000.

Sias, Richard, HJ Turtle, and Blerina Zykaj. 'Hedge Fund Crowds and Mispricing'. *Management Science* 62 (2016).

Simmons, Martin J. McMahon, and Daniel L. 'When Subchapter S Meets Subchapter C'. *The Tax Lawyer* 67, no. 2 (2014).

Sinclair, Darren. 'Self-Regulation Versus Command and Control? Beyond False Dichotomies'. *Law & Policy* 19, no. 4 (1997): 529-59.

Sjostrom, William K. 'The AIG Bailout'. *Washington and Lee Law Review* 66, no. 3 (2009): 943.

Skeel, David. 'The Euro Crisis: Lessons from Bear Stearns'. The Wall Street Journal, http://online.wsj.com/articles/SB10001424052970204002304576626932530739412.

Skeel, David. *The New Financial Deal: Understanding the Dodd-Frank Act and Its (Unintended) Consequences.* Wiley and Sons, 2011.

Skeel, David A. 'Single Point of Entry and the Bankruptcy Alternative'. In *Across the Great Divide: New Perspectives on the Financial Crisis*, edited by Martin Neil Bailey & John B Taylor, 14-10: Hoover Press, 2014.

Sklar, Ryan. 'Hedges or Thickets: Protecting Investors from Hedge Fund Managers' Conflicts of Interest'. *Fordham Law Review* 77 (2009): 3251.

Smaghi, Lorenzo Bini. 'Monetary Policy Transmission in a Changing Financial System: Lessons from the Recent Past, Thoughts About the Future, Speech at the Barclays Global Inflation Conference'. News release, June 14 2010.

Smits, René. *The European Central Bank, Institutional Aspects.* Kluwer Law International, 1997.

Sorkin, Andrew Ross. 'Shareholder Democracy Can Mask Abuses'. New York Times, Dealbook, http://dealbook.nytimes.com/2013/02/25/shareholder-democracy-can-mask-abuses/.

Soros, George. *The Alchemy of Finance: Reading the Mind of the Market*: Wiley, 1987.

Soskice, Peter Hall, and David, ed. *Varieties of Capitalism: The Institutional Foundations of Comparative Advantage*: Oxford University Press, 2002.

Spangler, Timothy. 'Clawbacks Becoming Fashionable on Wall Street'. http://www.forbes.com/sites/timothyspangler/2013/05/28/clawbacks-becoming-fashionable-on-wall-street/.

Speyer, Bernhard. 'EU Banking Union: Do It Right, Not Hastily!'. *Deutsche Bank Research EU Monitor* (July 2012).

Springford, John. 'Brexit and EU Regulation: A Bonfire of the Vanities?'. *Centre for European Reform* (February 2016).

Stefanini, Filippo. *Investment Strategies of Hedge Funds*. Wiley, 2006.

Stefano, Tascan Paolo, and Battiston. 'Diversification and Financial Stability'. *SRC Discussion Paper No. 10* (February 2014).

Steinberg, Julie. 'Fund of Hedge Funds Come with Heaps of Fees'. The Wall Street Journal, http://online.wsj.com/news/articles/SB10001424052702304448204579183973097089350.

Sterling, Shearman and. *Comparison of New EU Proposals on Proprietary Trading and Ring-Fencing Against US, UK, French and German Rules*. 26 February 2014.

Stokes, Eric. *Market Neutral Investing: Build Consistent Low-Risk Profits by Creating Your Own Hedged Portfolio*. Kaplan Business, 2004.

Storbeck, Olaf. 'Deutsche Bank's DWS Puts IPO Price at €32.50 a Share'. Financial Times, https://www.ft.com/content/de81fc28-2dfe-11e8-a34a-7e7563b0b0f4.

Story, Louise. 'A Debate as a Ban on Short-Selling Ends: Did It Make Any Difference?'. The New York Times, http://www.nytimes.com/2008/10/08/business/08short.html?_r=0.

Stout, Lynn. 'How Hedge Funds Create Criminals'. *Harvard Business Review*, December 13, 2010.

Stout, Lynn A. 'The Mechanisms of Market Inefficiency: An Introduction to the New Finance'. *Journal of Corporation Law* 28, no. 4 (2002): 635.

Stowell, David. *Investment Banks, Hedge Funds, and Private Equity*. Academic Press, 2012.

Strachman, Daniel A. *Getting Started in Hedge Funds*. 3rd ed.: Wiley, 2005.

Strachman, Daniel A. *Julian Robertson: Tiger in the Land of Bulls and Bears*. John Wiley and Sons, 2004.

Strasburg, Katherine Burton & Jenny. 'Jpmorgan, Renaissance Trail Hedge-Fund Gains in 2007'. Bloomberg, http://www.bloomberg.com/apps/news?pid=newsarchive&sid=aF2.5PL13F4o.

Street, State. *Hedge Funds: Rebuilding on a New Foundation*. August 2011.

Strine Jr, Leo E. 'One Fundamental Corporate Governance Question We Face: Can Corporations Be Managed for the Long Term Unless Their Powerful Electorates Also Act and Think Long Term?'. *Business Lawyer* 66 (2010).

Strömqvist, Maria. 'Hedge Funds and Financial Crises'. *Sveriges Riksbank Economic Review* (2009).

Strupczewski, Lefteris Papadimas, and Jan. 'EU, IMF Agree $147 Billion Bailout for Greece'. REUTERS, http://www.reuters.com/article/2010/05/02/us-eurozone-idUSTRE6400PJ20100502.

Stulz, René M. 'Financial Derivatives'. *The Milken Institute Review, Third Quarter* (2005).

Sudarsanam, Sudi, and Tim Broadhurst. 'Corporate Governance Convergence in Germany through Shareholder Activism: Impact of the Deutsche Boerse Bid for London Stock Exchange'. *Journal of Management & Governance* 16, no. 2 (2012): 235-68.

Sullivan, Ruth. 'Traditional Investors Adopt Activism'. The Financial Times, http://www.ft.com/intl/cms/s/0/62d5ea16-b253-11e2-a388-00144feabdc0.html.

Supervision, Basel Committee on Banking. *Basel III Leverage Ratio Framework and Disclosure Requirements*. January 2014.

Supervision, Basel Committee on Banking. *Basel III: The Liquidity Coverage Ratio and Liquidity Risk Monitoring Tools*. January 2013.

Supervision, Basel Committee on Banking. *Basel III: The Net Stable Funding Ratio*. October 2014.

Supervision, Basle Committee on Banking. *Sound Practices for Banks' Interactions with Highly Leveraged Institutions*. January 1999.

System, Board of Governors of the Federal Reserve. 'Enhanced Prudential Standards and Early Remediation Requirements for Covered Companies'. 5 January 2012.

Tappen, Jürgen Baur, and Falko. *Investmentrecht Luxembourg*. 2015.

Tarullo, Daniel K. *Banking on Basel: The Future of International Financial Regulation*. Peterson Institute, 2008.

Taylor. '"Twin Peaks": A Regulatory Structure for the New Century'. *Centre for the Study of Financial Innovation London*, no. 20 (1995).

Temple, Peter. *Private Equity: Examining the New Conglomerates of European Business*. Wiley, 1999.

Teodorczuk, Tom. 'Only a Third of Hedge Funds Charge "2 and 20" Fees, Says Expert'. Financial News, https://www.fnlondon.com/articles/only-a-third-of-hedge-funds-charge-2-and-20-fees-says-expert-20181108.

Tett, Gillian. 'Archegos Avalanche Shows Cracks Are Hidden Under the Surface'. Financial Times, https://www.ft.com/content/4459a6b2-b842-4d21-b19b-bda138a5bfdf.

The Group of Thirty, Working Group on Financial Reform. *Financial Reform: A Framework for Financial Stability*. 2009.

Thévenoz, Luc. 'The Rescue of UBS by the Swiss Confederation'. In *International Monetary and Financial Law*, edited by Mario Giovanoli and Diego Devos, 378-91: Oxford University Press, 2010.

Thierry, Foucault. 'Where Are the Risks in High-Frequency Trading'. *Banque de France, Financial Stability Review* 20 (April 2016).

Titcomb, James. 'HSBC: "The UK Has Rejected the Concept of Universal Banking"'. The Telegraph, http://www.telegraph.co.uk/finance/newsbysector/banksandfinance/11582516/HSBC-shares-jump-after-profits-smash-forecasts.html.

Tracy, Scott Patterson, and Ryan. 'Fed Gives Banks More Time to Sell Private Equity, Hedge Fund Stakes'. The Wall Street Journal, http://www.wsj.com/articles/fed-gives-banks-more-time-to-sell-private-equity-hedge-fund-stakes-1418933398.

Ueda, Kenichi, and Fabian Valencia. 'Central Bank Independence and Macro-Prudential Regulation'. *Economics Letters* 125, no. 2 (2014): 327-30.

Vaughan, David A. 'Selected Definitions of "Hedge Fund"'. *Comments for the U.S. Securities and Exchange Commission Roundtable on Hedge Funds* (14-15 May 2003).

Vedant Misra, Marco Lagi, Yaneer Bar-Yam. 'Evidence of Market Manipulation in the Financial Crisis'. *arXiv preprint arXiv:1112.3095* (2011).

Ventoruzzo, Marco. 'Comparing Insider Trading in the United States and in the European Union: History and Recent Developments'. *No. 257 European Corporate Governance Institute (ECGI)-Law Working Paper*, no. 257 (2014).

Viñals José, Pazarbasioglu Ceyla, Surti Jay, Narain Aditya, Erbenova Michaela, and Chow Julian. 'Creating a Safer Financial System: Will the Volcker, Vickers and Liikanen Structural Measures Help?'. *IMF Discussion Note* SDN/13/4 (14 May 2013).

Vletter-van Dort, and Hélène M. 'Some Challenges Facing European Central Banks as Supervising Authority'. *European Company and Financial Law Review* 9, no. 2 (2012): 131-55.

Wagner, Wolf. 'In the Quest of Systemic Externalities: A Review of the Literature'. *CESifo Economic Studies* 56, no. 1 (2010): 96-111.

Walker Marcus, Forelle Charles and Enrich David. 'Ailing Ireland Accepts Bailout'. The Wall Street Journal, http://online.wsj.com/news/articles/SB10001424052748703567304575628362883493310?mg=reno64-wsj.

Wardwell, Davis Polk. 'A Fund by Any Other Name: The Convergence of Hedge Funds and Private Equity Funds'. *Private Equity Newsletter* (May 2006): 1.

Wetherilt Anne, Benos Evangelos. 'The Role of Designated Market Makers in the New Trading Landscape'. *Bank of England Quarterly Bulletin* Q4 (2012).

Whelan, Karl. 'The ECB's Role in Financial Supervision'. *Working Paper, UCD Centre for Economic Research* WP09/15 (2009).

Whitehead, Charles K. 'The Volcker Rule and Evolving Financial Markets'. *Harvard Business Law Review* 1, no. 1 (2011).

Wigglesworth, Sam Jones, and Robin. 'Hedge Funds Profit in Land of Greek Opportunity'. The Financial Times, http://online.wsj.com/news/articles/SB10001424052748703709804575201330937572258.

Wilhelm, Alan D. Morrison, and William J. 'The Demise of Investment-Banking Partnerships: Theory and Evidence'. Oxford Financial Research Center Working Paper, http://papers.ssrn.com/sol3/papers.cfm?abstract_id=569109.

Wilhelm, Alan D. Morrison, and William J. *Investment Banking: Institutions, Politics, and Law.* Oxford University Press, 2008.

Wilmarth, Arthur E. 'Citigroup: A Case Study in Managerial and Regulatory Failures'. *Indiana Law Review* 47, no. 1 (2014): 69-137.

Wilmarth, Arthur E. 'Transformation of the Us Financial Services Industry, 1975-2000: Competition, Consolidation, and Increased Risks'. *The University of Illinois Law Review* (2002).

Wilmarth, Arthur E. 'The Dark Side of Universal Banking: Financial Conglomerates and the Origins of the Subprime Financial Crisis'. *Connecticut Law Review* 41, no. 4 (2009).

Wolff, Nicolas Véron, and Guntram B. 'From Supervision to Resolution: Next Steps on the Road to European Banking Union'. *No. PB13-5 Policy Brief, Peterson Institute For International Economics* (February 2013).

Woll, Cornelia. 'Beyond Ideological Battles: A Strategic Analysis of Hedge Fund Regulation in Europe'. *Les Cahiers Europeens de Sciences Po.* 2 (2011).

Worrachate, Anchalee. 'Bond Liquidity Seen Worsening by BofA as Regulations Tighten'. Reuters, http://www.bloomberg.com/news/articles/2015-11-04/bond-liquidity-seen-worsening-by-bank-of-america-merrill-lynch.

Wyman, Oliver. *The Effects of Short Selling Public Disclosure of Individual Positions on Equity Markets*. 2011.

Wymeersch, Eddy. 'The Single Supervisory Mechanism or 'SSM', Part One of the Banking Union'. *No. 255 National Bank of Belgium Working Paper* (2014).

Wymeersch, Eddy. 'The Structure of Financial Supervision in Europe: About Single Financial Supervisors, Twin Peaks and Multiple Financial Supervisors'. *European Business Organization Law Review* 8, no. 02 (2007): 237-306.

Yellen, Janet. 'The Asian Financial Crisis Ten Years Later: Assessing the Past and Looking to the Future, Speech to the Asia Society of Southern California' news release, 6 February 2007.

Zavvos, George S, and Stella Kaltsouni. 'The Single Resolution Mechanism in the European Banking Union: Legal Foundation, Governance Structure and Financing'. Ch. 117 In *Research Handbook on Crisis Management in the Banking Sector*, edited by Matthias Haentjens and Bob Wessels, 117: Edward Elgar, 2015.

Zuckerman, Gregory. *The Greatest Trade Ever: The Behind-the-Scenes Story of How John Paulson Defied Wall Street and Made Financial History*. Crown Business, 2010.

Table of Statues

Index

EUROPEAN COMPANY LAW SERIES

1. Steef M. Bartman (ed.), *European Company Law in Accelerated Progress*, 2006 (ISBN 978-90-411-2529-3)
2. Karen Vandekerckhove, *Piercing The Corporate Veil: A Transnational Approach*, 2007 (ISBN 978-90-411-2591-0)
3. Beate Sjåfjell, *Towards a Sustainable European Company Law: A Normative Analysis of the Objectives of EU Law, with the Takeover Directive as a Test Case*, 2009 (ISBN 978-90-411-2768-6)
4. Cornelis de Groot, *Corporate Governance as a Limited Legal Concept*, 2009 (ISBN 978-90-411-2873-7)
5. Adriaan F.M. Dorresteijn, Christoph Teichmann, Erik Werlauff, Tiago Monteiro & Nadia Pocher, *European Corporate Law*, Third Edition, 2017 (ISBN 978-90-411-8593-8)
6. Gert-Jan Vossestein, *Modernization of European Company Law and Corporate Governance: Some Considerations on its Legal Limits*, 2010 (ISBN 978-90-411-2592-7)
7. Catalin Stefan Rusu, *European Merger Control: The Challenges Raised by Twenty Years of Enforcement Experience*, 2010 (ISBN 978-90-411-3259-8)
8. Sabrina Bruno & Eugenio Ruggiero, *Public Companies and the Role of Shareholders: National Models Towards Global Integration*, 2011 (ISBN 978-90-411-3423-3)
9. Hanne S. Birkmose, Mette Neville & Karsten Engsig Sørensen (eds), *The European Financial Market in Transition*, 2012 (ISBN 978-90-411-3360-1)
10. Hanne S. Birkmose, Mette Neville & Karsten Engsig Sørensen (eds), *Boards of Directors in European Companies: Reshaping and Harmonising Their Organisation and Duties*, 2013 (ISBN 978-90-411-4141-5)
11. Christoph Van der Elst, *Executive Directors' Remuneration in Comparative Corporate Perspective*, 2015 (ISBN 978-90-411-5607-5)
12. Hanne S. Birkmose, *Shareholders' Duties*, 2017 (ISBN 978-90-411-6670-8)
13. Alan S. Gutterman, *Sustainability and Corporate Governance: A Practice Guide to Implementing a Sustainability Governance System*, 2018 (ISBN 978-90-411-9975-1)
14. Jan De Bruyne, *Third-Party Certifiers*, 2019 (ISBN 978-94-035-1091-0)
15. Hanne S. Birkmose, Mette Neville & Karsten Engsig Sørensen (eds), *Abuse of Companies*, 2019 (ISBN 978-94-035-0892-4)
16. Ivan Romashchenko, *Related Party Transactions and Corporate Groups: When Eastern Europe Meets the West*, 2020 (ISBN 978-94-035-1701-8)

17. Patryk Filipiak & Anna Hrycaj, *European Insolvency Proceedings: Commentary on Regulation (EU) 2015/848 of the European Parliament and of the Council of 20 May 2015 on Insolvency Proceedings (Recast)*, 2021 (ISBN 978-94-035-3410-7)
18. Alexandros Seretakis, *Regulating Hedge Funds in the EU*, 2022 (ISBN 978-94-035-3512-8)

www.ingramcontent.com/pod-product-compliance
Ingram Content Group UK Ltd.
Pitfield, Milton Keynes, MK11 3LW, UK
UKHW020801290926
15470UKWH00003B/879

9 789403 535128